Grenville Clark
Feb. 1938
31 Nassau St.
N.Y. City

FREEDOM OF SPEECH

BY

ZECHARIAH CHAFEE, Jr.
Professor of Law in Harvard University

NEW YORK
HARCOURT, BRACE AND COMPANY

FREEDOM *of* SPEECH

BY
ZECHARIAH CHAFEE, Jr.
PROFESSOR OF LAW IN HARVARD UNIVERSITY

"GIVE YOUR MIND SEA ROOM"

NEW YORK
HARCOURT, BRACE AND COMPANY

COPYRIGHT, 1920, BY
HARCOURT, BRACE AND HOWE, INC.

TO
LEARNED HAND
UNITED STATES DISTRICT JUDGE
FOR THE SOUTHERN DISTRICT OF NEW YORK
WHO DURING THE TURMOIL OF WAR
COURAGEOUSLY MAINTAINED
THE TRADITION OF ENGLISH-SPEAKING FREEDOM
AND GAVE IT NEW CLEARNESS AND STRENGTH
FOR THE WISER YEARS TO COME

CONTENTS

CHAPTER			PAGE
I.	Freedom of Speech in War Time		1
II.	Opposition to the War with Germany		40
	I.	The Espionage Acts of 1917 and 1918	42
	II.	Masses Publishing Co. v. Patten	46
	III.	The District Court Cases	56
	IV.	The Human Machinery of the Espionage Acts	66
	V.	The Supreme Court Decisions	87
	VI.	Censorship and Exile	106
	VII.	State Espionage Acts	110
	VIII.	Reflections During a Technical State of War	113
III.	A Contemporary State Trial—The United States v. Jacob Abrams et al.		120
	I.	The District Court	125
	II.	The Supreme Court	148
IV.	Legislation against Sedition and Anarchy		161
	I.	The Normal Law Against Violence and Revolution	165
	II.	The Normal Criminal Law of Words	169
	III.	The Difference Between the Normal Law and the New Legislation	173
	IV.	Radical Meetings and the Red Flag	180
	V.	Criminal Anarchy and Criminal Syndicalism	187
	VI.	The Federal Sedition Bills	194

CONTENTS

CHAPTER		PAGE
VII.	The Constitutionality of a Federal Sedition Law	199
VIII.	The Wisdom and Expediency of a Federal Sedition Law . . .	207

V. THE DEPORTATIONS 229
    I. The Statute as to Deportable Radicals   230
    II. The Administrative Machinery for Deporting Radicals . . . 232
    III. The Raids of January, 1920 . . 241
    IV. The Arrest of American Citizens for Deportation 252
    V. A Review of the Actual Cases of Radicals Held for Deportation . . 256
        (1) Communists—Guilt by Association and Government Spies   256
        (2) Industrial Workers of the World 272
        (3) Anarchists 275
    VI. The Deportations and the Bill of Rights   280
    VII. Suggested Changes in Our Deportation Policy 291

VI. JOHN WILKES, VICTOR BERGER, AND THE FIVE MEMBERS 294
    I. John Wilkes 295
    II. The Raids of 1763 and the Raids of 1919 296
    III. The Exclusion of Wilkes from the House of Commons 311
    IV. The Exclusion of Victor L. Berger from the House of Representatives . . 315
    V. The Five Socialist Members of the New York Assembly 332

VII. FREEDOM AND INITIATIVE IN THE SCHOOLS . . 365

CONTENTS

APPENDICES

APPENDIX		PAGE
I.	Bibliography on Freedom of Speech	377
	A. General and Historical; *B.* The War; *C.* Radical Activities in the United States and Peace-time Restrictions upon Freedom of Speech; *D.* Power of a Legislature to Exclude or Expel for Opinions; *E.* Schools.	
II.	Index of Reported Cases under the Espionage Acts of 1917 and 1918	387
III.	Text and Construction of the Espionage Act of 1918	395
IV.	Normal Law of Four Jurisdictions Against Actual or Threatened Violence	398
V.	State War and Peace Statutes Affecting Freedom of Speech	399
Index of Cases		407
General Index		411

FREEDOM OF SPEECH

CHAPTER I

FREEDOM OF SPEECH IN WAR TIME

And though all the winds of doctrine were let loose to play upon the earth, so Truth be in the field, we do injuriously by licensing and prohibiting to misdoubt her strength. Let her and Falsehood grapple; who ever knew Truth put to the worse, in a free and open encounter?—MILTON, *Areopagitica*.

NEVER in the history of our country, since the Alien and Sedition Laws of 1798, has the meaning of free speech been the subject of such sharp controversy as to-day. Over nineteen hundred prosecutions and other judicial proceedings during the war, involving speeches, newspaper articles, pamphlets, and books, have been followed since the armistice by a widespread legislative consideration of bills punishing the advocacy of extreme radicalism. It is becoming increasingly important to determine the true limits of freedom of expression, so that speakers and writers may know how much they can properly say, and governments may be sure how much they can lawfully and wisely suppress. The United States Supreme Court has recently handed down several decisions upon the Espionage Act, which put us in a much better position than formerly to discuss the war-time aspects of the general problem of liberty of speech. Therefore, instead of beginning with an abstract treatment of that problem, I shall take the concrete situation of opposition to war, and from it endeavor to work out the fundamental principles of the whole subject. These can afterwards be tested by their application to radical agitation in peace.

It is already plain, I hope, that this book is an inquiry into the proper limitations upon freedom of speech, and is in no way an argument that any one should be allowed to say whatever he wants anywhere and at any time. We can all agree from the very start that there must be some point where the government may step in, and my main purpose is to make clear from many different angles just where I believe that point to lie. We ought also to agree that a man may believe that certain persons have a right to speak or other constitutional rights, without at all identifying himself with the position and views of such persons. In a country where John Adams defended the British soldiers involved in the Boston Massacre and Alexander Hamilton represented British Loyalists and General Grant insisted upon amnesty for Robert E. Lee, it is surprising how in the last three years it has been impossible for any one to uphold the rights of a minority without subjecting himself to the accusation that he shared their opinions. If he urged milder treatment of conscientious objectors, he was a pacifist. If he held that the treaty with Germany should not violate the terms of the armistice, he was a pro-German. This popular argument reached its climax when an opponent of the disqualified Socialist assemblymen informed the world that he had always suspected Governor Hughes of being disloyal.

I am not an atheist, but I would not roast one at the stake as in the sixteenth century, or even exclude him from the witness-stand as in the nineteenth. Neither am I a pacifist or an anarchist or a Socialist or a Bolshevik. I have no sympathy myself with the views of most of the men who have been imprisoned since the war began for speaking out. The only one, I suppose, of all that number with whom I could sit down for half an hour's conversation without losing my temper is Mr. Bertrand Russell. My only interest is to find whether or not the treatment which they have received accords with freedom of speech. That principle may be invoked just as eagerly in future years by conservatives. Whatever political or economic opinion falls within the scope of the

First Amendment ought to be safeguarded from governmental interference by every man who has sworn to uphold the Constitution of the United States, no matter how much he disagrees with those who are entitled to its protection or how lofty the patriotism of those who would whittle away the Bill of Rights into insignificance.

A friend of Lovejoy, the Abolitionist printer killed in the Alton riots, said at the time that we are more especially called upon to maintain the principles of free discussion in case of unpopular sentiments or persons, as in no other case will any effort to maintain them be needed.[1]

The free speech clauses of the American constitutions are not merely expressions of political faith without binding legal force. Their history shows that they limit legislative action as much as any other part of the Bills of Rights. The United States Constitution as originally drafted contained no guaranty of religious or intellectual liberty, except that it forbade any religious test oath and gave immunity to members of Congress for anything said in debates. Pinckney, of South Carolina, had sought to insert a free speech clause, grouping liberty of the press with trial by jury and habeas corpus as " essentials in free governments." His suggestion was rejected by a slight majority as unnecessary, in that the power of Congress did not extend to the press, a natural belief before Hamilton and Marshall had developed the doctrine of incidental and implied powers. Hamilton himself defended the omission on the ground that liberty of the press was indefinable and depended only on public opinion and the general spirit of the people and government for its security, little thinking that he himself would frame a definition now embodied in the constitutions of half the states.[2] The citizens of the states were not satisfied, and the absence of the guaranty of free-

[1] Edward Beecher, *Alton Riots,* Alton, Ill., 1838 (Widener Library). A bibliographical note to this and other chapters will be found in Appendix I.
[2] The various types of free speech clauses are given in *Index Digest of State Constitutions,* N. Y. State Cons. Conv. Comm., 1915, pp. 700-702,

dom of speech was repeatedly condemned in the state conventions and in outside discussion. Virginia, New York, and Rhode Island embodied a declaration of this right in their ratifications of the federal Constitution. Virginia expressly demanded an amendment and Maryland drafted one in its convention, basing it on a very significant reason, to be mentioned shortly. At the first session of Congress a Bill of Rights, including the present First Amendment, was proposed for adoption by the states, and became part of the Constitution November 3, 1791. Massachusetts, Virginia, and Pennsylvania already had similar provisions, and such a clause was eventually inserted in the constitutions of all other states. Thus the guaranty of freedom of speech was almost a condition of the entry of four original states into the Union, and is now declared by every state to be as much a part of its fundamental law as trial by jury or compensation for property taken by eminent domain. Such a widely recognized right must mean something, and have behind it the obligation of the courts to refuse to enforce any legislation which violates freedom of speech.

We shall not, however, confine ourselves to the question whether a given form of federal or state action against pacifist and similar utterances is void under the constitutions. It is often assumed that so long as a statute is held valid under the Bill of Rights, that document ceases to be of any

956-958. Twenty-three state constitutions follow Hamilton (note 65, *infra*) in making truth a defense to criminal libel if published with good motives. The first was *New York Constitution*, 1821, Art. 7, § 8. See *Reports of New York Constitutional Convention of 1821*, pp. 167, 487. All but five states have a clause resembling another sentence of the New York section: "Every citizen may freely speak, write, and publish his sentiments, on all subjects, being responsible for the abuse of that right; and no law shall be passed, to restrain, or abridge the liberty of speech, or of the press." Massachusetts, Mississippi, New Hampshire, Vermont, and South Carolina retain a short clause much like the federal Constitution. The express exception of "abuse" was first made by Pennsylvania in 1790 (note 36, *infra*); but since I regard such an exception as implied in the United States form, I have assumed in this book that there is no difference in legal effect. The effect of the Hamiltonian clause is discussed by Henry Schofield, "Freedom of the Press in the United States," **9** *Proc. Am. Sociolog. Soc.* 88 ff., cited hereafter as Schofield.

importance in the matter, and may be henceforth disregarded. On the contrary, a provision like the First Amendment to the federal Constitution,

> Congress shall make no law respecting an establishment of religion, or prohibiting the free exercise thereof; or abridging the freedom of speech, or of the press; or the right of the people peaceably to assemble, and to petition the Government for a redress of grievances,

is much more than an order to Congress not to cross the boundary which marks the extreme limits of lawful suppression. It is also an exhortation and a guide for the action of Congress inside that boundary. It is a declaration of national policy in favor of the public discussion of all public questions. Such a declaration should make Congress reluctant and careful in the enactment of all restrictions upon utterance, even though the courts will not refuse to enforce them as unconstitutional. It should influence the judges in their construction of valid speech statutes, and the prosecuting attorneys who control their enforcement. The Bill of Rights in a European constitution is a declaration of policies and nothing more, for the courts cannot disregard the legislative will though it violates the Constitution.[3] Our Bills of Rights perform a double function. They fix a certain point to halt the government abruptly with a " Thus far and no farther "; but long before that point is reached they

---

[3] A. V. Dicey, *Law of the Constitution*, 8 ed., 130: "This curious result therefore ensues. The restrictions placed on the action of the legislature under the French constitution are not in reality laws, since they are not rules which in the last resort will be enforced by the Courts. Their true character is that of maxims of political morality, which derive whatever strength they possess from being formally inscribed in the constitution and from the resulting support of public opinion. What is true of the constitution of France applies with more or less force to other polities which have been formed under the influence of French ideas."

Probably some Americans anticipated only the same effect from our bills of rights, not realizing that an unconstitutional statute would be held unenforceable. Spencer said in the North Carolina Convention: "If a boundary were set up, when the boundary is passed, the people would take notice of it immediately." 4 *Elliot's Debates* (2 ed.) 175.

urge upon every official of the three branches of the state a constant regard for certain declared fundamental policies of American life.[4]

Our main task, therefore, is to ascertain the nature and scope of the policy which finds expression in the First Amendment to the United States Constitution and the similar clauses of all the state constitutions, and then to determine the place of that policy in the conduct of war, and particularly the war with Germany. The free speech controversy of the last two years has chiefly gathered about the federal Espionage Act. This Act contains a variety of provisions on different subjects, such as the protection of ships in harbors, spy activities, unlawful military expeditions, etc., but the portion which concerns us, Title I, section 3, discussed at length in the next chapter, as it has been interpreted by the courts, makes criminal several kinds of spoken or written opposition to this or any future war, and imposes a maximum penalty of $10,000 fine or twenty years' imprisonment, or both. Any material violating this section may, under Title XII of the Act, be excluded from the mails. This statute has been enacted and vigorously enforced under a constitution which provides: "Congress shall make no law . . . abridging the freedom of speech, or of the press."

Clearly, the problem of the limits of freedom of speech in war time is no academic question. On the one side, thoughtful men and journals are asking how scores of citizens can be imprisoned under this constitution only for their open disapproval of the war as irreligious, unwise, or unjust. On the other, federal and state officials point to the great activities of German agents in our midst and to the unprecedented extension of the business of war over the whole nation, so that in the familiar remark of Ludendorff, wars are no

---

[4] "No doubt our doctrine of constitutional law has had a tendency to drive out questions of justice and right, and to fill the mind of legislators with thoughts of mere legality, of what the constitution allows."— J. B. Thayer, *Legal Essays*, 38. See his quotation from 1 Bryce, *American Commonwealth*, 1 ed., 377.

longer won by armies in the field, but by the *morale* of the whole people. The widespread Liberty Bond campaigns, and the shipyards, munition factories, government offices, training camps, in all parts of the country, are felt to make the entire United States a theater of war, in which attacks upon our cause are as dangerous and unjustified as if made among the soldiers in the rear trenches. The government regards it as inconceivable that the Constitution should cripple its efforts to maintain public safety. Abstaining from countercharges of disloyalty and tyranny, let us recognize the issue as a conflict between two vital principles, and endeavor to find the basis of reconciliation between order and freedom.

At the outset, we can reject two extreme views in the controversy. First, there is the view that the Bill of Rights is a peace-time document and consequently freedom of speech may be ignored in war. This view has been officially repudiated.[5] At the opposite pole is the belief of many agitators that the First Amendment renders unconstitutional any Act of Congress without exception " abridging the freedom of speech, or of the press," that all speech is free, and only action can be restrained and punished. This view is equally untenable. The provisions of the Bill of Rights can not be applied with absolute literalness, but are subject to exceptions.[6] For instance, the prohibition of involuntary servitude in the Thirteenth Amendment does not prevent military conscription, or the enforcement of a " work or fight" statute. The difficulty, of course, is to define the principle on which the implied exceptions are based, and an effort to that end will be made subsequently.

---

[5] Report of the Attorney General of the United States (1918), 20: " This department throughout the war has proceeded upon the general principle that the constitutional right of free speech, free assembly, and petition exist in war time as in peace time, and that the right of discussion of governmental policy and the right of political agitation are most fundamental rights in a democracy."

[6] Robertson v. Baldwin, 165 U. S. 275, 281 (1897); Selective Draft Law Cases, 245 U. S. 366, 390 (1918); Claudius v. Davie, 175 Cal. 208 (1917); State v. McClure, 105 Atl. 712 (Del. Gen. Sess., 1919).

Since it is plain that the true solution lies between these two extreme views, and that even in war time freedom of speech exists subject to a problematical limit, it is necessary to determine where the line runs between utterances which are protected by the Constitution from governmental control and those which are not. Many attempts at a legal definition of that line have been made, but two mutually inconsistent theories have been especially successful in winning judicial acceptance, and frequently appear in the Espionage Act cases.

One theory construes the First Amendment as enacting Blackstone's statement that "the liberty of the press . . . consists in laying no *previous* restraints upon publications and not in freedom from censure for criminal matter when published." [7] The line where legitimate suppression begins is fixed chronologically at the time of publication. The government cannot interfere by a censorship or injunction *before* the words are spoken or printed, but can punish them as much as it pleases *after* publication, no matter how harmless or essential to the public welfare the discussion may be. This Blackstonian definition found favor with Lord Mansfield,[8] and is sometimes urged as a reason why civil libels should not be enjoined,[9] so that on this theory liberty of the press means opportunity for blackmailers and no protection for political criticism. The same definition was adopted by a few American judges in early contempt proceedings and prosecutions for libel.[10] The Federalist judges of that time were so noto-

[7] 4 Blackstone, *Commentaries*, 151.

[8] King v. Dean of St. Asaph, 3 T. R. 428, 431 (1784): "The liberty of the press consists in printing without any previous license, subject to the consequence of law."

[9] See Roscoe Pound, "Equitable Relief Against Defamation and Injuries to Personality," 29 *Harv. L. Rev.* 651, and recent federal cases in 32 *ibid.* 938 n. Dean Pound discusses two views besides Blackstone's. The view mentioned as Story's is really that of St. George Tucker, whom Story was criticising. 2 Story, *Constitution*, § 1886.

[10] McKean in Respublica v. Oswald, 1 Dall. 319 (Pa., 1788), and Trial of William Cobbett, Wharton's State Trials, 322 (Pa., 1797), Yeates in Respublica v. Dennie, 4 Yeates 267 (Pa., 1805); Parker in Comm. v. Blanding, 3 Pick. 304 (Mass., 1825). See Schofield in 9 *Proc. Am. Sociolog. Soc.* 69.

rious for their slavish adherence to English authorities in disregard of our own constitutions and statutes,[11] that their Blackstonian statements should have little weight in the construction of constitutional guaranties. However, one of these cases was in Massachusetts, whence Justice Holmes carried the Blackstonian definition into the United States Supreme Court.[12] Fortunately he has now repudiated this interpretation of freedom of speech,[13] but not until his dictum had had considerable influence, particularly in Espionage Act cases.[14] Of course, if the First Amendment does not prevent prosecution and punishment of utterances, the Espionage Act is unquestionably constitutional.

This Blackstonian theory dies hard, but it ought to be knocked on the head once for all. In the first place, Blackstone was not interpreting a constitution, but trying to state the English law of his time, which had no censorship and did have extensive libel prosecutions. Whether or not he stated that law correctly, an entirely different view of the liberty of the press was soon afterwards enacted in Fox's Libel Act, so that Blackstone's view does not even correspond to the English law of the last hundred and twenty-five years. Furthermore, Blackstone is notoriously unfitted to be an authority on the liberties of American colonists, since he upheld the right of Parliament to tax them, and was pronounced by one of his own colleagues to have been " we all know, an anti-republican lawyer." [15]

Not only is the Blackstonian interpretation of our free speech clauses inconsistent with eighteenth-century history, soon to be considered, but it is contrary to modern decisions, thoroughly artificial, and wholly out of accord with a common-sense view of the relations of state and citizen. In

[11] Beveridge's *Marshall*, III, 23 ff. See page 22, *infra*.
[12] Patterson *v.* Colorado, 205 U. S. 454, 462 (1907).
[13] Schenck *v.* U. S., 249 U. S. 47 (1919); Abrams *v.* U. S., 250 U. S. 616 (1919).
[14] Masses Pub. Co. *v.* Patten, 246 Fed. 24 (1917); U. S. *v.* Coldwell, Bull. Dept. Just., No. 158, page 4.
[15] 1 Blackstone, *Commentaries,* 109; Willes, J., in Dean of St. Asaph's Case, 4 Doug. 73, 172 (1784).

some respects this theory goes altogether too far in restricting state action. The prohibition of previous restraint would not allow the government to prevent a newspaper from publishing the sailing dates of transports or the number of troops in a sector. It would render illegal removal of an indecent poster from a billboard or the censorship of moving pictures before exhibition, which has been held valid under a free speech clause.[16] And whatever else may be thought of the decision under the Espionage Act with the unfortunate title, United States *v.* The Spirit of '76,[17] it was clearly previous restraint for a federal court to direct the seizure of a film which depicted the Wyoming Massacre and Paul Revere's Ride, because it was " calculated reasonably so to excite or inflame the passions of our people or some of them as that they will be deterred from giving that full measure of co-operation, sympathy, assistance, and sacrifice which is due to Great Britain, as an ally of ours," and " to make us a little bit slack in our loyalty to Great Britain in this great catastrophe."

On the other hand, it is hardly necessary to argue that the Blackstonian definition gives very inadequate protection to the freedom of expression. A death penalty for writing about socialism would be as effective suppression as a censorship. The government which holds twenty years in prison before a speaker and calls him free to talk resembles the peasant described by Galsworthy:[18]

> The other day in Russia an Englishman came on a street-meeting shortly after the first revolution had begun. An extremist was addressing the gathering and telling them that they were fools to go on fighting, that they ought to refuse and go home, and so forth. The crowd grew angry, and some soldiers were for making a rush at him; but the chairman, a big burly peasant, stopped them with these words: " Brothers, you know that our

---

[16] Mutual Film Corporation *v.* Industrial Commission of Ohio, 236 U. S. 230, 241 (1915).

[17] 252 Fed. 946 (D. C. S. D. Cal., 1917), Bledsoe, J. See also Goldstein *v.* U. S., 258 Fed. 908 (C. C. A. 9th, 1919).

[18] John Galsworthy, " American and Briton," 8 *Yale Rev.* 27 (October, 1918). *Cf.* Boswell's Johnson, ed. G. B. Hill, IV, 12.

FREEDOM OF SPEECH IN WAR TIME 11

country is now a country of free speech. We must listen to this man, we must let him say anything he will. But, brothers, when he's finished, we'll bash his head in!'"

Cooley's comment on Blackstone is unanswerable:[19]

> ... The mere exemption from previous restraints cannot be all that is secured by the constitutional provisions, inasmuch as of words to be uttered orally there can be no previous censorship, and the liberty of the press might be rendered a mockery and a delusion, and the phrase itself a byword, if, while every man was at liberty to publish what he pleased, the public authorities might nevertheless punish him for harmless publications, ... Their purpose [of the free-speech clauses] has evidently been to protect parties in the free publication of matters of public concern, to secure their right to a free discussion of public events and public measures, and to enable every citizen at any time to bring the government and any person in authority to the bar of public opinion by any just criticism upon their conduct in the exercise of the authority which the people have conferred upon them. ... The evils to be prevented were not the censorship of the press merely, but any action of the government by means of which it might prevent such free and general discussion of public matters as seems absolutely essential to prepare the people for an intelligent exercise of their rights as citizens.

If we turn from principles to precedents, we find several decisions which declare the constitutional guarantee of free speech to be violated by statutes and other governmental action which imposed no previous restraint, but penalized publications after they were made.[20] And most of the deci-

---

[19] Cooley, *Constitutional Limitations*, 7 ed., 603, 604.

[20] Louthan *v.* Commonwealth, 79 Va. 196 (1884)—statute punishing school superintendent for political speeches; Atchison, etc. Ry. *v.* Brown, 80 Kans. 312 (1909)—service-letter statute, making employer liable to civil action if he failed to furnish a discharged employee a written statement for the true reason for discharge. St. Louis, etc. Ry. Co. *v.* Griffin, 106 Texas 477 (1914), same; Wallace *v.* Georgia Ry. Co., 94 Ga. 732 (1894), same; *Ex parte* Harrison, 212 Mo. 88 (1908),—statute punishing voters' leagues for commenting on candidates for office without disclosing the names of all persons furnishing the information; State *ex rel.* Metcalf *v.* District Court, 52 Mont. 46 (1916)—contempt proceedings for criticism of judge for past decision; State *ex rel.* Ragan *v.* Junkin, 85 Neb. 1 (1909),—statute invalidating nomination of candidates by conventions or any other method except primaries; State *v.* Pierce, 163 Wis. 615 (1916)—corrupt practices act punishing political

sions in which a particular statute punishing for talking or writing is sustained do not rest upon the Blackstonian interpretation of liberty of speech,[21] but upon another theory, now to be considered. Therefore, it is possible that the severe punishments imposed by Title I, section 3, of the Espionage Act, violate the First Amendment, although they do not interfere with utterances before publication.[22]

A second interpretation of the freedom of speech clauses limits them to the protection of the use of utterance and not to its "abuse." It draws the line between "liberty" and "license." Chief Justice White [23] rejects:

the contention that the freedom of the press is the freedom to do wrong with impunity and implies the right to frustrate and defeat the discharge of those governmental duties upon the performance of which the freedom of all, including that of the press, depends. . . . However complete is the right of the press to state public things and discuss them, that right, as every other right, enjoyed in human society, is subject to the restraints which separate right from wrong-doing.

A statement of the same view in another peace case is made by Judge Hamersley of Connecticut: [24]

Every citizen has an equal right to use his mental endowments, as well as his property, in any harmless occupation or manner; but he has no right to use them so as to injure his fellow-citizens or to endanger the vital interests of society. Immunity in the mischievous use is as inconsistent with civil liberty as prohibition

---

disbursements outside one's own county except through a campaign committee; State v. Printing Co., 177 Pac. 751 (N. M., 1918)—contempt. Some of these decisions are open to dispute on the desirability of the statutes, and some are opposed by other cases for that reason, but in their repudiation of the Blackstonian test they furnish unquestioned authority.

[21] Examples in such cases of express repudiation of the Blackstonian doctrine are found in Schenck v. United States, 249 U. S. 47 (1919); State v. McKee, 73 Conn. 18 (1900); State v. Pioneer Press Co., 100 Minn. 173 (1907); Cowan v. Fairbrother, 118 N. C. 406, 418 (1896).

[22] Title XII of the Espionage Act does impose previous restraint on publications which violate the Act by authorizing the Postmaster General to exclude them from the mails. See page 108, *infra*.

[23] Toledo Newspaper Co. v. United States, 247 U. S. 402, 419 (1918).
[24] State v. McKee, 73 Conn. 18, 28 (1900).

FREEDOM OF SPEECH IN WAR TIME 13

of the harmless use. . . . The liberty protected is not the right to perpetrate acts of licentiousness, or any act inconsistent with the peace or safety of the State. Freedom of speech and press does not include the abuse of the power of tongue or pen, any more than freedom of other action includes an injurious use of one's occupation, business, or property.

The decisions in the war are full of similar language,[25] of which a few specimens will suffice:

In this country it is one of our foundation stones of liberty that we may freely discuss anything we please, provided that that discussion is in conformity with law, or at least not in violation of it.

No American worthy of the name believes in anything else than free speech; but free speech means, not license, not counseling disobedience of the law. Free speech means that frank, free, full, and orderly expression which every man or woman in the land, citizen or alien, may engage in, in lawful and orderly fashion.

No one is permitted under the constitutional guaranties to commit a wrong or violate the law.

Just the same sort of distinction was made by Lord Kenyon during the French revolution:

The liberty of the press is dear to England. The licentiousness of the press is odious to England. The liberty of it can never be so well protected as by beating down the licentiousness.

This exasperated Sir James Fitzjames Stephen into the comment, "Hobbes is nearly the only writer who seems to me capable of using the word 'liberty' without talking nonsense."[26]

A slightly more satisfactory view is adopted by Cooley,[27] that the clauses guard against repressive measures by the

[25] Mayer, J., in United States v. Phillips, Bull. Dept. Just., No. 14 (S. D. N. Y., 1917), 5; and United States v. Goldman, Bull. Dept. Just., No. 41 (S. D. N. Y., 1917), 2; Van Valkenburgh, J., in United States v. Stokes, Bull. Dept. Just., No. 106 (W. D. Mo., 1918), 12. See also United States v. Pierce, Bull. Dept. Just., No. 52 (S. D. N. Y., 1917), 22, Ray, J.; United States v. Nearing, Bull. Dept. Just., No. 192 (S. D. N. Y., 1917), 4, Mayer, J.; United States v. Wallace, Bull. Dept. Just. 4 (Ia., 1917), 4, Wade, J.

[26] 2 *Hist. Crim. Law* 348 n.

[27] Cooley, *Constitutional Limitations*, 7 ed., 605; quoted by Hough, J., in Fraina v. United States, 255 Fed. 28, 35 (C. C. A. 2d, 1918).

several departments of government, but not against utterances which are a public offense, or which injure the reputation of individuals.

We understand liberty of speech and of the press to imply not only liberty to publish, but complete immunity from legal censure and punishment for the publication, so long as it is not harmful in its character, when tested by such standards as the law affords.

To a judge obliged to decide whether honest and able opposition to the continuation of a war is punishable, these generalizations furnish as much help as a woman forced, like Isabella in *Measure for Measure*, to choose between her brother's death and loss of honor, might obtain from the pious maxim, " Do right." What is abuse? What is license? What standards does the law afford? To argue that the federal Constitution does not prevent punishment for criminal utterances begs the whole question, for utterances within its protection are not crimes. If it only safeguarded lawful speech, Congress could escape its operation at any time by making any class of speech unlawful. Suppose, for example, that Congress declared any criticism of the particular administration in office to be a felony, punishable by ten years' imprisonment. Clearly, the Constitution must limit the power of Congress to create crimes. But how far does that limitation go? Cooley suggests that the constitutional guaranties must be interpreted in the light of the contemporary common law of blasphemy, obscenity, and defamation, but flatly denies that they enact the common law of sedition and libels against the government.[28] Conditions in 1791 must be considered, but they do not arbitrarily fix the division between lawful and unlawful speech for all time.

Clearly, we must look further and find a rational test of what is use and what is abuse. Saying that the line lies between them gets us nowhere. And " license " is too often " liberty " to the speaker, and what happens to be anathema to the judge.

[28] *Ibid.* **604, 612 ff.**

We can, of course, be sure that certain forms of utterance, which have always been crimes or torts at common law, are not within the scope of the free speech clauses. The courts in construing such clauses have, for the most part, done little more than place obvious cases on this or that side of the line. They tell us, for instance, that libel and slander are actionable, or even punishable, that indecent books are criminal, that it is contempt to interfere with pending judicial proceedings, and that a permit can be required for street meetings; and on the other hand, that some criticism of the government must be allowed, that a temperate examination of a judge's opinion is not contempt, and that honest discussion of the merits of a painting causes no liability for damages. But when we ask where the line actually runs and how they know on which side of it a given utterance belongs, we find little answer in their opinions.

We do have two very able judicial statements which take us far toward the ultimate solution of the problem of the limits of free speech, but they unfortunately lack the weight of binding adjudications, for one is a decision by Judge Learned Hand which was subsequently reversed on appeal and the other a dissenting opinion by Justice Holmes. Therefore, it is regrettable that when Justice Holmes spoke for all members of the United States Supreme Court in the earlier Espionage Act decisions, he did not feel at liberty to go beyond the particular facts before him into a fuller exposition of fundamental principles, and make articulate for us that major premise, under which judges ought to classify words as inside or outside the scope of the First Amendment. He, we then hoped, would concentrate his great abilities on fixing the line. Instead, like other judges, he told us that certain plainly unlawful utterances are, to be sure, unlawful.

The First Amendment . . . obviously was not intended to give immunity for every possible use of language. . . . We venture to believe that neither Hamilton nor Madison, nor any other competent person then or later, ever supposed that to make criminal the counselling of a murder . . . would be an unconstitutional interference with free speech.[29]

The most stringent protection of free speech would not protect a man in falsely shouting fire in a theater and causing a panic.[30]

How about the man who gets up in a theater between the acts and informs the audience honestly, but perhaps mistakenly, that the fire exits are too few or locked? He is a much closer parallel to Frohwerk or Debs. How about James Russell Lowell when he counseled, not murder, but the cessation of murder, his name for war? The question whether such perplexing cases are within the First Amendment or not cannot be solved by the multiplication of obvious examples, but only by the development of a rational principle to mark the limits of constitutional protection.

"The gradual process of judicial inclusion and exclusion,"[31] which has served so well to define other clauses in the federal Constitution by blocking out concrete situations on each side of the line until the line itself becomes increasingly plain, has as yet been of very little use for the First Amendment. The cases are too few, too varied in their character, and often too easily solved, to develop any definite boundary between lawful and unlawful speech. Even if some boundary between the precedents could be attained, we could have little confidence in it unless we knew better than now the fundamental principle on which the classification was based. Indeed, many of the decisions in which statutes have been held to violate free speech seem to ignore so seriously the economic and political facts of our time, that they are precedents of very dubious value for the inclusion and exclusion process.[32] Nearly every free speech decision, outside such hotly litigated portions as privilege and fair comment in defamation, appears to have been decided largely by intuition.

[29] Frohwerk v. United States, 249 U. S. 204 (1919).
[30] Schenck v. United States, 249 U. S. 47 (1919).
[31] Miller, J., in Davidson v. New Orleans, 96 U. S. 97, 104 (1877).
[32] See note 20, *supra*.

In the next chapter I shall return to the opinions of Justice Holmes and Judge Hand. For the moment, however, it may be worth while to forsake the purely judicial discussion of free speech, and obtain light upon its meaning from the history of the constitutional clauses and from the purpose free speech serves in social and political life.

The framers of the First Amendment make it plain that they regarded freedom of speech as very important—" absolutely necessary " is Luther Martin's phrase. But they say very little about its exact meaning. That should not surprise us if we recall our own vagueness about freedom of the seas. Men rarely define their inspirations until they are forced into doing so by sharp antagonism. Therefore, it is not until the Sedition Law of 1798 made the limits of liberty of the press a concrete and burning issue that we get much helpful expression of opinion on our problem.[33] Before that time, however, we have a few important pieces of evidence to show that the words were used in the Constitution in a wide and liberal sense.

On October 26, 1774, the Continental Congress issued an address to the inhabitants of Quebec, declaring that the English colonists had five invaluable rights, representative government, trial by jury, liberty of the person, easy tenure of land, and freedom of the press:[34]

> The last right we shall mention regards the freedom of the press. The importance of this consists, besides the advancement of truth, science, morality and arts in general, in its diffusion of liberal sentiment on the administration of government, its ready communication of thoughts between subjects, and its consequential promotion of union among them, whereby oppressive officials are shamed or intimidated into more honorable and just modes of conducting affairs.

In 1785 Virginia, which was the first state to insert a clause protecting the liberty of the press in its constitution (1776), enacted a statute drawn by Jefferson for Establish-

---
[33] See Appendix I for references on the Law of 1798.
[34] Journal of the Continental Congress, Vol. I (ed. 1800), p. 57.

ing Religious Freedom.³⁵ This opened with a very broad principle of toleration: "Whereas, Almighty God hath created the mind free; that all attempts to influence it by temporal punishments or burthens, or by civil incapacitations, tend only to beget habits of hypocrisy and meanness——" While this relates specifically to religion, it shows the trend of men's thoughts, and the meaning which "liberty" had to Jefferson long before the bitter controversy of 1798.

One other framer of our government has stated his views on this matter in less solemn language, Benjamin Franklin.³⁶ In discussing the brief "freedom of speech" clause in the Pennsylvania Constitution of 1776, he said in 1789, that if by the liberty of the press were to be understood merely the liberty of discussing the propriety of public measures and political opinions, let us have as much of it as you please. On the other hand, if it means liberty to calumniate another there ought to be some limit; but he has been at a loss to imagine any that may not be construed an infringement of the sacred *liberty of the press*. At length, however, he thinks he has found one that instead of diminishing general liberty shall augment it; he means *the liberty of the cudgel*. If, however, it should be thought that this proposal of his may disturb the public peace, he would humbly recommend to our legislators to take up the consideration of both liberties, that of the *press*, and that of the *cudgel*, and by an explicit law mark their extent and limits. Thus Franklin construed this clause so widely as even to grant immunity from private libel actions. Next year the Pennsylvania Constitution was amended to impose responsibility for the abuse of the liberty, but no such exception was thought necessary in the United States Constitution, probably because private libels were not within the purview of the federal law.

The most significant evidence of the meaning of the First

---

³⁵ See note 66, *infra*.
³⁶ *Works*, ed. A. H. Smyth, X, 36 ff. See Pa. Cons. (1776), c. I, sect. 12; Pa. Cons. (1790), Art. IX, sect. 7.

FREEDOM OF SPEECH IN WAR TIME 19

Amendment is the reason given by the Maryland convention of 1788 to the people for including such a clause in the proposed federal Bill of Rights:[37] "In prosecutions in the federal courts, for libels, the constitutional preservation of this great and fundamental right may prove invaluable." This is, of course, absolutely inconsistent with any Blackstonian limitation of the right to absence of a censorship.

If we apply Coke's test of statutory construction, and consider what mischief in the existing law the framers of the First Amendment wished to remedy by a new safeguard, we can be sure that it was not the censorship. This had expired in England in 1695, and in the colonies by 1725.[38] For years the government here and in England had substituted for the censorship rigorous and repeated prosecutions for criminal libel or seditious libel, as it was often called, which were directed against political discussion, and for years these prosecutions were opposed by liberal opinion and popular agitation. Primarily the controversy raged around two legal contentions of the great advocates for the defense, such as Erskine and Andrew Hamilton. They argued, first, that the jury and not the judge ought to decide the libellous nature of the writing, and secondly, that the truth of the charge ought to prevent conviction. The real issue, however, lay much deeper. Two different views of the relation of rulers and people were in conflict. According to one view, the rulers were the superiors of the people, and therefore must not be subjected to any censure that would tend to diminish their authority. The people could not make adverse criticism in newspapers or pamphlets, but only through their lawful representatives in the legislature, who might be petitioned in an orderly manner. According to the other view, the rulers are agents and ser-

[37] 2 Elliot's Deb. (2 ed.) 511; see the same argument in newspaper letters given in *Pennsylvania and the Federal Constitution*, ed. J. B. McMaster and F. D. Stone, 151, 181. The second letter suggests the possibility of a prohibitive stamp tax as in Massachusetts to crush the press.

[38] Macaulay, *History of England*, Chap. XXI; C. A. Duniway, *Freedom of Speech in Massachusetts*, 89 note.

vants of the people, who may therefore find fault with their servants and discuss questions of their punishment or dismissal, and of governmental policy.

Under the first view, which was officially accepted until the close of the eighteenth century, developed the law of seditious libel. This is defined as "the intentional publication, without lawful excuse or justification, of written blame of any public man, or of the law, or of any institution established by law." There was no need to prove any intention on the part of the defendant to produce disaffection or excite an insurrection. It was enough if he intended to publish the blame, because it was unlawful in him merely to find fault with his masters and betters. Such, in the opinion of the best authorities, was the common law of sedition.[39]

It is obvious that under this law liberty of the press was nothing more than absence of the censorship, as Blackstone said. All through the eighteenth century, however, there existed beside this definite legal meaning of liberty of the press, a definite popular meaning: the right of unrestricted discussion of public affairs. There can be no doubt that this was in a general way what freedom of speech meant to the framers of the Constitution. Thus Madison in 1799 bases his explanation of the First Amendment on "the essential difference between the British Government and the American constitutions." In England, he says, Parliament is omnipotent and all the ramparts for protecting the rights of the people are reared only against the royal prerogative. Therefore, exemption from the censorship of the king's appointees is the only freedom secured to the press. In the United States, however, the people and not the government possess the absolute sovereignty, and the legislature as well as the executive is under limitations of power. The effective

[39] Madison, Report on the Virginia Resolutions, 1799, 4 Ell. Deb. (2 ed.) 596 ff.; 2 Stephen, *History of the Criminal Law*, 299, 353, and Chap. XXIV., *passim;* Schofield, in 9 *Proc. Am. Sociol. Soc.* 70 ff., gives an excellent summary with especial reference to American conditions.

security of the press requires that it should be exempt not only from previous restraint by the executive as in England, but from legislative restraint also through the subsequent penalty of laws. After this repudiation of the Blackstonian doctrine, Madison goes on to reject the theory that the legislature is free to punish anything which was criminal at English common law. Here again, he says, the different natures of the two governments must have its effect and contemplate a different degree of liberty in the use of the press. A government which is " elective, limited and responsible " in all its branches may well be supposed to require " a greater freedom of animadversion " than might be tolerated by one that is composed of an irresponsible hereditary king and upper house, and an omnipotent legislature. This inference is favored, he continues, by the actual English practice. " Notwithstanding the general doctrine of the common law, on the subject of the press, and the occasional punishment of those who use it with a freedom offensive to the Government, it is well known that with respect to the responsible measures of the Government, where the reasons operating here become applicable there, the freedom exercised by the press and protected by public opinion far exceeds the limits prescribed by the ordinary rules of law." [40]

This contemporary testimony corroborates the conclusion of Professor Schofield:

One of the objects of the Revolution was to get rid of the English common law on liberty of speech and of the press. . . . Liberty of the press as declared in the First Amendment, and the English common-law crime of sedition, cannot co-exist.[41]

The few early judicial decisions [42] to the contrary ought not to weigh against the statements of Franklin, Jefferson,

[40] Madison's Report on the Virginia Resolutions, 4 Ell. Deb. (2 ed.) 596-598. The same distinction was made by Erastus Root, *Report of the New York Constitutional Convention of 1821*, p. 489. See also *Speeches of Charles Pinckney*, 1800, p. 116 ff.
[41] Schofield, 76, 87.
[42] Cases in note 10; Charge to the Grand Jury of Judge Addison (who was born and educated in the United Kingdom), Addison Ch. (Pa.)

and Madison, and the general temper of the time. These judges were surely wrong in holding as they did that sedition was a common-law crime in the federal courts, and in other respects they drew their inspiration from British precedents and the British bench instead of being in close contact with the new ideas of this country. "Indeed," as Senator Beveridge says, "some of them were more British than they were American." "Let a stranger go into our courts," wrote one observer, "and he would almost believe himself in the Court of the King's Bench." [43] Great as was the service of these judges in establishing the common law as to private rights, their testimony as to its place in public affairs is of much less value than the other contemporary evidence of the men who sat in the conventions and argued over the adoption of the Constitution. The judges forgot the truth emphasized by Maitland: "The law of a nation can only be studied in relation to the whole national life." I must therefore strongly dissent, with Justice Holmes,[44] from the position sometimes taken in arguments on the Espionage Act, that the founders of our government left the common law as to seditious libel in force and merely intended by the First Amendment "to limit the new government's statutory powers to penalize utterances as seditious, to those which were seditious under the then accepted common-law rule." [45] The founders had seen seventy English prosecutions for libel since 1760, and fifty convictions under that common-law rule, which made conviction easy.[46] That rule had been detested in this country ever since it was repudiated by jury and populace in

---

270. Marshall's Minority Report in opposition to Madison's is chiefly devoted to establishing an implied power of the government to protect itself against libels. His discussion of the First Amendment, while undoubtedly opposed to my view, is little more than a repetition of Blackstone. *The Address of the Minority in the Virginia Legislature,* etc. (Library of Congress, Class E 327, Book A 22; extracts in U. S. reply brief in Debs *v.* U. S.)

[43] Beveridge's *Marshall*, III, 23-29.
[44] Abrams *v.* U. S., 250 U. S. 616 (1919).
[45] W. R. Vance, in "Freedom of Speech and the Press," 2 *Minn. L. Rev.* 239, 259.
[46] 2 May, *Constitutional History of England,* 2 ed., 9 note.

the famous trial of Peter Zenger, the New York printer, the account of which went through fourteen editions before 1791.[47] The close relation between the Zenger trial and the prosecutions under George III in England and America is shown by the quotations on reprints of the trial and the dedication of the 1784 London edition to Erskine, as well as by reference to Zenger in the discussions preceding the First Amendment.[48] Nor was this the only colonial sedition prosecution under the common law, and many more were threatened.[49] All the American cases before 1791 prove that our common law of sedition was exactly like that of England, and it would be extraordinary if the First Amendment enacted the English sedition law of that time, which was repudiated by every American and every liberal Englishman,[50] and altered through Fox's Libel Act by Parliament itself in the very next year, 1792. We might well fling at the advocates of this common law view the challenge of Randolph of Roanoke, " whether the common law of libels which attaches to this Constitution be the doctrine laid down by Lord Mansfield, or that which has immortalized Mr. Fox? "[51] The First Amendment was written by men to whom Wilkes and Junius were household words, who intended to wipe out the common law of sedition, and make further prosecutions for criticism of the government, without

[47] 17 How. St. Tr. 675 (1735). The fullest account of Zenger and the trial is given by Livingston Rutherford, *John Peter Zenger*, New York, 1904. Rutherford's bibliography lists thirteen editions of the account of the trial before 1791. The Harvard Law School Library contains four of these (London, 1738; London, 1752; London, 1765; New York, 1770), and also an undated copy without specified place, differing from any listed by Rutherford. See also the life of Zenger's counsel, Andrew Hamilton, by William Henry Loyd, in 1 *Great American Lawyers* 1.
[48] Newspaper letter, reprinted in *Penn. and the Fed. Cons.*, 151.
[49] C. A. Duniway, *Freedom of the Press in Massachusetts*, 91, 93, 115, 123, 130, and note. In 1767 Chief Justice Hutchinson charged the grand jury on Blackstonian lines, "This Liberty means no more than a Freedom for every Thing to pass from the Press without a License." *Ibid.*, 125.
[50] 2 May, *Constitutional History of England*, Chap. IX; 2 Stephen, *History of the Criminal Law*, Chap. XXIV.
[51] 3 Beveridge's *Marshall* 85.

any incitement to law-breaking, forever impossible in the United States of America.

It must not be forgotten that the controversy over liberty of the press was a conflict between two views of government, that the law of sedition was a product of the view that the government was master, and that the American Revolution transformed into a working reality the second view that the government was servant, and therefore subjected to blame from its master, the people. Consequently, the words of Sir James Fitzjames Stephen about this second view have a vital application to American law.[52]

To those who hold this view fully and carry it out to all its consequences there can be no such offense as sedition. There may indeed be breaches of the peace which may destroy or endanger life, limb, or property, and there may be incitements to such offenses, but no imaginable censure of the government, *short of a censure which has an immediate tendency to produce such a breach of the peace,* ought to be regarded as criminal.

The repudiation by the constitutions of the English common law of sedition, which was also the common law of the American colonies, has been somewhat obscured by judicial retention of the two technical incidents of the old law after the adoption of the free speech clauses. Many judges, rightly or wrongly, continued to pass on the criminality of the writing and to reject its truth as a defense,[53] until statutes or new constitutional provisions embodying the popular view on these two points were enacted.[54] Doubtless, a jury will protect a popular attack on the government better than a judge, and the admission of truth as a defense lessens the evils of suppression. These changes help to substitute the modern view of rulers for the old view, but they

---

[52] 2 Stephen, *History of the Criminal Law*, 300. The italics are mine. See also Schofield, 9 *Proc. Am. Sociol. Soc.*, 75.

[53] Duniway, *supra*, Chap. IX; Commonwealth v. Clap, 4 Mass. 163 (1808); Commonwealth v. Blanding, 3 Pick. (Mass.) 304 (1825).

[54] Examples are: Pa. Cons. 1790, Art. 9, § 7; N. Y. Session Laws, 1805, c. 90; N. Y. Cons., 1821, Art. VII, § 8; Mass. Laws, 1827, c. 107. See Schofield, *op. cit.*, 95-99.

are not essential. Sedition prosecutions went on with shameful severity in England after Fox's Libel Act [55] had given the jury power to determine criminality. The American Sedition Act of 1798, which President Wilson declares to have " cut perilously near the root of freedom of speech and of the press," [56] entrusted criminality to the jury and admitted truth as a defense. On the other hand, freedom of speech might exist without these two technical safeguards. The essential question is not, who is judge of the criminality of an utterance, but what is the test of its criminality. The common law and the Sedition Act of 1798 made the test blame of the government and its officials, because to bring them into disrepute tended to overthrow the state. The real issue in every free speech controversy is this—whether the state can punish all words which have some tendency, however remote, to bring about acts in violation of law, or only words which directly incite to acts in violation of law.

If words do not become criminal until they have " an immediate tendency to produce a breach of the peace," there is no need for a law of sedition, since the ordinary standards of criminal solicitation and attempt apply. Under those standards the words must bring the speaker's unlawful intention reasonably near to success. Such a limited power to punish utterances rarely satisfies the zealous in times of excitement like a war. They realize that all condemnation of the war or of conscription may conceivably lead to active resistance or insubordination. Is it not better to kill the serpent in the egg? All writings that have even a remote tendency to hinder the war must be suppressed.

Such has always been the argument of the opponents of free speech. And the most powerful weapon in their hands, since the abolition of the censorship, is this doctrine of indirect causation, under which words can be punished for a supposed bad tendency long before there is any probability that they will break out into unlawful acts. Closely related

[55] 32 Geo. III, c. 60 (1792).
[56] 3 Woodrow Wilson, *History of the American People*, 153.

to it is the doctrine of constructive intent, which regards the intent of the defendant to cause violence as immaterial so long as he intended to write the words, or else presumes the violent intent from the bad tendency of the words on the ground that a man is presumed to intend the consequences of his acts. When rulers are allowed to possess these weapons, they can by the imposition of severe sentences create an *ex post facto* censorship of the press. The transference of that censorship from the judge to the jury is indeed important when the attack on the government which is prosecuted expresses a widespread popular sentiment, but the right to jury trial is of much less value in times of war or threatened disorder when the herd instinct runs strong, if the opinion of the defendant is highly objectionable to the majority of the population, or even to the particular class of men from whom or by whom the jury are drawn.

Under Charles II trial by jury was a blind and cruel system. During part of the reign of George III it was, to say the least, quite as severe as the severest judge without a jury could have been. The revolutionary tribunal during the Reign of Terror tried by a jury.[57] It is worth our frank consideration, whether in a country where the doctrine of indirect causation is recognized by the courts twelve small property-holders, who have been through an uninterrupted series of patriotic campaigns and are sufficiently middle-aged to be in no personal danger of compulsory military service, are fitted to decide whether there is a tendency to obstruct the draft in the writings of a pacifist, who also happens to be a socialist and in sympathy with the Russian Revolution. This, however, is perhaps a problem for the psychologist rather than the lawyer.

Another significant fact in sedition prosecutions is the well-known probability that juries will acquit, after the excitement is over, for words used during the excitement, which are as bad in their tendency as other writings prose-

[57] 1 Stephen, *History of the Criminal Law*, 569.

cuted and severely punished during the critical period. This was very noticeable during the reign of George III. It is also interesting to find two juries in different parts of the country differing as to the criminal character of similar publications or even the same publication. Thus Leigh Hunt was acquitted for writing an article, for the printing of which John Drakard was convicted. The acquittal of Scott Nearing and the conviction by the same jury of the American Socialist Society for publishing his book form an interesting parallel.[58]

The manner in which juries in time of excitement may be used to suppress writings in opposition to the government, if bad tendency is recognized as a test of criminality, is illustrated by the numerous British sedition trials during the French Revolution. These were after the passage of Fox's Libel Act. For instance, in the case just mentioned, Drakard was convicted for printing an article on the shameful amount of flogging in the army, under a charge in which Baron Wood emphasized the formidable foe with whom England was fighting, and the general belief that Napoleon was using the British press to carry out his purpose of securing her downfall.[59]

It is to be feared, there are in this country many who are endeavoring to aid and assist him in his projects, by crying down the establishment of the country, and breeding hatred against the government. Whether that is the source from whence the paper in question springs, I cannot say, but I advise you to consider whether it has not that tendency. You will consider whether it contains a fair discussion—whether it has not a manifest tendency to create disaffection in the country and prevent men enlisting into the army—whether it does not tend to induce the soldier to desert from the service of his country. And what considerations can be more awful than these? . . .

The House of Parliament is the proper place for the discussion of subjects of this nature . . . It is said that we have a right to

[58] Judge Mayer has decided that there is not such inconsistency in the two verdicts as to warrant a new trial. American Socialist Society *v.* United States, 260 Fed. 885 (1919).
[59] 31 How. St. Tr. 495, 535 (1811).

discuss the acts of our legislature. That would be a large permission indeed. Is there, gentlemen, to be a power in the people to counteract the acts of the parliament, and is the libeller to come and make the people dissatisfied with the government under which he lives? This is not to be permitted to any man,—it is unconstitutional and seditious.

The same emphasis on bad tendency appears in Lord Ellenborough's charge at Leigh Hunt's trial, although it failed to secure his conviction.

Can you conceive that the exhibition of the words "One Thousand Lashes," with strokes underneath to attract attention, could be for any other purpose than to excite disaffection? Could it have any other tendency than that of preventing men from entering into the army?[60]

The same desire to nip revolution in the bud was shown by the Scotch judges who secured the conviction of Muir and Palmer for advocating reform of the rotten boroughs which chose the House of Commons and the extension of the franchise, sentences of transportation for seven and fourteen years being imposed.[61]

The right of universal suffrage, the subjects of this country never enjoyed; and were they to enjoy it, they would not long enjoy either liberty or a free constitution. You will, therefore, consider whether telling the people that they have a just right to what would unquestionably be tantamount to a total subversion of this constitution, is such a writing as any person is entitled to compose, to print, and to publish.

American sentiment about sedition trials was decisively shown by an expedition to New South Wales to rescue Muir, a sort of reverse deportation.

[60] 31 How. St. Tr. 367, 408, 413 (1811).
[61] 2 May, *Constitutional History*, 38-41, on the trials of Muir and Palmer. Philip A. Brown, *The French Revolution in English History*, 97. Fourteen years appears to have been the longest sentence for sedition imposed in Scotland during the French wars. Four years was the longest in England. See note 80 in Chapter II, *infra*, for sentences under the Espionage Act. Compare with these charges that of Van Valkenburgh, J., in United States *v.* Rose Pastor Stokes, *infra*, and the remarks of Judge Clayton in the Abrams trial in Chapter III.

In the light of such prosecutions it is plain that the most vital indication that the popular definition of liberty of the press, unpunishable criticism of officials and laws, has become a reality, is the disappearance of these doctrines of bad tendency and presumptive intent. In Great Britain they lingered until liberalism triumphed in 1832,[62] but in this country they disappeared with the adoption of the free speech clauses.

The revival of those doctrines is a sure symptom of an attack upon the liberty of the press.

Only once in our history prior to 1917 has an attempt been made to apply those doctrines. In 1798 the impending war with France, the spread of revolutionary doctrines by foreigners in our midst, and the spectacle of the disastrous operation of those doctrines abroad,—facts that have a familiar sound to-day—led to the enactment of the Alien and Sedition Laws.[63] The Alien Law allowed the President to compel the departure of aliens whom he judged dangerous to the peace and safety of the United States, or suspected, on reasonable grounds, of treasonable or secret machinations against our government. The Sedition Law punished false, scandalous, and malicious writings against the government, either House of Congress, or the President, if published with intent to defame any of them, or to excite against them the hatred of the people, or to stir up sedition or to excite resistance of law, or to aid any hostile designs of any foreign nation against the United States. The maximum penalty was a fine of two thousand dollars and two years' imprisonment. Truth was a defense, and the jury had power to determine criminality as under Fox's Libel Act. Despite the inclusion of the two legal rules for which reformers had contended, and the requirement of an actual

---

[62] That they may not have wholly disappeared even yet is indicated by the definition of sedition in Stephen's *Digest of Criminal Law*, which should have no application to American law. See also House Judiciary Hearings on S. 3317 etc., 66th Cong., 2d Sess., p. 277.

[63] Act of June 25, 1798, 1 Stat. at L., 570; Act of July 14, 1798, 1 Stat. at L., 596. See Bibliography for other references on these Acts.

intention to cause overt injury, the Sedition Act was bitterly resented as invading the liberty of the press. Its constitutionality was assailed on that ground by Jefferson, who pardoned all prisoners when he became President, Congress eventually repaid all the fines, and popular indignation at the Act and the prosecutions wrecked the Federalist party. In those prosecutions words were once more made punishable for their judicially supposed bad tendency, and the judges reduced the test of intent to a fiction by inferring the bad intent from this bad tendency.

Whether or not the Sedition Act was unconstitutional, and on that question Jefferson seems right, it surely defeated the fundamental policy of the First Amendment, the open discussion of public affairs. Like the British trials, the American sedition cases showed, as Professor Schofield demonstrates,[64] " the great danger . . . that men will be fined and imprisoned, under the guise of being punished for their bad motives, or bad intent and ends, simply because the powers that be do not agree with their opinions, and spokesmen of minorities may be terrorized and silenced when they are most needed by the community and most useful to it, and when they stand most in need of the protection of the law against a hostile, arrogant majority." When the Democrats got into power, a common-law prosecution for seditious libel was brought in New York against a Federalist who had attacked Jefferson. Hamilton conducted the defense in the name of the liberty of the press.[65] This testimony from Jefferson and Hamilton, the leaders of both par-

[64] Schofield, *op. cit.*, 91, and 92 note.
[65] People *v.* Croswell, 3 Johns. Cas. 337 (1804). New York had then no constitutional guarantee of liberty of the press, but Hamilton urged that under that right at common law truth was a defense and the jury could decide on criminality. He defined liberty of the press as "The right to publish, with impunity, truth, with good motives, for justifiable ends though reflecting on government, magistracy, or individuals." See Schofield, *op. cit.*, 89 ff., for criticism of this definition as not in the common law and as too narrow a definition of the conception of free speech. However, it is embodied in many state constitutions and statutes. Two out of four judges agreed with Hamilton.

ties, leaves the Blackstonian interpretation of free speech in America without a leg to stand on. And the brief attempt of Congress and the Federalist judges to revive the crime of sedition had proved so disastrous that it was not repeated during the next century.

The lesson of the prosecutions for sedition in Great Britain and the United States during this revolutionary period, that the most essential element of free speech is the rejection of bad tendency as the test of a criminal utterance, was never more clearly recognized than in Jefferson's preamble to the Virginia Act for establishing Religious Freedom.[66] His words about religious liberty hold good of political and speculative freedom, and the portrayal of human life in every form of art.

To suffer the civil Magistrate to intrude his powers into the field of opinion, and to restrain the profession or propagation of principles on supposition of their ill tendency, is a dangerous fallacy, which at once destroys all religious liberty, because he being of course judge of that tendency, will make his opinions the rule of judgment, and approve or condemn the sentiments of others only as they shall square with or differ from his own.

Although the free speech clauses were directed primarily against the sedition prosecutions of the immediate past, it must not be thought that they would permit unlimited previous restraint. They must also be interpreted in the light of more remote history. The framers of those clauses did not invent the conception of freedom of speech as a result of their own experience of the last few years. The idea had been gradually molded in men's minds by centuries of conflict. It was the product of a people of whom the framers were merely the mouthpiece. Its significance was not fixed by their personality, but was the endless expression of a

---

[66] Act of December 26, 1785, 12 Hening's *Statutes at Large of Virginia* (1823), c. 34, page 84. Another excellent argument against the punishment of tendencies is found in Philip Furneaux, *Letters to Blackstone*, 2 ed., 60-63, London, 1771; quoted in State *v.* Chandler, 2 Harr. (Del.) 553, 576 (1837), and in part by Schofield, *op. cit.*, 77.

civilization.[67] It was formed out of past resentment against the royal control of the press under the Tudors, against the Star Chamber and the pillory, against the Parliamentary censorship which Milton condemned in his *Areopagitica*, by recollections of heavy newspaper taxation, by hatred of the suppression of thought which went on vigorously on the Continent during the eighteenth century. Blackstone's views also had undoubted influence to bar out previous restraint. The censor is the most dangerous of all the enemies of liberty of the press, and ought not to exist in this country unless made necessary by extraordinary perils.

Moreover, the meaning of the First Amendment did not crystallize in 1791. The framers would probably have been horrified at the thought of protecting books by Darwin or Bernard Shaw, but "liberty of speech" is no more confined to the speech they thought permissible than "commerce" in another clause is limited to the sailing vessels and horse-drawn vehicles of 1787. Into the making of the constitutional conception of free speech have gone, not only men's bitter experience of the censorship and sedition prosecutions before 1791, but also the subsequent development of the law of fair comment in civil defamation, and the philosophical speculations of John Stuart Mill. Justice Holmes phrases the thought with even more than his habitual felicity.[68] "The provisions of the Constitution are not mathematical formulas having their essence in their form; they are organic living institutions transplanted from English soil."

It is now clear that the First Amendment fixes limits upon the power of Congress to restrict speech either by a censorship or by a criminal statute, and if the Espionage Act exceeds those limits it is unconstitutional. It is sometimes argued that the Constitution gives Congress the power to declare war, raise armies, and support a navy, that one provision of the Constitution cannot be used to break down

---

[67] 1 Kohler, *Lehrbuch des Bürgerlichen Rechts*, I, § 38.
[68] Gompers *v.* United States, 233 U. S. 604, 610 (1914).

another provision, and consequently freedom of speech cannot be invoked to break down the war power.[69] I would reply that the First Amendment is just as much a part of the Constitution as the war clauses, and that it is equally accurate to say that the war clauses cannot be invoked to break down freedom of speech. The truth is that all provisions of the Constitution must be construed together so as to limit each other. In a war as in peace, this process of mutual adjustment must include the Bill of Rights. There are those who believe that the Bill of Rights can be set aside in war time at the uncontrolled will of the government.[70] The first ten amendments were drafted by men who had just been through a war. The Third and Fifth Amendments expressly apply in war. A majority of the Supreme Court declared the war power of Congress to be restricted by the Bill of Rights in *Ex Parte* Milligan,[71] which cannot be lightly brushed aside, whether or not the majority went too far in thinking that the Fifth Amendment would have prevented Congress from exercising the war power under the particular circumstances of that case. If the First Amend-

[69] United States *v.* Marie Equi, Bull. Dept. Just., No. 172, 21 (Ore., 1918), Bean, J.

[70] Henry J. Fletcher, "The Civilian and the War Power," 2 *Minn. L. Rev.* 110, expresses this view. See also Ambrose Tighe, "The Legal Theory of the Minnesota 'Safety Commission' Act," 3 *Minn. L. Rev.* 1.

[71] 4 Wall. (U. S.) 2 (1866). The judges all agreed that Congress had not authorized the trial of the petitioner by a military tribunal. The majority, per Davis, J., took the ground that the government cannot have recourse to extraordinary procedure until there are extraordinary conditions to justify it and that under the Bill of Rights the decision of Congress that such procedure is necessary can be reviewed by the courts. The minority, per Chase, C. J., declared that Congress is sole judge of the expediency of military measures in war time, and that the war power is not abridged by any Amendment. The majority view on this matter may be accepted by one who questions their opinion that military tribunals are never justified outside the theater of active military operations in a place where the civil courts are open. It may be that military tribunals are necessary where the machinery of the civil courts cannot adequately meet the situation (3 *Minn. L. Rev.* 9), but the civil courts must eventually decide whether their machinery was adequate or not. Otherwise, in any war, no matter how small or how distant, Congress could put the whole country under military dictatorship.

ment is to mean anything, it must restrict powers which are expressly granted by the Constitution to Congress, since Congress has no other powers.[72] It must apply to those activities of government which are most liable to interfere with free discussion, namely, the postal service and the conduct of war.

The true meaning of freedom of speech seems to be this. One of the most important purposes of society and government is the discovery and spread of truth on subjects of general concern. This is possible only through absolutely unlimited discussion, for, as Bagehot points out, once force is thrown into the argument, it becomes a matter of chance whether it is thrown on the false side or the true, and truth loses all its natural advantage in the contest. Nevertheless, there are other purposes of government, such as order, the training of the young, protection against external aggression. Unlimited discussion sometimes interferes with these purposes, which must then be balanced against freedom of speech, but freedom of speech ought to weigh very heavily in the scale. The First Amendment gives binding force to this principle of political wisdom.

Or to put the matter another way, it is useless to define free speech by talk about rights. The agitator asserts his constitutional right to speak, the government asserts its constitutional right to wage war. The result is a deadlock. Each side takes the position of the man who was arrested for swinging his arms and hitting another in the nose, and asked the judge if he did not have a right to swing his arms in a free country. "Your right to swing

[72] United States Constitution, Art. I, § 1: "All legislative powers herein granted shall be vested in a Congress." Amendment X: "The powers not delegated to the United States by the Constitution, nor prohibited by it to the States, are reserved to the States respectively or to the people."

"This government is acknowledged by all to be one of enumerated powers. The principle that it can exercise only the powers granted to it, would seem too apparent."—Marshall, C. J., in McCulloch *v.* Maryland, 4 Wheat. (U. S.) 316, 405 (1819). See also Taney, C. J., in *Ex parte* Merryman, Taney, 236, 260 (1861), and Brewer, J., in Kansas *v.* Colorado, 206 U. S. 46, 81 (1907).

FREEDOM OF SPEECH IN WAR TIME 35

your arms ends just where the other man's nose begins." To find the boundary line of any right, we must get behind rules of law to human facts. In our problem, we must regard the desires and needs of the individual human being who wants to speak and those of the great group of human beings among whom he speaks. That is, in technical language, there are individual interests and social interests, which must be balanced against each other, if they conflict, in order to determine which interest shall be sacrificed under the circumstances and which shall be protected and become the foundation of a legal right.[73] It must never be forgotten that the balancing cannot be properly done unless all the interests involved are adequately ascertained, and the great evil of all this talk about rights is that each side is so busy denying the other's claim to rights that it entirely overlooks the human desires and needs behind that claim.

The rights and powers of the Constitution, aside from the portions which create the machinery of the federal system, are largely means of protecting important individual and social interests, and because of this necessity of balancing such interests the clauses cannot be construed with absolute literalness. The Fourteenth Amendment and the obligation of contracts clause, maintaining important individual interests, are modified by the police power of the states, which protects health and other social interests. The Thirteenth Amendment is subject to many implied exceptions, so that temporary involuntary servitude is permitted to secure social interests in the construction of roads, the prevention of vagrancy, the training of the militia or national army. It is common to rest these implied exceptions to the Bill of Rights upon the ground that they existed in 1791 and long before, but a less arbitrary explanation is desirable. Not everything old is good. Thus the antiquity of peonage

---

[73] This distinction between rights and interests clarifies almost any constitutional controversy. The distinction originated with von Ihering. For presentation of it in English, see John Chipman Gray, *Nature and Sources of the Law*, § 48 ff.; Roscoe Pound, "Interests of Personality," 28 *Harv. L. Rev.* 453.

does not constitute it an exception to the Thirteenth Amendment; it is not now demanded by any strong social interest. It is significant that the social interest in shipping which formerly required the compulsory labor of articled sailors is no longer recognized in the United States as sufficiently important to outweigh the individual interest in free locomotion and choice of occupation. Even treaties providing for the apprehension in our ports of deserting foreign seamen have been abrogated by the La Follette Seamen's Act. The Bill of Rights does not crystallize antiquity. It seems better to say that long usage does not create an exception to the absolute language of the Constitution, but demonstrates the importance of the social interest behind the exception.[74]

The First Amendment protects two kinds of interests in free speech. There is an individual interest, the need of many men to express their opinions on matters vital to them if life is to be worth living, and a social interest in the attainment of truth, so that the country may not only adopt the wisest course of action but carry it out in the wisest way. This social interest is especially important in war time. Even after war has been declared there is bound to be a confused mixture of good and bad arguments in its support, and a wide difference of opinion as to its objects. Truth can be sifted out from falsehood only if the government is vigorously and constantly cross-examined, so that the fundamental issues of the struggle may be clearly defined, and the war may not be diverted to improper ends, or conducted with an undue sacrifice of life and liberty, or prolonged after its just purposes are accomplished. Legal proceedings prove that an opponent makes the best cross-examiner. Consequently it is a disastrous mistake to limit criticism to those who favor the war. Men bitterly hostile to it may point out evils in its management like the secret treaties, which

---

[74] This paragraph rests on Butler *v.* Perry, 240 U. S. 328 (1916); Robertson *v.* Baldwin, 165 U. S. 275, 281 (1897); Bailey *v.* Alabama, 219 U. S. 219 (1911); Act of March 4, 1915, c. 153, § 16, U. S. Comp. Stat., 1918, § 8382 *a;* Hurtado *v.* California, 110 U. S. 516 (1884).

its supporters have been too busy to unearth. If a free canvassing of the aims of the war by its opponents is crushed by the menace of long imprisonment, such evils, even though made public in one or two newspapers, may not come to the attention of those who had power to counteract them until too late.[75]

The history of the last five years shows how the objects of a war may change completely during its progress, and it is well that those objects should be steadily reformulated under the influence of open discussion not only by those who demand a military victory, but by pacifists who take a different view of the national welfare. Further argument for the existence of this social interest becomes unnecessary if we recall the national value of the opposition in former wars.

The great trouble with most judicial construction of the Espionage Act is that this social interest has been ignored and free speech has been regarded as merely an individual interest, which must readily give way like other personal desires the moment it interferes with the social interest in national safety. The judge who has done most to bring social interests into legal thinking said years ago, " I think that the judges themselves have failed adequately to recognize their duty of weighing considerations of social advantage. The duty is inevitable, and the result of the often proclaimed judicial aversion to deal with such considerations is simply to leave the very ground and foundation of judgments inarticulate and often unconscious." [76] The failure of the courts in the past to formulate any principle for drawing a boundary line around the right of free speech has not only thrown the judges into the difficult questions

---

[75] " Senator Borah—'Then we had no knowledge of these secret treaties so far as our Government was concerned until you reached Paris?'

" The President—'Not unless there was information at the State Department of which I knew nothing.' "—*N. Y. Times,* Aug. 20, 1919.

[76] Oliver Wendell Holmes, "The Path of the Law," 10 *Harv. L. Rev.* 457, 467.

of the Espionage Act without any well-considered standard of criminality, but has allowed some of them to impose standards of their own and fix the line at a point which makes all opposition to this or any future war impossible. For example:

> No man should be permitted, by deliberate act, or even unthinkingly, to do that which will in any way detract from the efforts which the United States is putting forth or serve to postpone for a single moment the early coming of the day when the success of our arms shall be a fact.[77]

The true boundary line of the First Amendment can be fixed only when Congress and the courts realize that the principle on which speech is classified as lawful or unlawful involves the balancing against each other of two very important social interests, in public safety and in the search for truth. Every reasonable attempt should be made to maintain both interests unimpaired, and the great interest in free speech should be sacrificed only when the interest in public safety is really imperiled, and not, as most men believe, when it is barely conceivable that it may be slightly affected. In war time, therefore, speech should be unrestricted by the censorship or by punishment, unless it is clearly liable to cause direct and dangerous interference with the conduct of the war.

Thus our problem of locating the boundary line of free speech is solved. It is fixed close to the point where words will give rise to unlawful acts. We cannot define the right of free speech with the precision of the Rule against Perpetuities or the Rule in Shelley's Case, because it involves national policies which are much more flexible than private property, but we can establish a workable principle of classification in this method of balancing and this broad test of certain danger. There is a similar balancing in the determination of what is "due process of law." We can insist

---

[77] United States v. "The Spirit of '76," 252 Fed. 946. Another good example is United States v. Schoberg, Bull. Dept. Just., No. 149.

upon various procedural safeguards which make it more probable that a tribunal will give the value of open discussion its proper weight in the balance. Fox's Libel Act is such a safeguard, and others will be considered in the next chapter. And we can with certitude declare that the First Amendment forbids the punishment of words merely for their injurious tendencies. The history of the Amendment and the political function of free speech corroborate each other and make this conclusion plain.

CHAPTER II

OPPOSITION TO THE WAR WITH GERMANY

Vital as is the necessity in time of war not to hamper acts of the executive in the defense of the nation and in the prosecution of the war, of equal and perhaps greater importance, is the preservation of constitutional rights.—JUDGE MAYER, in *Ex parte* Gilroy, 257 Fed. 110, 114 (1919).

ON April 6, 1917, Congress declared war against Germany. On May 18 it enacted the Selective Service Act for raising a National Army. The people, by an overwhelming majority, believed conscription to be a necessary and just method of waging an unavoidable war, and the machinery for enforcing the draft by civilian aid was admirably planned. "The result," says Attorney General Gregory,[1] "was that the ultimate opposition to the draft by those liable was surprisingly small, considering the persistent propaganda carried on against the policy of the law and against its constitutionality." And his Assistant, Mr. John Lord O'Brian, adds, "No anti-draft propaganda had the slightest chance of success." The decision of the Supreme Court sustaining the validity of the statute[2] merely fulfilled the general expectation.

Besides the military and civilian organization for reaching the men who were liable to registration and subsequently called into service, the government had at its disposal several criminal statutes enacted during the Civil War, which it could and did use to punish conspiracies to resist recruiting and conscription by riots[3] and other forcible means, or seeking by speeches and publications to induce men to evade the

---

[1] Report of the Attorney General, 1917, p. 74. "Civil Liberty in War Time," John Lord O'Brian, 42 Rep. N. Y. Bar Assn. 275, 291 (1919), cited hereafter as O'Brian.

[2] Selective Draft Law Cases, 245 U. S. 366 (1918).

[3] Bryant *v.* U. S., 257 Fed. 378 (C. C. A., 1919); Orear *v.* U. S., 261

draft.[4] In some respects, however, these statutes were felt to be incomplete. It was not a crime to persuade a man not to enlist voluntarily, and an attempt by an isolated individual to obstruct the draft, if unsuccessful, was beyond the reach of the law, unless his conduct was sufficiently serious to amount to treason. The treason statute, the only law on the books affecting the conduct of the individual, was of little service,[5] since there was considerable doubt whether it applied to utterances. Therefore, although it is probable that under the circumstances the existing conspiracy statutes would have met any serious danger to the prosecution of the war, new legislation was demanded.

If the government had been content to limit itself to meeting the tangible needs just mentioned, the effect on discussion of the war would probably have been very slight, for treason, conspiracies, and attempts constitute a direct and dangerous interference with the war, outside the protection of freedom of speech as defined in the preceding chapter. Two additional factors, however, influenced the terms of the new statutes, and even more the spirit in which they were enforced. First, came the recollection of the opposition during the Civil War, which was handled under martial law in so far as it was suppressed at all, a matter which I shall take up later. Some persons, full of old tales of Copperheads, were for stigmatizing all opponents of this war as traitors. Senator Chamberlain of Oregon introduced a bill which made the whole United States " a part of the zone of operations conducted by the enemy," and declared any person who endangered or interfered with the successful operation of our forces by publishing anything

---

Fed. 257 (C. C. A., 1919); U. S. v. Reeder, Bull. Dept. Just., No. 161 (1918); Reports of the Attorney General, 1917, p. 75; 1918, p. 45.

[4] Emma Goldman v. U. S., 245 U. S. 474 (1918); Wells v. U. S., 257 Fed. 605 (C. C. A., 1919); U. S. v. Phillips, Bull. Dept. Just., No. 14 (1917); and other cases in the bulletins; Reports of the Attorney General, *supra*.

[5] O'Brian, 277. Among the treason cases of the war were U. S. v. Werner, 247 Fed. 708 (1918), and Nelles, Espionage Act Cases, 4, cited hereafter as Nelles; U. S. v. Robinson, 259 Fed. 685 (1919); U. S. v. Fricke, 259 Fed. 673 (1919). See Bibliography, on treason.

to be a spy subject to trial by court martial and the penalty of death. The bill was dropped upon receipt of a letter from the President, in which he attacked the constitutionality and advisability of the law.[6] Whatever control was exercised over civilians should be through the ordinary courts, and it was evident that the conspiracy statutes did not make that possible on a large scale. The second factor was the fear of German propaganda and the knowledge of legislation and administrative regulations guarding against it in Great Britain [7] and Canada.[8] Although we did not adopt the British administrative control, which combined flexibility with possibilities of despotism, it was easy to forget our own policy of non-interference with minorities and put the United States also in a position to deal severely with written and spoken opposition to the war.

I. *The Espionage Acts of* 1917 *and* 1918

The result of these various influences was the third section of Title I of the Espionage Act. As originally enacted on June 15, 1917, this section established three new offenses: [9]

(1) Whoever, when the United States is at war, shall willfully make or convey false reports or false statements with intent to interfere with the operation or success of the military or naval

[6] "Freedom of Speech and of the Press in War Time: the Espionage Act," Thomas F. Carroll, 17 *Mich. L. Rev.* 663 note; cited hereafter as Carroll. Such a bill seems clearly unconstitutional in view of the Fifth Amendment and *Ex parte* Milligan. See note 71 in Chapter I.

[7] The Defense of the Realm Consolidation Act, 1914, 5 Geo. 5, c. 8, § 1, gives His Majesty in Council power "to issue regulations." A very wide scope is given to this power by the House of Lords in Rex *v.* Halliday (1917) A. C. 260, Lord Shaw of Dunfermline dissenting. See 31 *Harv. L. Rev.* 296. Regulation 27 of the Orders in Council makes various forms of speech, writing, etc., offenses. Regulation 51 A provides for the seizure of publications on warrant, and Regulation 56 (13) for the punishment of press offenses. See Pulling, *Defense of the Realm Manual*, revised monthly. These regulations have been construed in Norman *v.* Mathews, 32 T. L. R. 303, 369 (1915); Fox *v.* Spicer, 33 T. L. R. 172 (1917); Rex *v.* Bertrand Russell, *infra*, note 37. The practical effect has been to establish an administrative censorship. H. J. Laski, *Authority in the Modern State*, 101.

[8] Carroll, 17 *Mich. L. Rev.* 621 note.

[9] Act of June 15, 1917, c. 30, Title I, § 3. The numerals are inserted by me.

forces of the United States or to promote the success of its enemies (2) and whoever, when the United States is at war, shall willfully cause or attempt to cause insubordination, disloyalty, mutiny, or refusal of duty, in the military or naval forces of the United States, (3) or shall willfully obstruct the recruiting or enlistment service of the United States, to the injury of the service or of the United States, shall be punished by a fine of not more than $10,000 or imprisonment for not more than twenty years, or both.

Although most of the Espionage Act deals with entirely different subjects, like actual espionage, the protection of military secrets, and the enforcement of neutrality in future conflicts between other nations, the section just quoted is buttressed by four provisions. Section 4 of the same Title punishes persons conspiring to violate section 3, if any one of them does any act to effect the object of the conspiracy. Section 5 imposes a penalty of $10,000 or two years' imprisonment for harboring or concealing any person suspected of committing or being about to commit any of the offenses already mentioned. Title XI authorizes the issue of search warrants for the seizure of property used as the means of committing a felony, which would include violations of the section just quoted. It was under this provision that the moving-picture film was confiscated in the *Spirit of '76* case, and raids were made on the offices of anti-war organizations. Finally, Title XII made non-mailable any matter violating the Act, or advocating treason, insurrection, or forcible resistance to any law of the United States, directed that it should not be conveyed or delivered, and imposed heavy penalties for attempting to use the mails for its transmission.

Attorney General Gregory reports that, although this Act proved an effective instrumentality against deliberate or organized disloyal propaganda, it did not reach the individual casual or impulsive disloyal utterances. Also some District Courts gave what he considered a narrow construction of the word "obstruct" in clause (3), so that, as he puts it, "most of the teeth which we tried to put in were taken out." [10]

[10] 4 *Am. Bar Assoc. Journ.* 306.

These individual disloyal utterances, however, occurring with considerable frequency throughout the country, naturally irritated and angered the communities in which they occurred, resulting sometimes in unfortunate violence and lawlessness and everywhere in dissatisfaction with the inadequacy of the Federal law to reach such cases. Consequently there was a popular demand for such an amendment as would cover these cases.[11]

The history of what then happened in Congress is not without interest. The Attorney General asked for a brief amendment of the Act by the addition of attempts to obstruct the recruiting service, and the punishment of efforts intentionally made for the purpose of discrediting and interfering with the flotation of war loans. The Senate Committee on the Judiciary, being thus stirred up, took the bit in its teeth, and decided to stamp on all utterances of a disloyal character. It went for a model of legislation affecting freedom of discussion to a recent sedition statute of the state of Montana, and borrowed a large number of its clauses for the new federal law. While this measure was pending in Congress it was proposed to incorporate a provision exempting anti-war utterances if made with good motives and for justifiable ends. Mr. Gregory informed Congress that the experience of his department had shown "that some of the most dangerous types of propaganda were either made from good motives or else that the traitorous motive was not provable," and that the defense would "in effect destroy the value of the Espionage Act as a weapon against propaganda." The bill became law without the proviso.

This amendment of May 16, 1918,[12] which is sometimes called the Sedition Act, inserted "attempts to obstruct" in the third of the original offenses, and added nine more offenses, as follows: (4) saying or doing anything with intent to obstruct the sale of United States bonds, except by

[11] The history of the amendment is taken from Report of the Attorney General of the United States (1918), 18; and O'Brian, 302. See *Montana Laws*, 1918, sp., c. 11.

[12] The full text of this Amendment is in Appendix III.

way of bona fide and not disloyal advice; (5) uttering, printing, writing, or publishing any disloyal, profane, scurrilous, or abusive language, or language intended to cause contempt, scorn, contumely or disrepute as regards the form of government of the United States; (6) or the Constitution; (7) or the flag; (8) or the uniform of the Army or Navy; (9) or any language intended to incite resistance to the United States or promote the cause of its enemies; (10) urging any curtailment of production of any things necessary to the prosecution of the war with intent to hinder its prosecution; (11) advocating, teaching, defending, or suggesting the doing of any of these acts; and (12) words or acts supporting or favoring the cause of any country at war with us, or opposing the cause of the United States therein. Whoever commits any one of these offenses in this or any future war is liable to the maximum penalty of the original act, $10,000 fine or twenty years' imprisonment, or both.

The buttressing provisions of the Act of 1917 apply to this 1918 Act and the non-mailable provision is made still more severe. The Postmaster General can now, if "on evidence satisfactory to *him*" he thinks anything mailed constitutes any one of the twelve offenses of the Sedition Act, prevent the sender from receiving any mail at all, however innocent. Without any jury trial or hearing before a judge, the citizen in question becomes for the post-office an outlaw.

The Espionage Act of 1918 has been defended on the ground that when the public found that many obnoxious utterances were regarded by United States District Attorneys as outside the simple Act of 1917, loyal people would take matters into their own hands. Two lynchings and many horsewhippings and tar-and-featherings had occurred, and over two hundred miners, mostly members of the I. W. W., were forcibly deported from their homes in Bisbee, Arizona, into the desert.[13] Congress responded to this outcry by the

[13] See note 11. Many cases of mob violence are listed on pp. 5-13 of *War-time Prosecutions and Mob Violence*, N. Y., 1919. The Bisbee deportations were held not to be a federal crime, U. S. *v.* Wheeler, 254 Fed. 611 (1918). State prosecutions are now pending.

passage of the Sedition Law. Doubtless some governmental action was required to protect pacifists and extreme radicals from mob violence, but incarceration for a period of twenty years seems a very queer kind of protection. If Congress had adopted some plan by which persons outside the existing conspiracy statutes whose speeches and writings were really causing trouble could be tried and confined until the actual emergency was passed, and in no case beyond the termination of hostilities, this would have prevented every danger to such men, and, what is more, every danger from them, and would have accorded with the preventive but not punitive policy pursued by Lincoln in the Civil War toward his most disloyal opponents. Instead, many persons convicted under the Espionage Act remained out on bail for months, often until the war was over, so that all the preventive purposes of the statute were defeated, and then were sent to prison for years.[14]

The chief importance of the new crimes created by the Espionage Act of 1918 is in their effect on future wars, for the amendment came so late in this war that all the big cases, except the Abrams prosecution, turned on the meaning of the three original offenses of the 1917 Act or on "attempts to obstruct." As the Abrams case is reserved for a chapter by itself, I shall hereafter in this chapter confine myself to those three offenses except when I expressly refer to the statute of 1918.

II. *Masses Publishing Co.* v. *Patten*

The framers of the First Amendment knew that the right to criticise might weaken the support of the Government in a time of war. They appreciated the value of a united public opinion at such a time. They were men who had experienced all those things in the war of the Revolution, and yet they knew too that the republic which they were founding could not live unless the right of free speech, of freedom of the press was maintained at such a time. They balanced these considerations and then wrote the First Amendment.—JUDGE CHARLES F. AMIDON.

[14] O'Brian, 311.

THE WAR WITH GERMANY

The Espionage Act of 1917 seems on its face constitutional under the interpretation of the First Amendment reached in this book, but it may have been construed so extremely as to violate the Amendment. Furthermore, freedom of speech is not only a limit on Congressional power, but a policy to be observed by the courts in applying constitutional statutes to utterance. The scope of that policy is determined by the same method of balancing social interests. The boundary line of punishable speech under this Act was consequently fixed at the point where words come close to injurious conduct by that judge who during the war gave the fullest attention to the meaning of free speech,— Judge Learned Hand, of the Southern District of New York.

In Masses Publishing Co. v. Patten [15] Judge Hand was asked to enjoin the postmaster of New York from excluding from the mails the August issue of *The Masses*, a monthly revolutionary journal, which contained several articles, poems, and cartoons attacking the war. When notified of the exclusion, the publisher had offered to delete any passages pointed out by the postmaster, but was refused such information. After suit was started, the postmaster, while objecting generally that the whole purport of the number was unlawful, since it tended to encourage the enemies of the United States and hamper the government in the conduct of the war, specified four cartoons, entitled "Liberty Bell," "Conscription," "Making the World Safe for Capitalism," and "Congress and Big Business"; also a poem, which declared Emma Goldman and Alexander Berkman, who were in prison for conspiracy to resist the draft, to be "elemental forces"—

> Like the water that climbs down the rocks;
> Like the wind in the leaves;
> Like the gentle night that holds us.

He also objected to three articles admiring the "sacrifice" of conscientious objectors, and praising Goldman and Berkman as "friends of American freedom."

[15] 244 Fed. 535 (S. D. N. Y., 1917).

The Espionage Act, it will be remembered, made non-mailable any publication which violated the criminal provisions of the section already quoted. One important issue was, therefore, whether the postmaster was right in finding such a violation. The case did not raise the constitutional question whether Congress could make criminal any matter which tended to discourage the successful prosecution of the war, but involved only the construction of the statute, whether Congress had as yet gone so far. Judge Hand held that it had not and granted the injunction. He refused to turn the original Act, which obviously dealt only with interference with the conduct of military affairs,[16] into a prohibition of all kinds of propaganda and a means for suppressing all hostile criticism and all opinion except that which encouraged and supported the existing policies of the war, or fell within the range of temperate argument. As Cooley pointed out long ago, you cannot limit free speech to polite criticism, because the greater a grievance the more likely men are to get excited about it, and the more urgent the need of hearing what they have to say.[17] The normal test for the suppression of speech in a democratic government, Judge Hand insists, is neither the justice of its substance nor the decency and propriety of its temper, but the strong danger that it will cause injurious acts. The Espionage Act should not be construed to reverse this national policy of liberty of the press and silence hostile criticism, unless Congress had given the clearest expression of such an intention in the statute.

Congress had shown no such intention. Moreover, whether

---

[16] The plain fact that the original Espionage Act is a military statute and not a sedition statute is also recognized by United States *v.* Fontana, Bull. Dept. Just., No. 148 (N. D. 1917), Amidon, J.; United States *v.* Wishek, Bull. Dept. Just., No. 153 (N. D., 1917), Amidon, J.; United States *v.* Henning, Bull. Dept. Just., No. 184 (Wis., 1917), Geiger, D. J.; and implied by other cases. The large number of cases which ignore the clear meaning of the statute is astounding in view of the rule that criminal statutes must be construed strictly.

[17] Cooley, *Constitutional Limitations*, 7 ed., 613.

THE WAR WITH GERMANY

or not it could create a personal censorship of the press under the war power, it had not yet done so. Since the portions of *The Masses* selected by the postmaster did not actually advocate violence, he had no right to suppress the magazine " on the doctrine that the general tenor and animus of the paper were subversive to authority and seditious in effect."

The tradition of English-speaking freedom has depended in no small part upon the merely procedural requirement that the state point with exactness to just that conduct which violates the law. It is difficult and often impossible to meet the charge that one's general ethos is treasonable.

Judge Hand places outside the limits of free speech one who counsels or advises others to violate existing laws. Language is not always exempt from punishment. " Words are not only the keys of persuasion, but the triggers of action, and those which have no purport but to counsel the violation of law cannot by any latitude of interpretation be a part of that public opinion which is the final source of government in a democratic state." It is also true, he says, that any discussion designed to show that existing laws are mistaken in means or unjust in policy may result in their violation. Nevertheless, if one stops short of urging upon others that it is their duty or their interest to resist the law, he should not be held to have attempted to cause illegal conduct. If this is not the test, the 1917 Act punishes every political agitation which can be shown to be apt to create a seditious temper. The language of the statute proves that Congress had no such revolutionary purpose in view.

According to this view, criminality under the Espionage Act of 1917 would be determined by an objective test, the nature of the words used. The jury could pass on this much better than on questions of political and economic tendency. Moreover, the Act would have a meaning easily understood by the opponents of the war. They could safely engage in discussion of its merits and the justice of war policies, so long as they refrained from urging violation of laws. The Act, thus interpreted, does not go to the limits of Congressional power as I have construed them. Under some circumstances an expression of opinion which does not counsel any unlawful act may be highly dangerous. Even Mill would punish a statement that grain-dealers are starvers of the poor, or that private property is robbery, when delivered orally to an excited mob assembled before the house of a grain-dealer.[18] A scathing analysis of the incompetence of the commanding general circulated among the troops on the eve of battle would be a direct and dangerous interference with the war. But military law would deal with this offense within the lines, and the law of illegal assembly will come into play elsewhere, as in Mill's case. There is no need to make the expression of opinion in itself criminal. It has not been so normally in this country, especially not under federal law, and the Espionage Act of 1917 (unlike that of 1918) contains nothing to indicate such an interference with the attainment and dissemination of truth. That statute by its terms fills in the gap between the treason and the conspiracy laws by reaching the individual who actually attempts or incites interference with the war, whether by acts like assaulting a recruiting officer or by words whose tenor shows that they have very little to do with the social interest in truth, since they do not discuss the merits of the war, but counsel immediate and injurious acts. In other words, Congress was punishing dangerous acts and such words as had all the effect of acts, because they could have no other purpose but a direct and dangerous interference with the war.

There was during the war no finer judicial statement of the right of free speech than these words of Judge Hand:

Political agitation, by the passions it arouses or the convictions it engenders, may in fact stimulate men to the violation of law.

[18] Mill, *Liberty,* opening of c. 3.

THE WAR WITH GERMANY

Detestation of existing policies is easily transformed into forcible resistance of the authority which puts them in execution, and it would be folly to disregard the causal relation between the two. Yet to assimilate agitation, legitimate as such, with direct incitement to violent resistance, is to disregard the tolerance of all methods of political agitation which in normal times is a safeguard of free government. The distinction is not a scholastic subterfuge, but a hard-bought acquisition in the fight for freedom.

Look at the Espionage Act of 1917 [19] with a post-armistice mind, and it is clear that Judge Hand was right. There is not a word in it to make criminal the expression of pacifist or pro-German opinions. It punishes false statements and reports—necessarily limited to statements of fact—but beyond that does not contain even a provision against the use of language. It differs entirely from the Act of 1918, and from state laws making utterances criminal for their own sake as nuisances or breaches of the peace. Utterances (except false statements) are punishable, if at all, because of their relation to specified acts. Clauses (2) and (3) punish successful interference with military affairs and attempts to interfere, which would probably include incitement.[20] The tests of criminal attempt and incitement are well settled.[21] The first requirement is the intention to bring about the overt criminal act. But the law does not punish bad intention alone, or even everything done with a bad intention. A statute against murder will not be construed to apply to discharging a gun with the intention to kill a man forty miles away. Writing a letter to a firm in San Francisco requesting a shipment of liquor into Alaska is not an attempt to import liquor into Alaska until it is brought near the borders, headlands, or waters of that territory. Attempts and incitement to be punishable must come danger-

---

[19] See page 42, *supra,* for text of the Act.

[20] Attempts do not ordinarily include solicitation, see Beale, *infra,* 16 *Harv. L. Rev.* 491, 506 note 1; but attempts to commit offenses under the 1917 Espionage Act would naturally be by incitement.

[21] Joseph H. Beale, "Criminal Attempts," 16 *Harv. L. Rev.* 491; U. S. *v.* Stephens, 12 Fed. 52. See also 32 *Harv. L. Rev.* 417.

ously near success, and bad intention is merely one modifying factor in determining whether the actual conduct is thus dangerous. A speaker is guilty of solicitation or incitement to a crime only if he would have been indictable for the crime itself, had it been committed, either as accessory or principal.[22] Of course his liability when nothing really happens will not be greater than if his conduct leads to actual crime. Now even in that event, at common law the utterer of written or spoken words is not criminally liable merely because he knows they will reach those who may find in them the excuse for criminal acts. The assassin of President McKinley may have been influenced by the denunciatory cartoons of "Willy and his Papa" in the Hearst newspapers, but the artist was not an accessory to the murder.

Wharton, a leading writer on criminal law, shows how wise the common law was in refusing to establish any rule of indirect causation with respect to utterances:

For we would be forced to admit, if we hold that solicitations to criminality are generally indictable, that the propagandists, even in conversation, of agrarian or communistic theories are liable to criminal prosecutions; and hence the necessary freedom of speech and of the press would be greatly infringed. It would be hard, also, we must agree, if we maintain such general responsibility, to defend, in prosecutions for soliciting crime, the publishers of Byron's *Don Juan,* of Rousseau's *Émile,* or of Goethe's *Elective Affinities.* Lord Chesterfield, in his letters to his son, directly advises the latter to form illicit connections with married women; Lord Chesterfield, on the reasoning here contested, would be indictable for solicitation to adultery. Undoubtedly, when such solicitations are so publicly and indecently made as to produce public scandal, they are indictable as nuisances or as libels. But to make bare solicitations or allurements indictable as *attempts,* not only unduly and perilously extends the scope of penal adjudication, but forces on the courts psychological questions which they are incompetent to decide, and a branch of business which would make them despots of every intellect in the land.[23]

[22] See Beale, *supra,* 16 *Harv. L. Rev.* 491, 505. Under the federal statutes he would be a principal. Rev. Stat. §§ 5323, 5427; March 4, 1909, c. 321, § 332; U. S. Comp. Stat., 1918, § 10506 (Crim. Code, § 332).
[23] Wharton, *Criminal Law,* I (9 ed.), § 179.

On the contrary, the rule has always been that, to establish criminal responsibility, the words uttered must constitute dangerous progress toward the consummation of the independent offense attempted and amount to procurement, counsel, or command to commit the forbidden acts.[24] This standard can be applied, not only to attempts to cause insubordination and obstruction of the draft, where the ultimate result would be a crime, but also to the persuasion of men not to volunteer. Their failure to enlist is not a crime, but is a serious injury to the government. The speaker is interfering with the right of the army to a free labor market, in a manner analogous to picketing and boycotting in private business, which often constitute civil wrongs, compensated by damages.[25] Such interference may justly be made criminal, but only if it is direct and dangerous, for the measure of liability ought not to be larger than for solicitation to a criminal result like evasion of the draft.[26]

Consequently, no one should have been held under clauses (2) and (3) of the Espionage Act of 1917 who did not satisfy these tests of criminal attempt and incitement. As Justice Holmes said in Commonwealth v. Peaslee,[27] "It is a question of degree." We can suppose a series of opinions, ranging from "This is an unwise war" up to "You ought to refuse to go, no matter what they do to you," or an audience varying from an old women's home to a group of drafted men just starting for a training camp. Somewhere in such a range of circumstances is the point where direct causation begins and speech becomes punishable as incitement under the ordinary standards of statutory construction

[24] 4 Blackstone's *Commentaries* 36.
[25] Gompers v. Bucks Stove and Range Co., 221 U. S. 418 (1911); Vegelahn v. Guntner, 167 Mass. 92 (1896). The boycott may become a crime under the Sherman Law, Loewe v. Lawlor (Danbury Hatters' Case), 208 U. S. 274 (1908).
[26] See Hand in U. S. v. Nearing, 252 Fed. 223, 227 (1918). The same principle applies to interference with Liberty Bond sales under the 1918 Act.
[27] 177 Mass. 267, 272 (1901). See also his opinion in Swift v. U. S., 196 U. S. 375, 396 (1905).

and the ordinary policy of free speech, which Judge Hand applied. Congress could push the test of criminality back beyond this point, although eventually it would reach the extreme limit fixed by the First Amendment, beyond which words cannot be restricted for their remote tendency to hinder the war.[28] In other words, the ordinary tests punish agitation just before it begins to boil over; Congress could change those tests and punish it when it gets really hot, but it is unconstitutional to interfere when it is merely warm. And there is not a word in the 1917 Espionage Act to show that Congress did change the ordinary tests or make any speech criminal except false statements and incitement to overt acts. Every word used, "cause," "attempt," "obstruct," clearly involves proximate causation, a close and direct relation to actual interference with the operations of the army and navy, with enlistment and the draft. Finally, this is a penal statute and ought to be construed strictly. Attorney General Gregory's charge that judges like Learned Hand "took the teeth" out of the 1917 Act [29] is absurd, for the teeth the government wanted were never there until other judges in an excess of patriotism put in false ones.

Nevertheless, Judge Hand was reversed [30] on a point of administrative law, that the postmaster's decision must stand unless clearly wrong,[31] but the Circuit Court of Appeals thought it desirable to reject his construction of the Espionage Act and substitute the view that speech is punishable under the Act " if the natural and reasonable effect of what is said is to encourage resistance to law, and the words are used in an endeavor to persuade to resistance." His objective test of the nature of the words was considered un-

[28] See the quotation from Justice Brandeis, page 99, *infra*.

[29] See note 10, *supra*.

[30] Masses Pub. Co. *v.* Patten, 245 Fed. 102 (C. C. A. 2d, 1917), Hough, J., stayed the injunction; *ibid.* 246, Fed. 24 (C. C. A. 2d, 1917), Ward, Rogers, and Mayer, JJ., reversed the order granting the injunction.

[31] See for authorities against this proposition, 32 *Harv. L. Rev.* 417, 420. See page 106, *infra,* VI. Censorship; also Chapter V.

THE WAR WITH GERMANY

sound. Advice in direct language was repudiated as a requisite of guilt. Judge Hough used the Sermon on the Mount as a precedent for the government's war policy: "It is at least arguable whether there can be any more direct incitement to action than to hold up to admiration those who do act. . . The Beatitudes have for some centuries been considered highly hortatory, though they do not contain the injunction: 'Go thou and do likewise.'" It is possible that the Court of Appeals did not intend to lay down a very different principle from Judge Hand, but chiefly wished to insist that in determining whether there is incitement one must look not only at the words themselves but also at the surrounding circumstances which may have given the words a special meaning to their hearers. Judge Hand agrees with this, and regards Mark Antony's funeral oration, for instance, as having counseled violence while it expressly discountenanced it. However, the undoubted effect of the final decision in Masses v. Patten was to establish the old-time doctrine of remote bad tendency in the minds of district judges throughout the country. By its rejection of the common-law test of incitement,[32] it deprived us of the only standard of criminal speech there was, since there had never been any well-considered discussion of the meaning of "freedom of speech" in the First Amendment.

As a result of this and similar decisions, the district judges ignored entirely the first element of criminal attempt and solicitation, that the effort, though unsuccessful, must approach dangerously near success. They repudiated the test of guilt under the Act laid down by Judge Hand, that the words must in themselves urge upon their readers or hearers a duty or an interest to resist the law or the appeal for volunteers, and substituted the test that the words need only have a tendency to cause unrest among soldiers or to make recruiting more difficult. The remaining element,

[32] See the review of Masses v. Patten by Learned Hand, J., in U. S. v. Nearing, 252 Fed. 223, 227 (1918). Judge Rogers may not have realized he was rejecting it (246 Fed. 38), but the test of common-law incitement has never been applied to the Act by a District Judge since.

intention to cause the bad overt action, they retained. This new standard of guilt allowed conviction for any words which had an indirect effect to discourage recruiting and the war spirit, like the poem about Emma Goldman and the wind, if only the intention to discourage existed. Intention thus became the crucial test of guilt in any prosecution of opposition to the government's war policies, and this requirement of intention became a mere form since it could be inferred from the existence of the indirect injurious effect.[33] A few judges, notably Amidon of North Dakota, have stemmed the tide, but of most Espionage Act decisions what Jefferson and Stephen and Schofield said about the prosecutions under George III and the Sedition Act of 1798 can be said once more, that men have been punished without overt acts, with only a presumed intention to cause overt acts, merely for the utterance of words which judge and jury thought to have a tendency to injure the state. Judge Rogers was right in saying[34] that the words of the Espionage Act of 1917 bear slight resemblance to the Sedition Law of 1798, but the judicial construction is much the same, except that under the Sedition Law truth was a defense.

III. *The District Court Cases*

The effect of the prosecutions under this Act has, no doubt, been beneficial in maintaining law and order.—Report of the Attorney General, 1919.

The revival of the doctrines of bad tendency and constructive intent always puts an end to genuine discussion of public matters. It is unnecessary to review the two thousand Espionage Act prosecutions in detail, but a few general results may be presented here. The courts have treated opinions as statements of fact and then con-

[33] Masses Pub. Co. *v.* Patten, 246 Fed. 24, 39 (1917), Ward, J.; and Rogers, J.: "The court does not hesitate to say that, considering the natural and reasonable effect of the publication, it was intended willfully to obstruct recruiting."
[34] *Ibid.* 29.

demned them as false because they differed from the President's speech or the resolution of Congress declaring war. Their construction of this first clause of the Act will be considered in connection with the Supreme Court decisions. Under the second and third clauses against causing insubordination or obstructing recruiting, only a few persons have been convicted for actually urging men to evade the draft or not to enlist. Almost all the convictions have been for expressions of opinion about the merits and conduct of the war. It became criminal to advocate heavier taxation instead of bond issues, to state that conscription was unconstitutional though the Supreme Court had not yet held it valid, to say that the sinking of merchant vessels was legal, to urge that a referendum should have preceded our declaration of war, to say that war was contrary to the teachings of Christ. Men have been punished for criticising the Red Cross and the Y.M.C.A., while under the Minnesota Espionage Act it has been held a crime to discourage women from knitting by the remark, " No soldier ever sees these socks." [35] It was in no way necessary that these expressions of opinion should be addressed to soldiers or men on the point of enlisting or being drafted. Most judges held it enough if the words might conceivably reach such men. They have made it impossible for an opponent of the war to write an article or even a letter in a newspaper of general circulation because it will be read in some training camp where it might cause insubordination or interfere with military success. He cannot address a large audience because it is liable to include a few men in uniform; and some judges have held him punishable if it contains men

---

[35] State v. Freerks, 140 Minn. 349 (1918). References to all cases mentioned by name in succeeding paragraphs will be found indexed in Appendix II. Among the many other cases illustrating the statements of this paragraph may be mentioned the trials of Sandberg, Miller, Nagler, Goldsmith, Kaufman, Weist, Kirchner, Shaffer, Albers, Krafft, Boutin, Granzow, Hitchcock, Weinsberg, Denson, Von Bank, White (all in Appendix II). A few of these convictions have been reversed, but this does not excuse the conduct of the trial courts. See also the Supreme Court cases discussed *infra*. See 32 *Harv. L. Rev.* 417, and other references in Appendix I. The facts of many cases are in *War-time Prosecutions and Mob Violence*.

between eighteen and forty-five, since they may be called into the army eventually; some have emphasized the possible presence of shipbuilders and munition-makers. All genuine discussion among civilians of the justice and wisdom of continuing a war thus becomes perilous.

Judge Van Valkenburgh, in United States v. Rose Pastor Stokes, would even make it criminal to argue to women against a war, by the words, " I am for the people and the government is for the profiteers," because what is said to mothers, sisters, and sweethearts may lessen their enthusiasm for the war, and " our armies in the field and our navies upon the seas can operate and succeed only so far as they are supported and maintained by the folks at home." The doctrine of indirect causation never had better illustration than in his charge. It shows how a very able judge of large experience can be swept from his moorings by war passion. Furthermore, although Mrs. Stokes was indicted only for writing a letter, the judge admitted her speeches to show her intent, and then denounced the opinions expressed in those speeches in the strongest language to the jury as destructive of the nation's welfare, so that she may very well have been convicted for the speeches and not for the letter.

Just as Lord Kenyon, while trying a man who happened to sympathize with the French Revolution, went out of his way to emphasize its massacres as a consequence of theories like the defendant's,[36] so Judge Van Valkenburgh denounced the Russian Revolution as " the greatest betrayal of the cause of democracy the world has ever seen," and made use of Mrs. Stokes' declared sympathy with that Revolution, an offense not punishable even under the Espionage Act, to show how dangerous it was for her to talk about profiteers.

Of course, the jury convicted Mrs. Stokes after such a charge. They found that the words, " I am for the people, and the government is for the profiteers," were a false statement, known to be false and intended and calculated to inter-

[36] Rex. v. Cuthell, 27 How. St. Tr. 642, 674 (1799).

fere with the success of our military and naval forces, that they were an attempt to cause insubordination in those forces, and that they obstructed recruiting. The judge sentenced her to ten years in prison. The Circuit Court of Appeals set aside this conviction in March, 1920, but it stood all during the war as a stern example that it was a heinous crime to discuss profiteering, because of " the possible, if not probable effect on our troops."

A case in the Second Circuit makes it equally perilous to urge a wider exemption for conscientious objectors because this tends to encourage more such objectors, a close parallel to the English imprisonment of Bertrand Russell.[37]

Many men have been imprisoned for arguments or profanity used in the heat of private altercation, on a railroad train, in a hotel lobby, or at that battle-ground of disputation, a boarding-house table.[38] In one case,[39] two strangers came to a farmhouse and asked the owner if he could let them have some gasoline, saying that they had been stranded out in the country. He not only gave them the gasoline, but invited them to dinner. An argument arose during the meal, and the farmer used scurrilous and presumably unpatriotic language in the presence of his guests, two hired men, two nieces, and some children. The guests reported his language, and he was convicted of a willful attempt to cause disloyalty, insubordination, mutiny, and refusal of duty in the military and naval forces of the United States. Even unexpressed thoughts have been prosecuted through an ingenious method of inquisition. A German-American who had not subscribed to Liberty bonds was visited in his house by a committee

[37] Fraina *v.* United States, 255 Fed. 28 (C. C. A. 2d, 1918), for conspiracy and not under the Espionage Act; Rex *v.* Bertrand Russell, Littell's *Living Age,* Feb. 15, 1919, p. 385.

[38] For instance, Sandberg, Albers, Goldsmith, Denson. But Judge Bourquin refused to let the jury pass on such evidence in the case of V. Hall, involving " kitchen gossip and saloon debate."

[39] U. S. *v.* Harshfield, 260 Fed. 659 (C. C. A., 8th, 1919), reversing the conviction. In Schoberg *v.* U. S., 264 Fed. 1, under 1918 Act, three elderly German Americans, hobnobbing together in the cobbler's shop of one of them and growling about the war, were convicted by means of a dictagraph.

who asked his reasons and received a courteous reply that he did not wish either side to win the war and could not conscientiously give it his aid. He was thereupon arrested and held in confinement until released by a district court.[40]

A few concrete cases of convictions that have been upheld will show how the Espionage Act operates to punish expressions of opinion.

J. P. Doe, son of the great Chief Justice of New Hampshire, while living in Colorado because of bad health, mailed an "endless chain" letter, to be sent "to friends of immediate peace," which stated that although the President and Secretary of State had said Germany had broken her promise to end submarine warfare, Germany had made no such promise, but had reserved in the *Sussex* note complete liberty of decision as to the future. Doe's statement was a legitimate inference from the note, whatever its bearing on the merits of our position—and this he did not discuss. Yet he was convicted for it, the alleged intent to obstruct recruiting being evidenced by passages from a long personal letter to his sister. The Court of Appeals said it was a fair construction of the circular that Doe intended to convey the idea that the United States was wrong in relying on the alleged promise as a cause of war; "such an argument would have a direct tendency to obstruct the recruiting and enlistment service." Doe was sentenced to eighteen months in prison.

Robert Goldstein, who had been connected with D. W. Griffith in producing "The Birth of a Nation," a well-known moving-picture film of the Civil War, planned a similar presentation of the Revolution in a film called "The Spirit of '76," which contained such scenes as Patrick Henry's Speech, the Signing of the Declaration of Independence, and Valley Forge. After a year and a half of work the picture was finished, just before the outbreak of our war with Germany. The film was displayed in Los Angeles to the

---

[40] United States *v.* Pape, 253 Fed. 270 (1918). State *v.* Ludemann, 172 N. W. (Minn.) 887 (1919), *acc.*

THE WAR WITH GERMANY 61

usual audience, which was not shown to contain either soldiers or sailors. The government thereupon indicted Goldstein for presenting a play designed and intended to arouse antagonism, hatred and enmity between the American people, particularly the armed forces, and the people of Great Britain, particularly their armed forces, when Great Britain was " an ally " of the United States, because one scene, the Wyoming Massacre, portrayed British soldiers bayoneting women and children and carrying away girls. The film was seized, the business was thrown from prosperity into bankruptcy with a loss of over $100,000, and Goldstein was convicted of attempting to cause insubordination, etc., in the armed forces and sentenced to ten years in the federal penitentiary at Steilacoom, Washington. His punishment for depicting the origin of this nation has been commuted to three years.[41]

Rev. Clarence H. Waldron, of Windsor, Vermont, was charged with handing to five persons, among whom were a woman, two men apparently above military age, and another clergyman, a pamphlet to show where he himself stood on the war. The judge in his charge quoted the following statements from the pamphlet:

Surely, if Christians were forbidden to fight to preserve the Person of their Lord and Master, they may not fight to preserve themselves, or any city they should happen to dwell in. Christ has no kingdom here. His servants must not fight.

The Christian may not go to "the front" to repel the foe— for there he is required to kill men.

They (referring to the Twelve Apostles) knew the force of their Lord's example, and whether to save themselves or to save others—never, never use the sword.

Better a thousand times to die than for a Christian to kill his fellow.

[41] 258 Fed. 908; 252 Fed. 946. This conviction has been defended on two grounds. (1) That Goldstein inserted the massacre at the public performance, though he had omitted it at a preliminary representation before officials. If they had no right to censor by previous restraint any way (cf. Dailey v. Superior Court, 112 Cal. 94), this fact seems immaterial. In any event it does not merit three years in jail. (2) That he had attempted to finance the enterprise by appeal to the anti-British sentiments of German-Americans. As this was before we entered the war, it should have no bearing whatever even if true.

I do not say that it is wrong for a nation to go to war to preserve its interests, but it is wrong to the Christian, absolutely, unutterably wrong.

Under no circumstances can I undertake any service that has for its purpose the prosecution of war.

Mr. Waldron was convicted for causing insubordination and obstructing recruiting, and sentenced to fifteen years in prison.[42]

D. H. Wallace, an ex-British soldier, was sentenced to twenty years for saying:

That when a soldier went away he was a hero and that when he came back flirting with a hand organ he was a bum, and that the asylums will be filled with them; that the soldiers were giving their lives for the capitalists, that 40 per cent of the ammunition of the allies or their guns was defective because of graft.

Wallace went insane and died in jail.

D. T. Blodgett was given the same sentence by the same judge, Wade, for circulating a pamphlet urging the voters of Iowa not to re-elect the Congressmen who voted for conscription, and reprinting an argument of Thomas E. Watson, of Georgia, against the constitutionality of the Draft Act. This was before its validity had been upheld by the Supreme Court. Judge Wade charged that the government had passed the Espionage Act, "realizing that it must protect the feeling and spirit of the American people against the work of those who defy authority; it was not intended for ninety-five per cent of the American people, but necessary for the few who will not heed the judgment of the ninety-five per cent; who assume to know more than all the others put together. It is not a harsh Act." He recalled the draft riots of the Civil War, and suggested that Blodgett had felt that a little mutiny might aid his political cause. "Just look at this that he wants drafted men to buy:"

In Washington City it is a carnival, a wild extravagance; an orgy of prodigal waste; a Bacchanalian revel of men who act as

[42] He was pardoned after a year in prison.

though they were drunk on power and had lost every sense of shame, duty and responsibility. The huge appropriations made will accrue to the benefit of the classes. Great is the gathering of the vultures at the National Capital, for never before has there been such a carcase inviting them to the feast. Three thousand millions of dollars in one appropriation, and the vultures fiercely shrieking for more.

" There is no better way," said the judge, " of unsettling the confidence of the people and stirring their souls against the war than to paint it as a war of capitalism, organized by capitalists and for capitalists, and painting the officers of the government as representing willing tools of Wall Street. There is no better way."

Undoubtedly in all these cases, intention to cause insubordination or obstruct recruiting was made a test of guilt. It may seem to many persons that, so long as a speaker talks with such a purpose it makes no difference whether he satisfies Judge Hand's objective standard by saying, " Don't enlist, don't register, shoot over the enemies' heads," or whether he confines himself to statements about the horrors of a modern battlefield and opinions about the legality of the German entry into Belgium. Very likely the moral quality of the two methods is the same; the tendency to prevent enlistment may be the same. But the reason that makes it, if not unconstitutional, at least very unwise, to punish the second type of utterance, the expression of fact or opinion, is that it is only by absence of penalties for such utterances that a self-governing people can learn and disseminate the truth on public affairs. The first type of utterance, on the other hand, has practically no value for such a purpose. When the public is interested, bad motives ought not to deprive it of the benefit of what is said. Opposition to governmental action through discussion, like opposition to private action through law-suits, is the alternative to the use of force. If the law should require litigants to have good motives, it might as well shut up the courts. In the same way, truth is truth, and just as valuable to the public, whether it comes from the most enthusiastic supporter of the war or from a pro-German, and in order to get the truth, conflicting views must be allowed. What a pacifist says about the extravagance of Congress or bad camp conditions during the influenza epidemic or the desire of France for the left bank of the Rhine, may be worth hearing and acting on, and it will be just as important, although he does it with the hope of hindering the war. If disclosures like those made by Admiral Sims are true, they would have been very valuable if made by some private citizen during the war, and no less so if printed in Berger's *Milwaukee Leader*. So long as the speaker creates no great danger of losing the war, so long as the discouraging effects of his utterances can be checked by the draft organization, the four-minute men, and the general loyalty, it is wiser to let him talk for the sake of possible good.

The last case reviewed, Judge Wade's trial of Blodgett, brings out my point clearly. Every one will admit that Congress may properly consider ending a war. If so, the men to favor this must be elected, as many of them were in 1864, and the election will be a poor expression of the popular will unless it is preceded by discussion of the merits of beginning and continuing the war. Once more, that discussion will have little value for the formation of opinion if the presence of a man within draft age brings it within the scope of the Espionage Act, and if those who oppose the war vigorously are cowed into silence by twenty-year sentences. It must never be forgotten that the Espionage Act applies to all future wars, and the next one may be as questionable as those of 1812 and 1846. The same considerations apply to the right of petitioning Congress and high officials, which is expressly secured by the First Amendment. Twenty-seven South Dakota farmers were opposed to the draft and believed that an unduly high quota was exacted from their county. They petitioned various state officers, asking a new arrangement, a referendum on the war, payment of war expenses from taxation and repu-

THE WAR WITH GERMANY 65

diation of war debts. As an alternative they threatened defeat to the officers, their party, and the nation. Foolish as this petition was, it stated a grievance which deserved inquiry. Instead, the twenty-seven were sentenced to more than a year in prison. This conviction, Attorney General Gregory declares to have been " one of the greatest deterrents against the spread of hostile propaganda, and particularly that class of propaganda which advanced and played upon the theme that this was a capitalists' war." Yet after it had served this suppressive purpose, and reached the Supreme Court, he confessed that the conviction was erroneous.[43]

In the same way, punishment of alleged evil tendency coupled with unlawful intention limits the general influence of the press on legislation and administrative policies, which is a recognized part of American democracy. Undoubtedly, the statement that $640,000,000 had been spent on aeroplanes without a single machine in France had as great a tendency to weaken the national morale as any event of the war. The District Court test makes it criminal for an editor to mention that fact with the purpose of turning public opinion against the war. It is true that no prosecutions were brought on that account, but are we any worse off without them? Was it not an advantage to have the fact as widely known as possible so as to produce a complete alteration of government methods? And so with respect to the territorial and commercial aims of our associates in the war, which have caused us so much concern since the armistice. In short, the truth may be told with a bad purpose, but it is none the less truth; and the most dangerous falsehoods (like the report of the premature armistice, which probably cost a very great loss of production of munitions), may be committed from motives of the highest patriotism. Even on the assumption, which I shall soon show to be questionable, that all the

[43] Baltzer case; Report of Attorney General, 1918, 48. Jared Peck was indicted under the Sedition Act of 1798 for circulating a petition to Congress for the repeal of the Act.—Beveridge's *Marshall*, III, 42 note.

persons convicted under the Espionage Act intended to hinder the war, intention is a very poor test of the truth and value of reports and opinions, and in effect results in the punishment of men, not for any actual or probable injury, but for their state of mind.

IV. *The Human Machinery of the Espionage Acts*

If there be a scintilla of real *evidence* that seditious rags are infecting the Native Army, nobody would refuse suppression. Only you won't forget that in moments of excitement, such as this may become, people are uncommonly liable to confuse suspicions and possibilities with certainty and reality.—MORLEY, *Recollections*. Letter to the Viceroy of India.

A less obvious but not less vital objection to the District Court test is its unfitness for practical administration. Even if we decide that the man who makes discouraging utterances in war time with a bad intention deserves punishment, we ought not to lay down a rule of law to punish him, unless we can be sure that in its actual operation it will catch him and let the man with good intention go. A rule is not desirable simply because it reads well. It must also work well. The law is not self-operating and it cannot pick out the bad man automatically. It must discover him through human machinery, and the defects of this machinery are the very greatest reason for preserving an immunity of speech from prosecution far wider than the District Court test.

"We have to consider," said Macaulay of a theory of criminal law very similar to this test,[44] " not merely the goodness of the end, but also the fitness of the means. . . . There is surely no contradiction in saying that a certain section of the community may be quite competent to protect the persons and property of the rest, yet quite unfit to direct our opinions."

---

[44] Essay on Southey's *Colloquies*. The whole is worth re-reading to-day, especially the warning against a Paul Pry government, declaring what we shall think and what we shall drink.

Jefferson pointed out in the Virginia Toleration Statute, quoted in the first chapter,[45] the unfitness of this machinery for discriminating between utterances of good tendency and utterances of bad tendency. Its unsuitability to separate good from bad intention is just as great.[46] The trouble with the District Court test is, that in making intention the crucial fact in criminality, it exposes all who discuss heated questions to an inquiry before a jury as to their purposes. That inquiry necessarily is of the widest scope and if the general attitude of the person is singular and intransigeant, there is an insufficient protection. You cannot tell a man's intention by looking at his forehead, you must look through it to the inside of his head, and no judge and jury are capable of looking through the skull of a man who has done nothing but talk, to see what goes on inside. It is true that intention is material in other crimes, such as murder, but in dealing with an overt criminal act the intention is evidenced by many other acts, which are a kind of fact with which the jurymen are familiar and capable of dealing. On the other hand, the intention in making utterances is evidenced by inferences drawn from the supposed bad tendency of the words themselves, and by other utterances, which will also be viewed under the obnoxious test of bad tendency. For instance, in the Stokes and Doe cases the judge admitted speeches or letters not included in the indictment. In many cases opinions expressed before the United States entered the war have also been admitted, opinions which the defendants then shared with many persons who afterwards supported the war. No matter how carefully the judge instructs the jury to disregard such prior language except as evidence of intention,

---

[45] See page 31, *supra*.

[46] "It seems to me perfectly clearly established, that no official yet born on this earth is wise enough or generous enough to separate good ideas from bad ideas, good beliefs from bad beliefs, and that the utmost that anybody can ask of a government, is that if it is efficient it should detect and run down criminal acts; that beyond reaching words which are the direct and immediate incitement to criminal acts, no government dare go."—Walter Lippmann, Bull. League of Free Nations Assn., Mar., 1920.

there can be no doubt that it is human nature to lump together all the utterances, inside and outside the indictment, and decide whether or not the defendant deserves punishment for everything he said. The Abrams case in the next chapter will bring this out very clearly.

The parallelism with the French revolutionary trials is often curiously close. Just as Lord Ellenborough could see no motive for Leigh Hunt's attack on flogging in the army except to cause a mutiny, so the District Court judges have often been ready to infer a similar criminal intent from talk of profiteering or Wall Street. It is easy for the supporters of a war to class all its opponents as traitors, forgetting that some of them argue against it merely because they cannot bear to see what seems to them a needless conflict, cripple or destroy the lives of thousands of their fellow-countrymen. A lawyer who has defended many Espionage Act cases tells me that there was much speculation among his clients as to whether they actually possessed the requisite criminal intent. A few of them admitted to him that they had it, and there is not much question that some of the utterances which were prosecuted were made with the purpose of obstructing recruiting or the draft, although the danger of their doing so was usually non-existent. But it is impossible to read over the various cases without coming to the conclusion that most of the defendants had no real intention to cause trouble, but were only engaged in heated altercations or expounding economic doctrines.

A saw is a very good thing, but not to shave with, and a judge and jury are an excellent instrument to pass on overt acts. They are also well-fitted to decide the effect of words upon the reputation of an individual, when the harmfulness of the language can be easily tested by common-sense standards, and its counterbalancing benefit to the public, if any, is indicated by well-established principles of law as to privilege and fair comment. But they are not trained and they are not able to apply such vague and misleading

THE WAR WITH GERMANY

tests of the criminality of utterances as bad tendency and presumptive intent.

It is on this account that I have spent so much time in emphasizing the difference between Judge Hand's test and the District Court test, in what may seem to many of my readers a mere interest in technicalities, far removed from the broad principles of freedom of speech. They forget that the technical rules of the common law are often the greatest safeguards of freedom. As Sir Henry Maine said, "Substantive law has at first the look of being gradually secreted in the interstices of procedure." [47] It is only necessary to recall the tremendous importance to human liberty of such procedural regulations as the Habeas Corpus Act, Fox's Libel Act, and the rule that no man shall be compelled to give evidence against himself. This is the great value of Judge Hand's test, which was the only sort of rule about war-time utterances which should have been permitted. If it was not the correct interpretation of the language of the Espionage Act, then an act with different language ought to have been passed. Even if not the only constitutional construction, it was the only workable construction. His rule gave the jury something definite to consider, the actual nature of the words and the danger of interference with the armed forces. The District Court test left them nothing but speculation upon the remote political and economic effect of words and the probable condition of mind of a person whose ideas were entirely different from their own.

In peaceable and quiet times, our legal rights are in little danger of being overborne; but when the wave of power lashes itself into violence and rage, and goes surging up against the barriers which were made to confine it, then we need the whole strength of an unbroken Constitution to save us from destruction.[48]

Judge Hand's test would have been a sea-wall against these surging waves, but the District Court test was nothing but a mud-bank which was rapidly swept away.

[47] *Early Law and Custom*, 389.
[48] Jeremiah Black, arguing in *Ex parte* Milligan, 4 Wall. 2, 75 (1866).

No one reading the simple language of the Espionage Act of 1917 could have anticipated that it would be rapidly turned into a law under which opinions hostile to the war had practically no protection. Such a result was made possible only by the District Court test and by the tremendous wave of popular feeling against pacifists and pro-Germans during the war. This feeling was largely due to the hysterical fear of spies and other German propaganda. All of us on looking back to 1917 and 1918 are now sure that the emotions of ourselves and every one else were far from normal. I remember hearing one woman in a railroad train say to another, "Yes, my brother was going to France with the Y.M.C.A., but the sailing of his boat has been put off and put off. I don't like to say that it's German propaganda, but it certainly looks like it."

Mr. John Lord O'Brian, Assistant to the Attorney General in the prosecution of the most important Espionage Act cases, gives a vivid account of the false stories of enemy activities within the United States, put forth through the medium of press dispatches, pamphlets of patriotic societies, and occasionally speeches on the floor of Congress:[49]

A phantom ship sailed into our harbors with gold from the Bolsheviki with which to corrupt the country; another phantom ship was found carrying ammunition from one of our harbors to Germany; submarine captains landed on our coasts, went to the theater and spread influenza germs; a new species of pigeon, thought to be German, was shot in Michigan; mysterious aeroplanes floated over Kansas at night, etc. Then there were the alleged spies themselves,—Spoermann, alleged intimate of Bernstorff, landed on our coasts by the U-53, administrator of large funds, caught spying in our camps, who turned out to be a plumber from Baltimore. Several other alleged spies caught on the beaches signaling to submarines were subsequently released because they were, in the several cases, honest men, one of whom had been changing an incandescent light bulb in his hotel room,

---

[49] 52 N. Y. Bar Assn. Rep. 281 (1919). Judge G. W. Anderson, who was U. S. District Attorney in Massachusetts in 1917, says, " More than ninety-nine per cent of the advertised and reported pro-German plots never existed."—21 *New Republic* 251.

another of whom was trying to attract the attention of a passerby on the beach, etc. There was no community in the country so small that it did not produce a complaint because of failure to intern or execute at least one alleged German spy. These instances are cited, not to make light of the danger of hostile activities, nor to imply that incessant vigilance was not necessary in watching the German activities, but to show how impossible it was to check that kind of war hysteria and war excitement which found expression in impatience with the civil courts and the oft-recurring and false statement that this government showed undue leniency toward enemies within our gates.

Yet not one case under this part of the statute shows the slightest evidence that the utterances were actuated by German money or German plans. Mr. O'Brian says it is doubtful if even the I.W.W. had any degree of German support. Besides this fear of spies another influence which made fair trials under the Espionage Act very difficult was the passion for becoming spies. Not only did the American Protective League act as auxiliary to the Department of Justice, but as the same authority says:[50]

Throughout the country a number of large organizations and societies were created for the purpose of suppressing sedition. All of these were the outgrowth of good motives and manned by a high type of citizens. The membership of these associations ran into the hundreds of thousands. One of them carried full page advertisements in leading papers from the Atlantic to the Pacific, offering in substance to make every man a spy chaser on the payment of a dollar membership fee. These associations did much good in awakening the public to the danger of insidious propaganda, but no other one cause contributed so much to the oppression of innocent men as the systematic and indiscriminate agitation against what was claimed to be an all-pervasive system of German espionage.

It is obvious that the presence of members of these societies on juries made a just determination of such vague facts as the bad tendency of utterances and the intention of the defendant impossible. Once more we have a curious parallel-

[50] O'Brian, 279, 292, 297. On the I.W.W., 299.

ism with the experiences of England during the French Revolution:[51]

> Another agency was evoked by the spirit of the times, dangerous to the liberty of the press, and to the security of domestic life. Voluntary societies were established in London and throughout the country, for the purpose of aiding the executive Government in the discovery and punishment of seditious writings or language. . . . These societies, supported by large subscriptions, were busy in collecting evidence of seditious designs, often consisting of anonymous letters, often of the report of informers, liberally rewarded for their activity. They became, as it were, public prosecutors, supplying the Government with proof of supposed offenses, and quickening its zeal in the prosecution of offenders. Every unguarded word at the club, the market-place or the tavern, was reported to these credulous alarmists and noted as evidence of disaffection.
>
> Such associations were repugnant to the policy of our laws, by which the Crown is charged with the office of bringing offenders to justice, while the people, represented by juries, are to judge, without favor or prejudice, of their guilt or innocence. But here the people were invited to make common cause with the Crown against offenders, to collect the evidence, and prejudge the guilt. How then could members of these societies assist in the pure administration of justice, as jurymen and justices of the peace? In the country especially was justice liable to be warped.

Attorney General Gregory corroborates Mr. O'Brian's statement:[52]

> The department has also been hampered by the circulation of unfounded reports, running into the hundreds, of supposed unpunished alien enemy activities in the way of fires alleged to have been caused by enemy agents, alleged uses of poison by enemy agents, alleged uses of ground glass, alleged damage to Red Cross supplies, etc. In view of the necessity for constant vigilance on the part of the public, it has not always seemed advisable to this department to enter into controversies as to the truth of these irresponsible reports.

It was with the country in the atmosphere above described that the laws affecting free speech received the severest test

[51] May, *Constitutional History*, II, 36.   [52] Report, 1918, 23.

thus far placed upon them in our history.[53] It is obvious that a country full of would-be spies chasing imaginary spies and finding only pro-Germans and pacifists is a very unfit place for the decision of those psychological questions, which, as Wharton pointed out,[54] inevitably arise from the prosecution of utterances. It may be helpful to examine briefly the effect of this atmosphere upon the three main parts of the human machinery through which the Espionage Act necessarily operated, namely, the prosecuting officials, the juries, and the trial judges.

The Assistants to the Attorney General in charge of the administration of the Espionage Act were John Lord O'Brian of Buffalo, so frequently quoted in these pages, and Alfred Bettman of Cincinnati. Although these men enforced the statute in accordance with the District Court test, which in my opinion made the maintenance of a real freedom of speech impracticable, nevertheless they were firm believers in that principle and singularly free from the effects of war emotion. In particular, great praise must be given to their thorough investigation of hundreds of convictions, as a result of which the sentences imposed by the judges were in many instances commuted by the President to a small fraction of their original length.[55] Unfortunately, it was very hard for these officials in Washington to impress their ideas of fairness and open discussion upon some of their subordinates and upon the public, and consequently to keep control of prosecutions throughout the country. Mr. O'Brian sums up this local situation:

It has been quite unnecessary to urge upon the United States Attorneys the importance of prosecuting vigorously, and there has been little difficulty in securing convictions from juries. On the contrary, it has been necessary at all times to exercise caution in order to secure to defendants accused of disloyalty the safeguard of fair and impartial trials. In addition to the causes already recited there were the patriotic agitations continually

[53] O'Brian, 299.
[54] See page 52, *supra*.
[55] Report of the Atty. Gen., 1919, Exhibit 21.

being carried on by the Liberty Loan speakers, four-minute men and others, all of which worked the whole country up to a pitch of intense patriotism, resulting in instinctive aversion toward anyone even under suspicion for disloyalty.

The situation became particularly serious after the passage of the Espionage Act of 1918. Despite the very wide scope given the Act of 1917 by the judges, it did after all require some connection between the expressions of opinion and the raising of our armed forces and did not punish disloyal utterances as such. Before the Amendment, isolated disloyal utterances had been treated in many parts of the country as incitement to disorder and had been summarily disposed of under a rather generous interpretation of state or local laws providing punishment for disorderly conduct. The Act of 1918 threw upon the law machinery of the Federal Government a great burden which it was ill-adapted to assume. It was almost impossible for the law officials to keep abreast of the complaints, and the result everywhere tended to encourage impatience with the action of civil tribunals.

The general publicity given the statute through the newspapers and, in many cases, through employers, who circularized their employees with copies of the act (calling attention to the dangers of strike activities), fanned animosities into flame, vastly increasing the amount of suspicion and complaints throughout the country. This, in turn, resulted in a large increase in the amount of prosecutions, backed up by strong local patriotic sentiment. Up to the time that this statute went into practical operation the United States Attorneys throughout the country, except in genuine cases of treason, had each acted as the supreme law official of his district, exercising on his own account full discretion in all matters as to prosecution.[56]

Under these circumstances, on May 23, 1918, the Attorney General issued to all United States attorneys a circular about the amended act. It stated that the prompt and aggressive enforcement of the act was of the highest importance, but it

---

[56] O'Brian, 304, 305, 309. See the facts of some of the local cases in *War-time Prosecutions*, 27 ff., listing 126 convictions under local laws (a few under state sedition statutes).

was also of great importance that it should be administered with discretion and should not be permitted to become the medium whereby efforts were made to suppress honest, legitimate criticism of the administration or discussion of government policies, or for personal feuds or persecution.[57] It is obvious that this circular simply transferred the strain from the judge and jury to another portion of the human machinery, the district attorney, who is a government official, and naturally less impartial. Opinions may differ as to the wisdom of enacting a very broad criminal statute which enables the government to deal with persons who are really dangerous and ignore others who are actually within its terms. Such irregularity of application is certainly novel in our system of criminal law. It has been well said that this circular " converts every United States attorney into an angel of life and death clothed with the power to walk up and down his district, saying, ' This one will I spare, and that one will I smite.' If the law leaves it to the district attorney to determine when an act shall be prosecuted as a crime and when it shall not be, how is a citizen to know when he is exercising his constitutional right, and when he is committing a crime? Of course such conduct in administering criminal law, punishable by imprisonment for twenty years, simply converts government into a government of men and not of law." The Department of Justice eventually realized this, wide divergencies appearing in the theories entertained by the various prosecuting attorneys, so that the Attorney General about a month before the end of the war issued a circular directing district attorneys to send no more cases to grand juries under the Espionage Act of 1918, without first submitting a statement of facts to the Attorney General and receiving by wire his opinion as to whether or not the facts constituted an offense under the Act.[58] " This circular," says Mr. O'Brian, " is suggestive of the immense pressure brought to bear throughout the war upon the Department of Justice in all parts of the country for

[57] Rep. Atty. Gen., 1918, 674.   [58] *Ibid.;* O'Brian, 306.

indiscriminate prosecution demanded in behalf of a policy of wholesale repression and restraint of public opinion." Doubtless this circular made it possible for the Attorney General to weed out mere " clamor " cases, but it came too late in the war to have any practical effect. Until that time all persons who were opposed to the war were practically at the mercy of the local district attorneys, and under the District Court test of the 1917 Act or the express language of the 1918 Act prosecution almost invariably resulted in conviction.

For the human machinery broke down at a second point— the jury. It is sometimes suggested that a jury trial gives a sufficient protection for freedom of speech, and that public sentiment will inevitably reflect itself in verdicts of acquittal if the prosecution seems unjust.[59] It is undoubtedly true that in England freedom of discussion is, as Dicey says, " little else than the right to write or say anything which a jury, consisting of twelve shopkeepers, think it expedient should be said or written." In my first chapter, however, I have endeavored to show that this protection is entirely inadequate and that the constitutional provision must mean much more. It is only in times of popular panic and indignation that freedom of speech becomes important as an institution, and it is precisely in those times that the protection of the jury proves illusory. As the Assistant to the Attorney General admits, " There has been little difficulty in securing convictions from juries."

Judge Amidon, who has had much experience in Espionage Act cases, says:

Only those who have administered the Espionage Act can understand the danger of such legislation. When crimes are defined by such generic terms, instead of by specific acts, the jury becomes

[59] *E.g.*, W. R. Vance in 2 *Minn. L. Rev.* 260; 33 *Harv. L. Rev.* 448. In England freedom of speech is necessarily protected only by jury trial plus the common law rules of criminal attempt and solicitation, unlawful meetings, etc. See Dicey, *Law of the Constitution,* chapters VI and VII. Without the guidance of these rules the jury would be far less valuable. Hence the merit of Judge Hand's test.

the sole judge, whether men shall or shall not be punished. Most of the jurymen have sons in the war. They are all under the power of the passions which war engenders. For the first six months after June 15, 1917, I tried war cases before jurymen who were candid, sober, intelligent business men, whom I had known for thirty years, and who under ordinary circumstances would have had the highest respect for my declarations of law, but during that period they looked back into my eyes with the savagery of wild animals, saying by their manner, "Away with this twiddling, let us get at him." Men believed during that period that the only verdict in a war case, which could show loyalty, was a verdict of guilty.

There are strong indications of other influences which accentuated the effect of the general war emotion, of circumstances which resemble the situation in England during the French Revolution, when the juries were chosen largely from men much opposed to the prisoners.[60] Mr. O'Brian tells [61] how the administration of the Act was affected by economic conflicts growing out of the activities of the Non-Partisan League and the I.W.W. Although the Attorney General insisted upon the doctrine that guilt was personal and refused to proscribe any group as such, the effect on juries in federal and state prosecutions was probably serious. For instance, in the trial of the president of the Non-Partisan League, under the Minnesota Espionage Act, the jury was chosen from the regular term panel of thirty-two men, which in turn was selected by lot from a total panel of one hundred and forty-four, picked from among the voters by the County Commissioner. Three "triers" also aided, who are charged with hostility to the League. Although the farmers of Jackson County were sharply divided into members of the Non-Partisan League and bitter opponents with practically no neutrals, and the League candidate at the last election had fallen only thirty-one short of a majority, the panel of one hundred and forty-four contained not a single member of the League, but consisted of men from sections of the county which League organizers and speakers were

[60] May, II, 36, 87.   [61] O'Brian, 295.

barred from visiting. The defense had only four peremptory challenges. The jury was not segregated, but was subjected to the heat of popular discussion during the trial.[62]

This was not a federal case, but similar problems are raised by the method of selecting juries in the federal courts. As long ago as the Sedition trials of 1798 the method of securing indictments and convictions met with public condemnation because of the men from whom and by whom the jury were chosen. Mr. Beveridge says,[63] "In many states the United States Marshals selected what persons they pleased as members of the grand juries and trial juries. These officers of the National courts were, without exception, Federalists; in many cases, Federalist politicians. When making up juries they selected only persons of the same manner of thinking as that of the marshals and judges themselves. So it was that the juries were nothing more than machines that registered the will, opinion, or even inclination of the National judges and the United States District Attorneys. In short, in these prosecutions, trial by jury in any real sense was not to be had."

It would certainly be improper without a very elaborate investigation to assert that such conditions exist in federal juries at the present time. The method of selection varies so much that generalization is impossible. There can be no doubt, however, that in some districts a wide power of selection, otherwise than by lot, is exercised by the officials. Federal juries in civil cases are considered by members of the bar to be superior in quality to state juries, and this is accounted for by the practice of the officials to go through the lists carefully and exclude persons who are considered undesirable. While this method may not have been exercised with any desire to prejudice the

[62] See Bibliography on Townley trial.
[63] Beveridge's *Marshall*, III, 42. F. M. Anderson, "The Enforcement of the Alien and Sedition Laws," Rep. Am. Hist. Assn. (1912), 125, says that the grand juries were composed preponderantly, if not exclusively, of Federalists; that the Callender trial jury was drawn in a manner that went far toward justifying the charge of packing, and that other juries could scarcely be called impartial.

THE WAR WITH GERMANY

jury in Espionage Act cases, the jury might naturally be limited to men of means who were not likely to understand at all the position of a person opposed to the war for economic reasons. On the other hand, federal jurors in New York City are said by a member of the Department of Justice to be inferior to those in the state courts. The government had more difficulty there in securing convictions in war cases than almost anywhere else, and this was attributed by some of the government counsel to the presence on the jury list of many persons with radical tendencies of thought. Without framing any conclusions myself on this extremely delicate matter, I shall present certain statements made on behalf of the defendants in various cases as material for criticism and subsequent investigation by other persons interested in this field.

Max Eastman in his account of the Debs case speaks from the point of view, obviously partisan but worth attention, of one who has himself been on trial under the Espionage Act: [64]

As to the jury . . . they were about seventy-two years old, worthy fifty to sixty thousand dollars, retired from business, from pleasure, and from responsibility for all troubles arising outside of their own family. An investigator for the defense computed the average age of the entire venire of 100 men; it was seventy years. Their average wealth was over $50,000. In the jury finally chosen every man was a retired farmer or a retired merchant, but one, who was a contractor still active. They were none of them native to leisure, however, but men whose faces were bitterly worn and wearied out of all sympathy with a struggle they had individually surmounted.

Berger's counsel made the following statement to the Committee of the House of Representatives: [65]

---

[64] "The Trial of Eugene Debs," 1 *Liberator*, No. 9 (Nov., 1918), 9.
The charge of Mayer, J., in United States v. Phillips, was so favorable to the defendant that, I am informed by an eyewitness, an acquittal was generally expected in the court-room, but the defendants were convicted.

[65] Victor L. Berger: Hearings before the Special Committee, I, 636.

On the selection and composition of the jury, I want to say that out of a panel that was examined of fully 50 there was only one laboring man who appeared, out of a 90 per cent. population of that judicial district, on the panel, and he was promptly treated as though he were a spy in camp. The jury was made up of a number of insurance brokers of the city of Chicago, of a number of very wealthy farmers, retired farmers, I think five, all men of much acreage and wealth in Illinois, and two bankers. Racially, it was utterly unrepresentative. I mean the whole panel was utterly unrepresentative of the racial, national, or industrial composition of the masses of the people in that district. . . . It is the marshal's personal selection. It is the most extraordinary thing and the judicial system of our country ought to be corrected, because he is the appointee of the civil administration.

Whether or not these accusations are just, they certainly present a problem in the trial of persons of radical inclinations, which must be solved in the future with considerable thought. The solution should not only give justice, but be so plain as to satisfy all classes, in so far as that is possible, that they are getting justice.

The third point at which the human machinery breaks down in the enforcement of a sedition law is the trial judges. Some of the English charges against agitators have already been mentioned. It is well known that one of the worst features of the Sedition Act of 1798 was its administration by the Federalist judges, which afterwards caused a determined assault upon the National Judiciary. In their charges to grand juries, they lectured and preached on religion, on morality, on partisan politics. At the trials, freedom of speech was ignored, no distinction was made between fact and opinion, and prosecutions for " wholly justifiable political criticisms—some of them trivial and even amusing "— were allowed to go to the jury. Although the deportment of the judges, with the exception of Chase, was substantially correct and the charges were usually right in what they said, convictions followed because of what was omitted or

See John Wurts, " The Jury System under Changing Social Conditions," 47 *Am. L. Rev.* 67; Mamaux v. U. S., 264 Fed. 816.

THE WAR WITH GERMANY

because the jury should have been prevented by a direction of acquittal from passing on the cases at all.[66]

Some Espionage Act charges which merit a similar criticism have already been mentioned, and make it plain that in contrast to the Civil War judges who stood rock-ribbed for legality,[67] a few men on the present United States bench felt it to be their duty to deliver stump speeches to the jury as if they were soliciting subscriptions to a Liberty Loan. One more instance may be given.

Judge Aldrich in a New Hampshire case charged:[68]

> These are not times for fooling. The times are serious. Nobody knows what is going to happen to our institutions within the next year, or the next month. Out West they are hanging men for saying such things as this man is accused of saying. They are feeling outraged by such expressions to such extent that they are taking the law into their own hands. Now, that is a very bad thing to do. We do not want that in New Hampshire, but we do want a courageous enforcement of the law.

Besides this attitude toward opposition to the war in general, some judges have expressed an attitude on economic questions which seriously affects not only the enforcement of Espionage Act cases but of the Deportation law and of a federal peace-time Sedition law, should one be enacted. A considerable portion of hostility to the declaration of war and conscription was due to the belief of radicals that it represented a sacrifice of working-class lives for the benefit of the wealthy. This belief was expressed by many members of the Non-Partisan League, the Socialist Party, and the Industrial Workers of the World. Sympathy with the Rus-

---

[66] Beveridge's *Marshall*, III, 30 note; II, 421; and III, 29-49 *passim;* F. M. Anderson, *op. cit.*, 126.

[67] *E.g.*, Taney's decision in *Ex parte* Merryman, Taney, 246 (1861); and the release of the Copperhead Milligan, 4 Wall. 2 (1866).

[68] U. S. v. Taubert, Bull. Dept. Just., No. 108. He was sentenced to three years for obstructing bond sales by saying, "This was a Morgan war and not a war of the people." There is nothing about bonds in the 1917 Act, but Judge Aldrich held it covered them because an army could not be raised without them and "the Government must not be embarrassed in those respects by unreasonable opposition."

sian Revolution was also a complicating factor. It was clearly the duty of the judges to keep their minds free from economic prejudices and to warn the jury that just because a defendant held unpopular radical views this in no way affected his guilt for interference with the war. Of course judges, like other men, are entitled to definite opinions on vital controversies of the day, and most of them will naturally favor only gradual changes in the present order, but the increasingly frequent part which radicalism is playing in legal proceedings of various kinds, and particularly in sedition prosecutions during and since the war, makes it essential that the judge hearing such cases shall have a scholarly and dispassionate attitude and an ability to discriminate between different schools of revolutionary thought. The warning of Justice Holmes deserves reprinting:[69]

When twenty years ago a vague terror went over the earth and the word socialism began to be heard, I thought and still think that fear was translated into doctrines that had no proper place in the Constitution or the common law. Judges are apt to be naif, simple-minded men, and they need something of Mephistopheles. We too need education in the obvious—to learn to transcend our own convictions and to leave room for much that we hold dear to be done away with short of revolution by the orderly change of law.

Consequently, it is a cause for grave concern when we find Judge Albert B. Anderson, who later enjoined the coal strike, using this language from the bench, even though in the particular case he made a very good decision:[70]

I think that about the least commendable sort of folks I know are these Russians, who have fled to this country, and are not anything like satisfied with what they have here. Why? Because we do not give them everything they want. Mary Antin was here not long ago and delivered an address, but she didn't simply want the Jews to have their rights. The trouble with Mary Antin

[69] Speeches by Oliver Wendell Holmes, 101; quoted in 29 *Harv. L. Rev.* 691.
[70] U. S. *v.* Zimmerman, Nelles, 10-12.

THE WAR WITH GERMANY

is that she wanted the Jews to have everything that we have got; and that is the way with this gentleman. . . . I do not like the word "Socialist" or these Socialists. The Socialist always flatters himself when he calls himself a Socialist. He means to leave the impression that he is more generous and more unselfish than the average run of men; but he doesn't want to be called an anarchist. . . . If I had time I would like to have somebody explain what it means except for the "have-nots" to take it away from the "haves". That is all there is to it; so I have not much patience with that sort of thing or soap-box orators. Why don't they go hire a hall?

One fears that he will not always add as he wisely did:

Free speech means the right to say foolish things as well as the right to say sensible things.

Judge Wade said in sentencing Mrs. O'Hare: [71]

Well, I tell you, if that is the sort of stuff the socialist party stands for, if its gospel is the gospel of hate, and contempt of religion and charity, it has not any place on the American soil either in times of war or times of peace.

The feeling against the I.W.W. was very bitter in the West, and convictions were numerous. One of these has been reversed because Judge Wolverton in Oregon charged: [72]

The I.W.W. is a disloyal and unpatriotic organization. Adherents thereof owe no allegiance to any organized government, and so far as the government is concerned the organization itself is thoroughly bad.

Contrast with this language the words of Judge Amidon in trying a member of the Non-Partisan League: [73]

The head and front of it is that the speech tended to array class against class. I have been on this earth quite a spell myself. I never have known of any great reform being carried through

---

[71] Nelles, 47.

[72] Kumpula v. U. S., 261 Fed. 49. Another case of reversal for the prejudicial attitude of the court is Rutherford v. U. S., 258 Fed. 855. See "Lawless Enforcement of Law," 33 *Harv. Law Rev.* 956.

[73] U. S. v. Brinton, Bull. Dept. Just., No. 132.

where the people whose established condition would be disturbed by the carrying out of the reform did not say that the people who were trying to bring about the reform were stirring up class against class. That is an argument that I know to be at least 3,500 years old from my knowledge of history, and it is repeated in every effort to change an existing condition.

Besides the war spirit and economic opinions, one more factor must be mentioned which may possibly have affected the Espionage Act cases, the supervision of United States judges by the Department of Justice. Here, as with regard to the methods of jury selection, I draw no conclusions whatever because of the insufficiency of data, but present the charge which has been made, that special agents have watched the proceedings of the courts and the district attorneys, swift to report to Washington any charge or action which has seemed to their excited temper not to measure up to the full standard of patriotic duty. In his book on Juridical Reform,[74] John D. Works, formerly Justice of the Supreme Court of California, and United States Senator for that state, points out:

Practically, Federal judges are selected by the Attorney General of the United States. All applications for appointment are referred to, investigated by, and reported upon by him, and, where there are a number of applicants, he recommmends to the President the one selected by him, and usually his recommendation is approved and the applicant of his choice appointed. The Attorney General is also the attorney of the Government in all its litigation before the judges he has selected. Not only this, but he assumes, and actually exercises, the right to investigate and supervise the course and conduct of these same judges, and has in some instances,—whether generally or not is not known,— made secret investigations of Federal judges through secret agents and without the knowledge of such judges.

If these charges are not proved untrue, a very serious danger in all sedition legislation is revealed, for there is no

[74] N. Y., 1919, pp. 123-125. Senator Works recommends that the power of selecting, recommending, and investigating judges be vested elsewhere than in the Department of Justice.

THE WAR WITH GERMANY 85

branch of the criminal law where convictions may on occasion become so important in the eyes of a government.

The number of Espionage Act judges who are guilty of actually prejudicial conduct at the trials is comparatively few, and in many respects the judges deserve the praise which Mr. O'Brian expresses [75] for giving great latitude to the defendant's proof [76] and urging upon the jury the necessity for the dispassionate consideration of evidence. The defect is, for the most part, not so much in what they said as in what they did not say. In the first place, despite the vagueness of the District Court test, common sense ought to have led them to withdraw many more cases of remote language from the jury, as Justice Brandeis has forcibly insisted in his *Tageblatt* opinion.[77] And whenever there was enough apparent relation to the raising of armies to justify the submission of the evidence to the jury, they should have cautioned them against convicting because the words might possibly and indirectly cause discontent in the forces or a refusal to enlist. The juries needed much more careful guidance on the issue of intent and far more discretion should have been exercised in the admission of prior utterances, because of the danger that the jury would convict the defendant as an undesirable citizen, who, taken all in all, ought to be shut up.[78] Furthermore, whenever a charge does mention freedom of speech, it is almost sure to say or imply that

---

[75] O'Brian, 310.

[76] On the importance of such a policy in political criminal trials, see Robert Ferrari in 3 *Minn. L. Rev.* 365, and 66 *Dial* 647 (June 28, 1919). *Cf.* the opportunity given Debs, Nearing, Eastman, and even the I.W.W.'s at Chicago to speak in their own defense with the refusal of the Minnesota state court to hear Townley, when at the close of his case he arose in the hot night with coat off to address the jury. 109 *Nation* 144.

[77] See page 100, *infra*. *Cf.* O'Brian, 309: "The chief difficulty on any trial has naturally been the question of what *quantum of evidence* would, as a matter of law, justify submitting to the jury the question of unlawful intent and the question of the reasonable and natural result of the utterance complained of."

[78] Admissibility of such utterances has been contested, but see the Abrams decision. *Cf.* People *v.* Molyneux, 168 N. Y. 264, a famous case of the other view. See Wigmore on Evidence, §§ 302, 367.

it has nothing to do with opposition to war and class such opposition with such extreme utterances like advocacy of a natural right to kill men or outrage women. Almost no emphasis is laid on the desirability of wide discussion so long as there is no real interference with the raising of armies, even discussion by those opposed to the war. The charge of Judge Augustus Hand in the trial of Max Eastman is a notable exception:[79]

> Every citizen has a right, without intent to obstruct the recruiting or enlistment service, to think, feel, and express disapproval or abhorrence of any law or policy or proposed law or policy, including the Declaration of War, the Conscription Act, and the so-called sedition clauses of the Espionage Act; belief that the war is not or was not a war for democracy; belief that our participation in it was forced or induced by powers with selfish interests to be served thereby; belief that our participation was against the will of the majority of the citizens or voters of the country; belief that the self-sacrifice of persons who elect to suffer for freedom of conscience is admirable; belief that war is horrible; belief that the Allies' war aims were or are selfish and undemocratic; belief that the Hon. Elihu Root is hostile to socialism, and that his selection to represent America in a socialistic republic was ill-advised.
>
> It is the constitutional right of every citizen to express his opinion about the war or the participation of the United States in it; about the desirability of peace; about the merits or demerits of the system of conscription, and about the moral rights or claims of conscientious objectors to be exempt from conscription. It is the constitutional right of the citizen to express such opinions, even though they are opposed to the opinions or policies of the administration; and even though the expression of such opinion may unintentionally or indirectly discourage recruiting and enlistment.

In one matter over which they had complete control, the District Court judges must bear a lasting blame. The only proceedings in our law comparable to the Espionage Act

[79] Nelles, 29, 30. As this charge was not reprinted in the Bulletins of the Department of Justice, it had no effect upon other district judges, except possibly in U. S. *v.* Debs, which permits "reasonable and tempered discussions." Bull. Dept. Just., No. 155, p. 12. Judge Clayton refused to repeat Judge Hand's words in his Abrams charge.

sentences are the sedition prosecutions under George III, with which so many parallels have been found. Indeed, at this point the parallelism breaks down. The longest sentences for sedition in England were four years, and even Braxfield and his Scotch colleagues did not exceed fourteen years, of transportation and not imprisonment. Our judges have condemned at least eleven persons to prison for ten years, six for fifteen years, and twenty-four for twenty years.[80] Judge Van Valkenburgh summed up the facts with appalling correctness in view of the virtual life terms imposed under the Espionage Act, when he said that freedom of speech means the protection of " criticism which is made friendly to the government, friendly to the war, friendly to the policies of the government." [81]

V. *The Supreme Court Decisions*

To me it seems simply a case of flagrant mistrial, likely to result in disgrace and great injustice, probably in life imprisonment for two old men, because this court hesitates to exercise the power, which it undoubtedly possesses, to correct, in this calmer time, errors of law which would not have been committed but for the stress and strain of feeling prevailing in the early months of the late deplorable war.—JUSTICE CLARKE, dissenting in the *Tageblatt* case.

The United States Supreme Court did not have an opportunity to consider the Espionage Act until 1919, after the armistice was signed and almost all the District Court cases had been tried. Several appeals from conviction had resulted

---

[80] These figures include only sentences stated in Rep. Atty. Gen., 1919, Exh. 21, and in the reported cases, listed in Appendix II, except the I.W.W. case (U. S. *v.* Haywood), which is omitted because I do not know how far the sentences were imposed because of counts under the old conspiracy statutes. There are, however, many unreported cases with long sentences, *e.g.*, 26 at Sacramento for ten years. No omission is made for reversals and commutations, because they do not lessen the responsibility of the district court judges, whose work is at this point under review. Indeed, there could be no more biting comment on the way these judges administered the Act than the enormous reductions in scores of sentences recommended by the Department of Justice. See Appendix II for instances.

[81] United States *v.* Rose Pastor Stokes, p. 14.

in a confession of error by the government,[82] but at last four cases were heard and decided against the accused.[83] Of these the Schenck case was one of the few reported prosecutions under the Act where there clearly was incitement to resist the draft. The defendants had mailed circulars to men who had passed exemption boards, which not only declared conscription to be unconstitutional despotism, but urged the recipients in impassioned language to assert their rights. Such utterances could fairly be considered a direct and dangerous interference with the power of Congress to raise armies, and were also counseling unlawful action within Judge Hand's interpretation of the statute. Consequently, no real question of free speech arose. Nevertheless, the defense of constitutionality was raised, and denied by Justice Holmes:

> We admit that in many places and in ordinary times the defendants in saying all that was said in the circular would have been within their constitutional rights. But the character of every act depends upon the circumstances in which it is done. . . . *The question in every case is whether the words used are used in such circumstances and are of such a nature as to create a clear and present danger that they will bring about the substantive evils that Congress has a right to prevent.* It is a question of proximity and degree. When a nation is at war many things that might be said in time of peace are such a hindrance to its effort that their utterance will not be endured so long as men fight and that no Court could regard them as protected by any constitutional right.

Although "the substantive evils" are not specifically defined, they mean successful interference with the particular power of Congress that is in question—in this instance, the war power. Since Congress is authorized to declare war and raise armies, it can expedite its task by punishing those who actually keep men out of the service, whether by starting a draft riot or by effectually persuading men not to register or not to enlist. And Congress can go one step farther. Be-

---

[82] Baltzer and Head cases, 249 U. S. 593.
[83] Schenck v. U. S., 249 U. S. 47 (1919); Sugarman v. U. S., *ibid.* 130; Frohwerk v. U. S., *ibid.* 204; Debs v. U. S., *ibid.* 211. The italics are mine.

THE WAR WITH GERMANY

sides punishing overt acts of interference with the war, it can prevent such acts from occurring by penalizing unsuccessful efforts to interfere, whether they are acts or words. But this desire to head off actual injury to the government is, we have seen, the basis of all suppression of discussion, unless it is limited very narrowly. In order to give force to the First Amendment, Justice Holmes draws the boundary line very close to the test of incitement at common law and clearly makes the punishment of words for their remote bad tendency impossible. Moreover, the close relation between freedom of speech and criminal attempts is indicated by the use of a phrase employed by the Justice in a leading attempt case, Commonwealth *v.* Peaslee.[84] Justice Holmes interprets the Espionage Act more widely than Judge Hand, in making the nature of the words only one element of danger, and in not requiring that the utterances shall in themselves satisfy an objective standard. Thus he loses the great administrative advantages of Judge Hand's test. But while the decision, like the District Courts, allows conviction for expressions of opinion uttered with a bad intention, it imposes additional requirements, which most trial courts had neglected. Words are criminal under the second and third clauses of the Act only because of their relation to the armed forces, and that relation must be so close that the words constitute " a clear and present danger " of injury to the raising of those forces or of mutiny and similar breaches of discipline. Words and intentions are not punishable for their own sake, or merely for their tendency to discourage citizens at war. Thus the opinion, especially the italicized sentence, substantially agrees with the conclusion reached by investigation of the history and political purpose of the First Amendment. The concept of freedom of speech received for the first time an authoritative judicial interpretation in accord with the purpose of the framers of the Constitution.

The Sugarman decision, written by Justice Brandeis, was much like the Schenck case, as there was evidence

[84] 177 Mass. 267, 272 (1901). See page 53, *supra.*

that the defendant had in a speech advised a number of registrants not to report for military service when called. The Espionage Act plainly covers such utterances, and they would have been criminal under the conspiracy statutes of the Civil War, if other persons had been associated with the speaker. The Frohwerk decision was more difficult, and Justice Holmes' opinion recognizes that if more evidence had been presented on the inadequately prepared record there might have been cause for reversal. The defendant had inserted several articles in the *Missouri Staats-Zeitung* on the constitutionality and merits of the draft and on the purposes of the war. Even in the Department of Justice there was considerable question whether these were not an advocacy of a change in governmental policy as distinguished from advocacy of obstruction of such policy, and it did not appear that there was any special effort to reach men who were subject to the draft. Justice Holmes thought, however, that on the record as it was the evidence might conceivably have been sufficient to sustain a conviction, since the circumstances and the intention, though not the words *per se*, might satisfy the danger-test.

It may be that all this might be said or written even in time of war in circumstances that would not make it a crime. We do not lose our right to condemn either measures or men because the country is at war. . . . But we must take the case on the record as it is, and of that record it is impossible to say that it might not have been found that the circulation of the paper was in quarters where a little breath would be enough to kindle a flame and that the fact was known and relied on by those who sent that paper out.

If the Supreme Court had applied this same standard of "clear and present danger" to the utterances of Eugene V. Debs, in the remaining decision, it is hard to see how he could have been held guilty. The test is not mentioned, however, but Justice Holmes is willing to accept the verdict as proof that actual interference with the war was intended and was the proximate effect of the words used. It is regrettable that he should have felt unable to go behind a verdict which had been found without any reference to the danger of the utterances. The point is that Judge Westenhaver did not instruct the jury according to the Supreme Court test at all, but allowed Debs to be found guilty, in Justice Holmes's words, because of the " natural *tendency* and reasonably probable effect " of his speech, and gave a fairly wide scope to the doctrines of indirect causation and constructive intent, so that the defendant could have been and probably was [85] convicted for an exposition of socialism, merely because the jury thought his speech had a tendency to bring about resistance to the draft. If the Supreme Court test is to mean anything more than a passing observation, it must be used to upset convictions for words when the trial judge did not insist that they must create " a clear and present danger " of overt acts.

Justice Holmes seems to discuss the constitutionality of the Espionage Act of 1917 rather than its construction. There can be little doubt that it is constitutional under any test if construed naturally, but it has been interpreted in such a way as to violate the free speech clause and the plain words of the statute, to say nothing of the principle that criminal statutes should be construed strictly. If the Supreme Court test had been laid down in the summer of 1917 and followed in charges by the District Courts, the most casual perusal of the utterances prosecuted makes it sure that there would have been many more acquittals. Instead, bad tendency and presumed intent have been the tests of criminality, tests which this article has endeavored to prove wholly inconsistent with freedom of speech, and any genuine discussion of public affairs.

The decision shows clearly the evils of the broad con-

[85] United States *v.* Debs, Bull. Dept. Just., No. 155 (N. D. Oh., 1918). See especially the last paragraphs on page 8, and page 15: " In deciding what the defendant's intention was, permit me to suggest to you these questions: Ought he not to have reasonably foreseen that the natural and probable consequences of such words and utterances would or *might* be to cause insubordination, etc.? "

struction of the Espionage Act, which rejected the objective standard of the meaning of the words used. Debs was convicted of an attempt to cause insubordination in the army and obstruct recruiting, yet no provocation to any such definite and particular acts was proved. He spoke to a convention of Socialists in support of their economic views, instancing the war as the supreme curse of capitalism. In a few sentences he approved the conduct of persons convicted of like offenses, saying, for example, that if Mrs. Stokes was guilty so was he. Her conviction has since been reversed. Not one word was designed for soldiers, not one word urged his hearers to resist the draft, objectionable as he considered it. Undoubtedly he admitted at his trial that he had obstructed the war—" I abhor war. I would oppose the war if I stood alone. When I think of a cold, glittering steel bayonet being plunged in the white, quivering flesh of a human being, I recoil with horror." But the only question before the jury was whether he had tried to obstruct it in the ways made unlawful in the statute. If all verbal or written opposition to the war furnishes a basis for conviction, because it is dangerous under the circumstances and indicates a criminal mind, then none but the most courageous will dare speak out against a future war.

"It is useless," writes Ernst Freund,[86] "to over-emphasize the substantive limitations of the constitution; the real securities of rights will always have to be found in the painstaking care given to the working out of legal principles. So long as we apply the notoriously loose common law doctrines of conspiracy and incitement to offenses of a political character, we are adrift on a sea of doubt and conjecture. To know what you may do and what you may not do, and how far you may go in criticism, is the first condition of political liberty; to be permitted to agitate at your

[86] Ernst Freund, "The Debs Case and Freedom of Speech," 19 *New Republic* 13 (May 3, 1919); and the correspondence in 19 *ibid.* 151 (May 31, 1919).

own peril, subject to a jury's guessing at motive, tendency and possible effect, makes the right of free speech a precarious gift."

The last sentence of the passage quoted from the Schenck case seems to mean that the Supreme Court will sanction any restriction of speech that has military force behind it, and reminds us that the Justice used to say when he was young, " that truth was the majority vote of that nation that could lick all others." [87] His liberalism seems in these decisions to be held in abeyance by his belief in the relativity of values. It is not by giving way to force and the majority that truth has been won. Hard it may be for a court to protect those who oppose the cause for which men are dying in France, but others have died in the past for freedom of speech.

After all, whatever we may think about such a close case as the Debs decision, it can best be regarded as a reason for repealing the Espionage Act, if it must be so construed. And surely the cause of freedom of speech profited in the long run from Justice Holmes's opinion in these three cases more than if he had favored reversal, for subsequent decisions prove that he would then have been in the minority and would not have been able, as he was, to announce with the backing of a unanimous court the rule of clear and present danger, which should serve as a guiding principle in the future. Already its application in the Circuit Courts of Appeals has led to the setting aside of some convictions,[88] and it ought to make impossible hereafter a repetition of some of the worst decisions under the Espionage Act.

That it has not, however, made freedom of speech secure is proved by the later interpretations of that statute in the Supreme Court. In November, 1919, came a second group of cases, of which one turned largely on procedure,[89]

---

[87] Oliver Wendell Holmes, "Natural Law," 32 *Harv. L. Rev.* 40 (1918).
[88] Kammann v. U. S., 259 Fed. 192; Harshfield v. U. S., 260 Fed. 659.
[89] Stilson v. U. S., 250 U. S. 583 (1919).

and the other, Abrams v. United States, has been reserved for a separate chapter, because it involves the special element of opposition to Russian intervention and because it furnishes a valuable example of the way political crimes, which were first known in this country because of the Espionage Act, are liable to be tried. Justice Holmes and Justice Brandeis have now and henceforth parted company with the rest of the court.

In the opening of 1920 came a third group of two decisions,[90] which were chiefly concerned with the first clause of the Espionage Act of 1917, punishing willfully published "false reports and statements with intent to interfere with the operation or success of the military or naval forces of the United States or to promote the success of its enemies." Thus far, very little has been said of this clause and of the District Court cases which construed it to apply to opinions about the causes of the war, or the influence of profiteers.

Conspicuous among such cases was the conviction of five officers of the corporation issuing the *Philadelphia Tageblatt*, a German-language daily and Sunday newspaper. After an acquittal on the charge of treason for publishing fifteen articles, which were most assuredly unpatriotic in tone, glorifying German strength and success, abusing our allies, and attacking the sincerity of the United States, they were indicted in nine counts under the Espionage Act for the same utterances and all found guilty. In Schaefer v. United States two defendants were discharged by the Supreme Court for want of responsibility for the articles. Three convictions (two for five years, one for two years) were affirmed by a majority of six speaking through Justice McKenna; Justice Brandeis filed a dissenting opinion on behalf of himself and Justice Holmes; and Justice Clarke, who had spoken for the majority in the Abrams case, now also dissented, not because he found any violation of the First Amendment, but upon the ground that the Act had

[90] Schaefer v. U. S., 251 U. S. 468; Pierce v. U. S., 40 Sup. Ct. 205.

been misinterpreted by the trial court, whose charge " was so utterly unadapted to the case . . . as to be valueless or worse as a direction to the jury."

This newspaper was so poor financially that it was not able to have any telegraphic service, and consequently filled its columns with clippings from other newspapers. As it did not print so many columns as they, it was necessarily obliged to cut and condense both the headlines and the body of the articles. It did not indicate the source of its articles or imply that they were complete copies. The falsity alleged by the government was not that the articles which were published were false in fact, but merely that they differed from the originals, and had been altered or mistranslated so as to bear a changed meaning which was depressing or detrimental to patriotic ardor. For instance, the news editor quoted an Amsterdam dispatch about the shortage of food in Holland because of our seizure of ships, and was convicted for adding a sentence of comment that our proposal for sending food would be rejected, although this sentence was not made part of the quotation, but was clearly indicated for what it was.[91] He was convicted for copying an account of the fall of Riga, and omitting one sentence from the original, " From this it can be concluded that the fall of Riga has united the opposing political factions in Russia." He was convicted because in translating a speech of Senator La Follette, predicting bread-lines as a consequence of the failure to tax profiteers, the word *Brot-riots* was used instead of *Brodreihen*. The wide divergence of opinion in the Court is indicated by Justice McKenna's statement, " There could be no more powerful or effective instruments of evil than two German newspapers organized and conducted as these papers were organized and conducted," as against that of Justice Brandeis, " To hold that such harmless additions to or omissions from news items, and such impotent expressions of editorial opinion, as were shown here, can af-

[91] U. S. *v.* Werner, 247 Fed. 708.

ford the basis even of a prosecution, will doubtless discourage criticism of the policies of the Government."

A comparison of the opinions of Justice McKenna and Justice Brandeis will form a valuable study in judicial method and in the two ways of solving any problem of freedom of speech. Of course we shall not find that total ignoring of the social interest in discussion, which blots many District Court cases, in a member of the Supreme Court. The difference between the two Justices is a difference in the degree of emphasis placed upon that interest and in their approach to the case. Since the limits of the right of freedom of speech in war time necessarily involve a conflict between the desirability of public knowledge of the truth about the war and the danger of defeat, it makes all the difference in the world whether the judge who sets out to determine those limits starts from the unqualified language of the First Amendment, which, unlike the Habeas Corpus clause, makes no exception of invasion,[92] and seeks to give to public opinion as much scope as is possible in view of the danger and the precise words of the statute; or whether he is primarily concerned to avert all influences which might conceivably delay or forfeit victory and is anxious not to go any farther to permit words of that tendency than seems absolutely necessary if we are to have any discussion about a war at all. Again, it makes all the difference in the world whether this judge is satisfied to say, " Free speech is not an absolute right, and when it or any right becomes wrong by excess is somewhat elusive of definition," without seeking to define it, or whether he insists that the preservation of this right must inevitably depend on the latitude allowed to the human machinery administering the law.

Justice McKenna approaches the problem from the side of the war power, and entrusts freedom of speech to the

[92] " Not one of these safeguards [in the Bill of Rights] can the President, or Congress, or the Judiciary disturb, except the one concerning the writ of *habeas corpus.*"—Field, J., in *Ex parte* Milligan, 2 Wall. 125.

jury's sense of fairness rather than to any guiding principles. In his opinion the restraints of the Espionage Act are not excessive or ambiguous, and the trial court gives sufficient protection to the right of free speech if it admonishes the jury to decide impartially after close attention to the evidence. The statute is directed against conduct which might cause our armies "to operate to defeat and the immeasurable horror and calamity of it." He is surprised that the Constitution should have been invoked to protect "the activities of anarchy or of the enemies of the United States." This is an argument always used to undermine freedom of speech, for if it does not protect criticism hostile to the government it has little value, and such criticism in the times when it is most needed is invariably denounced by the supporters of the government as revolution or treason. Only wide discussion and time can tell whether the activities of the opponents of our wars, James Russell Lowell, the Hartford Convention, William Graham Sumner, Vallandigham, were the activities of the enemies of the United States or of its friends.

To all the passages he applies the eighteenth-century tests of bad tendency and presumptive intent to see whether the evidence would justify conviction. The only limit on remoteness which he recognizes seems to depend on the will of the jury. Thus he says of the conviction for obstructing enlistment by a reprint from a Berlin paper, entitled "Yankee Bluff," which ridiculed the possibility of our giving any aid to the Entente, so slow were our war preparations, that the article might seem to its readers truly descriptive of American inability to combat German prowess and thereby "chill and check the ardency of patriotism and make it despair of success and in hopelessness relax energy both in preparation and in action." What was its purpose if not that? We cannot conclude that the observations were the mere expression of peevish discontent, but must take them at their word, as the jury did, and ascribe a more active and sinister aim. Success is unnecessary. The tendency of the articles and their efficacy were enough for offense, and this is all that "intent" and "attempt" mean. To require more would make the law useless, for it was passed in precaution, and the consequences of its violation might appear only in disaster. In other words, any newspaper editor who reprints German bragging is liable to imprisonment unless he can furnish a clean bill of health as to his loyal intentions.

Justice McKenna also regards it as criminal to predict turbulent resistance to a war, as in the La Follette report, or to say that the war was commenced without the people's consent. Of an article, attacking "the pro-British policy of the Government," he says, in language that leaves no room for questioning as to the righteousness of any war:

Its statements were deliberate and willfully false, the purpose being to represent that the war was not demanded by the people but was the result of the machinations of executive power, and thus to arouse resentment to it and what it would demand of ardor and effort. In final comment we may say that the article in effect justified the German aggressions.

Justice Brandeis, on the other hand, starts from the danger-test of freedom of speech in the Schenck case and from the actual words of the Espionage Act. He even goes back to an important circumstance preceding the statute, the recommendation of the War College for legislation to prevent injurious disclosures on military matters, to get help on the meaning of the "false statement clause."

Congress sought thereby to protect the American people from being willfully misled to the detriment of their cause by one actuated by the intention to further the cause of the enemy. Willfully untrue statements which might mislead the people as to the financial condition of the Government and thereby embarrass it; as to the adequacy of the preparations for war or the support of the forces; as to the sufficiency of the food supply; or willfully untrue statements or reports of military operations which might mislead public opinion as to the competency of the army or navy or its leaders [see "The Relation Between the Army and the Press in War Time," War College Publication, 1916]; or willfully untrue statements or reports which might mislead officials in the execution of the law, or military authorities in the disposition of the forces. Such is the kind of false statement and the only kind which, under any rational construction, is made criminal by the act. Could the military and naval forces of the United States conceivably have been interfered with or the success of the enemy conceivably have been promoted by any of the three publications set forth above?

And in connection with the " Yankee Bluff " article, he applied the same tests of danger and statutory wording to the recruiting clause of the 1917 Act, confirming the interpretation of the Act advanced earlier in this chapter:[93]

It is not apparent on a reading of this article—which is not unlike many reprints from the press of Germany to which our patriotic societies gave circulation in order to arouse the American fighting spirit—how it could rationally be held to tend even remotely or indirectly to obstruct recruiting. But as this court has declared . . . the test to be applied—as in the case of criminal attempts and incitements—is not the remote or possible effect. There must be the clear and present danger. Certainly men judging in calmness and with this test presented to them could not reasonably have said that this coarse and heavy humor immediately threatened the success of recruiting.

The most important part of his opinion is the repeated criticism of the administration of the statute in the trial below. The jury, however much instructed to be calm and unbiassed, were authorized to convict for any words which would lessen " our will to win, or, as it is generally expressed, our will to conquer." Jurymen need something more than " a sense of duty and a sense of justice." They need hard and fast tests of criminality, which will bring home to them the standard of " clear and present danger." And in this case that test should have prevented the evidence, so remote is it, from going to the jury at all. After quoting the words of the unanimous Court in the Schenck case, he said:

[93] Page 54, *supra*.

This is a rule of reason. Correctly applied, it will preserve the right of free speech both from suppression by tyrannous, well-meaning majorities and from abuse by irresponsible, fanatical minorities. Like many other rules for human conduct, it can be applied correctly only by the exercise of good judgment; and to the exercise of good judgment, calmness is, in times of deep feeling and on subjects which excite passion, as essential as fearlessness and honesty. The question whether in a particular instance the words spoken or written fall within the permissible curtailment of free speech is, under the rule enunciated by this Court, one of degree. And because it is a question of degree the field in which the jury may exercise its judgment is, necessarily, a wide one. But its field is not unlimited. The trial provided for is one by judge *and* jury; and the judge may not abdicate his function. If the words were of such a nature and were used under such circumstances that men, judging in calmness, could not reasonably say that they created a clear and present danger that they would bring about the evil which Congress sought and had a right to prevent, then it is the duty of the trial judge to withdraw the case from the consideration of the jury; and if he fails to do so, it is the duty of the appellate court to correct the error.

Then he emphasized a principle which has often been ignored in sedition trials, and which might have affected the Debs decision, as well as the Abrams case, that the appellate court ought not to determine the nature and possible effect of a speech or writing simply by culling here and there a sentence and presenting it separated from the context. It ought to be read as a whole, and often considered with other evidence which may control its meaning.

Finally, he warned the Court, in a passage which I shall quote later with reference to peace-time Sedition laws, that the sweeping application of a criminal statute to utterances with scant regard for the First Amendment would have disastrous consequences for freedom of speech in future periods of excitement. In truth, the passage of the simple language of the Espionage Act of 1917 was, little as we thought it at the time, the deadliest blow ever struck at a free press in the United States, and the beginning of a

THE WAR WITH GERMANY

series of encroachments on civil rights of every kind, whose full consequences we are dimly beginning to realize.

The latest decision is United States v. Pierce. This was a prosecution for distributing "The Price We Pay," one of those leaflets which, like "The Finished Mystery" of the Pastor Russell sect, figure in several Espionage Act cases. The pamphlet was a highly colored and sensational document by St. John Tucker, one of the defendants in the Berger case. It was issued by the national office of the Socialist Party at Chicago, and "contained much in the way of denunciation of war in general, the pending war in particular, something in the way of assertion that under Socialism things would be better, little or nothing in the way of fact or argument to support the assertion." The four defendants in New York had refrained from circulating it until after a prosecution of other persons in Maryland, based on the same pamphlet but under the conspiracy statutes for obstruction of the draft, had terminated in a directed acquittal on the ground that it was intended to get recruits for the Socialist Party, and not even an attempt to persuade men to disobey the draft law.[94] Pierce and his associates were then arrested and convicted. Seven judges through Justice Pitney sustained the conviction, while Justice Brandeis dissented with the concurrence of Justice Holmes.

The principal ground of conviction was the false statements clause. Justice Brandeis pointed out that the danger-test applies to this clause as much as the other two, and that three additional elements of crime must be established: (1) The statement or report must be of something capable of being proved false in fact. The expression of an opinion, for instance, whether sound or unsound, might conceivably afford a sufficient basis for the charge of attempting to cause insubordination, disloyalty or refusal of duty, or for the charge of obstructing recruiting; but, because an opinion is not capable of being proved false in fact, a statement

[94] U. S. v. Baker, 247 Fed. 124 (1917).

of it cannot be made the basis of a prosecution under this clause. (2) The statement or report must be proved to be false. (3) The statement or report must be known by the defendant to be false when made or conveyed.

Three passages, consisting of five sentences in all, were culled from this long document as constituting the false statements or reports:

1. Into your homes the recruiting officers are coming. They will take your sons of military age and impress them into the army. . . .
And still the recruiting officers will come; seizing age after age, mounting up to the elder ones and taking the younger ones as they grow to soldier size.
2. The Attorney General of the United States is so busy sending to prison men who do not stand up when the Star Spangled Banner is played, that he has no time to protect the food supply from gamblers.
3. Our entry into it was determined by the certainty that if the allies do not win, J. P. Morgan's loans to the allies will be repudiated, and those American investors who bit on his promises would be hooked.

Only the last passage need detain us. The first is clearly true, since "recruiting" was held in the Schenck case to include the draft, though a regular army major gravely testified at the trial that it had only to do with the volunteer service. The prediction that older and younger persons would be drafted was, of course, fulfilled. Yet the point was left to the jury. While civilians could not be prosecuted for sitting during the National Anthem, such an obviously figurative way of saying that the Attorney General was devoting important time to trivial sedition cases could not properly be regarded as a statement of fact within a twenty-year criminal penalty.[95]

Justice Pitney held that these passages satisfied the three requirements laid down by Justice Brandeis.

[95] Under a local law, J. W. Beckstrom of Chicago was, since the Pierce trial, fined $50 for refusing to stand when the "Star-Spangled Banner" was played in a theater.—*War-time Prosecutions*, 30.

THE WAR WITH GERMANY

On the points of intention and proximate cause he said that the jury might fairly believe that the leaflet " would have a tendency to cause insubordination "; and that it was intended to bring home to eligible men and especially to " their parents, sisters, wives, and sweethearts," a sense of impending personal loss, calculated to discourage men from entering the service, to arouse suspicion whether the chief law officer was not more concerned in enforcing the strictness of military discipline than in protecting the people against improper speculation in their food supply, and to produce a belief that our participating in the war was the product of sordid and sinister motives. One rubs his eyes and wonders whether he has dreamed himself back into the eighteenth century.

The most dangerous aspect of this case, however, is the decision that the opinion about the economic cause of the war is a false statement and known to be false. Justice Pitney says:

Common knowledge (not to mention the President's Address to Congress of April 2, 1917, and the Joint Resolution of April 6 declaring war, which were introduced in evidence) would have sufficed to show at least that the statements as to the causes that led to the entry of the United States into the war against Germany were grossly false; and such common knowledge went to prove also that defendants knew they were untrue. That they were false if taken in a literal sense hardly is disputed.

Justice Pitney is a great equity judge, and often a man is held subject to the equitable rights of others because he ought reasonably to know of them though in fact he does not, but such constructive notice has never before been made the basis of criminal responsibility. For example, a man purchasing land cannot get rid of a heavy recorded mortgage just because he was ignorant of it, but if he resells the land without mentioning this still unknown mortgage he is not guilty of obtaining money under false pretenses. Yet the Supreme Court is willing to say that men who wrangled with their neighbors for years about the capitalistic causes of the war and clung to their views with pig-headed devotion knew they were wrong just because they were in a small minority.

Consider where this leads. If opinions about the origin and justice of a war are to be regarded as false statements if the jury find them erroneous, the proof of truth or falsity involves logically all available evidence about the causes of the war, a staggering task. The proof surely ought not to be limited to the President's Message or the Resolution of Congress, for then conviction would be a foregone conclusion. Neither by sight nor by hearing can the jury investigate this "question of fact." It is a matter of inference from the complex and obscure political, economic, and social conditions of the nation or even of the world. The data for such a judgment, even if a jury had the very slightest capacity for making it, are not available during a war or for years afterwards. Imagine John Bright or James Russell Lowell trying to convince a jury that the Crimean or the Mexican Wars were due to sinister motives, a question on which men are still disputing.

What minority opinion can be safe in war time under Justice Pitney's test? Surely, language which is immune from civil defamation suits as comment on a public matter ought to be equally immune from the sterner rigors of the federal penitentiary. If everything an opponent of a war says is to be adjudged false because the jury and the Supreme Court disagree with it, and then he is declared to know it is false because most people think it so, the whole value of the First Amendment as a means of learning the truth about future wars is lost.

Into this technical reasoning, which virtually ignores the standard of clear and present danger and revives the District Court test of remotely injurious tendency, cuts the common sense of Justice Brandeis. The so-called statement of fact about the Morgan loans is, he says, merely a conclusion or deduction from facts. True, it is not a conclusion of law, but it is not an evidentiary fact. In its

THE WAR WITH GERMANY

essence it is the expression of a judgment, like the statements of many so-called historical facts. There is no exact standard of absolute truth by which to prove the assertion false.[96] Himself a strong supporter of the war, he recognizes nevertheless the possibility of divergent views:

The cause of a war—as of most human action—is not single. War is ordinarily the result of many co-operating causes, many different conditions, acts and motives. Historians rarely agree in their judgment as to what was the determining factor in a particular war, even when they write under circumstances where detachment and the availability of evidence from all sources minimizes both prejudice and other sources of error. For individuals, and classes of individuals, attach significance to those things which are significant to them. And, as the contributing causes cannot be subjected, like a chemical combination in a test tube, to qualitative and quantitative analysis so as to weigh and value the various elements, the historians differ necessarily in their judgments. One finds the determining cause of war in a great man, another in an idea, a belief, an economic necessity, a trade advantage, a sinister machination, or an accident. It is for this reason largely that men seek to interpret anew in each age, and often with each new generation, the important events in the world's history.

Not all who voted for the declaration of war did so for the President's reasons, and the previous debate, Justice Brandeis reminds us, includes many statements that the vast loans were instrumental in causing a sentiment through the nation in favor of war.

However strongly we may believe that these loans were not the slightest makeweight, much less a determining factor, in the country's decision, the fact that some of our representatives in the Senate and the House declared otherwise on one of the most solemn occasions in the history of the Nation, should help us to understand that statements like that here charged to be false are in essence matters of opinion and judgment, not matters of fact to be determined by a jury upon or without evidence; and

[96] Citing American School of Magnetic Healing v. McAnnulty, 187 U. S. 94, 104, which held that the Postmaster General could not exclude from the mails as fraudulent, proposals to cure disease by mental treatment, since the claim was not subject to proof as to its falsity.

that even the President's address, which set forth high moral grounds justifying our entry into the war, may not be accepted as establishing beyond a reasonable doubt that a statement ascribing a base motive was criminally false. All the alleged false statements were an interpretation and discussion of public facts of public interest. . . . To hold that a jury may make punishable statements of conclusions or of opinion, like those here involved, by declaring them to be statements of facts and to be false would practically deny members of small political parties freedom of criticism and of discussion in times when feelings run high and the questions involved are deemed fundamental.

It seems extremely ominous that at a time when the Supreme Court has shown such solicitude in the United States Steel Corporation and stock dividend cases,[97] and rightly as I believe, in protecting large bodies of capital from unlawful governmental action, it should have been so careless in its safeguarding of the fundamental human need of freedom of speech, so insistent in this sphere that the interests of the government should be secured at all costs. Progress is possible only through a genuine application of the great principle behind that Amendment which the Abrams, Schaefer, and Pierce decisions have reduced almost to a pious hope.

The fundamental right of free men to strive for better conditions through new legislation and new institutions will not be preserved, if efforts to secure it by argument to fellow citizens may be construed as criminal incitement to disobey the existing law—merely, because the argument presented seems to those exercising judicial power to be unfair in its portrayal of existing evils, mistaken in its assumptions, unsound in reasoning or intemperate in language.[98]

VI. *Censorship and Exile*

The Federal Government has restricted speech in two ways besides punishment. It possesses a virtual censorship in

[97] U. S. *v.* U. S. Steel Corp., 251 U. S. 417 (1920); Eisner *v.* Macomber, 40 Sup. Ct. 189 (1920).
[98] Brandeis, J., in Pierce *v.* U. S., *supra*.

war time over all criticism of its policies, and exercises this power at the arbitrary will of an administrative official, who is of course directly interested to preserve those policies from attack, especially when they touch his own department. That this official is not called a censor is immaterial. Under the Espionage Act the Postmaster General can exclude from the mails, the only profitable, and often the only possible means of effective publication, anything which he considers to be in violation of the statute. In no case during the war has any court set aside his decision by injunction or mandamus since Judge Hand was reversed as to the *Masses.* Some judges say that they will not review his ruling unless it is clearly wrong, which means never. Others declare that an opponent of the war does not come into court with clean hands and therefore cannot get judicial relief even though the ruling is illegal. And the power of the Postmaster General is not limited to the particular issue of the periodical which he declares non-mailable. For instance, after Mr. Burleson had suppressed the August number of the *Masses*, he refused to admit the September or any future issues to the second-class mailing privilege, even if absolutely free from any objectionable passages, on the ground that since the magazine had skipped a number, *viz.*, the July number, it was no longer a periodical, since it was not regularly issued! He took the same position as to Berger's *Milwaukee Leader*, and in both instance the courts sustained him, thus confirming his right to drive a newspaper or magazine out of existence for one violation as determined by him.

Let us now see what Mr. Burleson has considered to violate the Espionage Act. By no means did he limit himself to pro-German and pacifist articles and books, like Latzko's *Men in War*. He suppressed an issue of the *Public* for urging that more money be raised by taxes and less by loans. He suppressed Lenine's *Soviets at Work*, a purely economic pamphlet, although we were not at war with Russia. He suppressed the *Nation* of September 14, 1918, either for criticising the great slacker round-up in New York City,

108   FREEDOM OF SPEECH

which Mr. O'Brian states to have been in contravention of specific instructions from the Attorney General and a mistake which could not be condoned,[99] or more probably for attacking Mr. Gompers. He censored any adverse comment on the affairs of the British Empire. He censored a pamphlet by Lajpat Rai on India. He censored the *Freeman's Journal and Catholic Register* for reprinting Jefferson's opinion that Ireland should be a republic; the *Gaelic American* for denouncing the felicitous remarks of F. E. Smith during his flying trip to this country, and saying, "The clear-headed, keen-witted Yankees who read his bitter attack on the Irish will not wonder at the Irish for refusing to fight for a government of which Smith is a member"; and the *Irish World* for expressing the expectation that Palestine would not be a Jewish kingdom, but on the same footing as Egypt, and that the trend of French life and ideals for a century has been toward materialism. And finally, Thorstein Veblen's *Imperial Germany and the Industrial Revolution*, which was published in 1915, was recommended by Mr. Creel's Committee on Public Information as containing damaging data about Germany, and then excluded by Mr. Burleson from the mails.

This is clearly previous restraint and might seem forbidden by the Blackstonian definition, which, however, is held not to apply to the postal power.[100] This power, like the war power, ought to be subject to the requirements of free speech and due process of law, and there are dicta of the Supreme Court that it is not unlimited.[101] Although the post-office may not be strictly a common carrier,[102] it is in the nature of a public service company. Its functions have

---

[99] O'Brian, 292.

[100] Masses Pub. Co. *v.* Patten, 246 Fed. 24, 27 (1917), Rogers, J. The operation of our postal censorship is shown by material cited in the Bibliography. The cases are at the end of Appendix II. See also the Trading with the Enemy Act for regulation of the foreign language press. U. S. Comp. Stat. 1918, § 3115½ j.

[101] *Ex parte* Jackson, 96 U. S. 727 (1877); Public Clearing House *v.* Coyne, 194 U. S. 497, 507 (1904).

[102] Masses Pub. Co. *v.* Patten, 245 Fed. 102, 106 (1917), Hough, J.

THE WAR WITH GERMANY 109

been performed by private persons in the past, and if it were not unlawful, would probably be shared by them now because of the greater speed possible.[103] According to the political theories of Leon Duguit,[104] the government in furnishing public service must be judged by ordinary standards of public callings. If the United States owned the railroads, it ought not to make unreasonable discrimination among passengers any more than a private railroad corporation, and a similar limitation should apply to the postal power. The congressional restrictions which have been upheld by the courts may be considered as reasonable regulations in view of the nature of the service. Even opposition to the government may be entitled to some consideration by the post-office as by the judges, who frequently decide against the United States. It is clear that exclusion from the mails practically destroys the circulation of a book or periodical, and makes free speech to that extent impossible. To say, as many courts do, that the agitator is still at liberty to use the express or the telegraph,[105] recalls the remark of the Bourbon princess when the Paris mob shouted for bread, "Why don't they eat cake?"

Still another method of suppression of opinion has been used. Not only have we substantially revived the Sedition Act of 1798, but the Alien Act as well. Aliens have been freely deported under statutes passed during the war, to be discussed in a later chapter, and even naturalized citizens or native American women marrying foreigners are within the reach of this power. A former German subject who was naturalized in 1882 refused in 1917 to contribute to the Red Cross and the Young Men's Christian Association be-

[103] Something like this happened when the Western Union Telegraph Co. recently tried to carry "night-letters" by messengers on trains.

[104] *Law in the Modern State*, translated by F. and H. Laski, N. Y., 1919. See H. J. Laski in 31 *Harv. L. Rev.* 186; and his *Authority in the Modern State*, p. 378.

[105] This alternative is even less valuable when the government controls the express and the telegraph. The *New York World* was denied the opportunity to use the telegraph to distribute a criticism of Mr. Burleson. *Collier's Weekly*, May 17, 1919, p. 16.

cause he would do nothing to injure the country where he was brought up and educated. His naturalization certificate was revoked after thirty-five years on the presumption that his recent conduct showed that he took the oath of renunciation in 1882 with a mental reservation as to the country of his birth. He may therefore be deported as an enemy alien.[106]

VII. *State Espionage Acts*

Him that escapeth the sword of Hazael shall Jehu slay.—*The First Book of Kings.*

One would have supposed that the federal Espionage Act was a sufficient safeguard against opposition to the war, but many states were not satisfied with either its terms or its enforcement, and enacted similar but more drastic laws of their own.[107] These were particularly common in western states, where feeling ran high against the Non-Partisan League or the I.W.W. The most important of these statutes, that of Minnesota, made it unlawful to say "that men should not enlist in the military or naval forces of the United States or the State of Minnesota," or that residents of that state should not aid the United States in carrying on war with the public enemies.[108] There have been

---

[106] United States *v.* Wursterbarth, 249 Fed. 908 (N. J., 1918), Haight, J.; see also United States *v.* Darmer, 249 Fed. 989 (W. D. Wash., 1918), Cushman, J.; U. S. *v.* Kramer, 262 Fed. 395 (C. C. A., 5th, 1919); Schurmann *v.* U. S., 264 Fed. 917 (C. C. A., 9th, 1920).

[107] These statutes and the decisions under them are collected in Appendix V. Other state cases arising out of war utterances are: *Breaches of the peace:* People *v.* Nesin, 179 N. Y. App. Div. 869 (1917); People *v.* Whitaker (Cal.), Nelles, p. 53; *War-time Prosecutions,* p. 27.

Municipal Ordinance regulating newspapers invalid: Star *v.* Brush, 170 N. Y. Supp. 987 (1918); 172 N. Y. Supp. 851 (1918); New Yorker Staats-Zeitung *v.* Nolan, 105 Atl. 72 (N. J., 1918). *Conspiracy to compel newsdealer to handle distasteful newspaper:* Sultan *v.* Star Co., 174 N. Y. Supp. 52 (1919). *Ordinance prohibiting German opera:* Star Opera Co. *v.* Hylan, 109 N. Y. Misc. 132 (1919). *Libel in war controversy:* Van Lonkhuyzen *v.* Daily News, 195 Mich. 283, 161 N. W. 979 (1917), 170 N. W. 98 (1918). *Expulsion of college student for pacifism:* not reviewed, Samson *v.* Columbia, 101 N. Y. Misc. 146, 167 N. Y. Supp. 202 (1917).

[108] Minn. Laws, 1917, c. 463. This was superseded in 1919 by a

a very large number of prosecutions and many convictions under this statute, chiefly of members of the Non-Partisan League, culminating in the condemnation of its president.

Although these statutes have been held in several cases [109] to punish crimes within the jurisdiction of the states, it seems possible that the offenses named are, unless mere breaches of the peace, crimes against the United States, and therefore cognizable only in the federal courts. Of course, the same act may be both a federal and a state crime, for instance, counterfeiting, which injures United States money and is also a kind of cheating. Consequently, it is urged in support of these sedition statutes, that a violation of the Espionage Act is also a breach of the duty of citizens of a state to assist that state in performing its duty to support the nation in war, and that sedition, although directly aimed at the federal government, must indirectly affect the security of the state government. On the other hand, it has been held that treason against the United States cannot be prosecuted by the states [110] and interference with the federal war power is closely analogous. The argument that there is also interference with the states is open to question. They have no war powers; their control over the militia in so far as that was affected by any of the utterances prosecuted was taken out of their hands during the war; and although the state officers did render aid in the raising of troops, that does not make it a state function, any more than the assistance of a policeman in the arrest of a deserter renders him amenable to state law. The control was entirely in the hands of the federal government.

still more drastic act, to take care of future wars. Laws, 1919, c. 93. See cases in Appendix V and Bibliography on Townley Trial.

[109] State *v.* Holm, 139 Minn. 267 (1918); State *v.* Tachin, 106 Atl. 145, 108 Atl. 318, two JJ. dissenting (N. J., 1919); State *v.* Gibson, 174 N. W. 34 (Ia. 1919). But see *Ex parte* Meckel, 220 S. W. 81 (Tex. 1920), the only case holding a sedition statute unconstitutional.

[110] People *v.* Lynch, 11 Johns. (N. Y.) 549 (1814); *Ex parte* Quarrier, 2 W. Va. 569 (1866). The National Guard, when called into the service of the United States, were discharged from the state militia, U. S. Comp. Stat. 1918, § 2044a; S. T. Ansell, "Status of State Militia under the Hay Bill," 30 *Harv. Law Rev.* 712.

Even though the crime be not held exclusively within the jurisdiction of the United States, still this seems like one of those cases where the state government has at the most a power concurrent with that of Congress, which must cease to operate when Congress has determined the proper laws to apply to the subject-matter. For example, a state would have power to grant immunity from civil suits to persons in military service so long as there was no federal law on the subject, but when Congress passed the Soldiers' and Sailors' Civil Relief Act, a state law giving a less or a greater degree of protection became thereby invalid.[111] The same principle applies to regulations as to interference with the raising of armies.

For there can be no doubt that state acts like that in Minnesota conflict very seriously with the enforcement of the federal statute, so as to render the state legislation extremely undesirable even if not unconstitutional. If a man deserves to be prosecuted for his anti-war activities it is fair to presume that the Department of Justice will have him indicted under the ample provisions of the Espionage Act, and it is important that the control of proceedings should be in the hands of the Department, without parallel prosecutions by independent state officials. On the other hand, if Congress and the federal officials think it wise to allow much discussion of war aims and economic aspects, it is very unfortunate that their policy should be hampered by bitter prosecutions based on an entirely different policy and growing out of local hysteria or directed against opinions which are objectionable to influential political or economic groups in the state. Mr. O'Brian contrasts the federal policy of restraint against members of the Non-Partisan League and adherence to the fundamental principle that guilt is personal and that no class of individuals will be proscribed

---

[111] Konkel *v.* State, 168 Wis. 335 (1919), with a very full discussion; see State *v.* Darwin, 102 Wash. 402 (1918). *Cf.* Halter *v.* Nebraska, 205 U. S. 34 (1907); Houston *v.* Moore, 5 Wheat. 1 (1820). The dissenting opinions in S. *v.* Tachin, 108 Atl. 318, make the same point and also attack the N. J. statute as a violation of freedom of speech.

as a class, with the sweeping and severe action of Minnesota:[112]

> The result of its adoption increased discontent and the most serious cases of alleged interference with civil liberty were reported to the federal government from that state. Our view was that, while cases of individual guilt must be prosecuted with severity, class movements cannot be controlled or molded by indictments. Arbitrary repression or interference often adds to their dynamic force. But unfortunately the constructive teachings and arguments of persuasion necessary to deal with movements of this character were not at any time in evidence in these disturbed districts of the country.

If hostilities had continued for another year, these local statutes might have produced an alarming effect upon the output of the grain-producing states by breeding a suppressed but no less active hatred of the war in the Non-Partisan League, and might also in jailing members of the I.W.W., whom the Department of Justice was leaving alone, have blocked the conciliatory work of Colonel Disque in the spruce forests and of other federal agents in the copper regions.[113]

VIII. *Reflections During a Technical State of War*

I do not speak of what is past and gone; but in case of a future war what results will follow from your decision indorsing the Attorney General's views?—JEREMIAH BLACK, arguing in *Ex parte* Milligan, 2 Wall. 78.

The Espionage Act of 1917, as interpreted by the Supreme Court, suppresses free speech for all opponents of a war, but allows militant newspapers and politicians to block, by unbounded abuse, the efforts of the President to end a war by a just settlement. Congress reached the same result by the 1918 Act, making it criminal to "oppose the cause of the United States" in any war.

---

[112] O'Brian, 296.

[113] O'Brian, 299; Report to the President of the President's Mediation Commission. For a very harsh case of a ten-year sentence for the victim of a flag-kissing mob, *Ex parte* Starr, 263 Fed. 145 (1920).

The Espionage Act of 1918 is not limited to this war. The pacifists and Socialists were, I believe, wrong about that, but they may be right next time. They might have been right a few months ago had we been drawn into war with Mexico as carelessly as England was drawn into the war with Spain over Jenkins' ear. Balance military necessity in such a case against the harm of suppressing truth by a ten-year sentence. The government can argue better than its opponents, if it has any case at all, and at its back are public opinion, the press, the police, the army, to prevent their words from causing unlawful acts. And while national welfare doubtless demands that a just war be pushed to victory, it also demands that an unjust war be stopped. The only way to find out whether a war is unjust is to let people say so.

The 1918 clauses punishing attacks on the Constitution and our form of government raise still stronger objections. They have nothing to do with war. They may be used during some petty struggle with Haiti to arrest and imprison for twenty years an excitable advocate of the repeal of the Eighteenth Amendment or the abolition of the Senate. If there was one thing which the First Amendment was meant by our ancestors to protect, it was criticism of the existing form of government and advocacy of change, the kind of criticism which George III's judges punished. Even if the Act permits temperate discussion, which is doubtful, in view of the words about causing " contempt . . . or disrepute," it still abridges free speech, for the greater the need of change, the greater the likelihood that agitators will lose their temper over the present situation. It is impossible to speak respectfully of that portion of our Constitution and form of government which is represented by the electoral college, and much hatred has justly been directed to the clause for the return of fugitive slaves. Other parts may prove equally objectionable in the course of years. Particularly dangerous are the 1918 clauses about defamation of the army and navy. They would surely be invoked by advocates of compulsory military service against their opponents, if they wished to take advantage of any hostilities to fasten conscription upon the nation as a continuous policy. They make any scathing criticism of military methods a very perilous matter in future wars even for the most loyal and eminent civilians (no intent to favor the enemy being required by the statute), and raise the army and navy into a privileged position beyond the range of ordinary outspoken discussion, such as is enjoyed by no civilians. This is what the French army wanted during the Dreyfus affair, and a petty war will suffice to give it. Furthermore, if the language used does bring the army or navy into contempt, it is absolutely immaterial that the charge made is true.

That these predictions of what will happen in a petty war are by no means exaggerated is proved by what has been done under the Espionage Act in a time when there is no war at all—except by a legal fiction. First, the Attorney General, a year after the armistice, raided and closed the office of the *Seattle Union-Record*, because it urged the workers to kick the governing class into the discard at the next election, and said that the Centralia shootings were the culmination of a long series of illegal acts by ex-service men, pleading for law and order by rich and poor alike.[114] Secondly, thirteen months after the armistice, Mr. Burleson still kept the *New York Call* from the mails, and announced to the Supreme Court of the District of Columbia that in view of the facts, his exercise of judgment was " not subject to be reviewed, reversed, set aside, or controlled by a court of law." [115] Thirdly, fourteen months after all fighting had stopped three men were tried in Syracuse for distributing

[114] Anna Louise Strong, " A Newspaper Confiscated—and Returned," 109 *Nation* 738 (Dec. 13, 1919). Indictments of the editors for items published during the year after the armistice were quashed in U. S. *v.* Strong, 263 Fed. 789; U. S. *v.* Listman, *ibid.* 798; U. S. v. Ault, *ibid.* 800. For the other side, see Ole Hanson, *Americanism versus Bolshevism*, N. Y., 1920.

[115] United States of America *ex rel.* The Workingmen's Co-operative Publishing Association *v.* Burleson, Supreme Court, Dist. Col., Oct. Term, 1919, Law No. 63134. Answer of Respondent.

circulars in the autumn of 1919, describing ill-treatment of political prisoners, calling an amnesty meeting, and requesting that letters be written to the President and members of Congress. The leaflets quoted the First Amendment, *Ex parte* Milligan, and a speech by President Wilson. The defendants were convicted and sentenced to eighteen months in prison for disloyal language about our form of government and the military forces, language designed to bring them and the Constitution into contempt, inciting resistance to the United States, and obstruction of recruiting.[116]

The Supreme Court has never passed squarely on these sections of the Espionage Act of 1918, though some of them were involved in the Abrams case, and it is to be hoped that they will be declared unconstitutional. It would be better yet if they and the whole of section 3 were repealed.

Whatever be decided as to constitutionality, the Espionage Act prosecutions break with a great tradition in English and American law. Only once before has the United States tried to punish political crimes, and the Sedition Act of 1798 with its maximum of two years' imprisonment wrecked the Federalist party. The Mexican War produced the Biglow Papers, and every stanza in the opening poem would have violated a separate clause of the Espionage Act of 1918, if the slaveholders had drafted such a statute. We fought the Civil War with the enemy at our gates and powerful secret societies in our midst without an Espionage Act.

When the disloyal press was curbed by Burnside and his subordinates, they received sharp telegrams of revocation from Lincoln. The irritation produced by such acts was in his opinion "likely to do more harm than the publication would do."[117] Undoubtedly he permitted a very large number of arbitrary arrests by Seward and Stanton, or

[116] 21 *New Republic* 302 (Feb. 11, 1920); "Bringing the Constitution into Disrepute," 21 *ibid.* 330 (Feb. 18, 1920). U. S. *v.* Steene, 263 Fed. 130.

[117] J. F. Rhodes, *History of the United States*, III, 553; IV, 223-253, 267 note, 467, 473; VI, 78, 96. For Lincoln's refusal to allow General

THE WAR WITH GERMANY

under martial law in the border states. "Must I shoot a simple soldier boy who deserts, while I must not touch a hair of a wily agitator who induces him to desert?" But Lincoln's policy, apart from all questions of its legality, was very different in nature from most of the Espionage Act prosecutions and sentences. He was proceeding against men who were so far within the test of direct and dangerous interference with the war that they were actually causing desertions, and even then he acted to prevent and not to punish. Vallandigham was sent through into the Confederate lines, and left unmolested on his return. Lincoln would not have allowed an old man, a Presidential opponent and the choice of nine hundred thousand American citizens, to lie in prison for sincere and harmless, even though misguided, words, over a year after the last gun was fired.

If the North was a dictatorship, says Rhodes, the South was a socialized state, which was much closer to the situation of all the countries engaged in the World War. There the newspapers were probably under closer control, but there were no prosecutions.

And so in England. Bright and Cobden in the Crimean War, Morley and Lloyd George in the Boer War, were un-

---

Burnside and his subordinates to suppress the *Chicago Times* and other newspapers of Copperhead tendencies in Illinois, Indiana, and Ohio, see also Official Record of the Rebellion, Series II, Vol. V, 723, 741; Series III, Vol. III, 252. On number of arrests, Rhodes, IV, 230 note; Lincoln's Proclamation suspending *habeas corpus* for "aiders or abettors of the enemy," 13 Stat. at L. 734.

The case of *Ex parte* Vallandigham, 1 Wall. (U. S.) 243 (1863), is sometimes supposed to support the unlimited exercise of the war power to restrict speech. See Ambrose Tighe in 3 *Minn. L. Rev.* 1 (1918). The decision merely holds that the writ of *certiorari* does not lie to a military tribunal. Nothing is said as to the existence of some other remedy such as *habeas corpus*, or an action for false imprisonment. *Ex parte* Vallandigham, 28 Fed. Cas. 874 (1863), lends support to Mr. Tighe. The treatment of Vallandigham is considered illegal by Rhodes, *op. cit.*, IV, 245-252, and would seem so under *Ex parte* Milligan. On the South, Rhodes, V, 473, is contradicted by Edward A. Pollard, Jefferson Davis, p. 316. As late as May 19, 1864, a resolution was introduced in the Confederate Congress to inquire if legislation was necessary to prevent press disclosures of military information. 4 Journ. C. S. A. Cong., p. 60.

touched. Even in this war, while the terms of the Defense of the Realm Act are more sweeping than our statute, the administration has been less severe. Those who enforced it have allowed a wide range of discussion and imposed brief sentences, though they sat within sound of the German guns. And of all the nations at war, we alone, three thousand miles from the conflict, still refuse a general amnesty to political prisoners.[118]

Undoubtedly some utterances had to be suppressed. We have passed through a period of danger, and have reasonably supposed the danger to be greater than it actually was, but the prosecutions in Great Britain during a similar period of peril in the French Revolution have not since been regarded with pride. Action in proportion to the emergency was justified, but we have censored and punished speech which was very far from direct and dangerous interference with the conduct of the war. The chief responsibility for this must rest, not upon Congress which was content for a long period with the moderate language of the Espionage Act of 1917, but upon the officials of the Department of Justice and the Post-office, who turned that statute into a drag-net for pacifists, and upon the judges who upheld and approved this distortion of law. It may be questioned too, how much has actually been gained. Men have been imprisoned, but their words have not ceased to spread.[119] The poetry in the *Masses* was excluded from the mails only to be given a far wider circulation in two issues of the *Federal Reporter*. The mere publication of Mrs. Stokes' statement in the *Kansas City Star*, "I am for the people and the Gov-

---

[118] This was granted in Italy on November 19, 1918, before the signing of peace and in Germany before the armistice. The French amnesty was October 24, 1919. Sentences under the British Defense of the Realm Act have all expired, being very short; the longest, three years, was commuted to one year. This note comprises only seditious utterances in the war, not treasonable acts like the Bonnet Rouge affair or Irish convictions since the armistice.

[119] *Cf.* a similar experience of the Emperor Tiberius: Tacitus, *Annals*, IV, c. 35: "Punitis ingeniis, gliscit auctoritas." "A man who preaches in the stocks will always have hearers enough."—Dr. Johnson.

ernment is for the profiteers," was considered so dangerous to the morale of the training camps that she was sentenced to ten years in prison, and yet it was repeated by every important newspaper in the country during the trial. There is an unconscious irony in all suppression. It lurks behind Judge Hough's comparison of the *Masses* to the Beatitudes,[120] and in the words of Lord Justice Scrutton during this struggle against autocracy: " It had been said that a war could not be conducted on the principles of the Sermon on the Mount. It might also be said that a war could not be carried on according to the principles of Magna Charta." [121]

Those who gave their lives for freedom would be the last to thank us for throwing aside so lightly the great traditions of our race. Not satisfied to have justice and almost all the people with our cause, we insisted on an artificial unanimity of opinion behind the war. Keen intellectual grasp of the President's aims by the nation at large was very difficult when the opponents of his idealism ranged unchecked while the men who urged greater idealism went to prison. In our efforts to silence those who advocated peace without victory we prevented at the very start that vigorous threshing out of fundamentals which might to-day have saved us from a victory without peace.

[120] See page 55, *supra*.
[121] Ronnfeldt *v.* Phillips, 35 T. L. R. 46 (1918, C. A.).

CHAPTER III

A CONTEMPORARY STATE TRIAL—THE UNITED STATES *VS*. JACOB ABRAMS *ET AL*.

In this case sentences of twenty years imprisonment have been imposed for the publishing of two leaflets that I believe the defendants had as much right to publish as the Government has to publish the Constitution of the United States now vainly invoked by them.—JUSTICE HOLMES.

SHORTLY before eight o'clock, on the morning of August 23, 1918,[1] several men and boys were loitering at the corner of Houston and Crosby streets, in New York City, perched on sprinkler hydrants or standing about in talk, while they waited for the day's work to begin in the manufacturing building close by. One or two happened to look up and saw something being thrown from a window above and falling—the air was full of leaflets. Nothing of the kind had ever happened there before, and the workmen picked the papers up curiously from sidewalk and gutter. Some circulars in Yiddish they could not make head or tail of, but they read together others in English, which attacked the recent despatch of troops to Russia.

There has been so much misapprehension about the wording of these two leaflets that their text ought to be given in full.[2] That in English was as follows:

THE
HYPOCRISY
OF THE
UNITED STATES
AND HER ALLIES

"Our" President Wilson, with his beautiful phraseology, has hypnotized the people of America to such an extent that they do not see his hypocrisy.

[1] The sources for this case are in the Bibliography.
[2] The English pamphlet is Government's Exhibit No. 1, *Record*, p.

A CONTEMPORARY STATE TRIAL 121

Know, you people of America, that a frank enemy is always preferable to a concealed friend. When we say the people of America, we do not mean the few Kaisers of America, we mean the "People of America." You people of America were deceived by the wonderful speeches of the masked President Wilson. His shameful, cowardly silence about the intervention in Russia reveals the hypocrisy of the plutocratic gang in Washington and vicinity.

The President was afraid to announce to the American people the intervention in Russia. He is too much of a coward to come out openly and say: "We capitalistic nations cannot afford to have a proletarian republic in Russia." Instead, he uttered beautiful phrases about Russia, which, as you see, he did not mean, and secretly, cowardly, sent troops to crush the Russian Revolution. Do you see how German militarism combined with allied capitalism to crush the russian revolution?

This is not new. The tyrants of the world fight each other until they see a common enemy—WORKING CLASS—ENLIGHTMENT as soon as they find a common enemy, they combine to crush it.

In 1815 monarchic nations combined under the name of the "Holy Alliance" to crush the French Revolution. Now militarism and capitalism combined, though not openly, to crush the russian revolution.

What have you to say about it?

Will you allow the Russian Revolution to be crushed? YOU: Yes, we mean YOU the people of America!

THE RUSSIAN REVOLUTION CALLS TO THE WORKERS OF THE WORLD FOR HELP.

The Russian Revolution cries: "WORKERS OF THE WORLD! AWAKE! RISE! PUT DOWN YOUR ENEMY AND MINE!"

Yes friends, there is only one enemy of the workers of the world and that is CAPITALISM.

It is a crime, that workers of America, workers of Germany, workers of Japan, etc., to fight THE WORKERS' REPUBLIC OF RUSSIA.

AWAKE! AWAKE, YOU
WORKERS OF THE WORLD!
REVOLUTIONISTS

P. S. It is absurd to call us pro-German. We hate and despise German militarism more than do your hypocritical tyrants. We have more reasons for denouncing German militarism than has the coward of the White House.

245. Errors of punctuation, etc., are preserved. The translation of the Yiddish pamphlet is Government's Exhibit No. 2, *Record,* p. 247. Both measure 12x4½ inches, one page, printed on one side.

The Yiddish leaflet has been translated. This translation was accepted as correct by the government and the defense. Abrams, however, suggested a few changes during his testimony. It would be interesting to know how much stronger the Yiddish equivalent for "murder" at the end of the fourth paragraph is than the word for "kill."

Workers—Wake Up.

The preparatory work for Russia's emancipation is brought to an end by his Majesty, Mr. Wilson, and the rest of the gang; dogs of all colors!

America, together with the Allies, will march to Russia, not, "God Forbid," to interfere with the Russian affairs, but to help the Czecho-Slovaks in their struggle against the Bolsheviki.

Oh, ugly hypocrites; this time they shall not succeed in fooling the Russian emigrants and the friends of Russia in America. Too visible is their audacious move.

Workers, Russian emigrants, you who had the least belief in the honesty of our government must now throw away all confidence, must spit in the face the false, hypocritic, military propaganda which has fooled you so relentlessly, calling forth your sympathy, your help, to the prosecution of the war. With the money which you have loaned or are going to loan them, they will make bullets not only for the Germans but also for the Workers Soviets of Russia. Workers in the ammunition factories, you are producing bullets, bayonets, cannon, to murder not only the Germans, but also your dearest, best, who are in Russia and are fighting for freedom.

You who emigrated from Russia, you who are friends of Russia, will you carry on your conscience in cold blood the shame spot as a helper to choke the Workers Soviets. Will you give your consent to the inquisitionary expedition to Russia? Will you be calm spectators to the fleecing blood from the hearts of the best sons of Russia?

America and her Allies have betrayed (the workers). Their robberish aims are clear to all men. The destruction of the Russian Revolution, that is the politics of the march to Russia.

Workers, our reply to the barbaric intervention has to be a general strike! An open challenge only will let the government know that not only the Russian Worker fights for freedom, but also here in America lives the spirit of revolution.

Do not let the government scare you with their wild punishment

A CONTEMPORARY STATE TRIAL 123

in prisons, hanging and shooting. We must not and will not betray the splendid fighters of Russia. Workers, up to fight.

Three hundred years had the Romanoff dynasty taught us how to fight. Let all rulers remember this, from the smallest to the biggest despot, that the hand of the revolution will not shiver in a fight.

Woe unto those who will be in the way of progress. Let solidarity live! THE REBELS.

The Military Intelligence Police were notified, and sent two army sergeants, who climbed from floor to floor of the manufacturing building asking questions, until at a hat factory on the fourth story they arrested Rosansky, a young Russian, who eventually confessed that he had thrown out the circulars. Three men whom he had met at an anarchistic meeting a fortnight previously had handed him a package of leaflets the night before, and asked him to toss them from some window where people were passing. As he had a rendezvous with the same men that night, the Military Police with his aid captured six other Russians,—five men and a girl. The oldest man, Abrams, was twenty-nine, the youngest, Lipman, twenty-one, the same age as the girl, Molly Steimer. The sergeants went with some of the prisoners to their lodgings, three flights up a rear staircase on East 104th Street. It was an apartment of six rooms,— a front room with a table and some books, a cot, and a bookstand; two bedrooms, in one a bed, in the other a mattress on the floor; a dining-room so-called which had a catercornered closet containing a lot of books and papers and in the center large boxes like packing-boxes, used apparently for desks, and also some chairs and a long couch; a room that could be called a kitchen because it had a sink; and a rear room used by Molly Steimer, just a chair and some women's clothes hanging on the door. Such was the headquarters of the great conspiracy.

Shortly after midnight, Thomas J. Tunney, the Police Inspector who had questioned Rosansky in the morning, and author of *Throttled*, a book on bomb-plotters, examined the prisoners in the presence of several army sergeants, and obtained statements which were taken down stenographically. The prisoners refused to tell where the pamphlets were printed, but some of the sergeants, after finding a bill for a printing press and materials in Abrams' papers, learned from the seller that they had been sold to Abrams about July 15, partly on a chattel mortgage, and had been delivered at the basement of 1582 Madison Avenue. The Military Police entered the basement with a search warrant and discovered a motor driven press and a small hand press, bundles of blank paper of the same size as the English and Yiddish pamphlets, and English and Hebrew type of the style used in them. The side door of the basement had been broken in, plates and type were thrown on the chairs, torn pieces of both pamphlets had been set on fire in a pail and partly burned. Misprinted pamphlets and corrected proof lay crumpled upon the floor. Further investigation showed that Abrams had rented the basement from the janitress in mid-July for eight dollars a month, and that she had seen him and Lachowsky, another prisoner, working there together.

The prisoners, one of whom, Schwartz, died before trial, were indicted for conspiracy to violate four clauses of the Espionage Act of 1918.[3] The case promised to be decisive for two reasons. It was the only important prosecution for the new crimes created by the Espionage Act of 1918, although one such crime had been incidentally involved in the Debs trial. Consequently, the construction and constitutionality of this Sedition Act of 1918 would very probably be called in question. In the second place, the defendants were not prosecuted for pacifist or pro-German utterances, as in the general run of Espionage Act cases, but for agitation against the government's Russian policy. The Department of Justice had prevented several other prosecu-

[3] The conspiracy section of the Espionage Act is Act of June 15, 1917, c. 30, Title I, § 4; U. S. Comp. Stat., 1918, § 10212d, § 3 and the cases thereunder are in Appendix III. See page 44, *supra*.

tions of so-called Bolshevists for opposition to that policy, since no war had been declared against Russia. For example, no trial was ever held upon an indictment contemporaneous with that against the Abrams group which was presented in New York against Abraham Shiplacoff for a speech at a Socialist meeting, in which he compared the attitude of the Russian toward the American troops to the sentiments of our revolutionary patriots toward those " hired murderers," the Hessians. The appeal of the Abrams group to munition workers for a general strike was, however, regarded as more serious, and since the prosecution had got under way before the Department of Justice learned of it, it was allowed to proceed.[4]

I. *The District Court*

The trial of Abrams and his associates, except Schwartz, began on October 10, 1918, in the United States Court House in New York City before Judge Clayton of the Northern and Middle Districts of Alabama. Henry De Lamar Clayton was then sixty-one years of age. Belonging to a distinguished Alabama family he had graduated from the State University and practised law in Montgomery. For eighteen years he represented Alabama in Congress, serving eventually as Chairman of the Judiciary Committee of the House and giving his name to the well-known Clayton Act. In 1914 he was appointed to the United States bench. This was his first prominent Espionage Act case.

There were in the Southern District of New York three judges with extensive experience in the difficulties of war legislation. Judge Learned Hand had heard the equity suit of the *Masses* to obtain admission to the mails, and the demurrer of Scott Nearing. Judge Julius M. Mayer had sat on the Circuit Court of Appeals which reversed Judge Hand's decision in the *Masses* case, and had also tried

[4] Testimony of Alfred Bettman, Hearings before the Committee on Rules, 126.—*N. Y. Times,* Sept. 24, 1918.

Goldman and Phillips for opposing the draft. Judge Augustus N. Hand had presided at the trial of Max Eastman. If two corporations were litigating the validity of an important patent, they would be surprised to have the matter heard by a judge who had little experience in patent cases, especially if three judges trained in similar contests were available. In the Abrams trial, six persons risked the best part of their lives upon the decision of the perplexing problems of freedom of speech. The position of the defendants could hardly be understood without some acquaintance with the immigrant population of a great city, some knowledge of the ardent thirst of the East Side Jew for the discussion of international affairs. Yet because the New York dockets were crowded the Abrams case was assigned to a judge who had tried no important Espionage Act case, who was called in from a remote district where people were of one mind about the war, where the working class is more conspicuous for a submissive respect for law and order than for the criticism of high officials, where Russians are scarce and Bolshevists unknown.

The government was represented by Francis G. Caffey, United States Attorney, with John M. Ryan and S. L. Miller, Assistant United States Attorneys, of counsel. Harry Weinberger of New York appeared for the defendants. The jury was duly empaneled and sworn on Monday, October 14, and the trial ended on Wednesday, October 23.

The overt acts were proved without contradiction. Soon after United States troops were sent to Vladivostok, the group had begun meeting in the bare " third floor-back " on East 104th Street, where most of them lived, and decided to protest against the attack on the Russian Revolutions, with which as anarchists or Socialists they strongly sympathized. Schwartz, the dead prisoner, had written the Yiddish circular, and Lipman the English. Abrams, the oldest, bought the press. After printing five thousand copies of each circular he stopped for lack of funds. Lachowsky and Molly Steimer had distributed about nine

A CONTEMPORARY STATE TRIAL

thousand pamphlets, throwing them in the streets where there were the most working-people or passing them around at radical meetings. Rosansky's aid had been secured just before the arrests. There was no evidence that one person was led to stop any kind of war work, or even that the pamphlets reached a single munition worker.

The defense, besides contending that the Espionage Act was unconstitutional, maintained that it was not violated, and in particular that the criminal intent required by the express terms of the statute did not exist. Each count of the indictment [5] covered a conspiracy to violate one clause of the Act, as follows, according to the language of the statute. Certain phrases in the indictment which are not in the Act are enclosed in brackets.

Whoever, when the United States is at war, . . . shall willfully utter, print, write, or publish
(Count 1) any disloyal, . . . scurrilous, or abusive language about the form of government of the United States, . . .
(Count 2) or any language intended to bring the form of government of the United States . . . into contempt, scorn, contumely, or disrepute, . . .
(Count 3) or . . . any language intended to incite, provoke, or encourage resistance to the United States [in said war with the German Imperial Government], . . .
(Count 4) or shall willfully by utterance, writing, printing, publication, . . . urge, incite, or advocate any curtailment of production in this country of any thing or things, product or products [to wit, ordnance and ammunition] necessary or essential to the prosecution of the war in which the United States may be engaged, [to wit, said war with the Imperial German Government], with intent by such curtailment to cripple or hinder the United States in the prosecution of the war, . . .
shall be punished by a fine of not more than $10,000 or imprisonment for not more than twenty years or both.

As to the first crime charged, the publication of "disloyal, . . . scurrilous, or abusive language" about our form of government, the Espionage Act by its terms punishes the

[5] The indictment is in *Record,* 2-19.

act of publication, without any mention of intent. Although some district judges have considered that there must be an evil or wicked intention,[6] it has been contended with much force and on high authority [7] that the utterance of the words is in itself criminal regardless of the state of mind. On this view, all that is necessary is intention to publish. There need be no intention to be abusive or disloyal about the form of government. If so, the Espionage Act is in this respect much more rigorous than the Sedition Act of 1798, which created the crime of "publishing any false, scandalous and malicious writing against the government," but required intent to defame it or excite against it the hatred of the people or stir up sedition. Also the penalty was only two years' imprisonment, and truth was a defense under that Act, whereas now a statement in real or technical war time of the soundest truths about our form of government is punishable by twenty years in prison if only those truths are sufficiently damaging to be considered abusive or disloyal.

However this may be, intention to injure is certainly material on the other three counts. Furthermore, the first and second counts may be dismissed at this point from further discussion. First, these clauses of the Espionage Act of 1918 punishing attacks on the Constitution and our form of government seem clearly unconstitutional, as stated in the preceding chapter. Also, even if they are constitutional, there was no attack in the pamphlets on our form of government, but only upon those who were administering that government. Surely the phrase "capitalistic nation" does not constitute defamation of our political structure, which is compatible with other types of economic organization, such as national ownership of all industries. Although the heavy fines imposed on the defendants under

---

[6] United States *v.* Buessel, Bull. 131; United States *v.* Martin, Bull. 157; United States *v.* Equi, Bull. 172.

[7] 33 *Harv. L. Rev.* 442, 443, citing Learned Hand, J., in United States *v.* Curran, Bull. 140.

A CONTEMPORARY STATE TRIAL

these two counts called for some decision on their constitutionality or construction, the Supreme Court refused to make it, and Justice Clarke contented himself with suggesting that the distinction between abusing our form of government and abusing the President and Congress, the agencies through which it must function in time of war, might be only "technical."[8] If so, these sections of the Espionage Act must have been more frequently violated in Wall Street than in Harlem.

The controversy about this case must be limited to the third and fourth counts of the indictment. Aside from questions of constitutionality, the government had to establish the specific criminal intent required by the indictment and the Espionage Act. (1) It had to prove intention to publish the pamphlets, because of the word "willfully" and on general principles of the criminal law, which ordinarily requires intention to do the prohibited act. This the government undoubtedly did. (2) Under the fourth count it had to prove intention to produce curtailment of munitions, because the words "urge, incite, advocate" create an offense analogous to criminal solicitation, which involves a specific intent to bring about the overt act. There are some sentences in the Yiddish circular which show such an intention, although it is open to question whether an incidental portion of a general protest which is not shown to have come dangerously near success really constitutes criminal solicitation or amounts to advocating. (3) At all events, the main task of the government was to establish under both counts an additional intention to interfere with the war with Germany, and the question whether it proved anything more than an intention to obstruct operations in Russia is the vital issue of fact in the case.

Since we had not declared war upon Russia, protests against our action there could not be criminal unless they were also in opposition to the war with Germany. There are two conceivable theories of guilt, which might connect the

[8] Abrams v. United States, 250 U. S. 616, 623.

circulars with the war. First, that the despatch of troops to Siberia was "a strategic operation against the Germans on the eastern battle front," so that any interference with that expedition hindered the whole war. The second theory is, that the circulars intended to cause armed revolts and strikes and thus diminish the supply of troops and munitions available against Germany on the regular battle front.

Clearly the second theory is the only legitimate basis for conviction. That opposition intended to hinder the armed occupation of neutral territory and asserting it to be illegal should be *per se* criminal is so clearly a travesty on the defense of Belgium and a violation of the right of freedom of speech that this view has been unanimously rejected by the United States Supreme Court in the Abrams case, by the government's brief,[9] and by writers [10] who support the decision. They have all adopted the second theory of guilt and have taken it for granted that the jury followed the same course. They assume that the convictions represent a finding of fact by the jury that the defendants intended to interfere with operations against Germany itself and to embarrass or defeat the military plans of our government in Europe. Practically the whole of the discussion of the case has been confined to the question whether such a finding that they encouraged strikes and revolts justifies conviction. Nevertheless, I believe that an examination of the record makes it highly probable that these defendants were convicted on just the other theory for trying to hinder the Russian expedition.

As a state trial, this case cannot be understood without reference to the atmosphere in which the defendants wrote the circulars and the jury reached their verdict. I have no desire to venture into the Serbonian bog of the Russian Revolution, but a few undisputed facts must be recalled.[11] On

---

[9] Page 35 ff.
[10] Mr. Wigmore is a possible exception and may regard all Bolshevism as within the Espionage Act.
[11] The documents are in 7 *N. Y. Times Current History of the War,* VII (part 2) 273; VIII (part 1) 49; VIII (part 2) 465, 470;

January 8, 1918, two months after the establishment of the Soviet Government, President Wilson declared as the sixth of his Fourteen Points, that Russia must have " an unhampered and unembarrassed opportunity for the independent determination of her own political development," and that the treatment accorded her by her sister nations during the months to come would be " the acid test of their good-will." On March 11 he telegraphed the Pan-Soviet Congress, " May I not take advantage of the meeting of the Congress of Soviets to express the sincere sympathy " felt for the disastrous outcome of the Brest-Litovsk negotiations, and again promised that Russia should be secured " complete sovereignty and independence in her own affairs." Four months later a small body of American marines joined in the occupation of Murmansk, and shortly afterwards American troops were sent to Vladivostok. On August 3, an official statement from Washington announced that military intervention in Russia would only add to the confusion there and dissipate our forces on the western front. Consequently, we would not interfere with the political sovereignty of Russia or intervene in her local affairs, but would merely send a few thousand men to Vladivostok in co-operation with Japan, who had given a similar assurance. The only present object for which the American troops would be employed would be to help the Czechoslovaks against the armed German and Austrian prisoners who were attacking them, to guard military stores, and render acceptable aid to the Russians in the organization of their own self-defense; but we could not restrict the actions or interfere with the independent judgment of our associates.

A few days later Abrams and his friends wrote and printed the leaflet headed, " The Hypocrisy of the United States and her Allies."

IX (part I) 87. They are reprinted in *Russian-American Relations*, ed. Cumming and Pettit, N. Y., 1920. See Charles Cheney Hyde, " The Recognition of the Czechoslovaks as Belligerents," 13 *Am. J. Int. L.* 93 (1919).

The Soviet government failed to distinguish between military intervention and the arrival of foreign troops on Russian soil. The diplomatic breach was complete. Soon afterwards the newspapers were filled with accounts of Bolshevist atrocities. In September the United States recognized the Czechoslovaks as a belligerent government warring against Germany and Austria, with their capital in Washington and their chief army in Siberia, so that the seacoast of Bohemia was evidently the Pacific Ocean. On September 15 the United States Committee on Public Information published nation-wide in the press the documents [12] collected by its representative, Mr. Edgar Sisson, which were stated to show that the present heads of the Bolshevist government were merely hired German agents. No one who recalls the widespread popular identification of the Soviet Government with Germany in the summer and early autumn of 1918 can doubt that an October jury would inevitably regard pro-Bolshevist activities as pro-German, and consequently apply the first or Russian theory of guilt, besides having a prejudice against the defendants as sympathizers with the Russian Revolution, which could only be overcome by an exposition of the Russian situation from sources which had as yet found no expression in the newspapers.

Early on Friday, October 18, the fifth day of the actual trial, the government rested. Mr. Weinberger opened the case to the jury on behalf of the defendants, and called to the witness stand Colonel Raymond Robins. Mr. Robins had not abandoned without a struggle the retirement in which he had lived since his return from Russia. He had tried to avoid service of a subpœna, and the United States

---

[12] War Information Series, No. 20 (October, 1918); the documents, without the historical report, are in *Bolshevik Propaganda*, etc., p. 1125. The documents appeared in the public press by installments, beginning September 15, 1918. See the *New York Times* of that date. For criticism of their genuineness, see 16 *New Republic* 209 (September 21, 1918), 107 *Nation* 616 (November 23, 1918), and the anti-Bolshevist book, E. H. Wilcox, *Russia's Ruin*, New York, 1919. They are accepted as genuine by Étienne Antonelli, *La Russie Bolcheviste*, Paris, 1919.

marshal was on the point of breaking in the door of his apartment when it opened and Mr. George W. Wickersham came out. As Mr. Robins's personal counsel he agreed to his testifying, but accompanied him to and from the courtroom and sat at the counsel table during his examination.[13]

After a dozen introductory questions, the United States attorney objected to further examination, and the witness thereafter was obliged to remain silent while the defendants' counsel ran through a series of thirty unanswered questions in order to get them on the record. This was repeated with Albert Rhys Williams, and it was not considered worth while to call Edgar Sisson at all. The admissibility of their evidence raises problems that go to the heart of the case.

The first theory of guilt raised the complex question whether the Russian expedition was a part of the war. If this is a political question which must be answered in the affirmative on the mere *ipse dixit of* the government, the existence of a war enables the government to withdraw the most remote and questionable policies from the scope of ordinary discussion simply by labeling them a war matter. The annexation of Mexico to prevent its becoming a base for German operations, the use of American troops to put down strikes in England or Sinn Fein in Ireland, are no more remotely connected with the war with Germany than the Russian affair. On the other hand, if the relation of such an expedition to the war is put in issue to be decided by the jury, the defense ought to be able to call witnesses to disprove it. On this account, in the Abrams case, Raymond Robins and other eyewitnesses of Russian affairs were summoned to prove that the Bolshevist and Czechoslovak situation was such that our intervention was not anti-German; but this testimony and all questions of the constitutionality of intervention were excluded by Judge Clayton with the

---

[13] The summary of the Robins incident is taken from *Record*, 110-138; *New York Call*, October 19, 1918; conversation with Mr. Weinberger.

remark, "The flowers that bloom in the spring, tra la, have nothing to do with the case." [14]

This phase of the trial is very important for its demonstration of the enormous difficulties of proof into which we have brought ourselves in the United States by creating political crimes. Before the Espionage Act our criminal law punished men almost entirely for acts which take place in the tangible world and are proved by the evidence of our five senses. This Act punishes men for words which cause no injury, but have a supposedly bad tendency to harm the state, and also for intentions which are regarded as evil. Now, bad tendency and bad intention cannot be seen or heard or touched or tasted or smelled. They are, as we have seen, a matter of inference from the complex and obscure background of general conditions. Consequently, that background becomes, whether we admit witnesses or not, an issue in the case. The rules of evidence for the trial of overt criminal acts prove almost useless. Common sense makes it plain that a knowledge of Russian affairs was essential to a jury with the attitude of that moment, obliged to interpret the repeated references to Russia in the circulars, and as we shall see, told often by the judge that the defendants were guilty if their pamphlets were issued for the purpose of preventing the government from carrying on its operations in Russia.

All prosecutions for words will involve us in the same awkward dilemma that was suggested in connection with the "false statements" clause in the Pierce case. If we follow the logical course just indicated and allow the alleged promoter of sedition to bring in a mass of evidence from Russia or other dark and distant regions to show that neither he nor his utterances are liable to cause even remote injury to the national welfare, the prosecution is justly entitled to call other witnesses to establish the evil character of the agitation. Every sedition trial will be a rag-bag proceeding like the hearings about Bolshevism before the Overman

[14] *Record*, pp. 120, 132.

A CONTEMPORARY STATE TRIAL 135

Committee of the Senate. As Judge Clayton pointed out in the Abrams trial, the admission of Raymond Robins's testimony would open up a Pandora's box. The district attorney would offer on his side to prove that Trotsky had been bought by the German Government.

To use a vulgar expression, it would be "swiping" them on the other hand, and we would forget all about the issues in this case, and we would find ourselves trying Lenine and Trotsky, which is something I do not intend to do. I have enough trouble trying these people here in the United States, and God knows I am not going into Russia to try to try anybody there.[15]

On the other hand, if for the sake of speed and convenience we adopt the policy of Judge Clayton and exclude general testimony as to bad tendency, pinning the evidence down to the facts of publication and the precise intention of the defendants, we shall often do a grave injustice to the prisoners. The jury and even the judge may bring to the trial preconceived views of the bad tendency and evil purpose of utterances opposed to the existing economic and social order or to war policies supported by the great mass of the population. If no counter-evidence to show that the opinions of the defendants may be reasonable or honest is admitted from third persons like Raymond Robins, these presuppositions must inevitably remain. Even if a defendant is allowed a wide scope in testifying in his own behalf, he is often the sort of man whose arguments carry little weight. In other words, in spite of the judge's desire to exclude outside evidence on either side as to bad tendency and bad intention from the case, such evidence in favor of a bad tendency and a bad intention is often automatically admitted the moment that the jury enter the box, and no system of challenges can avoid it. During a war they have for months been supplied with evidence by the government and the loyal press, diametrically opposed to the utterances for which the prosecution is brought. Unless something is done to tear

[15] *Record*, 130, 131. For Pierce *v.* U. S., see page 101, *supra*.

the tribunal out of the fabric of public sentiment, a conviction is almost certain to result in prosecutions for political crimes, where the ordinary tests of the five senses play no part and men are forced to judge of the opinions and character of the prisoners by their own opinions and character as formed in the furnace of war. What Mr. Robins has since said and written makes it clear that his evidence would have been highly valuable to the defense.

Despite the practical inconveniences of such testimony as his in political prosecutions, it is the method pursued in countries where political crimes have existed when unknown in the United States. France, for instance, allows a "free defense," as in the *Affaire Dreyfus*. The defendant is not only allowed to say anything in his own favor, but may bring forward any witnesses he pleases, who express themselves fully and unhindered. Strange as it seems to us, the results are said to be very satisfactory.[16] Consequently, if we are going to continue to prosecute men for the bad political tendency of their disloyal or anarchistic utterances, we may have to adopt a similar wide-open policy in justice to the defendants.

Better far to reject both horns of the dilemma and refuse altogether to make tendency a test of criminality. If we are not willing to allow the free defense, we ought to abolish political crimes by the repeal of the Espionage Act and all other sedition statutes.

In the absence of any established technique for political crimes in this country, the exclusion of the Robins testimony was correct, since it did not bear directly on the only legitimate theory of guilt, but this only made it all the more imperative that Judge Clayton should repeatedly during the trial and in his charge insist to the jury that opposition

---

[16] Robert Ferrari, "The Trial of Political Prisoners Here and Abroad," 66 *Dial* 647 (June 28, 1919). The same method is pursued in French murder cases where "the honor of the family" is a defense, and perhaps instances like the Thaw trial show it is not wholly unknown in this country. See Walter F. Angell, "A Providence Lawyer at the Caillaux Trial," *Providence Daily Journal*, August 21, 1914.

A CONTEMPORARY STATE TRIAL 137

to our Russian policy was not in itself a crime. He ought to have cleared Russia and Bolshevism out of the case for good and all, and pounded home the proposition that the only issue under the third and fourth counts (which alone should have gone to the jury, if anything went at all) was whether the defendants intended by inducing strikes in munition factories and other forms of protest to interfere with the supply of munitions for use against Germany. No one who will put himself back into the atmosphere of October, 1918, can doubt that the jury would naturally regard pro-Bolshevist activities as pro-German, and that it was the duty of Judge Clayton to warn them explicitly against the Russian theory of guilt, and confine their attention to the pro-German theory. There is no adequate warning on this in the record.* Instead, Judge Clayton himself repeatedly proclaimed the unsound theory of guilt, that if the defendants intended to oppose the government's Russian policy, they had *ipso facto* violated the law.

Before the defendants had put in any material testimony, he said: [17]

Now the charge in this case is, in its very nature, that these defendants, by what they have done, conspired to go and incite a revolt; in fact, one of the very papers is signed ' Revolutionists,' and it was for the purpose of avoiding—a purpose expressed in the paper itself—the purposes of the Government and raising a state of public opinion in this country of hostility to the Government of the United States, so as to prevent the Government from carrying on its operations and prevent the Government from recognizing that faction of the Government of Russia, which the Government has recognized, and to force the Government of the United States to recognize that faction of the Government in Russia to which these people were friendly.

Now, they cannot do that. No man can do that, and that is the theory that I have of this case, and we might as well have it out in the beginning.

The court did tell the jury that this statement was not part of the evidence and should be disregarded in passing on

[17] *Record*, pp. 117, 118. *See p. 160 *infra*, note 68.

the issue of fact, but the harm was done and he took no steps to present any concrete alternative view. The second and legitimate theory of guilt was never stated by him, and it is doubtful if he himself ever realized the distinction or what really was in issue. Instead, he continued to apply the Russian theory in his cross-examination of Lipman, for it is one of the remarkable features of this case that most of the cross-examination of the prisoners was not by the district attorney, but by the court, who sometimes broke in upon the direct examination before half a dozen questions had been asked.[18] Lipman was testifying in response to his counsel that he had written the English pamphlet because the President after sending the telegram of sympathy to the Soviets had a few weeks later despatched a military expedition to Russia. Judge Clayton took over the witness: [19]

"The President, you thought, and all that he was doing ought to be stopped and broken up?" "I thought when I know he is elected by the people they should protest against intervention. . . . I did not want to break up. I called for a protest, which as I understand it, from my knowledge of the Constitution, the people of America had a right to protest." . . .

"Did you not intend to incite or provoke or encourage resistance to the Government of the United States?" "Not to the Government—never did."

"Who was acting for the Government if the President was not?" "I thought it was the Congress and Senate that was supposed to represent the people of America."

"The President is the executive head . . . You intended to incite opposition to what the President did?" "I did not. I intended to enlighten the people about the subject, for, as I stated, the papers were afraid to state it, and I thought it was the right time."

" . . . The Government acts through the President, and you intended to incite opposition to what he was doing?" "I intended to incite opposition to every wrong act I understood to be wrong."

[18] See the court's cross-examination of Abrams, *Record*, p. 163. The testimony not included in the *Record* shows much more questioning by the judge. See current issues of the *New York Times* and *New York Call;* Stenographer's Notes.
[19] *Record*, pp. 201-203.

A CONTEMPORARY STATE TRIAL 139

"You had the specific intention to make public opinion and arouse public opinion against intervention in Russia?" "Yes."

When the judge also kept saying that the defendants' opinion of the legality of the President's action could not justify them in breaking the law,[20] he made their anti-interventionist propaganda seem a crime in itself, and there was no need for the jury to consider whether they had any intention to prevent the shipment of munitions to the western front. There is nothing in the charge about such an intention, nothing to exclude Russian operations from the scope of the war. Therefore, it is very probable that the defendants were convicted on an erroneous theory of guilt, simply because they protested against the despatch of armed forces to Russia.

However, it is maintained that the defendants did intend to hinder the fighting against Germany and so were properly convicted on the second theory of guilt. There are three classes of evidence in the case bearing on their intention.

First, the two pamphlets speak for themselves. Both plainly protest against our Russian policy and not against the war. The English circular emphatically repudiates the charge of pro-Germanism. It is nearly all expository, but throws in a few general exhortations which have been tossed about in every Socialistic hall and street-meeting for seventy years since the Communist manifesto in 1848 until Justice Clarke discovered in 1918 that it was a crime in war time to say, "Workers of the World! Awake! Rise! Put down your enemy and mine. . . . Capitalism!"

"This," he declares, "is clearly an appeal to the 'workers' of this country to arise and put down by force the Government of the United States."[21]

If this be so, practically every Socialistic book or pamphlet violates the Espionage Act, and the belief of American Socialists that the Act was directed against their political

[20] *Record*, pp. 115-121, 130-138, 167, 172, 173. See also Stenographer's Notes of Testimony, *passim*.
[21] 250 U. S. @ 620 (1919).

existence as a party under the pretext of war finds ample justification. Military imagery ought not to be taken literally in radical propaganda, any more than in church hymns. Nothing could show better than this sentence of Justice Clarke's how peace-time statutes which are limited in terms to the advocacy of "force and violence" may be interpreted judicially to punish obnoxious radical opinions which call for working-class action without a single word to indicate that force is to be employed.

The Yiddish circular is more specific and calls for a general strike, which can no more be kept out of a radical pamphlet than King Charles's head could be barred from Mr. Dick's Memorial. We ought to hesitate a long while before we decide that Congress made such shop-worn exuberance criminal. Very likely, as Justice Clarke says, "This is not an attempt to bring about a change of administration by candid discussion," [22]—but how much political discussion is candid? If nothing but candid discussion is protected by the First Amendment, its value for safeguarding popular review of official acts is *nil*. And even if words like "fight" and "revolution" indicate violence, though often used in a peaceable sense, the advocacy of strikes and violence is not a crime under this indictment unless intended to resist and hinder the war with Germany.

The second group of evidence consists of two manuscripts which were seized at the time of the arrests without a search-warrant.[23] One, a yellow sheet of paper in handwriting, taken from Lipman, contains a passage about keeping the allied armies busy at home in order to save the Russian Revolution.[24] The other, some typewritten sheets found in

[22] *Ibid.* 622. Bagehot points out the danger of such a test: "The effect of all legislative interference in controversies has ever been to make an approximation to candor compulsory on one side but to encourage on the other side violence, calumny, and bigotry."—*Works*, Longmans' ed., X, 127.

[23] A contest could have been made on this point. See Chapter VI.

[24] Government's Exhibit 11, *Record*, pp. 250, 251. See also *Record*, pp. 45, 103; also 78, where Lipman, under examination by the military intelligence police, testified it meant soldiers were to be kept busy preventing and stopping protest meetings.

A CONTEMPORARY STATE TRIAL 141

a closet in Abrams' rooms on a pile of books and papers, urges at its close a similar policy, so that there will be no armies to spare for Russia, and adds that if arms are used against the Russian people, " so will we use arms, and they shall never see the ruin of the Russian Revolution." [25] Very little attention was given to these manuscripts in either brief on appeal, but Justice Clarke says, after quoting the passages just mentioned:

These excerpts sufficiently show, that while the immediate occasion for this particular outbreak of lawlessness, on the part of the defendant alien anarchists, may have been resentment caused by our government sending troops into Russia as a strategic operation against the Germans on the eastern battle front, yet the plain purpose of their propaganda was to excite, at the supreme crisis of the war, disaffection, sedition, riots, and, as they hoped, revolution, in this country for the purpose of embarrassing and if possible defeating the military plans of the Government in Europe.[26]

These excerpts form a small part of two long discussions wholly concerned with the wrong committed against Russia by both Germany and ourselves. The clear and only purpose is to stop Russian intervention. Much more important, these passages do not occur in the pamphlets for which the defendants were indicted. They are in manuscripts which were never printed. There is not the slightest testimony that any one intended to print them, or indeed that the author, Lipman, ever showed them to any one. What one man jots down and refrains from printing is very weak proof of what several other men intended when they printed something else. Finally, a comparison of the second or typewritten manuscript with the English pamphlet shows that it is only a first draft, and the omission in revision of all the passages on which Justice Clarke relies furnishes decisive

[25] Government's Exhibit 13, *Record*, pp. 252-255. See also *Record*, pp. 55, 104. The significant passages from both manuscripts are in 250 U. S. @ 622 (1919). Mr. Wigmore actually quotes these passages as forming part of the Yiddish pamphlet. 14 *Ill. L. Rev.* 544.
[26] 250 U. S. @ 623 (1919).

evidence that such language did not express the actual intention of the defendants. All talk about keeping soldiers busy and using arms was thrown out, and the postscript denouncing German militarism was added. In other words, the one portion of the draft which might conceivably be regarded as favorable to Germany was deliberately dropped before printing, and a paragraph was substituted hostile to Germany and repudiating pro-Germanism.

Thirdly, we have the testimony of the defendants on the vital issue, whether they intended to defend the Russian Revolution by the methods of impulsive youth or intended to hinder us in our war against German militarism. All were born in Russia and had remained citizens of that country during their few years in the United States. All were anarchists except Lipman, and he was a Socialist. Nothing in the case rebuts the natural inference that such persons were devoted to Russian radicalism and bitterly hostile to Imperial Germany.

Abrams, under cross-examination by the district attorney, said that he had offered his services to the President to go to Russia and fight Germany, but permission had been refused.[27] Under cross-examination by the court, he denied that he intended to obstruct and hinder the government of the United States. His object was to help Russia. He did not believe in governments and was a revolutionist, rebelling against the conditions of life from twelve years of age, but that was only his philosophy. It had nothing to do with the pamphlets, the purpose of which was to protest against intervention.[28] On direct examination he testified that this was his sole purpose; that every Russian revolutionist was in favor of America's crushing German militarism; that he would go to Russia to fight it any time he had a chance; that he would help send propaganda from Russia to Germany to start a revolution there, as he had done on the border of Austria and was sent to Siberia for it. As to the appeal for strikes, he called upon the workers here

[27] *Record*, pp. 197.   [28] *Record*, pp. 163, 164, 196.

A CONTEMPORARY STATE TRIAL 143

not to produce bayonets to be used against the workers in Russia.

"I say it is absurd I should be called a pro-German, because in my heart I feel it is about time the black spot of Europe should be wiped out."
"You are opposed to German militarism in every form?"
"Absolutely."
"You would overthrow it and help overthrow it if you could?" "First chance." [29]

The other defendants testified to the same effect, even Molly Steimer, the most inflexible, who says that if she ever had a doubt whether people ought to be governed by one another it has vanished since she came in contact with those who rule, and now refuses to apply for a pardon because she ought not to be released so long as thousands of other political prisoners are languishing in American jails. She stated her intention thus: "The war between the United States and Germany does not concern me, because I wish to see militarism throughout the entire world crushed by the workers. . . . I thought, and I do think it now, that the workers of the United States who are working in munition factories ought to stop producing munitions which are used for the killing of Russians. I care nothing about interfering with the war with Germany, because it does not matter to me."

There is not a word in the whole *Record* to show that any prisoner was opposed to the war with Germany or had any intention except an absorbing desire to protest against intervention in Russia.[30]

It is hard to see how the jury could have convicted on this evidence if they had been instructed that a specific intent to hinder the war with Germany was necessary, but the charge contains nothing on this point except a mere repetition of the words of the statute. There is no com-

[29] *Record,* pp. 182, 183; and see also 168, 180, 190.
[30] Lipman, page 138, *supra, Record,* pp. 77, 200, 203, 206; Lachowsky, *Record,* pp. 223; Steimer, *Record,* pp. 82, 216, 221, 222.

ment on those words, no attempt to distinguish between a general intention to publish and the required specific intent. Instead, the judge charged, "People who have circulars to distribute, and they intend no wrong, go up and down the streets circulating them."[31] During the trial, although the defendants' counsel reminded him that Russian meetings in New York had been broken up, Judge Clayton said he would leave it to the jury whether throwing pamphlets out of windows squared with good, honest intention, and whether being anarchists and wanting to break up all government squared with honesty and sincerity of purpose. Soon afterward he stated:

If it were a case where the defendant was indicted for homicide, and he was charged with having taken a pistol and put it to the head of another man and fired the pistol and killed the man, you might say that he did not intend to do that.

But I would have very little respect for a jury that would come in with a verdict that he didn't have any intent.[32]

Plainly these rulings of Judge Clayton ignore absolutely the specific intent to oppose or hinder the war with Germany, as demanded by the statute, and authorize the jury to convict the defendants for intention to publish the pamphlets and a generally bad mind.

The verdict against Abrams, Lipman, Lachowsky, Rosansky, and Molly Steimer was guilty on all four counts. The sixth prisoner, Prober, was acquitted, for insufficient evidence of connection with the leaflets. The district attorney's office, which thought he had distributed leaflets at radical meetings, cites his acquittal as evidence of the fairness of the jury.

There is little of the heroic about these defendants and much that is repellent. Their beliefs were, as Justice Holmes called them, "the creed of ignorance and immaturity." Abrams was a sufficiently prominent radical to preside at a meeting in New York where Trotsky spoke. He and Lipman, who were subject to the draft as citizens of a nation

[31] *Record*, pp. 237, 238.   [32] *Record*, pp. 159-161.

still technically associated with ours in the war although our troops were fighting the compatriots of these men, have been indicted on strong evidence for stealing and forging draft cards. Two defendants, while out on bail after conviction, tried to escape as stowaways from New Orleans to Yucatan. Molly Steimer used her temporary freedom to distribute anarchistic leaflets in the New York streets, and was sent to Blackwell's Island, where she was regarded as incorrigible. Yet all this, bad as it is, in no way justifies their conviction under the Espionage Act. It is a fundamental principle of our law that men must not be punished in one case for other crimes, especially if not yet proved. If these prisoners are guilty of other offenses, they can be prosecuted for them. Such guilt and all their undesirable qualities cannot take the place of the essential and absent intention to hinder the war with Germany, and do not lessen the bad effects of this case as a precedent for the suppression of public protests against governmental action on the ground of its illegality.

Two features of the trial demand a passing notice. The method by which confessions were obtained from the defendants after arrest was not raised on appeal, since the overt acts were proved in other ways, but their testimony, if it can be believed, throws a significant light on the question, important to criminologists, of the treatment which political prisoners may expect in this country, especially if they be obscure aliens. The deportation raids prove that abuses are possible, but such a conclusion cannot be reached in the Abrams case without a detailed investigation of the conflicting evidence. The army sergeants deny threats and force.[33] The assistant district attorney, who showed much consideration toward the prisoners, noticed no traces of violence on the morning after the arrest, and is convinced that none was used. On the other hand, the charges of brutality seem disquietingly specific and sincere.[34] The defendants and their

[33] *Record*, pp. 70, 75, 85. Stenographer's Notes, 742 ff., 752 ff.
[34] Stenographer's Notes, 471 ff., 587, 613, 660 ff., 709 ff., 716 ff., 722; and the pamphlet, *Sentenced to Twenty Years Prison*, passim.

counsel also insisted, though the influenza epidemic and the long interval since the arrest render it improbable, that Schwartz's fatal illness was caused by the violence of one soldier, whom Judge Clayton relieved from the necessity of telling whether or not he was called by his associates, "The Tiger." The court observed, "There is no evidence as to who killed Schwartz any more than there was any evidence as to who killed cock robin." [35]

Legal historians have always taken interest in the criminal judge who jests with the lives of men.[36]

"You keep talking about producers," said Judge Clayton to Abrams. "Now may I ask why you don't go out and do some producing? There is plenty of untilled land needing attention in this country."

. . . The witness said that he was an anarchist and added that Christ was an anarchist.

"Our Lord is not on trial here. You are. . . ." [37]

At another point the witness began some remarks about John D. Rockefeller.

"Now," said Judge Clayton, "suppose we eliminate Mr. Rockefeller. He is not on trial. However, I will say that it is quite true that Mr. Rockefeller is a man of considerable wealth and he has done a great deal of good. He has eliminated the hook-worm, which was the curse of childhood in large sections of our country; he has established and maintained a great research hospital, and in other ways used his wealth to better the condition of his fellows. We will now proceed with the case."

"We will now," said Mr. Weinberger, "ask the witness about his other writings. The Holy Alliance——"

"Cut out the Holy Alliance. That is not in the issue . . ."

---

[35] Stenographer's notes, 665.

[36] The judge's words are taken *verbatim* from the *New York Times*, October 22, 1918, which was so far from being prejudiced against him that on October 28 it said editorially, "Judge Henry D. Clayton deserves the thanks of the city and of the country for the way in which he conducted the trial," and praised his "half-humorous" methods.

[37] Braxfield replied to a similar comparison, "Muckle he made o' that; he was hanget." See the account of how he tried Muir for sedition in R. L. Stevenson, *Some Portraits by Raeburn*, and Philip A. Brown, *The French Revolution in English History*, London, 1918, 95-99.

A CONTEMPORARY STATE TRIAL 147

"When our forefathers of the American Revolution———" the witness began, but that was as far as he got.

"Your what?" asked Judge Clayton.

"My forefathers," replied the defendant.

"Do you mean to refer to the fathers of this nation as your forefathers? Well, I guess we can leave that out, too, for Washington and the others are not on trial here."

Abrams explained he called them that because, "I have respect for them. We all are a big human family, and I say 'our forefathers.' . . . Those that stand for the people, I call them father."[38]

The day after conviction the prisoners were called before Judge Clayton for sentence. The court said:[39]

"I am not going to permit anybody to start anything to-day. The only matter before this court is the sentencing of these persons. There will be no propaganda started in this court, the purpose of which is to give aid and comfort to soap-box orators and to such as these miserable defendants who stand convicted before the bar of justice."

When Lipman, the socialist, stepped forward to address the court and started to harangue about democracy, "You don't know anything about democracy," said Judge Clayton, "and the only thing you understand is the hellishness of anarchy." . . .

"These defendants took the stand. They talked about capitalists and producers, and I tried to figure out what a capitalist and what a producer is as contemplated by them. After listening carefully to all they had to say, I came to the conclusion that a capitalist is a man with a decent suit of clothes, a minimum of $1.25 in his pocket, and a good character.

"And when I tried to find out what the prisoners had produced, I was unable to find out anything at all. So far as I can learn, not one of them ever produced so much as a single potato.[40] The only thing they know how to raise is hell, and to direct it against the government of the United States. . . .

"But we are not going to help carry out the plans mapped out by the Imperial German Government, and which are being carried out by Lenine and Trotsky. I have heard of the reported fate of the poor little daughters of the Czar, but I won't talk

[38] Abrams' reply is in *Record*, p. 194.
[39] *New York Times*, October 26, 1918.
[40] Abrams and Lachowsky bound books, Lipman produced furs, Rosansky produced hats, Molly Steimer produced shirtwaists.

about that now. I might get mad. I will now sentence the prisoners."

Rosansky was given three years in prison, Molly Steimer fifteen years and $500 fine, Lipman, Lachowsky, and Abrams twenty years (the maximum), and $1,000 on each count. If they had actually conspired to tie up every munition plant in the country and succeeded the punishment could not have been more.[41]

"I did not expect anything better," said Lipman.
"And may I add," replied the judge, "that you do not deserve anything better."[42]

II. *The Supreme Court*

Seven judges of the Supreme Court were for affirmance of these convictions, Justice Clarke delivering the majority opinion. Justice Holmes read a dissenting opinion, in which Justice Brandeis concurred. The Supreme Court had only a limited power to correct any errors that may have occurred at the trial. It could not revise the sentences.[43] It could not set aside the verdict because its judges would have found differently on the facts themselves, but only if there was so little evidence of the required guilty intent that a reasonable jury could not have convicted. It would be very unlikely to grant a new trial for misdirection and failure to place properly before the jury the vital issue of specific intent to hinder the war, since no objection on this ground is

---

[41] It would not be treason for lack of overt acts. See Chapter VI. Therefore, they would be punishable only under the Espionage Act. The general statute on conspiracy to destroy by force the government of the United States imposes only six years. *Crim. Code*, § 6, U. S. Comp. Stat., 1918, § 10170. Conspiracies to limit the production of necessaries are punishable under the Lever Act by two years. Act of August 10, 1917, c. 53, § 9, 40 Stat. at L. 279, U. S. Comp. Stat., § 3115⅛ i.

[42] *New York Times*, supra. *Record*, p. 243, says, "I do not think you deserve anything less. Now, the next one."

[43] That excessive sentences may possibly constitute "cruel and unusual punishment" under the Eighth Amendment, see Weems *v.* United States, 217 U. S. 349 (1910), per McKenna, J., White and Holmes, JJ., dissenting.

noted in the bill of exceptions,[44] although as I have tried to show, the trial judge did nothing to enlighten the jury on the issues of specific intent and did much to becloud that difficult question, so that they very probably reached a verdict on entirely inadequate grounds,—the existence of intention to publish and to oppose Russian intervention. Only two real questions were before the court: the existence of the requisite evidence of specific intent under the third and fourth counts, the other two being disregarded, and whether the Espionage Act could constitutionally be interpreted to apply to this case.

The required specific intent to hinder the war with Germany is worked out by Justice Clarke in this way: " It will not do to say . . . that the only intent of these defendants was to prevent injury to the Russian cause." They intended a general strike of munition workers, *i.e.*, a curtailment of production. This plan necessarily involved, before it could be realized, the paralysis and defeat of the war program of the United States. Therefore, the defendants intended such an interference with the war, since " men must be held to have intended, and to be accountable for, the effects which their acts were likely to produce." [45]

The " unfortunate maxim " propounded by the Justice is a pure fiction.[46] Obviously our acts result in many probable consequences which we do not intend. If he means that the defendants were liable for such consequences even if they did not in fact intend them, he states a principle of law which is applicable to some crimes, but not to those in which the law requires a specific intent, as in the case at bar. In

---

[44] The Supreme Court has granted a new trial for unexcepted misdirection imperiling liberty. Wiborg v. U. S., 163 U. S. 632, 659 (1896). Accord, Skuy v. U. S., 261 Fed. 316 (C. C. A. 8th, 1919). See August v. United States, 257 Fed. 388 (C. C. A. 8th, 1919), which holds that Act of February 26, 1919, c. 48, amending Judicial Code, § 269, now authorizes an appellate court to look to the entire record and render judgment without regard to the technicality of want of exceptions. It is doubtful, however, if this statute does more than prevent reversals for non-prejudicial errors.

[45] 250 U. S. @ 621.

[46] Jeremiah Smith, " Surviving Fictions," 27 *Yale L. J.* 147, 156 (1917).

those crimes the defendant must actually have the defined state of mind.[47] Thus a man who broke into a barn at night and cut the sinews of a horse's leg to prevent his winning a race is not guilty of burglary with intent to kill a horse, even though in consequence of the injury the horse died.[48] It is needless to multiply examples. Even recklessness does not take the place of the state of mind demanded by the statute.[49] On the other hand, if he means that the jury may permissibly infer as a matter of fact from the doing of an act that the actor intends its ordinary consequences, this is true enough,[50] but such an inference is worthless if there is overwhelming express evidence that the defendant had an entirely different intention. That is the situation in the Abrams case, where the pamphlets and the defendants' testimony show that they intended to help Russia.

The majority opinion must rest on the first sentence quoted from Justice Clarke, that aiding Russia was not the only intent of these defendants. It is argued that they had two intents: (1) to help Russia, (2) to hinder the war by curtailment of production in order to accomplish that object; that it is immaterial which intent was principal and which subordinate, so long as both existed.[51] Thus if I throw a brick at a man behind a plate-glass window, my principal desire may be to hit him, but if that necessarily involves breaking the window and I know this fact, I have a secondary intention to break it and am guilty of intentional destruction of property, even though I would much rather not have broken the glass.[52] When a man was indicted for assault on another with intent to disfigure him by biting off his ear, it

[47] May, *Criminal Law*, 3 ed., § 34; 1 Bishop, *New Criminal Law*, 8 ed., § 335; Roberts v. People, 19 Mich. 401, 415 (1870); Ogletree v. State, 28 Ala. 693, 701 (1856).

[48] Dobbs' Case, 2 East P. C. 513 (1770).

[49] United States v. Moore, 2 Lowell (U. S.) 232 (1873).

[50] Jeremiah Smith, *op. cit.;* People v. Scott, 6 Mich. 287, 296 (1859).

[51] 1 Bishop, *New Criminal Law*, 8 ed., § 339; Rex v. Gillow, 1 Moody C. C. 85 (1825).

[52] *Cf.* Rex v. Pembliton, 12 Cox C. C. 607 (1874). A shooting analogy is given in 33 *Harv. L. Rev.* 444 note.

A CONTEMPORARY STATE TRIAL 151

was useless for him to argue that he only intended to injure but not to disfigure, since the disfigurement was a necessary and obviously a known consequence of the intended act.[53]

There are several answers to this argument that one who intends a curtailment of munitions for any purpose must know that fewer munitions will hinder the war and therefore must *ipso facto* intend to hinder the war. First, the analogy of the throwing and biting cases just stated is too simple to have any application to the Abrams case. There is no such obvious and mechanical chain of cause and effect in complex social conditions, and the obscure factors involved are entirely beyond the capacity of a jury to decide. The argument supposes (1) that the hindrance of the war is inevitable, (2) that this inevitable consequence must have been in the defendants' minds. Both steps are very questionable, and the opinion of a jury on either step should have no weight with an appellate court. Of the first Justice Holmes says, " An intent to prevent interference with the Revolution in Russia might have been satisfied without any hindrance to carrying on the war in which we were engaged." [54] Thus a very short strike that stopped intervention would have caused a very small loss in munitions for shipment to France, which would have been enormously offset by the release of troops and equipment previously diverted to Russia, and a different Russian policy might have created greater liberal enthusiasm in this country and elsewhere for the President's war aims. The second step ignores the belief of the defendants that a friendly Soviet Government would render valuable aid in attacking Imperial Germany by war, or at least by propaganda, whose effectiveness was proved within a fortnight after the conviction of Abrams and his friends.

Secondly, if every curtailment of munitions, whatever its purpose, is necessarily criminal under this Act, because of its alleged obvious and inevitable effect on the war, why does

[53] State *v.* Clark, 69 Iowa 196 (1886).
[54] 250 U. S. @ 628 (1919).

the Espionage Act take pains to limit the crime to "curtailment . . . *with intent* . . . *to cripple or hinder the United States in the prosecution of the war*"?[55] This clause is superfluous and meaningless, if every advocacy of curtailment involves such an intent. This clause about intent must add something to the rest of the definition of this crime. "Intent to hinder the war" clearly means more than the artificial lawyer-made intention to obstruct the war conjured up from any threat of a strike. The word "intent" in a very severe criminal statute and especially a statute limiting popular discussion must mean what any layman who wished to urge a strike in war time lawfully would assume it to mean, that interference with the war must not be the object of his exhortation, the purpose at which he aims. Such a man would be entrapped if "intent" means an incidental, undesired, and at the most a vaguely considered consequence of his utterances.[56] Strikes are not ordinarily illegal, and it would be startling if Congress intended to prohibit all incitement to them in war. Naturally the statute confined itself to strikes and similar measures that were specifically planned to interfere with the war.

This is not, as has been charged, a confusion of intent and motive.[57] It is absurd to say that "interference with the war was palpably the *direct* and desired effect which these appeals were intended to produce" and aid to Russia only a motive. Justice Clarke expressly recognizes that the

[55] It is significant that Justice Clarke omits this clause in quoting the indictment, and possibly he overlooked it altogether and assumed that intent to advocate curtailment of war essentials was the only intent specified in the Act.

[56] *Ibid.*, Holmes, J.: "When words are used exactly a deed is not done with intent to produce a consequence unless that consequence is the aim of the deed—unless the aim to produce it is the proximate motive of the specific act . . ." The Sabotage Act punishes defective manufacture of war essentials only if there is intent to interfere with the war or reason to believe that the act will interfere with it. Act of April 20, 1918.

[57] "Justice Holmes' Dissent," 1 *Review* 636 (December 6, 1919). This article also censures Justice Holmes for not quoting the passage about keeping the armies at home. I hope I have shown reasons why it should never have been quoted by any judge

"primary intent" was to help Russia.[58] The defendants intended to produce certain tangible results, notably protest meetings, which in turn were intended to produce another tangible result, the end of intervention. Their motive was love for Russia. Possibly they also intended as part of their machinery of protest to produce a general strike, if intent can exist without any expectation of success. Interference with the war was at the most an incidental consequence of the strikes, entirely subordinate to the longed for consequence of all this agitation, withdrawal from Russia. It is wholly unsound to label the conjectural war consequence intent and the absorbing Russian consequence motive.

Finally, this argument of inevitable hindrance proves too much. If these defendants were guilty under the fourth count, so was every other person who advocated curtailment in the production of war essentials, no matter what his purpose. The machinists in Bridgeport who struck in defiance of the arbitration of the National War Labor Board violated the Espionage Act, although they intended to obtain higher wages. The Smith and Wesson Company violated it in refusing to continue to manufacture pistols under another arbitration, although they intended to retain an open shop.[59] The coal miners last autumn violated that Act in calling a strike. The government should have threatened all these people with the twenty-year penalty of the Espionage Act instead of acting under its general war statutes or imposing the milder rigors of the Lever Act and an injunction.[60]

---

[58] 250 U. S. @ 621.

[59] See these two cases in Report of the Activities of the War Department in the Field of Industrial Relations During the War (Washington, 1919), 32-35.

[60] I have not troubled to apply similar reasoning to the third count of the indictment, because for reasons already stated I do not consider the pamphlets contained any advocacy of resistance to the United States. Consequently, that count should be disregarded like the first two. Holmes, J., says: "Resistance to the United States means some forcible act of opposition to some proceeding of the United States in pursuance of the war. . . . There is no hint at resistance to the United States as I construe the phrase." 250 U. S. @ 629 (1919).

In other words, the Supreme Court was construing not only a criminal statute which must be applied in a fashion which the laymen who are menaced by it will readily understand, but a statute limiting discussion and hence to be interpreted in the light of the First Amendment. It ought not to be assumed that Congress meant to make all discussion of any governmental measure criminal in war time simply because of an incidental interference with the war. The danger of the majority view is that it allows the government, once there is a war, to embark on the most dubious enterprises, and gag all but very discreet protests against these non-war activities. To give extreme concrete examples: Irish munition workers could not have been urged to strike had our government been sending arms to Dublin Castle, because this would have lessened munitions for France, since a machinist could not be sure that any particular shell or gun was going to Ireland. Incitement to armed resistance to an executive edict nationalizing women would be opposition that might paralyze the war, and therefore easily suppressed under this Act.

The majority opinion dismisses this matter of constitutionality in two sentences, citing decisions on the Espionage Act of 1917 to establish the validity of the far more objectionable provisions of the Act of 1918.[61] Furthermore, the court did not have to declare the clauses involved in the third and fourth counts void. Indeed, it cannot reasonably be doubted that they are constitutional when construed in accordance with the First Amendment. It is the same situation that Judge Hand pointed out in Masses *v.* Patten:[62] it is not a question of judicial refusal to enforce legislation, but of giving it a construction which will not limit discussion beyond the express terms of the Act. The words of the statute requiring a specific intent were presumably not meant by Congress to bear a meaning which would curb political agitation on matters unrelated to the war. The

[61] 250 U. S. @ 619.
[62] 244 Fed. 535, 538 (1917). See p. 48, *supra*.

statute uses the ordinary language of criminal solicitation and attempt, and does not expressly demand the punishment of words in the absence of immediate danger or a determined purpose in itself dangerous to cause actual obstruction of the war. Therefore, it was erroneous for the court to construe it so as to make the remote bad tendency and possible incidental consequences of these pamphlets a valid basis for conviction. And even if all advocacy of curtailment of munitions be considered dangerous, the intent clause limits the crime and should not have been ignored. While the decision of the majority has done a lasting injustice to the defendants, its effect on the legal conception of freedom of speech should be temporary in view of its meager discussion of the subject and the enduring qualities of the reasoning of Justice Holmes.

Although a dissenting opinion, it must carry great weight as an interpretation of the First Amendment, because it is only an elaboration of the principle of " clear and present danger " laid down by him with the backing of a unanimous court in Schenck v. United States. Since that case is reaffirmed by Justice Clarke this principle still remains law, greatly strengthened since the Abrams case by Justice Holmes's magnificent exposition of the philosophic basis of this article of our Constitution:

Persecution for the expression of opinions seems to me perfectly logical. If you have no doubt of your premises or your power and want a certain result with all your heart you naturally express your wishes in law and sweep away all opposition. To allow opposition by speech seems to indicate that you think the speech impotent, as when a man says that he has squared the circle, or that you do not care whole-heartedly for the result, or that you doubt either your power or your premises. But when men have realized that time has upset many fighting faiths, they may come to believe even more than they believe the very foundations of their own conduct that the ultimate good desired is better reached by free trade in ideas—that the best test of truth is the power of the thought to get itself accepted in the competition of the market, and that truth is the only ground upon which their wishes safely can be carried out. That at any rate is the theory of our

Constitution. It is an experiment, as all life is an experiment. Every year if not every day we have to wager our salvation upon some prophecy based upon imperfect knowledge. While that experiment is part of our system I think that we should be eternally vigilant against attempts to check the expression of opinions that we loathe and believe to be fraught with death, unless they so imminently threaten immediate interference with the lawful and pressing purposes of the law that an immediate check is required to save the country. . . . Only the emergency that makes it immediately dangerous to leave the correction of evil counsels to time warrants making any exception to the sweeping command. "Congress shall make no law abridging the freedom of speech." Of course I am speaking only of expressions of opinion and exhortations, which were all that were uttered here, but I regret that I cannot put into more impressive words my belief that in their conviction upon this indictment the defendants were deprived of their rights under the Constitution of the United States.

The preceding chapters have been written in support of this danger-test as marking the true limit of governmental interference with speech and writing under our constitutions, but an able and thoughtful criticism of Justice Holmes' dissent [63] makes it imperative to say something more on the subject. In the first place, the First Amendment is very much more than "an expression of political faith." It was demanded by several states as a condition of their ratification of the Federal Constitution, and is as definitely a prohibition upon Congress as any other article in the Bill of Rights. The policy behind it is the attainment and spread of truth, not merely as an abstraction, but as the basis of political and social progress. "Freedom of speech and of the press" is to be unabridged because it is the only means of testing out the truth. The Constitution does not pare down this freedom to political affairs only or to the opinions which are held by a majority of the people in opposition to the government. A freedom which does not extend to a minority, however small, and which affords them no protection when the majority are on the side of the government

[63] "The Espionage Act and the Limits of Legal Toleration," 33 *Harv. L. Rev.* 442 (January, 1920), by Day Kimball.

A CONTEMPORARY STATE TRIAL 157

would be a very partial affair, enabling the majority to dig themselves in for an indefinite future. The narrow view that the amendment does not protect a few of the people against the force of public opinion throws us back to the English trials during the French Revolution, and the Sedition Law of 1798, for which the United States through many years showed its repentance by pardoning all prisoners and repaying to them the fines imposed. These were none the less injurious to the cause of truth because they had the sanction of the majority.

Undoubtedly, although we are not infallible, we must assume certain opinions to be true for purposes of action; but this does not make it right or desirable to assume that they are true for the purpose of crushing those who hold a contrary doctrine.

There is the greatest difference between presuming an opinion to be true, because, with every opportunity for contesting it, it has not been refuted, and assuming its truth for the purpose of not permitting its refutation.[64]

The vote of the majority of the electorate or the legislature is the best way to decide what beliefs shall be translated into immediate action, and the government must resist if its opponents begin to carry on the conflict of opinions by breaking heads instead of counting them. But it is equally inadvisable for the government to seek to end a contest of ideas by imprisoning or exiling its intellectual adversaries. Force seems like force to its victim, whether or not it has the sanction of law. No one will question that the government must resist a revolt, however Utopian in purposes, but the inference that logically it must also condemn all utterances " aimed at such subversion or tending solely thither " ignores the difference of degree emphasized by the First Amendment. It is the unfailing argument of persecutors. The opinions to which they object are always conceived to aim at revolu-

[64] Mill, *Liberty*, c. II.

tion, violence, and nothing else, although such utterances are usually in large part the exposition of political and economic views. The advocates of parliamentary reform in England were condemned on just such reasoning. To throw overboard the danger-test, and permit " the suppression, whenever reasonably necessary, of utterances whose aims render them a menace to the existence of the state," inevitably substitutes jail for argument, since the determination of the vague test of " menace " depends on the tribunal's abhorrence of the defendant's views. It is no answer that this tribunal (outside of the crushing powers of the post-office and of the immigration officials in deportation cases) is a jury. A fitness to apply a common-sense standard to alleged criminal acts bears no resemblance to a capacity to appraise the bad political and social tendency of unfamiliar economic doctrines during panic. The Abrams case shows the capacity of a judge to decide such a question. The only tribunal which can pass properly on the menace of ideas is time.

We must fight for some of our beliefs, but there are many ways of fighting. The state must meet violence with violence, since there is no other method, but against opinions, agitation, bombastic threats, it has another weapon,—language. Words as such should be fought with their own kind, and force called in against them only to head off violence when that is sure to follow the utterances before there is a chance for counter-argument. To justify the suppression of the Abrams agitation because the government could not trust truth to win out against " the monstrous and debauching power of the organized lie " overlooks the possibility that in the absence of free discussion organized lies may have bred unchecked among those who upheld the course of the government in Russia.

The lesson of United States *v.* Abrams is that Congress alone can effectively safeguard minority opinion in times of excitement. Once a sedition statute is on the books, bad tendency becomes the test of criminality. Trial judges will

A CONTEMPORARY STATE TRIAL

be found to adopt a free construction of the act so as to reach objectionable doctrines, and the Supreme Court will probably be unable to afford relief.

Most of the discussion of the Abrams case has turned on the question whether the decision of the United States Supreme Court affirming these convictions was right or wrong. It seems to me much more important to consider the case as a whole, and ask how the trial and its outcome accord with a just administration of the criminal law.

The systematic arrest of civilians by soldiers on the streets of New York City was unprecedented, the seizure of papers was illegal, and the charges of brutality at Police Headquarters are very sinister. The trial judge ignored the fundamental issues of fact, took charge of the cross-examination of the prisoners, and allowed the jury to convict them for their Russian sympathies and their anarchistic views. The maximum sentence available against a formidable pro-German plot was meted out by him to the silly futile circulars of five obscure and isolated young aliens, misguided by their loyalty to their endangered country and ideals, who hatched their wild scheme in a garret, and carried it out in a cellar. "The most nominal punishment" was all that could possibly be inflicted, in Justice Holmes's opinion,[65] unless Judge Clayton was putting them in prison, not for their conduct, but for their creed. Yet they are condemned for their harmless folly to spend the best years of their lives in American jails. The injustice [66] is none the less because our highest court felt powerless to wipe it out. The responsibility is simply shifted to the pardoning authorities, who except for the release of the unlucky dupe Rosansky have as yet done nothing to remedy the injustice, and to Congress which can change or abolish the Espionage Act of 1918, so that in future wars such a trial and such sentences for the

[65] 250 U. S. @ 629 (1919).
[66] See Morley's indignation at the "thundering sentences" for sedition in India. 2 *Recollections* 269.

intemperate criticism of questionable official action [67] shall never again occur in these United States.[68]

[67] On armed intervention without Congressional authority, see the state papers of Seward and Fish in J. B. Moore, *Digest of International Law,* VI, 23 ff., and Moorfield Storey, "A Plea for Honesty," 7 *Yale Rev.* 260 (1918): "If any nation were to do any of these things to the United States, we should not doubt that it was making war on us."

[68] Criticism of the conclusions in this chapter has mainly been based upon certain passages in the stenographic minutes of the trial. These I have set out in full in 35 *Harv. L. Rev.* 13, 14. In order to allow for the slight effect which these passages may have had on the jury with respect to the issue of specific intent, I have modified a sentence on page 137, saying, "There is no adequate warning on this in the record," instead of, "There is no trace of such a warning in the record." Reconsideration of all the evidence has only strengthened my conclusions, that the jury certainly may have misunderstood the issue, and probably did misunderstand it, that the conduct of the trial by Judge Clayton was very unfair to the prisoners, and that the sentences recommended by the prosecuting officers and imposed by the court were much too severe; but I have not intended to charge that the prosecuting officers tried the case in an unfair manner. In November, 1921, the prisoners were released on the condition of their return to Russia at their own expense.

CHAPTER IV

LEGISLATION AGAINST SEDITION AND ANARCHY

If there be any among us who wish to dissolve this union, or to change its republican form, let them stand undisturbed, as monuments of the safety with which error of opinion may be tolerated where reason is left free to combat it. I know indeed that some honest men have feared that a republican government cannot be strong; that this government is not strong enough. But would the honest patriot, in the full tide of successful experiment, abandon a government which has so far kept us free and firm on the theoretic and visionary fear that this government, the world's best hope, may, by possibility, want energy to preserve itself? I trust not. I believe this, on the contrary, the strongest government on earth.—JEFFERSON's *First Inaugural*.

LONG before the armistice it became clear that the problem of freedom of speech would not end with the war, but would be raised for us in a different aspect and with added difficulties by the unaccustomed prevalence and outspoken expression of radical ideas. Despite my own adherence to traditional political and economic views, I believe that this phenomenon was bound to result from the war. The routine of the day's work ordinarily holds in check the eternal antagonism of the " have-nots " to the " haves," but habits of mechanical obedience and adjustment to the prevailing scheme of life were suddenly destroyed for many by the rapid shift to new scenes and occupations and a novel conviction of the power of unskilled labor. The immense amount of thought and discussion caused by the war during the three years preceding our entry has been often remarked. Such an overhauling directed popular attention to the part played by economic factors in the origin and conduct of the war. Many extreme radicals claimed therefrom fresh proof of the economic interpretation of history and the class struggle. The official emphasis on democracy against autocracy inevitably stimulated discussion of those two concepts and their application to industrial and other non-political fields. Labor programs in England and France crossed the ocean. Then came one of the earthquakes of history, from whose remote influence it was as impossible for us to escape as from the French Revolution which produced the Alien and Sedition Laws of 1798. Jefferson's *First Inaugural* states the controversy of to-day.

During the throes and convulsions of the antient world, dur^g the agonis^d spasms of infuriat^d man, seeking through blood & slaughter his long lost liberty, it was not wonderful that the agitation of the billows should reach even this distant & peaceful shore: that y^s sh^d be more felt & fear^d by some, & less by others, & sh^d divide opinions as to measures of safety.

Much of this radicalism had identified itself with the opposition to the war, and thereby been involved in prosecutions under the Espionage Act and the state laws. A few members of the Non-Partisan League were tried in the federal courts, and its leaders and several of the rank and file were convicted in Minnesota. Much use was made against Debs, Berger, and Mrs. O'Hare of the St. Louis Socialist platform, with its declaration for " continuous, active, and public opposition to the war, through demonstrations, mass petitions, and all other means within our power." The Industrial Workers of the World had taken advantage of the nation's hour of need to withhold assistance which they felt under no obligation to give. Their position was stated to Carleton Parker in plain language by one of their chiefs.

You ask me why the I.W.W. is not patriotic to the United States. If you were a bum without a blanket; if you had left your wife and kids when you went West for a job, and had never located them since; if your job never kept you long enough in a place to qualify you to vote; if you slept in a lousy, sour bunk-house, and ate food just as rotten as they could give you and get by with it; if deputy sheriffs shot your cooking cans full of holes and spilled your grub on the ground; if your wages were lowered on you when the bosses thought they had you

LEGISLATION AGAINST SEDITION

down; if there was one law for Ford, Suhr, and Mooney, and another for Harry Thaw; if every person who represented law and order and the nation beat you up, railroaded you to jail, and the good Christian people cheered and told them to go to it, how in hell do you expect a man to be patriotic? This war is a business man's war and we don't see why we should go out and get shot in order to save the lovely state of affairs that we now enjoy.

Parker, Colonel Disque, and the President's Mediation Commission had striven with much success to bring these irreconcilables into the great stream of national effort. Others thought coercion a better method to end the dangerous menace of sabotage and the recurrent strike. W. D. Haywood and one hundred more members of the I.W.W. were convicted and imprisoned under long sentences for threats and designs of tangible obstruction to war work.

This union of hostility to the war with strange economic and political doctrines set its mark on the later war legislation. The amended Espionage Act of 1918 included the clauses about defamation of our form of government and curtailment of production which played such a prominent part in the Abrams case. A federal Sabotage Act was enacted. States punished the advocacy of syndicalism and sabotage in their war statutes or more often by separate acts. Much of this legislation extended automatically to peace-time utterances, and when it did not, it was easy and natural to adapt it for that purpose by the omission of a few military phrases. In the legislative sessions which followed the armistice, emergency laws against anarchy and criminal syndicalism were adopted by state after state with a coincidence of time and phraseology which proved either a uniform danger throughout the country or the operation of M. Tarde's Laws of Imitation.

This coercive legislation was held by its supporters to have unanswerable justification in the succeeding outrages of 1919. A large number of bombs addressed to federal officials and judges were seized in the mails, and the houses of

Attorney General Palmer and several other individuals prominent in sedition prosecutions and legislation were wrecked by explosions, one of which caused loss of life. There was much street fighting at May Day Parades in Boston and Cleveland, and a clash of very obscure origin between the I.W.W. and the American Legion in Centralia, Washington, resulted in the death of five ex-service men, four shot and one lynched. Meanwhile, the Department of Justice and a special Senate Committee to investigate Bolshevism accumulated a mass of evidence on the large number of revolutionary periodicals and publications in the United States.

The presence in our midst of new forces that make for disorder and violence renders it desirable to review the resources of our law for dealing with insurrection, bombs, and assassination, and to examine calmly recent and pending legislation to prevent the promotion of anarchy. The disruption of our social and economic fabric by revolution, or even the continual recurrence of local outrages, would be so disastrous that they ought to be prevented in the wisest and most effective manner. Many persons take it for granted that any statute which is directed against those evils must be beneficial. That does not necessarily follow. If an emergency really exists, it behooves us all to keep cool, and consider with great care any new laws, and particularly the bills lately introduced in Congress, to see whether they are actually needed to combat the danger, whether they will really meet it, and whether in the haste and excitement of the moment our legislators may not be going much too far.

This country has been able without any anarchy acts to cope with several insurrections like Shay's Rebellion and the Dorr War, a considerable amount of anarchy, and a great many turbulent strikes. May it not be that a wise and vigorous enforcement of the ordinary criminal law will meet most, if not all, of the present danger?

I. *The Normal Law Against Violence and Revolution*

As far as state prosecutions are concerned, there has been very little need of specific legislation against anarchy and criminal syndicalism. Actual violence against government, life, and property is punishable everywhere. Those who plan or counsel such violence are liable even if they do not actively participate. When several policemen were killed by a bomb at the Haymarket in Chicago in 1886, Spies and other anarchists were convicted and executed though it was clear that some one else threw the bomb. Nor is it necessary that any criminal act shall take place. An unsuccessful attempt at a serious crime or a definite solicitation of another to commit it is punishable under the general criminal law. Chief Justice Morton of Massachusetts said in 1883, while upholding the sentence of one Flagg for urging another without success to burn down a barn: " It is an indictable offense at common law to counsel and solicit another to commit a felony or other aggravated offense, although the solicitation is of no effect, and the crime counseled is not in fact committed." Consequently the normal law of the states and the District of Columbia, apart from any legislation against anarchy, enables the police and the courts to deal vigorously with actual or threatened insurrection, explosions, or assassination.[1] The persons of the President and other federal officials are protected by these laws in the District and the various states. Thus the assassin of President McKinley was convicted in New York. If it is felt to be safer that crimes against such men should also be subject to prosecution in the federal courts, it may be that Congress has power so to provide, since any injury to them would seriously impede the operation of the national gov-

---

[1] For purposes of illustration I have added in Appendix IV references to the normal law of four jurisdictions which have lately been alarmed over anarchy. If the law of any other state is incomplete, a definite provision as to criminal attempt or solicitation will meet the need far more wisely than the enactment of a vague and sweeping act against anarchy.

ernment, although this is a question which requires subsequent consideration. If such a statute can be constitutionally enacted, it should punish not only actual injuries to officials, but also unsuccessful attempts and incitement of others to commit such injuries, for such abortive conduct would not be criminal in the United States courts unless expressly made so.[2]

No Congressional legislation is needed to make criminal any scheme to overthrow the United States Government by bombs or any other means. A glance at the first eight sections of the Federal Criminal Code suffices to prove this.[3] Levying war against the United States is treason punishable with death, and recruiting or enlisting for armed hostility against the United States is a serious crime. Conduct short of insurrection is penalized in section 6. "If two or more persons . . . conspire to overthrow, put down, or to destroy by force the Government of the United States, or to levy war against them, or to oppose by force the authority thereof, or by force to prevent, hinder, or delay the execution of any law of the United States," they are each liable to six years in prison or $5,000 fine or both. It is of course well settled that conspiracy does not have to succeed to be punishable. All that is required is a common design to commit a crime, and some overt act in pursuance of the design. The act may be entirely innocent in itself, and may consist in speech or publication. If any further protection against threatened revolution is needed, it is furnished by section 37 of the Criminal Code, which punishes with severity conspiracy "to commit any offense against the United States."[4]

[2] Section 332 of the U. S. Criminal Code punishes one who "aids, abets, counsels, commands, induces or procures" a crime; but this section has only been applied to men who have aided in a crime which has actually been committed. It probably can not be used against unsuccessful incitement. U. S. v. Rogers, 226 Fed. 512, so holds, though there is a suggestion that the crime need not be committed in Billingsley v. U. S., 249 Fed. 331. Section 4 raises the same question.
[3] U. S. Comp. Stat., 1918, §§ 10165-10172.
[4] *Ibid.*, § 10201.

LEGISLATION AGAINST SEDITION

Section 6 of the Criminal Code was enacted during the Civil War and was thought adequate to meet the real dangers of the Reconstruction Period in the South. However, Attorney General Palmer, in asking Congress for a new sedition law, alleges two defects in this section, which in his opinion destroy its usefulness in dealing with the present radical situation.[5] First, the section is limited to conspiracies and does not reach the isolated individual who threatens to overthrow the government. It may be a breach of the peace under state law but it is not now a federal crime if one man, all by himself, goes and hires a hall and tells his audience to start a revolution. This solitary talker was frequently held up at recent Congressional hearings as an example of existing danger to the country, until Mr. Alfred Bettman answered out of his long experience with sedition prosecutions during war service in the Department of Justice:[6]

> This man does it all by himself. Nobody encourages him. No organization supports or inspires him. He thinks up a rebellion all by himself. He hires a hall all by himself. Nobody helps him pay for it. He makes his speech all by himself. Nobody introduces him. He makes his speech. And nothing happens. That is your case. *Nothing happens.* Well, nothing happens.

Mr. Palmer's second objection grows out of a test case, in which Judge Hazel dismissed a prosecution under section 6 against three members of the El Ariete Society, a Buffalo anarchistic organization, for the circulation of a Spanish manifesto. The Attorney General states that this manifesto "clearly constitutes an appeal to the proletariat to arise and destroy the government of the United States by force and substitute Bolshevism or anarchy in place thereof"; and consequently that the failure of the prosecution shows that new legislation is necessary to meet such publications.

---

[5] Investigation Activities of the Department of Justice, 6.
[6] 21 *New Republic* 314 (February 11, 1920).

The case cited does not justify any such conclusion.[7] (1) The defendants were not proved to have any substantial connection with the manifesto, so that the judge could not do anything but discharge them even if its language violated every section of the Criminal Code. (2) Judge Hazel expressly found that the manifesto does not advocate the overthrow of the government by force. Undoubtedly it abuses the form of our government and its officials, advocates the organization of soviets, anarchy, and the destruction of the institutions of society, " but there is nothing contained in it that advocates the destruction of society by the use of violence, and it is open to the construction that it was designed to be sent out for the purpose of bringing about a change in the government by propaganda—by written documents."

A circular which is part of any actual plot to overthrow the government by unlawful acts would be punishable under section 6. This is plainly shown, not only by Judge Hazel's reasoning, but also by another decision affirming a conviction under this section for a conspiracy to circulate pamphlets advocating resistance to the execution by conscription of the war resolution of Congress.[8] On the other hand, a statute applying to the Ariete manifesto would necessarily make it criminal to express economic views and aims different from those which now prevail. Whether such legislation is desirable will soon be discussed, but clearly it is not needed to meet any present danger of revolution. If there is any real revolutionary plot to-day by Bolshevists, anarchists, or any one else, they can be tried, convicted, and sentenced to six years in prison under section 6 of the Criminal Code, and if this is not time enough a simple amendment of this section can make it longer.

One other feature of the existing federal law deserves attention. The chief danger from anarchists arises through

---

[7] The opinion of Judge Hazel in this case (U. S. *v.* Aso) should be read in full on pp. 15-22, Investigation Activities of the Department of Justice.

[8] Wells *v.* U. S., 257 Fed. 605 (C. C. A., 1919). See Chapter II, note 4.

LEGISLATION AGAINST SEDITION

the use of explosives, and if these are kept under federal control the country will be reasonably safe from bombs and dynamite. On October 6, 1917, Congress passed an elaborate statute making it unlawful, when the United States is at war, to manufacture, distribute, store, use, or possess explosives, fuses, detonators, etc., except under specified regulations which include a requirement for a government license given only after full information. This law was used during the war to impose sentences of eighteen months on bomb plotters who were shipping explosives without a license.[9] The statute is automatically suspended during peace, but Congress would do well to continue it, and could, it seems, accomplish this constitutionally under its powers to regulate interstate and foreign commerce and to conserve material needed for army and navy use. Under this statute it would be practically impossible for unauthorized persons to secure enough explosives to cause extensive damage.

With these suggested amendments to the federal statutes to protct the lives and persons of United States officials and regulate the use of explosives in peace, the normal law will be entirely adequate to guard us against dangerous anarchy. Violence, direct and dangerous provocation to violence, and conspiracies to bring about violence will be severely punished, and the instruments of outrage will be removed.

II. *The Normal Criminal Law of Words*

I have dwelt at such length upon the ordinary law in order to make it clear that the so-called anarchy acts, insofar as they are not unnecessary duplication of that law, go far beyond it and impose an entirely different test of criminality. To restate the matter in accordance with the reasoning in the first chapter, the normal criminal law is interested in preventing crimes and certain non-criminal interferences with governmental functions like refusals to enlist or to subscribe to bonds. It is directed primarily

[9] U. S. Comp. Stat., 1918, §§ 3115¼ a, ff.; Inspector Thomas J. Tunney, in *Bolshevik Propaganda*, 28.

against actual injuries. Such injuries are usually committed by acts, but the law also punishes a few classes of words like obscenity, profanity, and gross libels upon individuals, because the very utterance of such words is considered to inflict a present injury upon listeners, readers, or those defamed, or else to render highly probable an immediate breach of the peace. This is a very different matter from punishing words because they express ideas which are thought to cause a future danger to the State.

Undoubtedly, the existence of these verbal peace-time crimes subjects the argument of my first chapter to an acid test. They are too well-recognized to question their constitutionality, but I believe that if they are properly limited they fall outside the protection of the free speech clauses as I have defined them. My reason is not that they existed at common law before the constitutions, for a similar argument would apply to the crime of sedition, which was abolished by the First Amendment. The existence of a verbal crime at common law shows the presence of a social interest which must be weighed in the balance, but the free speech guaranties, as I have argued at length, enact a countervailing social interest in the attainment and dissemination of truth, which was insufficiently recognized by the common law. Nor do I base my conclusion on the historical fact that the framers of the constitutions wanted to safeguard political discussion, because their own statements of freedom of speech in the address to the people of Quebec, the Virginia Toleration Statute, and the opening clause of the First Amendment itself, prove that they also wanted to safeguard scientific and religious freedom, both of which would be greatly restricted by a sweeping application of the common law of obscenity and blasphemy. The true explanation is, that profanity and indecent talk and pictures, which do not form an essential part of any exposition of ideas, have a very slight social value as a step toward truth, which is clearly outweighed by the social interests in order, morality, the training of the young, and the peace of mind of those

LEGISLATION AGAINST SEDITION

who hear and see. Words of this type offer little opportunity for the usual process of counter-argument. The harm is done as soon as they are communicated, or is liable to follow almost immediately in the form of retaliatory violence. The only sound explanation of the punishment of obscenity and profanity is that the words are criminal, not because of the ideas they communicate, but like acts because of their immediate consequences to the five senses. The man who swears in a street car is as much of a nuisance as the man who smokes there. Insults are punished like a threatening gesture, since they are liable to provoke a fight. Adulterated candy is no more poisonous to children than some books. Grossly unpatriotic language may be punished for the same reasons. The man who talks scurriously about the flag commits a crime, not because the implications of his ideas tend to weaken the Federal Government, but because the effect resembles that of an injurious act such as trampling on the flag, which would be a public nuisance and a breach of the peace. This is a state but not a federal crime, for the United States has no criminal jurisdiction over offenses against order and good manners, although Congress may possibly have power to regulate the use of the national emblem. It is altogether different from sedition.

The absurd and unjust holdings in some of these prosecutions for the use of indecent or otherwise objectionable language furnish a sharp warning against any creation of new verbal crimes. Thus, the test of obscenity is very vague, and many decisions have utterly failed to distinguish nasty talk or the sale of unsuitable books to the young from the serious discussion of topics of great social significance. The white slave traffic was first exposed by W. T. Stead in a magazine article, "The Maiden Tribute." The English law did absolutely nothing to the profiteers in vice, but put Stead in prison for a year for writing about an indecent subject.[10]

---

[10] For a division among judges whether a book was indecent, see People v. Eastman, 188 N. Y. 478 (1907). The Bibliography contains references on this class of crime.

When the law supplies no definite standard of criminality, a judge in deciding what is indecent or profane may consciously disregard the sound test of present injury, and proceeding upon an entirely different theory may condemn the defendant because his words express ideas which are thought liable to cause bad future consequences. Thus musical comedies enjoy almost unbridled license, while a problem play is often forbidden because opposed to our views of marriage. In the same way, the law of blasphemy has been used against Shelley's *Queen Mab*, and the decorous promulgation of pantheistic ideas, on the ground that to attack religion is to loosen the bonds of society and endanger the state.[11] This is simply a roundabout modern method to make heterodoxy in sex matters and even in religion a crime. A Washington decision punishing a man for a newspaper article tending to defame George Washington is a serious restriction on historical writing.[12] Furthermore, the breach of the peace theory is peculiarly liable to abuse. It makes a man a criminal simply because his neighbors have no self-control and cannot refrain from violence. The *reductio ad absurdum* of this theory was the imprisonment of Joseph Palmer, one of Bronson Alcott's fellow-settlers at "Fruitlands," not because he was a communist, but because he persisted in wearing such a long beard that people kept mobbing him, until law and order were maintained by shutting him up.[13] A man does not become a criminal because some one else assaults him unless his own conduct is in itself illegal or may be reasonably considered a direct provocation to violence.[14] Thus all these crimes of injurious words must be kept within very narrow limits if they are not to give excessive opportunities for outlawing heterodox ideas.

---

[11] Austin W. Scott, "The Legality of Atheism," 31 *Harv. L. Rev.* 289 (1917).

[12] People *v.* Haffer, 94 Wash. 136 (1916), under statute. Even such a conservative as Dr. Johnson opposed liability for defamation of the dead.

[13] Clara E. Sears, *Bronson Alcott's Fruitlands*, c. IV.

[14] See the subsequent discussion of the right of assembly.

Besides these special classes of words which cause present injury, the normal law punishes speech which falls short of injury as an attempt or solicitation, but the first chapter has shown that this is only when the words come somewhere near success and render the commission of actual crime or other tangible obstruction of state activities probable unless the state steps in at once and penalizes the conduct before it ripens into injury. The law of attempts and solicitation is directed not against the words but against acts, and the words are punished only because that is the necessary way to avoid harmful acts. When A urges B to kill C and tells him how he can do it, this has nothing to do with the attainment and dissemination of truth, and besides there is genuine danger that the murder will take place long before discussion will prove it to be a mistaken scheme.

The two conspiracy cases mentioned in connection with the federal Criminal Code bring out neatly the boundary of the normal criminal law. The anti-draft pamphlets fell within its range because of the danger created by their language and the surrounding circumstances, and although unlike solicitations to murder they served a social interest in criticising the policies of the war, this was outweighed by the pressing peril to the social interest in the enforcement of war legislation. On the other hand, the Ariete manifesto was simply intemperate discussion of fundamental economic and political questions, and even if it had a remote tendency to injure the country by causing a revolution some day there was obviously plenty of time to present the other side before the revolution arrived.

III. *The Difference Between the Normal Law and the New Legislation*

We have seen and heard of revolutions in other States. Were they owing to the freedom of popular opinions? Were they owing to the facility of popular meetings? No, sir, they were owing to the reverse of these; and therefore, I say, if we wish to avoid the danger of such revolutions, we should put ourselves in a state as different from them as possible.—CHARLES JAMES FOX, 1795.

The existing law protects us from dangerous anarchy, but the anarchy acts reach out to the futile soap-box orator who advocates violence and in most cases to the Ariete manifesto which does not. These statutes are not directed against those who commit or actually plan violence, but against those who express or even hold opinions which are distasteful to the substantial majority of citizens. Some of them are so sweeping as to suppress agitation which is neither dangerous nor anarchistic. The people may be led to accept such statutes because they fear anarchy, but they will soon find that all sorts of radical and even liberal views have thereby become crimes. These acts have been drafted by men who are so anxious to avoid any disturbance of law and order that they have punished by long prison terms and heavy fines not only provocation to the use of force, but also the promulgation of any ideas which might possibly if accepted cause some one to use force.

In the past the American law has shown little sensitiveness to revolutionary utterances in time of peace, and has wisely treated most fulminations against the social fabric like a pot-shot at a man ten miles away. However, as Judge Hand pointed out,[15] all vigorous criticism of the form of government or the economic system or particular laws may by arousing passion or engendering conviction of the iniquity of existing conditions lead indirectly to violence. Even an ardent oration urging the repeal of a statute may lead hearers to disobey it. We are always tempted to apprehend such results from opinions to which we are opposed. It is easy to believe that doctrines very different from our own are so objectionable that they could only come into operation through force, so that their advocates must necessarily favor criminal acts. The difference between the expression of radical views and direct provocation to revolution is only

[15] See p. 50, *supra*.

LEGISLATION AGAINST SEDITION

a difference of degree, but it is a difference which the normal criminal law regards as all-important.

There are always men who want the law to go much farther and nip opinions in the bud before they become dangerous because they may eventually be dangerous. Thus, when Colley Cibber produced his adaptation of "Richard III," the Master of the Revels expunged the whole first act, fearing that the distresses of Henry VI would put weak people too much in mind of James II, also exiled in France.[16] Such an attitude is particularly common in a period of unrest like the present, especially during a foreign revolution or after assassinations, when coercion and violence follow each other in a vicious circle. We have seen how George III's judges transported men who wanted to abolish rotten boroughs and the limited franchise, because if the people of Great Britain possessed the same privileges as the French they might destroy the Constitution and imitate the Reign of Terror. Restoration France, after the assassination of the Duc de Berri, passed a law to suppress any journal "if the spirit resulting from a succession of articles would be of a nature to cause injury to the public peace and the stability of constitutional institutions." It was only with the disappearance of these *procès de tendance* that the press once more became free, and under the Republic one can urge a change in the form of government to monarchy or empire with impunity.[17]

Abolition of slavery could never be mentioned in the antebellum South because it might cause a negro uprising. A similar sensitiveness to possible bad results led to the prohibition of "Mrs. Warren's Profession" and "September Morn." Since almost any opinion has some dangerous tend-

---

[16] 3 Johnson's *Lives of the Poets* (ed. G. B. Hill), 292 note.
[17] A. Esmein, *Éléments de Droit Constitutionnel*, 6 ed., 1145, 1149; Ernst Freund in 19 *New Republic* 14 (May 3, 1919). In the same way the New York post-office objected to the general tenor and animus of the *Masses* as seditious without specifying any particular portion as objectionable, although the periodical offered to excerpt any matter so pointed out. Masses Pub. Co. *v.* Patten, 244 Fed. 535, 536, 543 (1917).

encies, it is obvious that its suppression on that account puts an end to thorough discussion. Writings which do not actually urge illegal acts should never be made criminal except perhaps in great emergencies like war or revolt when the mere statement of the author's view creates a clear and present danger of injurious acts. In time of peace the limitation of the punishment of speech to direct provocation to crime is the essential element of the freedom of the press.

The normal criminal law is willing to run risks for the sake of open discussion, believing that truth will prevail over falsehood if both are given a fair field, and that argument and counter-argument are the best method which man has devised for ascertaining the right course of action for individuals or a nation. It holds that error is its own cure in the end, and the worse the error, the sooner it will be rejected. Attorney General Gregory has defended the Espionage Act on the ground that propaganda is especially dangerous in a country governed by public opinion.[18] I believe this to be wholly wrong. Free discussion will expose the lies and fallacies of propaganda, while in a country where opinion is suppressed propaganda finds subterranean channels where it cannot be attacked by its opponents.

Russia under the Czar took no risks. It was afraid to wait for a clear and present danger of violence. It put the ax to the root of the tree. Five powerful methods were developed to reach anarchy and revolution in their earliest stages. The government censored and suppressed books and periodicals; it raided houses and seized men and their papers without process; it prosecuted them for their expression of opinions and for their membership in radical societies; it deported them to Siberia or abroad; it devised ingenious methods of weeding them out of the Duma.

These are not American methods. During the whole of the nineteenth century, not one of them was used against radicals in the United States. It is the American habit to take a chance on queer and objectionable opinions. Roger Williams did it when he discarded religious qualifications for

[18] Report of the Attorney General, 1918, 21.

LEGISLATION AGAINST SEDITION

office and citizenship, which even England was afraid to abandon wholly for another two hundred and fifty years. It is easy for us to forget now what a tremendous risk the founder of Rhode Island was thought to run and did run in those days of wild beliefs. The " livelie experiment " of religious freedom described in the Charter, which it was much on his heart to hold forth, was a very lively experiment indeed in its early years. And in the past the same courage has marked our policy toward radicalism. Anarchy and communism are nothing new in this country,—we have had them in all varieties, foreign and domestic, since the days of Brook Farm until we lived safely through thirty-four years of Emma Goldman. The normal law, which refrains from punishing words for their bad political tendency, has carried us through far worse crises than the present. In the midst of the great railroad strikes of 1877, when unemployment was larger than ever before or since, a big communist meeting was permitted in New York. The Seventh Regiment was kept in a conspicuous readiness to put down any actual disorder, but there was no interference with anything that was said. The speakers indulged in the wildest kind of talk, but it fell flat on the meeting just because there was no chance for a row.[19] Arthur Woods used the same wise policy when he became police commissioner of New York City during the hard times of the summer of 1914. Under his predecessor the police had been breaking up anarchistic meetings in Union Square every Saturday afternoon and the feeling was excited, defiant, and bitter. Threats were not disguised that since the police had " acted like agents of the capitalists," the crowds would come next time prepared to answer clubs and revolvers with bombs. Mr. Woods took office, and told the police to interfere in any actual disturbance, but not otherwise. Next Saturday, a large force of police was held within available distance, and a hundred plain-clothes men were scattered singly through the meeting, on the watch for signs of violence so that they could nip any attempt in the bud, but beyond

[19] J. F. Rhodes, *History of the United States*, VIII, 41.

that they were only to try to maintain an atmosphere of quiet and calm and radiate good nature. Mr. Woods says:

> The change of method was almost unbelievably successful. There was no disorder; the crowd was very large but very well behaved, and at the end of the meeting when everything was over and many had gone home, three cheers were proposed and given for the police.[20]

This courage, this tolerance, this friendly co-operation between government and people, with its visible creation of loyalty, this is the true Americanism. And the issue before us to-day is whether in a period of prosperity and tremendous demand for labor we shall throw overboard the American laws and the American methods which carried us safely through the turbulent early years of our history, through Reconstruction, through panics and Populism with its widespread agitation among the native-born population, and shall now shaking and shivering in every wind of doctrine that blows from Bolshevist Russia imitate even in part any of the five methods with which Czarist Russia fought radicalism up to the day of her stupendous ruin.

To this issue in its various aspects I shall devote the remainder of my book.

The interpretation of freedom of speech which I have endeavored to establish in the opening chapter applies in peace as in war. The various interests, individual and social, must once more be balanced against one another with full regard to the social interests in progress and the attainment and dissemination of truth. The resultant boundary-line of permissible speech is drawn back of the point where overt acts of injury to the state occur but not far from that point. The test laid down by the United States Supreme Court in the Schenck case still holds good:

> The question in every case is whether the words used are used in such circumstances and are of such a nature as to create a clear and present danger that they will bring about the sub-

[20] Arthur Woods, *Policeman and Public*, 73-78. Equally typical of American methods is his account of the meeting in Bowling Green Park.

stantive evils that Congress (or the state legislature) has a right to prevent.

The power of the government to restrict discussion is undoubtedly less in time of peace than in time of war because war opens dangers that do not exist at other times. The strength of the state in war time is chiefly occupied in fighting the enemy. In a great war the chances of success are uncertain, and a slight set-back due to hostile opinion at home may cause defeat. It is hard enough for the government to resist the human desire not to enlist and not to fight, without outside incitement from adverse views of the war. Thus, there are very plausible reasons for limiting the social interest for which I earnestly contend, the need of continuous contact with the facts and with sound conclusions. In peace, however, the social interest mainly affected by discussion is not the sorely-beset endeavor to save the country from a powerful enemy, but the interest in order. With this interest the mass of the population earnestly sympathizes. It is protected by an enormous body of otherwise unoccupied police and soldiers, who are now available to check any actual violence. This interest in order is not opposed by troops and guns from abroad but only by words, which it can afford to tolerate, confident in the support of public opinion. In war an evil and wholly unfounded opposition at home may upset the state. In peace, those who love disorder for its own sake are so few that a revolution is improbable unless there are very strong reasons for discontent. If the agitation is without merit the state can afford to ignore it. If it has merit the state cannot afford to suppress it without a hearing. Consequently, in peace governmental interference should be delayed as in the New York meeting of 1877 until the last possible moment before violence occurs.

Sometimes in peace other social interests besides order come into play and strengthen the case for restriction. Thus, the interest in morals is concerned with moving-picture plays and books for the young. Street meetings may interfere with the public traffic besides causing a greater probability of violence than do books. Once more, it is a question of balancing the interests, and it may be worth while to arrange for meetings in less-used side streets in the noon-hour or in specified public parks, even at some sacrifice of traffic. After all, a democracy may wisely refuse to regard the streets only as a place where people exercise and go out to make money. Parades and soap-box orators and big meetings make them an open-air school, which prepares directly for citizenship.

The anarchy acts are the first break with the American tradition. Most of them are not willing to run any risks as to opinions generally considered objectionable, but make opinions in themselves and for their own sake a crime, although there is no direct and dangerous interference with order and only a remote possibility that violence will ensue. The first chapter has shown the evils of bad political tendency as a test of criminality. These statutes in large part revive that test, and are not directed against bad acts, but are designed to protect the minds of grown men and women from bad talk and bad thoughts.

IV. *Radical Meetings and the Red Flag*

There are several types of anarchy acts.[21] The simplest is the red flag law, recently adopted by twenty-five states. The New York statute [22] makes it a misdemeanor to display the banner " in any public assembly or parade as a symbol or emblem of any organization or association, or in furtherance of any political, social, or economic principle, doctrine or propaganda." Other states go much further and forbid the display of the red flag anywhere. Some shrewdly guard against the wearing of red neckties or buttons or the evasive

[21] All the state legislation mentioned in this chapter is listed in Appendix V.
[22] N. Y. Laws, 1919, c. 409.

adoption of a green flag [23] by punishing the use of any emblem of any hue if it is "distinctive of bolshevism, anarchism, or radical socialism"; [24] or is "suggestive of any organized or unorganized group of persons who by their rules, creeds, purposes, practices, or efforts, espouse any theory or principle antagonistic to or subversive of the constitution or its mandates"; [25] or if it is employed with some other revolutionary intent. In West Virginia imprisonment for a year (five years for the second offense) may be imposed for the possession of any red or black flag, or the display of "any emblem of any nature whatever indicating sympathy or support of ideals, institutions, or forms of government, hostile, inimical, or antagonistic to the form or spirit of the constitution, laws, ideals, and institutions of this state or of the United States." [26] It is plain to any lawyer that when a vague and very wide range of commonplace and harmless conduct is made criminal merely on the basis of a bad intention, a man is condemned for his thoughts and nothing else. He may never have expressed those thoughts until they were brought out under cross-examination in a sedition trial. He is convicted simply by the jury's guess at the inside of his head. Men should be punished for what they do and not for what they think.

The way in which the red flag causes disorder is explained by Inspector Thomas J. Tunney, who played such a prominent part in the Abrams case and certainly cannot be considered unduly favorable to radicals: [27]

Senator OVERMAN. What effect does that red flag have on a crowd?

Mr. TUNNEY. It has the effect of creating a feeling on the part of Americans that they would like to assassinate everybody carrying the red flag; or at least, a large number of them feel that way.

[23] Testimony of Inspector Tunney and Raymond Robins, in *Bolshevik Propaganda*, 11, 838.
[24] Kans., Laws, 1919, c. 184.
[25] Wash., Laws, 1919, c. 181.
[26] W. Va., Laws, 1919, c. 24.
[27] *Bolshevik Propaganda*, 10, 11.

Senator OVERMAN. What effect does it have on the people who are in sympathy with carrying the red flag?

Mr. TUNNEY. It simply enthuses them, and they indulge in cheering and waving it in the air.

The Roxbury Riot of last May [28] is a practical demonstration of his statements and also illustrates some interesting points in the law of assembly. An unprejudiced account in the *Boston Herald* relates that the trouble was caused by the appearance of a red flag carried at the head of a large group of members of the Lettish Workmen's Association, who were marching from one meeting to another in a different hall. If this was a parade, it was illegal, for they had no permit, but no red flag law was in force. The account continues: " Everywhere in Roxbury small groups of men and boys were to be seen strolling along the streets armed with clubs and pieces of iron bar and pipe. It was difficult for the police to cope with every group for as fast as one would be dispersed another would gather. Nearly everybody with a facial indication of being a Lett or a Russian was attacked. It was useless for them to offer excuses for none were listened to. . . . As soon as it became generally known that the presence of a red flag was the cause of all the trouble soldiers and sailors began taking a hand. Each group carried at least one sailor or soldier and they inflicted severe punishment on the men in the parade or those discovered hiding in stores and houses afterwards."

Either just before the attack on the marchers began or soon afterwards, it is hard to tell which from the tumultuous testimony, the police demanded a permit and ordered the parade to disperse. They replied with cat-calls, and in the three-cornered disturbance that followed between radicals, patriots, and police, two policemen were injured. A large number of marchers received sentences of six to eighteen months in the Municipal Court for participating

---

[28] *Boston Herald*, May 2, 1919; trials in *ibid.*, May 6, 8, 14; letter of adverse comment, *ibid.*, May 16. Convictions upheld, Comm. *v.* Frishman, 126 N. E. (Mass.) 838 (1920).

LEGISLATION AGAINST SEDITION

in a riot or assaulting the police, and several of them have since been convicted by juries, but so far as I can ascertain none of their assailants was even tried.

These cases raise several questions of general interest as to the legality of radical meetings.[29] The radicals took the position that no permit was necessary to enable men to walk from one place to another, but only for an organized parade. Of course, the social interest in traffic already mentioned gives the city power to forbid unlicensed processions, but there is some question whether this particular body of people was not itself a part of traffic, without need for a permit. For example, is a license required for collegians to march from the stadium to the yard after a football victory with a red flag at their head? These are questions of fact for the jury. However, even if this gathering of Roxbury radicals had not been held illegal by the Massachusetts Supreme Court for want of a permit, it may well be that the order to disperse was valid on other grounds. Three such grounds have been suggested.

(1) Since any gathering of radicals is likely to be attacked, the easiest way to preserve the peace is to forbid and break up such gatherings. Therefore, it may be contended that a meeting which is not otherwise illegal may become so solely because it will excite violent and unlawful opposition. This is the doctrine of the long-beard case over again. Let us see how it works out with respect to meetings. The Salvation Army holds a service in a public place, knowing that a mock-organization called the Skeleton Army intends to molest it. The Skeleton Army appears, and begins to throw stones. The members of the Salvation Army are arrested by the police for holding an unlawful assembly. Obviously they must be released. Their guilt cannot be determined by the intolerance of wrong-doers.

---

[29] See Dicey, *Law of the Constitution*, c. VII, "The Right of Public Meeting," also my Bibliography. The Salvation Army case is Beatty *v.* Gillbanks, 9 Q. B. D. 308 (1882). German opera riots, Star Opera *v.* Hylan, 109 N. Y. Misc. 132 (1919). Opposed to my view of red flag riots, P. *v.* Burman, 154 Mich. 150 (1908).

Apart from the question of permits, and special regulation by ordinances and statutes, the police cannot treat a meeting as unlawful simply because it may probably or naturally lead others to attack it. And if a permit is refused on that ground alone, a small number of intolerant men by passing the word around that they intend to start a riot can prevent any kind of meeting, not only of radicals who want a revolution, but of socialists, of moderates like the Committee of '48, of negroes, of novel religious sects, of free-masons in an anti-masonic community. Indeed, on any such theory a gathering which expressed the sentiment of a majority of law-abiding citizens would become illegal because a small gang of hoodlums threatened to invade the hall. The proper remedy for these emergencies is police protection, to which men are entitled in public places, whether they are there singly or in groups.

(2) There is, however, a well-recognized exception to this principle. If the meeting is going to cause trouble, not just because of the unpopularity of its views but because it expresses them in offensive ways, it may be unlawful *per se*. This is an analogy to the verbal crimes already discussed. For example, the " Pillars of Fire " were not allowed by the Mayor of Plainfield, New Jersey, to hold street meetings for abusing Roman Catholics. They must hire a hall where no one would be forced to listen to them. It is sometimes supposed that a parade displaying the red flag is illegal at common law for the same reason that it would be if it carried an abusive caricature of the Pope, but the situations are not truly parallel. The red flag is not offensive in itself. Nobody minds it at an auction sale or a railroad crossing. The onslaught is not on an object but on the unpopular ideas of those who carry it, because most of us consider that such ideas have a tendency to produce injury in the future. This only brings us back to the first point, that a meeting is not illegal just for unpopularity. Bad tendency must not be a test of criminality. Thus, the Roxbury marchers were not violating the law because of the red

flag. On the other hand, their loud cries of, "To Hell with the Police! Hurrah Bolsheviki! To Hell with the American flag!" were so provocative of disorder as to render the parade unlawful even if a permit had been issued.

(3) Finally, after the order to disperse was given the gathering was undoubtedly illegal. That order was valid under a second exception to the general principle that unpopular meetings are not illegal meetings. Where a meeting which is originally lawful and inoffensive has in spite of this produced a disturbance, so that the only way to restore the peace is to put an end to the meeting, then there is a clear and present danger which justifies the suppression of ideas on this occasion. By the time the police arrived in the Roxbury affair, it was evident that the parade could not continue without a riot. Consequently, those who resisted or refused to obey the order thereby broke the law.

One more lesson of general application may be drawn from this incident, the danger that men of peculiar views who are charged with definite tangible crimes may be condemned in reality not for what they do but for what they think. Three clear offenses were possibly committed by the defendants, parading without a permit, assaulting policemen, and remaining in the parade after the order to disperse. Every one of these issues is a pure question of fact, on which the opinions of the defendants had not the slightest bearing. Yet the Municipal Court Judge, instead of limiting the examination of the prisoners to the question, "Did you do this on May 1?" himself inquired at length whether they believed in God, approved of soviets, or agreed with what the American flag stands for. In the same way, when the cases came before a jury in the autumn, the district attorney gave the impression that he was trying the prisoners, not for what they did in May, but for what they thought in October. And in the Municipal Court, the red flag, although it violated no statute, was clearly treated as an offense. The judge said: "The red flag means revolution, nothing else, and the day for the red flag is past in America. It means bloodshed; it cannot be interpreted otherwise. . . . Waving a red flag is a breach of the peace."

The policy behind even the mildest form of the red flag legislation resembles the rule of the British Government that the Uganda tribes must not wear war-paint except on the chief's birthday. If Americans cannot be trusted any more than African natives to avoid the psychological effects of color, well and good. So far, the exact meaning of the red flag seems rather obscure. Some say it stands for bloody revolution,[30] and others, the brotherhood of workingmen throughout the world.[31] It might be desirable to find out which is right before we forbid it. There is no doubt that its display on May Day, 1919, was accompanied by much lawlessness—chiefly on the part of the supporters of law and order. Until the opponents of force can restrain themselves from mobbing any parade which carries a red flag, it may be wise to prohibit its use. We ought to remember, however, that if it is made a forbidden symbol its emotional appeal when displayed in secret is immeasurably heightened. The resentment caused by such laws, which assert any suggestion of revolutionary action to be a heinous offense, will not be lessened by the recent respect paid by mayors, governors, and legislators to an acknowledged banner of revolution, the green, white, and yellow of Ireland. Once we admit that violence may be a justifiable mode of political action in another country which has the ballot and representative government, we cannot consistently make men outlaws merely for holding a similar theory in this country, however much we disagree with them. Massachusetts once had a

[30] Besides quotation above, see Rugg, C. J., in Comm. v. Karvonen, 219 Mass. 30 (1914).

[31] This is the explanation of all radicals whom I have questioned. See testimony of William Sidis in *Boston Herald*, May 14, 1919. This is confirmed by the expert and conservative opinion of Professor Samuel N. Harper, *Bolshevik Propaganda*, 101: "I think it is little more than a tradition . . . representing this mental protest . . . against what they consider the injustices of the present organization of society."

law prohibiting a red or black flag. This was declared constitutional,[32] and then repealed because it made the Harvard crimson illegal. It is to be hoped that other portions of this land of the brave will also be willing to face valiantly a piece of cloth. There is much merit in the North Dakotan remark that the only animal that is afraid of a red flag has a fence around him.

The man who insists on waving the red flag on all occasions has just as little common sense. Those who want to remake society on a basis of fellowship and mutual agreement may fairly be asked to begin by yielding something to the wishes of their neighbors. It is an undoubted fact that most people do dislike seeing the red flag in a parade or over a building, but if the Stars and Stripes are beside it nearly all their objection vanishes. A decent respect for the opinions of mankind ought to lead the radical to do this much for the happiness of others. Even if he is so thoroughly a man without a country that he has no attachment for the government which guards his home and educates his children, at least like a foreign vessel in our ports he might out of courtesy raise our banner beside his own. I do not believe that a man should be arrested for carrying a solitary red flag in the street any more than for wearing a sweater at a dance, but ordinary politeness ought to keep him from doing either. Surely, it is worth while for the radical to take the conciliatory step I suggest, and thus produce a friendlier atmosphere in the mass of the population, which may gain converts for his views and will certainly induce many thoughtful men to co-operate with him in the more moderate of his schemes for a better world.

V. *Criminal Anarchy and Criminal Syndicalism*

A much more important group of statutes takes its origin from the New York Anarchy Act of 1902, which was enacted soon after the assassination of President McKinley.[33]

[32] Comm. *v.* Karvonen, *supra.*
[33] N. Y. Penal Law, 1918, §§ 160-166.

Criminal anarchy is there defined as "the doctrine that organized government should be overthrown by force or violence, or by assassination . . ., or by any unlawful means." It is a felony to advocate this doctrine by speech or writing, and to join any society or any meeting for teaching or advocating it. The act can be rigorously enforced, because the owner or person in charge of any room or building who knowingly permits a meeting therein is severely punished, and the editor or proprietor of a periodical or publisher of a book which contains anarchistic matter is liable unless it was printed without his knowledge and authority and disavowed immediately. This statute lay idle for nearly twenty years,[34] but there have been several prosecutions in the last few months. Especially significant is the sentence of Benjamin Gitlow, a former Socialist member of the New York Assembly, to an imprisonment of five to ten years, under a ruling of Justice Weeks that the advocacy of a general strike without any direct reference to force, violence, or unlawful means is criminal anarchy, because it is camouflaged revolution.[35] The Washington statute of 1909 is very similar, but also makes it criminal to circulate any document having a tendency to encourage the commission of any breach of the peace or disrespect for law or any court. The ridiculous possibilities of such legislation are proved by the conviction of one Fox for encouraging disrespect for law by an article, "The Nude and the Prudes," declaring bathing suits superfluous. Justice Holmes found nothing unconstitutional in the prosecution, but caustically remarked, "Of course, we have nothing to do with the wisdom of the defendant, the prosecution, or the act."[36] The first danger to be avoided in legislation against anarchy is the imposition of heavy penal-

[34] The only case is a slander suit, in which "anarchist" was held a charge of crime. Von Gerichten *v.* Seitz, 94 App. Div. 130 (1904).
[35] *Boston Transcript,* February 17, 1920. House Judiciary Hearings, 155.
[36] Wash. Laws, 1909, c. 249, §312; State *v.* Fox, 71 Wash. 185 (1912); Fox *v.* Washington, 236 U. S. 273 (1915).

LEGISLATION AGAINST SEDITION

ties for slight offenses. Such penalties create that very hatred of our system of laws which it is our object to avoid.

Another pre-war statute, in New Jersey, punishing the advocacy of unlawful destruction of property or injury to persons, is much more restricted in its scope, and has been construed to enact the common law of criminal solicitation with an increased penalty. It was used to punish labor leaders in Paterson who urged clubbing strike-breakers out of the silk mills and using chemicals and other devices to make the product unmerchantable.[37] The recent Massachusetts anti-anarchy act of 1919 is very similar; it specifically penalizes the advocacy of killing, destruction of property, or violent revolution.[38] This Massachusetts act was reduced to its present form by repeated protests from liberals. Instead of legislating against anarchy and other radical doctrines as opinions, the Massachusetts and New Jersey statutes prohibit incitement to definite serious criminal acts. Such codifications of the common law serve the desirable purpose of letting speakers and writers know what they must not do. If these statutes are construed strictly like other penal statutes and applied with common sense and a realization, as Justice Hughes puts it, that "Hyde Park meetings and soap-box oratory constitute the most efficient safety-valve against resort by the discontented to physical force," [39] then they will enable New Jersey and Massachusetts to deal vigorously with any real danger of lawlessness without at the same time turning revolutionary opinions into crimes. Any state which considers legislation

---

[37] N. J. Laws, 1908, c. 278; the cases construing it are given in Appendix V. The possibilities of the misapplication of even such a narrow statute are shown by State v. Scott, reversing a conviction for an intemperate newspaper attack on the brutality of the Paterson police; and by the dissenting opinion in State v. Quinlan because the defendant was prejudiced by the elaborate inquiry at the trial into the doctrines of the I.W.W. For the comment of an I.W.W. on these cases, see the quotation from E. G. Flynn in Herbert E. Cory's *The Intellectuals and the Wage Workers*, N. Y., 1919, p. 208.

[38] Mass. Laws, 1919, c. 191.

[39] Brief for N. Y. Socialist Assemblymen, p. 41 (see Chapter VI).

of this type necessary ought to turn to these two statutes as model anti-anarchy acts.

Most of the legislation since 1917 has, however, been far more extensive. About one-third of the states have applied the New York statutory scheme to the new crime of criminal syndicalism, " the doctrine which advocates crime, physical violence, arson, destruction of property, sabotage, or other unlawful acts or methods as a means of accomplishing or effecting industrial or political ends, or . . . industrial or political revolution, or for profit." The advocacy of any unlawful act for such ends and the circulation of any book affirmatively suggesting criminal syndicalism or any unlawful act for such ends are among the offenses punishable by imprisonment from one to ten years. These acts are almost uniform in phraseology, Idaho having apparently supplied the original model. Some states depart from type into much vaguer phraseology. Thus, Arizona in an act which Governor Hunt allowed to become law without being willing to put his name to it makes it criminal to advocate the violation of " the constitutional or statutory rights of another as a means of accomplishing industrial or political ends." [40] Montana punishes in peace all the non-military crimes mentioned in the federal Espionage Act of 1918 as well as " any language calculated to incite or inflame resistance to any duly constituted state authority." [41] West Virginia makes criminal any teachings in sympathy with or favor of " ideals hostile to those now or henceforth existing under the constitution and laws of this state." [42]

These are but brief extracts from the legislation which has been enacted or invoked in almost every state during the last few years.[43] In addition, Mayor Hylan of New York wanted an ordinance to punish owners of buildings permitting an assemblage advocating " policies tending to incite the

[40] Ariz. Laws, 1918, sp., c. 12.
[41] Mont. Laws, 1919, c. 77.   [42] See note 26.
[43] For harsh applications of these statutes, see Clare Shipman, " The Conviction of Anita Whitney," 110 *Nation* 365 (March 20, 1920), California; " The Most Brainiest Man," *ibid.* 510 (April 17), Connecticut.

minds of people to a proposition likely to breed a disregard for law," and a Boston ordinance to forbid the display of anything that was sacrilegious or tended to promote immorality was also unsuccessful, but the Mayor of Toledo is said to have prohibited any meeting anywhere in the city "where it is suspected a man of radical tendencies will speak."

These statutes and regulations are, for the most part, different from the normal criminal law in three ways: (1) they label opinions as objectionable and punish them for their own sake because of supposedly bad tendencies without any consideration of the probability of criminal acts; (2) they impose severe penalties for the advocacy of small offenses as much as for serious crimes; (3) they establish a practical censorship of the press *ex post facto*. These statutes are no dead-letter. In particular, the Illinois law has been enforced by wholesale arrests in Chicago. Furthermore, the governors of other states are already granting the extradition of accused persons to Illinois. Under this policy, a state with a drastic sedition law like Montana will be able to hunt a man down in the most liberal part of the nation, and there will be practically no chance for a review by the United States Supreme Court. The United States has always refused to allow the extradition of persons charged by other countries with political crimes, even if the charge (as often happened with Russians) involved the advocacy of violence and revolution.[44] Since state governors under the Constitution cannot be compelled to permit extradition,[45] it is to be hoped that in future they will follow the wise policy of the national government.

The state anarchy acts are constitutional under the test laid down by the United States Supreme Court in the

[44] See the state papers in 4 *Moore's Digest of International Law* 332 ff. The possible exception of anarchists who actually cause explosions (*ibid.* 354) may be disregarded, since we are dealing at most with unsuccessful incitement to anarchy, and in general with the expression of revolutionary views and membership in revolutionary organizations, which would clearly be political crimes and unextraditable.

[45] Kentucky *v.* Dennison, 24 How. (U. S.) 66 (1860).

Schenck case, insofar as they are employed to meet a "clear and present danger" of unlawful conduct. It is probable that the open advocacy of sabotage and the doctrines of revolutionary syndicalism, against which most of these statutes are directed, does present a sufficient danger to bring such speech within the range of legislative discretion, and a few decisions have already so held.[46] On the other hand, the clauses of these statutes which make it criminal *ipso facto* to belong to organizations like the Industrial Workers of the World, although the accused has never expressed any agreement with the violent portions of its economic theory, raise serious difficulties. This is not punishing a man for what he does, or even for what he says, but for what some one else says, which he may possibly not approve. There are so many reasons why a workman is led to join the labor union to which his fellows belong, that the law should hesitate to attribute to him an active support of every plank in its platform. Apart from questions of constitutionality, it is dubious policy to make membership in a labor union a crime no matter how much we may disagree as I do with its aims and methods. That was the policy of the English Combination Acts of the early nineteenth century. The attempt to break up trade unions by imprisonment was defended because of the violence which had accompanied some of their activities, but the imposition of severe penalties on men who had taken no part in that violence simply strengthened the unions and increased their bitterness. My own hope is that eventually the state may provide an impartial tribunal for the settlement of industrial disputes,[47] just as it formerly brought blood-feuds and quarrels over boundaries into the King's courts. Until that time comes, although my own sympathies and direct inter-

[46] State *v.* Boyd, 86 N. J. L. 75; State *v.* Moilen, 140 Minn. 112. But see 20 *Colum. L. Rev.* 232 (February, 1920); *Ex parte* Meckel, 220 S. W. 81 (Tex. 1920); dissent in State *v.* Tachin, 108 Atl. 318 (N. J. 1919).

[47] Henry B. Higgins, "A New Province for Law and Order," 29 *Harv. L. Rev.* 13, 32, *ibid.* 189, summarizes the Australian experience.

ests are on the side of the employers, I believe it to be a grave error for the state to intervene against the workingmen until immediate violence is threatened. The parties should be left to contend by economic methods. I know that many who would believe in such a policy as regards the American Federation of Labor will not approve its extension to the revolutionary unions. Nevertheless, those who investigated the I.W.W. on behalf of the government during the war found that the causes for its existence were deep-rooted economic factors,[48] and not any wide-spread desire for political changes or violence for its own sake. Until those factors are dealt with directly, the use of the tremendous power of the state on behalf of the employers and the conservative unions, while it may produce a superficial weakening of revolutionary unionism, is sure to intensify its hostility to the state and the belief that government is only the organ of capital. For instance, the men who have been enjoined by a judge at Spokane " from continuing as members of the I.W.W." [49] will not thereby be turned into enthusiastic supporters of the country's laws or alter their economic views. Indeed, careful observers already report a rapid shift of members of the I.W.W. into the A. F. of L., where they are safe from prosecution, and can do infinitely more damage than when they were in the open.[50]

When the anarchy acts go still farther and punish discussions of the general strike, or condemn words and symbols, which are inoffensive in themselves, for their bad social, economic, or political tendencies, they clearly infringe the danger-test and ought to be declared void. But I do not think we ought to let the discussion of the state and federal sedition laws turn on the controversy whether they are unconstitutional. The free speech clauses, as I said at the outset of this book, are a declaration of American policy

[48] The Bibliography lists material on the I.W.W.
[49] 109 *Nation* 843 (January 3, 1920).
[50] John Graham Brooks, *Labor's Challenge to the Social Order*, c. XX; Roger Baldwin, conversations; from a different angle, Ole Hanson, *Americanism versus Bolshevisim*, c. XII.

as well as an extreme limit upon legislative power. The most difficult questions are raised by the application of the anarchy acts to the advocacy of " force and violence," when no immediate violence is liable to take place. Although I do not feel sure that such speech can constitutionally be punished when there is no danger of immediate violence, still both Justice Holmes and Judge Learned Hand would agree that the nature of the words used is an essential factor, apart from the surrounding circumstances, in deciding whether the danger does exist, and the common law cases on solicitation support this view. But even if the statute is constitutional, the most important questions still remain, whether it is expedient and in accord with American traditions, and how it shall be construed. On these points what I have already said of the syndicalism statutes has bearing, but it is upon this ground of sound policy that every thoughtful American ought to consider the proposed federal Sedition Law.

VI. *The Federal Sedition Bills*

Nothing less than a very great national danger should lead us to abandon the American policy of courage and tolerance and re-enact the first Sedition Act in time of peace since the disaster of 1798. The burden of proof rests fairly on those who advocate such a doubtful step. It has already been shown that it is not called for by any immediate danger of revolution, since the Criminal Code will deal with that, and indeed what has been said of the enormously exaggerated accounts of pro-German plots during the war ought to show that " the Red menace " is probably a similar panic.[51] It is of course impossible for a private citizen to assert that no danger exists to justify the officials in their statement that this legislation is necessary, but he may properly assume that the documents in which they set forth that state-

[51] See page 70, *supra*, and the speech of George W. Anderson at the Harvard Liberal Club, reported in " The Red Hysteria," 21 *New Republic* 250 (January 28, 1920); and *Boston Herald*, January 13, 1920.

ment embody the principal facts on which it is based. If they have not yet supplied the vital facts, they ought to do so, and not ask this country to reverse its policy of six-score years at a mere trumpet-blast of danger.

The main documents in the case are furnished by the most distinguished supporter of sedition legislation, Mr. A. Mitchell Palmer. In an official Report,[52] he has asked Congress not only to enact an unprecedented statute, but for fear this may not be enough he has also suggested that Congress recommend the passage of similar legislation by all the states. The seditious writer will then be run to earth by the five hundred agents of the Department of Justice, with the aid of twelve thousand policemen and fifty prosecuting attorneys in New York City, and a multitude of others throughout the land. Thus, we can meet " the present intolerable situation." Why is it intolerable? The Attorney General says that he needs the legislation because of four facts: (1) the presence of " 60,000 radically inclined individuals " whose histories have been compiled by his agents; (2) the circulation of 471 " radical newspapers " besides other publications, all of which are " one of the most potent and far-reaching influences in stirring up discontent, race prejudice, and class hatred in this country " and " more than any other one thing, perhaps, are responsible for the spread of the Bolshevik, revolutionary, and extreme radical doctrines "; (3) the fact that the Trading with the Enemy Act, which requires that the local postmaster shall receive a translation of every publication in a foreign language criticising the policies of any government before distribution of any sort expires with the war, and the lapse of this censorship will create a difficult problem in dealing with " radical propaganda of a more violent character "; (4) " practically all of the radical organizations have endeavored to enlist negroes on their side."

[52] Investigation Activities of the Dept. of Justice, Sen. Doc. No. 53 (66th Cong., 1st Sess.), Wash., 1919. See also his evidence in House Judiciary Hearings and Palmer Deportations Testimony.

If the Attorney General had limited himself to a statute punishing successful and unsuccessful attacks upon federal officials and property, he would have performed a real service in filling gaps in the federal law against violence. Legislation against his hypothetical man who approaches the Chief Justice with a bomb in his hand would not affect freedom of speech. But it should be clearly understood that Mr. Palmer asked much more than this when he sought to legislate out of existence the four kinds of propaganda just mentioned on the ground that these theories and doctrines might conceivably lead to future assaults and revolutions.

In a circular letter sent to the editors of leading magazines,[53] Mr. Palmer shows even more plainly that he is seeking to use the power of the government, not against actual or threatened violence, but against bad ideas. After submitting copies of various publications of the Soviet Government, he states that these documents alone demonstrate: (1) " that the present aim of the Russian Government and its officers is to foment and incite discontent, aiming towards a revolution in this country; (2) that the entire movement is a dishonest and criminal one, in other words, an organized campaign to acquire the wealth and power of all countries for the few agitators and their criminal associates." Among other qualities of Bolshevism: " It advocates the destruction of all ownership in property, the destruction of all religion and belief in God. . . . The sabotizing of public thought is an essential of this movement."

The Department, as far as existing laws allow, intends to keep up an unflinching war against this movement no matter how cloaked or dissembled. We are determined that this movement will not be permitted to go far enough in this country to disturb our peace or create any widespread distrust of the people's government.

There is a menace in this country. It may not be the menace of revolution. . . . My one desire is to acquaint people like you

[53] Reprinted in 110 *Nation* 190 (February 14, 1920). See also Palmer Deportations Testimony, for emphasis on the atheism of prominent radicals as an argument for their deportation.

with the real menace of evil-thinking which is the foundation of the Red movement.

That a Quaker should employ prison and exile to counteract evil-thinking is one of the saddest ironies of our time, and particularly that he should justify this by the religious heresy of his opponents. After all that Milton and Bagehot and Mill have said of the unwisdom of influencing the mind by temporal punishments and burdens, after Justice Holmes's warning against attempts to check by force " the expression of opinions that we loathe and believe to be fraught with death," even those who disagree with Bolshevism, anarchism, and revolutionary syndicalism as strongly as I do myself will need no further argument to realize that as theories they must be defeated in some other way. To conduct arguments by violence, even if that violence is employed by government officials under the guise of law, is contrary to sound political policy and to the constitutional guaranties of freedom of speech.

Besides the draft Sedition Act recommended by the Attorney General, which goes so far as to punish writings which " tend to indicate sedition," Congress has under consideration about seventy similar bills, of which three have attracted public notice.[54] These are the Overman Bill, a peace-time replica of the sedition section of the Espionage Act of 1918, reported in 1919 by the Senate sub-committee to investigate Bolshevism, as the fruit of its labors; the Sterling Bill, the best drawn of the four, passed by the Senate in January, 1920; and the Graham Bill, a very drastic measure with a death penalty and a sweeping postal censorship, which the House Judiciary Committee substituted for the Sterling Bill and recommended for immediate enactment. Its reasons were the attack on Mr. Palmer's house, the shooting of soldiers at Centralia, " numerous other instances of outrage aimed at the existence of our institutions," and the

[54] S. 1686; S. 3317; H. R. 11430; Investigation Activities of the Dept. of Justice, 14; see also Report No. 542, H. R. (66th Cong., 2d Sess.). Congress adjourned, June, 1920, without any enactment.

vigor and extent of anarchistic teachings as revealed by recent investigations. The Committee does not show why the existing law is not adequate to deal with all these facts except the presence of pernicious and dangerous ideas. Attorney General Palmer refused to support the Graham Bill, and the House Rules Committee decided after several hearings that it was too unsatisfactory to be given any priority in the order of business. Some of these bills impose a maximum sentence of twenty years for unlawful discussion, and in addition aliens are to be deported and naturalized citizens are to be denaturalized and turned loose on the world as men without a country. Indeed, Senator McKellar of Tennessee wanted to go one step farther and deport native-born Americans to a penal colony in Guam, so that we also might have our Devil's Island or Siberia.[55]

Energetic opposition to all four bills by the American Federation of Labor and many kinds of other organizations and by the most conservative newspapers and periodicals, makes it improbable that any of them will become law. At all events the kaleidoscopic state of sedition legislation in Congress induces me to avoid going into the details of any pending bill. Instead, I am going to assume for purposes of discussion that Congress may eventually have before it a very simple measure, from which all the obviously objectionable features of the four bills mentioned will be eliminated. This hypothetical bill is limited by its terms to the advocacy of assassination of federal officials, and the use of "force or violence" for the overthrow of our government or all governments, or the attainment of changes in our Constitution and laws. It punishes the individual who urges such "force or violence" orally or in writing, and also any one who imports from abroad or transports from state to state any book or other printed matter which advocates such "force or violence."

It is improbable that power will be given to the Postmaster General to exclude such material from the mails, fo

[55] Amendment offered to S. 3317, December 4, 1919.

the strongest hostility to the pending bills was directed to such a power. Even if it be said that the Blackstonian test does not forbid the government to control the use of its own machinery, the post-office, it is clear to every newspaper that its exclusion from the mails is equivalent to an absolute censorship. If Mr. Burleson or his successor can exercise the same power in peace that he had during the war to suppress political discussion which he deems objectionable, he has at hand a much more powerful weapon than the Sedition Act of 1798. A newspaper editor fears being put out of business by the administrative denial of the second-class mailing privilege much more than the prospect of prison subject to a jury trial. Even if the periodical is given the right of judicial review, this is of little practical value because of the ruin of circulation during the delay before a court hearing. The same considerations apply to a censorship of the foreign-language press, although this presents special problems and dangers. Consequently, the bill before us for discussion imposes no previous restraint, but makes the advocacy of " force or violence " a crime, punishable by a long term in prison and a heavy fine.

Two questions are raised. (A) How far is such a measure constitutional? (B) How far is it wise and expedient?

VII. *The Constitutionality of a Federal Sedition Law*

The constitutional problem involves three points, affirmative power to punish, the treason clause, and the free speech clause.[56]

1. What clause in the Constitution gives the United States power to punish seditious utterances? The states face no such difficulty, for they possess all power that is not expressly denied to them by their constitutions, and can reach objectionable writings under their general police

[56] For a full discussion with citation of cases, see H. W. Biklé, " The Jurisdiction of the United States over Seditious Libel," 41 *Am. L. Reg.* (N. S.) 1 (1902). His conclusions as to the First Amendment differ very much from mine.

power and criminal jurisdiction. The United States Government, on the other hand, has only the powers which are expressly granted to it by its organic document. Most of the discussion in 1787-88 over the need of a free speech clause in the federal Constitution and most of the controversy over the constitutionality of the Sedition Act of 1798 turned on this point. Much has happened since, however, to indicate that the United States has this power to punish verbal opposition unless prohibited by some negative clause in the Constitution. The epoch-making decisions of Marshall show that the government does not have to rely on any one specific grant of power. The Constitution as a whole creates a nation with officers and functions and in Article I, Section 8, gives to Congress the right " to make all laws which shall be necessary and proper for carrying into execution the foregoing powers, and all other powers vested by this Constitution in the government of the United States, or in any department or officer thereof." Consequently, no express provision is required to enable the government to operate one or more national banks, or exclude aliens from its shores. Its courts can punish contempts committed against them. The United States Supreme Court has already decided in the Neagle case that the Federal Government has power to protect the lives of its judges engaged in the discharge of judicial duties and in other decisions that it can safeguard even prisoners in its custody. The same principle applies to the President or any other official and it seems immaterial whether they are at the moment occupied with business. Their work may be hindered by threats and other utterances as well as by acts. Similarly words which interfere with express functions of the government like the war power fall within its criminal jurisdiction. The conviction of Emma Goldman for issuing pamphlets urging disobedience to the draft, and all the Espionage Act cases prove this beyond question. It is of course true that revolutionary speeches do not affect any specific function of the government, but they do affect its

LEGISLATION AGAINST SEDITION

existence, the most important result of the Constitution. Therefore, on this point I conclude that the United States has affirmative power to protect its own life and the lives of its officers, not only from revolution and assassination, but also from attempts and solicitation directed toward these ends, and even from discussion which might have a remote tendency to produce such evils, unless that power is restricted by either the treason clause or the First Amendment.

2. Section 3 of Article III, which relates to the judicial power of the United States, provides: " Treason against the United States shall consist only in levying war against them, or in adhering to their enemies, giving them aid and comfort. No person shall be convicted of treason unless on the testimony of two witnesses to the same overt act, or on confession in open court. The Congress shall have power to declare the punishment of treason, but no attainder of treason shall work corruption of blood, or forfeiture except during the life of the person attainted."

We shall in discussing the Berger case return to the question of what is treason in war when there are " enemies," but in peace, treason is narrowly limited in this country to " levying war," and Chief Justice Marshall decided in the case of Aaron Burr that that crime requires an actual assemblage of forces. Consequently, the conduct we have in mind is not punishable as treason under our Constitution. Does this prevent it from being punishable otherwise? Under the English treason statute of 25 Edw. III, c. 2, very many kinds of action which interfered with the state were defined as treason. The courts construed these clauses very widely to reach as " constructive treasons," conduct very remote from the defined crimes.[57] This practice became so notorious that the framers of the Constitution wisely prevented it by rejecting most of the English categories and narrowly restricting the evidence on which conviction can be secured. Can Congress accomplish these undesired results by calling the same conduct, not treason but sedition or something else?

[57] 2 Stephen, *History of the Criminal Law*, c. 23 on High Treason.

For example, under the English statute it was treason to "compass or imagine the death of our lord the king." This was interpreted to include threats against him. By analogy, it would be treason to threaten the life of the President, if our Constitution had not definitely provided otherwise. Congress in 1917 created the crime of threats against the President.[58] Is such a statute an unconstitutional evasion of the treason clause?

Again, if the *Biglow Papers* were not "aid and comfort to the enemy"—a problem to which I shall return in the sixth chapter—could Congress treat them as severely as if they were treasonable by creating the crime of seditious libel with a punishment of death? A similar question was put to the counsel for the United States in the Abrams case by Justice Brandeis, who got the reply, "Of course, we wouldn't go that far." But if Congress and the Department of Justice have power to go that far, the value of the treason clause is considerably weakened. All the acts which were constructive treasons under the English law could be made criminal without even the security of two witnesses or the provisions against corruption of the blood and forfeiture.

On the other hand, it is argued that the treason clause is not placed among the restrictions on Congress. It simply prevents the courts from construing the word "treason" in a statute to extend beyond the constitutional definition, even if the statute gives it a wider definition. Congress is not prohibited from punishing on other grounds and under other names crimes which were treason in England, if these are within the federal criminal jurisdiction. The same act might be both treason and something else. Thus killing the king was treason and murder. Congress can punish the murder of the President but not the treason. Or rather, it can punish it not as murder, but as an interference with an express function of the government. It is settled that the United States can prevent assaults on federal judges

[58] U. S. *Comp. Stat.*, § 10200 a, Act of February 14, 1917, c. 64. See 32 *Harv. L. Rev.* 724.

though that is analogous to treason in England. Counterfeiting money was treason there and is expressly punishable under the Constitution.

This argument seems to me more satisfactory when applied to active interferences with specific functions of the government, than when extended to utterances which have a tendency to weaken the sovereignty of the state as a whole. Are they treason in England plus something else? Was it not this tendency to weaken which made them constructive treason, and when they cannot be criminal on that account, does not all ground of jurisdiction fail?

This is a problem somewhat foreign to my province, so that I prefer not to state a definite conclusion, which can only be reached after more judicial interpretation of the treason clause.

3. The First Amendment seems clearly to be violated by many clauses in pending federal sedition bills, which punish words merely for their assumed tendency to produce bad consequences in the remote future, for instance, that section of the Graham Bill which excludes from the mails under heavy penalty " printed matter . . . whereby the use of force . . . is . . . defended . . . as a means towards the accomplishment of industrial, economic, social, or political change, or whereby an appeal is made to racial prejudice the intended or probable result of which appeal is to cause rioting or the resort to force and violence within the United States . . ." The first clause would affect every history of the American Revolution, Macaulay's *History of England*, and W. R. Thayer's *Life of Cavour*. The second would suppress all but the most carefully guarded presentations of the wrongs of the negro.[59] This attempt to enlist popular support for attacks on radicalism by uniting fear of the blacks to fear of the reds has become a favorite device of late. Attorney General Palmer hints that negroes must not be allowed to join radical organizations. The Lusk

---

[59] Ho. Cal. No. 129, § 6. For restrictions of race-irritation in moving-picture films, see W. Va. Laws, 1919, c. 117.

Committee seizes an unanswered letter *to* the Rand School suggesting the spread of socialism among the negroes (without a word about violence) and presents it as a menacing scheme adopted *by* the School "for the spreading of Bolshevist propaganda among negroes in the South," so that the *New York Times* runs front-page head-lines: "Moves to Close the Rand School—District Attorney Takes Steps Toward Revoking Radical Institution's Charter—Planned Negro Uprising."[60]

The Sedition Act of 1798 was also a violation of the First Amendment, especially as it included criticism of the President and Congress, which was very remotely injurious to the United States.[61]

If, however, we consider a federal bill such as I have suggested, which, like the Massachusetts and New Jersey Anti-Anarchy Acts, eliminates all clauses obviously punishing bad tendency and penalizes only the advocacy of force and violence, much more difficult questions of constitutionality arise. It may be helpful to examine various kinds of utterances successively. If one directly incites another to murder an official and the murder takes place, the speaker is, of course, punishable. The same holds good, even if the incitement proves unsuccessful. If the speaker does not solicit any particular person, but eloquently appeals to a large audience for some new Charlotte Corday, or if naming no specific victim he urges the assassination of an indefinite number of men from some hated group, the case is not altered. Even if he alleges the loftiest motives, the social interest in truth and progress is far outweighed by the interest in order, and there is a direct interference with the safety of life. When he does not ask for any future killing, but merely glorifies such an event in the past, the danger lessens and the power to punish becomes more uncertain.[62]

---

[60] *New York Times*, June 28, 1919; see also July 9.

[61] See page 29, *supra*. Biklé admits it was probably invalid for the reason stated above.

[62] For opposing views on the question whether praise of a criminal

The time elapsed is perhaps an element. A distinction might be drawn between praise of the assassin of McKinley, and " Cæsar had his Brutus, Charles I. his Cromwell." Yet even Patrick Henry's speech might be held advocacy of force and within the hypothetical Sedition Law. A further step is the discussion of tyrannicide as an abstract proposition of morality. Mill was willing to allow the fullest liberty even for this,[63] but it is probable that assassination is so easily carried out that there is always a sufficiently clear and present danger of its occurrence to bring such discussions within the range of legislative discretion.

Advocacy of revolution is much less dangerous except in extraordinary times of great tension. The chances of success are so infinitesimal that the probability of any serious attempt following the utterances seems too slight to make them punishable by the Federal Government. This is especially true if the speaker urges revolution at some future day, so that no immediate check is required to save the country. Even if several men talk like this with very bad intentions, they should not be held guilty of conspiracy under section 6 of the United States Criminal Code unless the danger-test is satisfied. There is no " clear and present danger " in a revolution announced for 1948.

The Federal Government has nothing to do with the question whether such discussion is a public nuisance or a breach of the peace under state law. Johann Most was convicted on both sides of the Atlantic for advocacy of assassination,[64] but those decisions are based on present injury to the peace and not on danger to the rulers. When, however, the audience joins in the speaker's inflammatory utterances the assembly becomes unlawful, and may possibly constitute a conspiracy under the federal Criminal Code. Thus, Most at a New York meeting on the morrow of the Spies execu-

can be considered incitement to crime, see Masses Pub. Co. *v.* Patten, 244 Fed. 535; 245 Fed. 102.

[63] Mill, *Liberty,* note at opening of c. II.

[64] Reg. *v.* Most, 7 Q. B. D. 244 (1881); P. *v.* Most, 171 N. Y. 423 (1902).

tions doomed to an early death the prosecuting attorney; the trial judge; the Supreme Court of Illinois; "the highest murderers in the land, the Supreme Court of the United States"; and the Governor of Illinois. His hearers exhibited warm approval, and when he said, "The day of revolution is not far distant," one of the audience rose and said excitedly: "Why not to-night, for we are ready and prepared?" The address by itself appears to have been deemed insufficient to support a criminal prosecution, but he was convicted of participating in an unlawful assembly.[65] Possibly there was also a conspiracy within the United States Criminal Code, but the absence of any real danger to the Federal Government makes this improbable.

This case shows how much the danger of utterances is affected by surrounding circumstances as well as by the words used. A soap-box orator on a street-corner shouting to casual passers-by is far less perilous than if he delivers the same address in a hall overcrowded with sympathetic listeners. A pamphlet is less dangerous than any speech, a book than a pamphlet. A threat of revolution over the family tea-table is innocuous. Every one will admit that these considerations affect the wise drafting and enforcement of sedition legislation, and some at least hold that they may decrease the danger from objectionable utterances until they sink below the minimum limit of Congressional power. Thus, Freund says:[66]

The doctrine that crime may under given conditions become justifiable or that it may have a tendency to arouse the public conscience should not in itself be held to constitute a crime. It is clear that an exposition of social wrong or injustice must be allowed, nor can the necessary liberty of agitation be said to be overstepped by appeals to sentiment rather than to reason; and if it is said that appeal to sentiment is appeal to passion and must lead to disorder and violence, it must be answered that this was always the plea upon which political agitation was

[65] P. v. Most, 128 N. Y. 108 (1891); see Freund on the Police Power, § 477.
[66] *Op. cit.*, §§ 476, 478.

formerly suppressed. Not even the fact that an adherent of the doctrine commits a crime is conclusive that the teaching of the doctrine amounts to incitement; for the crime may as well have been induced by a morbid brooding over conditions which are the cause of social discontent. . . . The constitutional guaranty of freedom of speech and press and assembly demands the right to oppose all government and to argue that the overthrow of government cannot be accomplished otherwise than by force. . . . It is probably true to say . . . that it is impossible to strike at anarchism as a doctrine without jeopardizing valuable constitutional rights.

Nevertheless, the Abrams and Schaefer decisions in the Supreme Court should deter any one from predicting unconstitutionality under the First Amendment for the Threats against the President Act, or the Sterling Bill, or the hypothetical statute I have been considering, which is carefully limited to "force and violence." The "nature of the words used" may be held to create sufficient danger to support the restriction on freedom of speech. Moreover, the real issues of constitutional law, as in Masses v. Patten and the Abrams trial, are likely to arise from a loose construction of the statute, even if its wording is valid. Therefore, I consider it a much more fertile subject of discussion to turn to the wisdom and policy of a federal sedition law against the advocacy of "force and violence."

VIII. *The Wisdom and Expediency of a Federal Sedition Law*

No one knows what blasphemy is or what sedition is, but all know that they are vague words which can be fitted to any meaning that shall please the ruling powers.—WALTER BAGEHOT.

"No man," says Attorney General Palmer, "can go further than I will go in his earnestness to protect the people in the guaranty of free speech." Nevertheless, he insists that there must be a dead-line, and this he finds it easy to draw at the place where there is a threat or promise or necessary implication of the use of physical force or violence.[67] So long as Congress does no more than punish this sort of language, how can any one reasonably object? The public seems at first sight to get no benefit from such talk, and clearly the speaker has no claim to encouragement. Men may well inquire how the interest of society in the attainment of truth and progress is served by threats to kill officials, blow up buildings, and bring in the dictatorship of the proletariat with a holocaust of vengeance. Consequently, the question whether a law against the advocacy of force and violence is wise may be thought to admit only of an affirmative answer.

I believe, however, that the problem is far less simple than it seems. Although the opponent of the proposed legislation apparently occupies a very bad position, that of standing up for force and violence, yet it may be possible to show that such legislation is dangerous, far more dangerous than the agitation it expects to suppress. If a federal law against violent talk and writings which create no immediate danger of injurious action is not only constitutional but highly desirable and necessary, why is it that we have had only one such law in the past, and that one a stupendous failure? Even the state laws against inflammatory utterances as breaches of the peace have been used very sparingly against soap-box orators and revolutionary literature. We have refused to make arrests unless there was a real danger that the lawlessness which was advocated would immediately take place. Surely, there is nothing to be ashamed of in urging a continuance of this traditional American policy.

Most of us believe that our Constitution makes it possible to change all bad laws through political action. We ought to disagree vehemently with those who urge violent methods, and whenever necessary take energetic steps to prevent them from putting such methods into execution. This is a very different matter from holding that all discussion of the de-

[67] Testimony before House Judiciary Committee, *New York Times*, February 5, 1920. House Judiciary Hearings, 21.

sirability of resorting to violence for political purposes should be ruthlessly stamped out. There is not one among us who would not join a revolution if the reason for it be made strong enough. Californians would take up arms against an amendment passed by Congress and the other state legislatures for the cession of California to an Oriental power. And talk about violence is far more common. Tobacco will not follow alcohol into oblivion without some murmurs of a fight from the most peaceable citizens.

The United States is the last place on earth where mere talk about resistance and revolution ought to be treated as inherently vicious and intolerable. The founders of the colonies broke the religious laws of England before they came here and some of them engaged in a large-sized rebellion. The founders of the United States urged the destruction of property by the destruction of tea and the burning of stamped paper. They went further. They advocated the overthrow of this or any other government by force and violence when they adopted a well-known document which reads, "That whenever any form of government becomes destructive of these ends, it is the right of the people to alter and abolish it."

If a federal statute against the advocacy of force and violence had been enacted in the Abolition period, several distinguished citizens of Massachusetts would have been criminals. Wendell Phillips advocated opposition to the Fugitive Slave Law, and his statue is in the Public Gardens of Boston. William Lloyd Garrison did so, and his statue is on Commonwealth Avenue. The Overseers of Harvard College dismissed a law teacher, Edward G. Loring, because he carried out his oath of office as United States Commissioner by enforcing that law, and for the same reason both houses of the Massachusetts legislature requested the Governor to remove him from a probate judgeship, and he was removed. Theodore Parker, George L. Stearns, Thomas Wentworth Higginson, and Frank B. Sanborn contributed funds to send John Brown to Harper's Ferry to use force and violence.

These men believed that some bad laws are so powerfully supported that the only way to obtain their repeal is to violate them. They believed that no decent man could sit silent and inactive while the Fugitive Slave Law was enforced. Perhaps they were all of them wrong. Some of them were clearly liable as accessories to criminal acts. I insist that such acts must be punished, however noble the motive. But we cannot honor and praise these men for their courageous onslaughts on established evils, and at the same time pronounce it a heinous crime for any one to-day to urge the removal of wrongs by force. Above all, we cannot draw a distinction between those days and ours on the ground that the government was bad then and is now good. I believe that to be true, but time alone will prove which is right, the left-wing Socialist or I. We must not forget how Braxfield justified his ferocious sentences by saying that the British Constitution of 1794 was the best in the world. The law and order men of 1774 and 1854 did not consider their governments and laws bad. They would have been glad to incarcerate Otis and Adams, Garrison and Sumner, if they had had Mr. Palmer's bill in force. Yet the advocates of repression in those days were not a race of tyrants. They were respectable citizens just like ourselves. They were merely mistaken. Can we be any more sure of our infallibility than of theirs? And how do we know that we are infallible until we hear the men on the other side, however excitable and given to threats?

This is not indifferentism. We must take our stand for private property if we believe in it, put our backs to the wall, and fight for it with all our strength. Nevertheless, there are many ways of fighting. The American policy is to meet force by force, and talk by talk.

Furthermore, as soon as the danger-test is abandoned, bad tendency inevitably becomes the standard of criminality. Any attempt to distinguish between liberty and license will

LEGISLATION AGAINST SEDITION

break down in administration for sheer vagueness, and sooner or later officials will swing toward the view of Lord Holt in 1704: [68]

> If men should not be called to account for possessing the people with an ill opinion of the government, no government can subsist; for it is very necessary for every government, that the people should have a good opinion of it. And nothing can be worse to any government, than to endeavor to produce animosities as to the management of it. This has always been looked upon as a crime, and no government can be safe unless it be punished.

England in the eighteenth century and Russia in the nineteenth [69] applied this test of bad tendency. The United States has hitherto preferred to follow the principle of Madison: [70]

> Some degree of abuse is inseparable from the proper use of everything; and in no instance is this more true, than in that of the press.

Consequently, the President's Message is attempting the impossible when it supports Mr. Palmer's sedition bill on this high ground: [71] "With the free expression of opinion and with the advocacy of political change, however fundamental, there must be no interference, but toward passion and malevolence tending to incite crime and insurrection under guise of political evolution there should be no leniency." No one has yet invented a gun which will kill a wolf in sheep's clothing and will not hit a sheep. We should all be glad to have a law, "Bad men shall be imprisoned," if it would work, but we know that it would not. A law against "passion and malevolence" is just as bad. Far wiser is the statement of the former Democratic President, just quoted, far

---

[68] Tuchin's Case, Holt 424 (1704).
[69] See the summary of Russian law in Freund, *op. cit.*, § 471 note.
[70] Report on the Virginia Resolutions, 4 Elliot's Deb. (2 ed.), 598. Marshall told Talleyrand the same truth, Beveridge, II, 329.
[71] *New York Times*, December 3, 1919.

wiser the language in a later part of Mr. Wilson's own Message, which seems so inconsistent with the endorsement of the Sedition Bill that it might almost be the work of another man:

The only way to keep men from agitating against grievances is to remove the grievances. An unwillingness even to discuss these matters produces only dissatisfaction and gives comfort to the extreme elements in our country which endeavor to stir up disturbances in order to provoke Governments to embark upon a course of retaliation and repression. The seed of revolution is repression.

Most acts of violence urged as a reason for sedition legislation, the Gimbel bombs, the May explosions, the Centralia shooting, followed immediately on some act of suppression, —the Debs decision, the Roxbury Riot sentences, the Massachusetts Anti-Anarchy Act, raids on I.W.W. offices and statutes against Syndicalism. The men responsible for these outbreaks should be tried and severely punished if found guilty, as much as the Southern lynchers and the Omaha mob that nearly hanged the mayor. It is an altogether different matter to make these affairs the basis of further suppression. The advocates of such a policy are doing their best to get this country into the vicious circle of outrages, coercion,—coercion, outrages, from which John Morley spent his whole official career vainly trying to extricate Ireland and India.[72]

Contrast the American policy of punishing acts and letting talk run to waste. We have stuck by the schoolboy maxim, "Sticks and stones will break my bones, but words will never hurt me." Recent riots which have nothing to do with radicalism show that our criminal machinery is very unsuccessfully dealing with acts of violence. That is its absorbing task. It has no more time than it ever had to bother with the men who merely talk. If there is any immediate danger of revolution, the Attorney General should

[72] See especially the fine letter on the Phœnix Park murders, in his *Recollections*, I, 178.

LEGISLATION AGAINST SEDITION

be employing the Criminal Code instead of asking for a sedition law. If there is not, as he himself admits, then, much as every one of us dislikes the advocate of force and violence, we shall be wise if we seek remedial and not punitive methods to make his talk of no effect. In particular, let me mention three concrete reasons why a sedition law will fail to accomplish its purpose of getting the really bad man and leaving valuable discussion untouched.

In the first place, simple as a law against incitement to force and violence appears on its face, it will be a very difficult statute to construe, unless the courts adhere closely to the ordinary rules of criminal attempt. Of course, the man who shouts, " We want to kill the President and blow up the Capitol," presents no difficulties, and he is the man whom most people who discuss the proposed statute suppose it is meant to reach. These few plain cases, which are almost labeled " force and violence," will form only a very small part of the prosecutions. For instance, the Attorney General wants to imprison the editors of radical newspapers who have, he says, " a subtle way " of placing their propaganda for the overthrow of the government before their readers, but the reader understands what is meant.[73] The question is whether he or any one else can draft a statute which makes it possible for fallible human beings to distinguish good attacks on the government from bad attacks which sound as if they were good. Jeffreys, Braxfield, and Kenyon, thought they were punishing " passion and malevolence," but posterity has condemned them for interfering with the " advocacy of orderly political change."

Whatever law is passed will be used to prosecute speeches and books full of general language. The question whether such language is advocacy of force and violence must of course be determined by a judge and jury. Such men are trained to decide about overt acts, but problems of " subtle " propaganda are an entirely different matter. The normal law of criminal attempt offers to this tribunal a considerable

[73] Investigation Activities of the Dept. of Justice, 11.

amount of tangible fact. There is, of course, a mental element, the intention of the defendant to bring about the criminal act, but in addition the jury must find a clear and present danger to society in view of the nature of the words *and the surrounding circumstances*. Now, unless the proposed sedition law practically codifies the ordinary rules of attempt, the most tangible factor of the crime disappears; the jury can disregard the absence of danger in the external situation, and look merely at the intention of the prisoner and the nature of his words. This must be so, for the federal act is expressly intended to prevent the remote possibility of revolution and punish violent language for its own sake. Consequently, the jury are cut loose entirely from overt acts and the world of the five senses. They are adrift on a sea of speculation.

At the very outset the same controversy will arise as in Masses *v.* Patten. It is the old question of Mark Antony's funeral oration. Does a man advocate force and violence when he uses comparatively innocent words with the intention of producing assassination and revolution? Or must the statute be confined to words which taken by themselves are directly provocative of assassination and revolution?

Even this latter and narrower view involves great difficulties of application. This is evident from the experience of the courts with existing federal legislation based on the same " force and violence " principle. The statute making " matter of a character tending to incite arson, murder, or assassination " indecent and non-mailable, has not yet been much construed,[74] but abundant litigation has been caused by the statute which imposes imprisonment of five years maximum upon any one who knowingly and willfully makes a threat to take the life of the President or inflict bodily harm upon him.[75] The threat need not be communicated to the President, and if in a letter it need not be seen by any one

---

[74] U. S. Comp. Stat., 1918, § 10381; Magon *v.* U. S., 248 Fed. 201 (C. C. A., 1918).
[75] U. S. Comp. Stat., 1918, § 10200 a; see 32 *Harv. L. Rev.* 724.

LEGISLATION AGAINST SEDITION

except officials, so that the element of dangerous circumstances is eliminated. Already it has proved very hard to decide what words constitute a threat, and some of the practical effects of the statute should discourage imitation. A Syracuse woman of German descent, exasperated by her fellow employees who continually picked on her and called her the Kaiser, finally burst out that she would poison the President if she had him there. She pleaded guilty before Judge Ray, and was fined $300, " not because the court regarded her as a dangerous person, but to show all quick-tempered or alien-minded persons that they must not threaten to do the President bodily harm or utter unpatriotic sentiments in such times as these." [76] In another case, the words were, " I wish Wilson was in hell, and if I had the power I would put him there." The judges held this revolting language to be a threat to kill the President, because how could he be in hell unless he were dead? [77]

The kind of language which will be held to advocate force and violence under a peace-time Sedition Law may be clearly foreshadowed by the construction which the Supreme Court in the Abrams decision put upon the exhortation:

Workers of the World! Awake! Rise! Put down your enemy and mine! Yes, friends, there is only one enemy of the workers of the world and that is Capitalism.

Here is not a word to indicate violence or negative the use of political and economic pressure, but Justice Clarke declares:

This is clearly an appeal to the workers of this country to arise and put down by force the Government of the United States.

---

[76] A Memorandum concerning Political Prisoners within the Jurisdiction of the Dept. of Justice in 1919, 22, (in Harv. Law School Library).

[77] U. S. v. Clark, Bull. Dept. Just., No. 101; affd., 250 Fed. 449 (C. C. A., 1918).

If he is right, the traditional language of socialism becomes advocacy of "force or violence," as has already been held of the general strike under the similar terms of the New York Anarchy Act. If Justice Clarke is wrong, lesser judges may err. In either case, the Sedition Law will become a drag-net for every form of radicalism.

So far I have assumed that the nature of the words will determine criminality, and that if a man uses the ordinary language of political agitation with intent to produce a revolution, he will not be punishable. I doubt very much if the Act will receive any such narrow construction. When Judge Hand held in Masses v. Patten that the equally simple terms of the Espionage Act of 1917 would not be violated if the speaker stopped short of urging upon others that it was their duty or their interest to resist the law, he was reversed, and the upper court said that if the defendant is endeavoring to persuade to resistance, it is not necessary that the incitement to crime shall be direct. Enough "if the natural and reasonable effect of what is said is to encourage resistance." [78] The majority of the Supreme Court took the same position in the Schaefer case. In short, of the three elements of criminal attempt, (1) bad intention, (2) dangerous words, and (3) dangerous external circumstances, the third vanishes entirely, the second is whittled down to require only words of a bad tendency, and the first alone remains intact. And since the judges who construed the Espionage Act of 1917 will also construe the Sedition Law, they will probably interpret it in much the same way. We have traveled very far from the realm of overt acts.

It is unnecessary to repeat the argument of the first chapter and the experience of the eighteenth century in England, that the risk of the suppression of opinion is very great when the bad political tendency of words and the bad intention of the defendant become the only tests of criminality. Furthermore, we must not forget that we can never

[78] 244 Fed. @ 540; 246 Fed. @ 38.

LEGISLATION AGAINST SEDITION

be sure that the tendency is bad or the intention evil. These are not visible facts. We have to depend on the opinions of the judge and jury as to the merits of the tendency and the morality of what they can guess about the inside of a man's head. Of course, one evidence and often the main evidence of bad intention will be the supposed bad tendency of the language he employs. In short, any peace-time Sedition Law is open to exactly the objections which Jefferson stated in the Virginia Toleration Act,[79] that when the expression of opinion is made criminal, the tribunal will acquit or convict accordingly as the sentiments of the prisoner square with or differ from its own.

To recapitulate, we began to discuss the Sedition Law with the assumption that it would punish only the man who talks out-and-out revolution and whom we know to intend out-and-out revolution. Such a man seems entitled to no protection. Now we see that we are not dealing with such a man at all. We must encounter much vaguer language and we can never be sure that a man's mind is bad. In its actual application the law must necessarily convict any man whom the judge and jury consider to be using language of bad political tendency with a bad intention, whether or not the judge and jury are right. The desirability of the statute ought to depend very largely on the question whether human beings are likely to be right in forming such a judgment. The answer is that history shows they are very liable to be wrong.

Without the slightest imputation of corruption or malice, we can all agree that a juryman's judgment of the remote political and economic effects of a book or speech is inevitably warped by his own views to a much greater degree than if he is determining the path of a bullet or the value of a house or even the effect of a lie on a woman's reputation. And the moral quality of another's mind is even more difficult to determine fairly when there is no criminal act, as in ordinary crimes, to check it up by. A bad intention is

[79] Page 31, *supra*.

easily inferred from what we consider bad opinions. The consequence of such vague standards is that objectionable men and doctrines are easily decided to be advocating violence. Thus, a Winnipeg strike leader has just been prosecuted for sedition, solely on the ground in one count of the indictment that he " seditiously " published two verses of Isaiah, beginning, " Woe unto them that decree unrighteous decrees." [80] Intention, that is, presumed intention, becomes the essence of the crime, and the thing actually done immaterial. Once more, the prisoner is convicted, not for what he does but for what he thinks.

Whether we believe that the Espionage Act decisions were necessary in time of war or not, we ought to hesitate to enact in peace a statute which is sure to be construed as widely as the simple words of the 1917 Act, and to subject all adverse criticism of the government to the risk of suppression so forcibly presented by Justice Brandeis in a recent Espionage Act case: [81]

> The jury which found men guilty for publishing news items or editorials like those here in question must have supposed it to be within their province to condemn men not merely for disloyal acts but for a disloyal heart; provided only that the disloyal heart was evidenced by some utterance. To prosecute men for such publications reminds of the days when men were hanged for constructive treason. To hold that such harmless additions to or omissions from news items, and such impotent expressions of editorial opinion, as were shown here, can afford the basis even of a prosecution will doubtless discourage criticism of the policies of the Government. To hold that such publications can be suppressed as false reports, subjects to new perils the constitutional liberty of the press, already seriously curtailed in practice under powers assumed to have been conferred upon the postal authorities. Nor will this grave danger end with the passing of the war. The constitutional right of free speech has been declared to be the same in peace and in war. In peace, too, men may differ widely as to what loyalty to our country demands; and an intolerant majority, swayed by passion or by fear, may be

---

[80] " Quoting Isaiah in Winnipeg," A. V. Thomas, 109 *Nation* 850 (January 3, 1920). The case was afterwards dropped. 110 *ibid.* 292.
[81] Schaefer *v.* U. S., 251 U. S. 466, 493 (1920), dissenting opinion.

prone in the future, as it has often been in the past, to stamp as disloyal opinions with which it disagrees. Convictions such as these, besides abridging freedom of speech, threaten freedom of thought and of belief.

Secondly, men who use revolutionary language should not be suppressed in the absence of very serious and pressing danger, because they almost always have a grievance. Very few people want to smash things for the fun of it like small boys breaking windows. Whether the grievance is well founded or not, the defenders of the existing order ought to know about it so that they may correct it or show by counter-argument that it does not exist. The agitator would be much wiser and more effective if he expressed his case calmly without threats, but we ought not to punish him for this mistake. He is not an educated man, he is not a lawyer, he is not accustomed to weighing his words carefully, and he is only too apt in a heated argument to let himself go. And on the whole, society gains if he is free to do so. The worse the grievance, the more likely the victim is to get angry and urge violent measures. Yet that is the grievance which most needs removal.[82] Reformers who get excited are pretty sure to take the position that force is justifiable if peaceful methods fail to gain what they consider right. Even the supporters of existing institutions have been known to lose their tempers and suggest lamp-posts and ropes. In the past we have felt it wiser to let the opponents of the government talk than to cause much greater bitterness in them and in their friends by throwing them into prison. Nor will this treatment silence those who are really dangerous. A friend of mine wants all "Bolshevists" shut up till the jails are so crowded that their feet

[82] See the thoughtful statement by Judge Cooley in his *Constitutional Limitations* (7 ed.) 613, of the great danger of a rule aganist intemperate discussion, ending: "If they exceed all the proper bounds of moderation, the consolation must be, that the evil likely to spring from the violent discussion will probably be less, and its correction by public sentiment more speedy, than if the terrors of the law were brought to bear to prevent the discussion." Mill adds very strong arguments against the same rule at the close of c. 2 of his *Liberty*.

hang out of the windows, but the daily letters from political prisoners in the radical newspapers show that their tongues hang out too. Putting radicals to death is the only way to get rid of them, and for that we have lost our nerve. Anything less only increases their power for harm. If they can say, " This government of capitalists denies us a decent life and now it won't even let us tell our wrongs," the natural conclusion is, " If it will not let us talk, our only resort is to fight." The passage last quoted from the President's Message hammers this truth home.

Thirdly, a Sedition Act will suppress much discussion which is not within its terms. Men assume that such a law affects only a speech or a book which devotes itself entirely to the advocacy of violence. This is not so. For instance, any small conservative group in the community which wants to prevent radical agitators from bringing disagreeable facts to public attention will be enabled by such a statute to go through their speeches and pamphlets with a fine-tooth comb and probably find a sentence here or there which can be interpreted (in the light of the Abrams decision) as advocating revolution. Thus, it will be possible to imprison almost any radical agitator in the absence of any real danger of revolution. Of course, trivial offenses will not be punished in ordinary times, but during the excitement of a great strike or some other widespread unrest the partisans of law and order will hardly be able to resist the temptation to make use of this law to bottle up labor leaders and other agitators whom they fear and dislike. Witness the sentences of ten, fifteen, twenty years imposed upon leading Socialists under the Espionage Act, so that further activity on their part is conveniently prevented during the time they are likely to live. And in a government of laws and not of men, no one human being ought to be entrusted with the power to give or withhold the heavy sentences of a Sedition Law for the light offenses included within its provisions.

The effect of a Sedition Law upon books is even more injurious. An *ex post facto* censorship of the press is created by the provision that a book which advocates force and violence must not be sold or imported from abroad or transported from state to state. It may be asked, why should any one honestly want to possess a book which urges revolution or even the violation of law? Why should we allow such books to come into the country or be put on sale? It must be remembered that a book falls under the penalties of the law if only a part of it is revolutionary. There are many books and pamphlets which for the most part contain elaborate discussions of social and economic questions, which it is very desirable to read. Here and there the writer is so impressed with the hopelessness of legal change in the present system that he advocates resort to force if nothing else serves. That alone will render circulation of the whole book a heinous crime under this Act. Many of the classics of modern economics will be put on this new Index Expurgatorius. The law will prevent a loyal citizen from obtaining from abroad or another state the works of Marx, Proudhon, Bakunin, or Stirner, and will make it criminal for a loyal bookseller to buy these books for him.

One particular instance will show the evil of such a statute. Harvard University is now planning to collect in its library all books, pamphlets, posters, and other material relating to the Russian Revolution. After the French Revolution nothing of the sort was attempted for many years, and in consequence all collections of documents of that period are very imperfect. It is the intention of the Harvard Library to avoid such a loss in the case of the Russian Revolution, which everybody, no matter what his opinion of it may be, recognizes as one of the great events in the history of the world. Most of the pending sedition bills would make it a crime to import a large part of this material from Russia or even transport it from New York to Cambridge.

Furthermore, if any one who obtains this revolutionary material runs the risk of long imprisonment, sober men who would read and refute it will leave it alone, and it will still fall into the hands of agitators who are willing to take chances. The bulk of the people will be virtually ignorant of what the left-wing radicals are really planning. One of the most effective weapons against anarchy was an exhaustive article in the *New York Times* [83] translating anarchistic passages from the foreign language press. It warned the American people of the thought which we ought to seek to counteract by education, Americanization, constructive propaganda, and the cure of grievances. Such an article would be criminal under most of the proposed legislation. The Attorney General's Report to the Senate could not be distributed because of its extracts from the revolutionary press. Prosecutions of radical newspaper editors cannot be fully reported in the daily press, so that the public cannot know what men are convicted for, and it will be possible for the government under cover of such a practice to withhold from the people knowledge of punishment for legitimate political discussion. Even officials cannot lawfully import revolutionary literature under these bills, and an exception in their favor would be an insult to the citizens of the United States. This law is a kindergarten measure which assumes that the American people are so stupid and so untrustworthy that it is unsafe to let them read anything about anarchy and criminal syndicalism because they would immediately become converted. Above all, we shall not be able to meet this great danger of lawlessness if we refuse to look the enemy in the face. The habits of the ostrich are instinctive in many human beings, but they have not been conspicuous for success.

Even if we could wisely dispense with these left-wing books, much less radical publications will become criminal if advocacy of revolution by force and violence is punished. For example, one of the sanest discussions of contemporary thought, which has had a large sale in this country, is Bertrand Russell's *Proposed Roads to Freedom*. Further distribution will become a crime because of its extracts from

[83] June 8, 1919.

LEGISLATION AGAINST SEDITION

the Communist Manifesto of 1848: "The Communists disdain to conceal their views and aims. They openly declare that their ends can be attained only by the forcible overthrow of all existing social conditions. Let the ruling classes tremble at a Communistic revolution."

Or take his quotation from an anarchist song:

> Si tu veux être heureux,
> Nom de Dieu!
> Pends ton propriétaire.[84]

Of course, any anti-socialistic book which gives an adequate historical account of its opponents will fall under the same condemnation.

And we shall have some surprises nearer home. It is advocacy of revolution by force and violence to write: "I hold a little rebellion now and then is a good thing, and as necessary in the political world as storms in the physical."[85] Out go the works of Thomas Jefferson. It is advocacy of change of government by assassination to say, "The right of a nation to kill a tyrant in cases of necessity can no more be doubted than to hang a robber, or kill a flea."[86] Jefferson is followed by his old antagonist, John Adams, the author of the Sedition Law of 1798. The Declaration of Independence will be barred in this country as it was once upon a time in the Philippines, since it is a most eloquent advocate of change in the form of government by force without stint or limit. And the censorship can hardly overlook Lincoln's First Inaugural:

> This country with its institutions belongs to the people who inhabit it. Whenever they shall grow weary of the existing government, they can exercise their constitutional right of amending it, or their revolutionary right to dismember or overthrow it.

[84] Russell, *op. cit.*, 17, 53.
[85] Writings of Jefferson, ed. P. L. Ford, IV, 362; see also 370 and 467.
[86] Works of John Adams, ed. C. F. Adams, VI, 130.

It may be objected that of course no one will be prosecuted for selling such books. Perhaps not, but do we as a fair-minded people want a statute under which the very ideas which will be immune when cloth-bound in a respectable bookstore will constitute a penitentiary offense in a Yiddish handbill?

If this legislation is to be enforced with any impartiality, it must necessarily cut us off from our own revolutionary heritage and from the economic and political thought of Europe in our own time. During the last five years this nation has entered into the affairs of the world for the realization of noble aims. It cannot do this and at the same time propose to pass its existence for the next score of years like some Lady of Shalott, shut off from the turbulent life of European mankind.

Much more could be said, but I hope it is now clear that the really bad man is only an incidental victim of any federal Sedition Law in time of peace. Indeed, it is only too probable that he will be ingenious enough to hide his tracks and escape. Meanwhile, the law will suppress the discussion of public questions at point after point.

During the war the advocates of strong measures assured those who thought our traditional freedom of speech in peril, that suppression would disappear when the fighting stopped, and remarked with Lincoln that a man could not contract so strong an appetite for emetics during temporary illness as to persist in feeding upon them during the remainder of his healthful life.[87] The war is over, actually if not technically, the Espionage Act has suspended any widespread operation till the next conflict, but nearly every state in the Union has proceeded to make the expression of certain opinions criminal, and Congress is now considering a much more rigorous Espionage Act for times of peace. The truth is that persecution of unpopular doctrines is not an emetic at all, but a drug. A nation can-

[87] Letter to Erastus Corning and others (June 12, 1863), *Works of Lincoln,* ed. Nicolay and Hay, VIII, 309.

LEGISLATION AGAINST SEDITION

not indulge in an orgy of intolerance and console itself like Rip Van Winkle with the thought that "This time doesn't count!" Nobody enjoyed gasless Sundays or sugarless coffee so much that we are likely to continue them in peace, but the pleasure of being able to silence the pro-Germans and pacifists and Socialists who had irritated us in 1915 and 1916 was so agreeable in 1917 and 1918 that it will be abandoned with extreme reluctance, and we long for more suppression to satisfy the appetite which has been created contrary to our former national tradition of open political discussion.

Consequently we ought to cross-question acutely our present conviction that the repression of ideas is essential to the public safety, and ask ourselves how far that conviction results from the mood of the moment. Indeed, it may be conjectured that just as some soldiers were given ether to make them go "over the top" better, so a nation cannot enter whole-heartedly into the horrors of a war without some benumbing of its reasoning powers, from which it may not yet have recovered. Is it not psychologically probable that our minds have been so shaken by excitement, fear, and hatred, so stretched to one absorbing purpose, that they are slow to return to normal, and that we still crave something to fear and hate, some exceptional cause for which we can continue to evoke enthusiasm?

A very serious situation confronts us. For three years the government has pursued the policy advocated by Judge Van Valkenburgh when he tried Rose Pastor Stokes for her denunciation of profiteering:[88] "The President could not stop in the face of the enemy and effect domestic reforms. We do not ordinarily clean house and hang out the bedding when there is a thunderstorm on. We wait until it is over, go dirty a little longer." A good deal of soiled linen has accumulated, and the consequences are far from agreeable. The discussion of the radicals is bound to be doubly violent because it was postponed, and now it can be postponed no

[88] Bull. Dept. Just., No. 106, p. 18.

longer unless we mean to suppress it altogether. By doing that we shall not end it, but only drive it underground.

A Sedition Law is not the proper way to deal with anarchy. Outside of a few intellectuals, anarchy is the creation of discontent, and this law will increase discontent. Nothing adds more to men's hatred for government than its refusal to let them talk, especially if they are the type of person anarchists are, to whom talking a little wildly is the greatest joy of life. Besides, suppression of their mere words shows a fear of them, which only encourages them to greater activity in secret. A widespread belief is aroused that the government would not be so anxious to silence its critics unless what they have been saying is true. A wise and salutary neglect of talk, coupled with vigorous measures against plans for actual violence and a general endeavor to end discontent, is the best legal policy toward anarchy and criminal syndicalism.

To quote from an extra-judicial decision of Justice Holmes:[89]

With effervescing opinions, as with the not yet forgotten champagnes, the quickest way to let them get flat is to let them get exposed to the air.

Undoubtedly, there are elements in our population, small in number, but reckless and aggressive, who are ready to act on incitement to revolution, but the real danger lies in the existence of large masses of unthinking radicals. This danger cannot be met directly by clubbing such men into loyalty. We must first understand the causes of their discontent, studying with open minds all the existing information, and then take constructive steps to end that discontent and substitute positive ideals for those we want to drive out. To modernize an old illustration from Herbert Spencer, any one who has watched a tinsmith mend a crum-

[89] Letter to the Harvard Liberal Club, reprinted in 21 *New Republic* 250, and *Boston Herald,* January 13, 1920.

pled mud-guard on an automobile will observe that he never pounds the protuberant spot. To do so would either be ineffective or would simply raise a hump at some other place. Instead, he begins at a distance and hammers all around the critical point, gradually drawing the metal away from it until all is symmetrical as before.

If we have taken reasonable precautions against violence, we should not be disappointed at not securing absolute unanimity among our population on political and economic matters. If Americanism means anything concrete, it certainly means tolerance for opinions widely different from our own, however objectionable they seem to us. Such is the tradition handed down to us by Roger Williams and Thomas Jefferson. In the past we have been proud to believe that the arguments for law and order, the common sense of the American people, including those who have come from Europe to help build our industries, and the noble qualities of our institutions, would win out over any revolutionary talk or writing. The proposed Sedition Bills show a serious distrust in these three great stabilizing forces of American life. Not for the sake of the radicals, but for our own sake, should we oppose this unprecedented legislation, whose enforcement will let loose a horde of spies and informers, official and unofficial, swarming into our private life, stirring up suspicion without end, making all attacks on government either impotent or unsafe. The supporters of this gag-law assume that our patriotism and our institutions are so weak as to crumble away at any talk of revolution. Surely that time has not come, will never come. Let us put an end once for all to this cowardice, and take to heart the words of a great English Liberal: [90]

> We talk much—and think a great deal too much—of the wisdom of our ancestors. I wish we could imitate the courage of our ancestors. They were not ready to lay their liberties at the feet of the Government upon every vain or imaginary alarm.

[90] Lord John Russell, quoted in G. W. E. Russell, *Prime Ministers*, N. Y., 1919, 21.

There should be no legislation against sedition and anarchy. We must legislate and enforce the laws against the use of force, but protect ourselves against bad thinking and speaking by the strength of argument and a confidence in American common sense and American institutions, including that most characteristic of all, which stands at the head of the Bill of Rights, freedom of thought.

CHAPTER V

THE DEPORTATIONS

That imprisonment should continue an hour longer than it ought by law, or that there should be constraint of limb or voice that the law does not allow, is ever a consideration that should call off courts of justice from the ordinary deliberations on matters of property, however great, until this question be determined and this great wrong, if it be one, be redressed.— WILLIAM M. EVARTS, *Argument in the Lemmon Slave Case.*

As long as Congress refuses to follow the disastrous precedent of 1798 and enact a peace-time Sedition Law, the government cannot do much to suppress "evil-thinking" among citizens of the United States. It is not entirely powerless, for violent anarchistic books and periodicals can be excluded from the mails, and the Espionage Act will remain in force as long as we are at war with Germany; in other words, for an indefinite future. As we have seen, Mr. Burleson has not scrupled to use it in his effort to wreck the *New York Call*, and Mr. Palmer, while professing to limit the Act to "acts and utterances which tended to weaken the waging of actual hostilities,"[1] prosecuted and convicted Socialists for requesting an amnesty for political prisoners months after the armistice, and closed up the *Seattle Union-Record* a year after the last shot was fired. The outcry which these high-handed acts have drawn from even the conservative press has deterred the Attorney General from much independent action, though his agents are frequently reported as co-operating with state officials in raids under local anarchy acts on radical headquarters.

In the absence of a new Sedition Law against radical citizens, the government has seized upon the new Alien Law and used it with relentless vigor. The first conspicuous event

[1] Investigation Activities of the Department of Justice, 6.

was the sailing of the transport "Buford" on December 21, 1919, with two hundred and forty-nine Russians. This was followed in January by a carefully prepared round-up in all parts of the country in which over four thousand persons were arrested under deportation charges.

While the right of the Federal Government to punish sedition is open to serious doubt, there can be no question of its affirmative power to exclude aliens from this country or to deport them even though they are admitted. Although no clause in the Constitution expressly gives this power, it has been held by the United States Supreme Court in the Chinese Exclusion Cases to be an incident of the sovereignty and right of self-preservation necessarily conferred by the Constitution upon the government it created.[2]

I. *The Statute as to Deportable Radicals*

Various classes of aliens besides the Chinese have long been subject to exclusion and expulsion for such obvious objections as conviction of crime, insanity, pauperism, etc., but it was not until 1903 that the possession or expression of opinions was first made a disqualification. In consequence of the death of President McKinley, Congress refused entry to the United States to anarchists, persons advocating the forcible overthrow of our government or all government, or the assassination of public officials, as well as persons disbelieving in or opposed to all organized government or belonging to organizations teaching such disbelief or opposition.[3] Other types of extreme radicals were added by subsequent legislation.[4] The present statute, enacted toward the close of the war, specifies the following proscribed classes:[5]

[2] Nishimura Ekiu *v.* U. S., 142 U. S. 651, 659 (1892); see other cases in 1 Willoughby on the Constitution, 251 ff.

[3] Act, March 3, 1903, c. 1012, §§ 2, 38.

[4] Act, February 20, 1907, c. 1134, §§ 2, 38; Act, February 5, 1917, c. 29, in U. S. Comp. Stat., 1918, §§ 4289¼ b and jj.

[5] Act of October 16, 1918, c. 186; U. S. Comp. Stat., 1919 Supp., § 4289¼ b. This has been amended since the events narrated in this

THE DEPORTATIONS

Aliens who are anarchists; aliens who believe in or advocate the overthrow by force or violence of the Government of the United States or of all forms of law; aliens who disbelieve in or are opposed to all organized government; aliens who advocate or teach the assassination of public officials; aliens who advocate or teach the unlawful destruction of property; aliens who are members of or affiliated with any organization that entertains a belief in, teaches, or advocates the overthrow by force or violence of the Government of the United States or of all forms of law, or that entertains or teaches disbelief in or opposition to all organized government, or that advocates the duty, necessity, or propriety of the unlawful assaulting or killing of any officer or officers, either of specific individuals or of officers generally, of the Government of the United States or of any other organized government, because of his or their official character, or that advocates or teaches the unlawful destruction of property.

Such aliens are not only refused admission and put out if they succeed in getting in, but if they acquire these views or join these associations after their entry into this country, they are to be deported without any time limit, no matter how long before 1918 they came to the United States.

Like the federal "force and violence" bills discussed in the preceding chapter, this statute at first sight seems to apply to really bad men, and to effect nothing but desirable results. Once again, however, we ought to defer judgment until we have examined the actual operation of the statute. The life of a law is not in its words, but in its enforcement. In this case we do not have to rely on inference and argument with respect to the future, for the deportation laws have been in existence long enough to provide us with abundant data from past experience, upon which we may base our decision as to the wisdom and justice of this national course of action.

chapter to include aliens convicted under the Espionage Act and other war statutes (Act, May 10, 1920, No. 197), or advocating sabotage, or injury to property, or assaults on officials for any reason; giving or lending money is proof of advocacy or membership (Act, June 5, 1920, No. 262). On the last statute, see John Lord O'Brian, "The Menace of Administrative Law," address to Maryland Bar Association, June 25, 1920.

II. *The Administrative Machinery for Deporting Radicals*

> " I'll be judge. I'll be jury,"
> Said cunning old Fury;
> " I'll try the whole cause,
> And condemn you to death."—*Alice in Wonderland.*

The most important question with any legislation which affects human happiness is, what kind of men administer its provisions? Are they an impartial judge and jury, a government official, a secret council, a star chamber? The answer to this question in our problem is the following sentence: [6]

In every case where any person is ordered deported from the United States under the provisions of this Act, or by any law or treaty, the decision of the Secretary of Labor shall be *final*.

No judge or jury passes on the important question whether an alien who has lived here for many years actually holds or has expressed any of the objectionable views specified as grounds for deportation. No judge or jury decides whether he belongs to an objectionable organization or whether it really is objectionable. All these vital issues of fact are determined by the Secretary of Labor, or more often by his subordinates, the immigration officials. And there is for all practical purposes no appeal from those officials to any court, not even to the Supreme Court of the United States. The law takes the position that deportation is not a criminal proceeding and involves no punishment. It is simply an exercise of the right of every sovereign state to determine who shall reside within its borders. Therefore, the foreigner who is expelled without a hearing in court, no matter how long he has lived in the United States, no matter if he must leave a house and other cherished possessions behind him, is not deprived of life, liberty, or property without due process of law.

[6] U. S. Comp. Stat., 1918, § 4289¼ jj. Italics mine.

THE DEPORTATIONS

Such wide powers have not been acquired by the executive branch of our government all at once or without a struggle.[7] The doctrine that administrative decisions on questions of fact may be made conclusive without any judicial review originated in our law in controversies growing out of the distribution of public property. When the government is giving away money which it has acquired under a treaty or is making free grants of public land, it may justly annex whatever conditions it pleases to its gifts and delegate to anybody it selects the power to say how and where those gifts shall go. The recipients of its generosity cannot complain if they must dispense with judicial proceedings and abide by the decision of some administrative body like the Land Department. If they are denied relief by such officials, they lose nothing which they had before.

Similar powers were soon accorded from obvious necessity to tax officials. The collection of the public revenues would become impossible if every dispute of fact over the value of an imported scarf or the size of an income could be carried by the disgruntled taxpayer into the courts. The complexity of the business and the requirement of speed make it very desirable that administrative officers should execute any valid tax law without interruption so long as no issue of law is involved; on the other hand, their decisions do not affect the liberty of the citizen or interfere with the normal activities of his life.

When the doctrine was extended to exclusion from the mails, its effect became much more serious. The business man who wishes to communicate with prospective buyers and sources of supply is not a recipient of public bounty like the occupant of free land. While he does make use of governmental machinery, he pays for what he gets, and in sub-

---

[7] The leading cases are in 2 Willoughby on the Constitution, c. LXIV. A very valuable article by the Assistant Secretary of Labor, Louis F. Post, is "Administrative Decisions in Connection with Immigration," 10 *Pol. Sci. Rev.* 251 (1916). This supports my conclusions. The same volume contains several other articles on administrative decisions. See the Bibliography for further references on the Post-office.

stance the transaction is like buying municipal water or riding on a national railway. The opportunity to obtain essential services is a condition of earning a livelihood and very possibly of life itself. If a city cuts off a man's water, he cannot dig a well; if he is kept off the trains, he cannot walk; and in the same way the factory or newspaper which is excluded from the mails is denied any other practicable means of systematic intercourse. The decision virtually ruins its business. All questions of constitutionality aside, Congress ought to consider the advisability of continuing to place such a destructive power in the Postmaster General instead of in an impartial tribunal which would not be both judge and prosecuting attorney. Questions of the weight and contents of letters are administrative like tariff valuations, but the tax department does not furnish an analogy for exclusion orders in the post-office for fraud and other reasons, because such controversies are comparatively few and similar in nature to those which courts are accustomed to settle, besides being far-reaching in their consequences to the community as well as to the prohibited periodical. The cases I have already discussed of exclusion from the mails for alleged indecency or disloyalty show the possibilities of danger when the attainment and dissemination of truth are regulated by the arbitrary will of one man.

All these considerations apply *à fortiori* to deportation, and especially deportation for opinions. Exclusion of a newly arrived alien by administrative fiat is not a serious hardship, for he simply returns to his old life and takes up the threads where he recently dropped them, but expulsion after long residence is another affair. The matter at stake here is not a gift from the government, or the payment of a tax which leaves substantial property untouched, or even the existence of a business. Liberty itself, long-established associations, the home, are at the mercy of a bureaucracy. Although technically Justice Gray was right in saying that it is not a punishment to deport an alien who has been domiciled here many years, but only a method of removing him to his own country because he has not complied with the conditions for residence imposed by our government,[8] nevertheless, practically it is nothing but a punishment, which, as Justice Field pointed out, is " beyond all reason in its severity."

As to its cruelty nothing can exceed a forcible deportation from a country of one's residence, and the breaking up of all the relations of friendship, family, and business there contracted. The laborer may be seized at a distance from his home, his family, and his business and taken before the judge [now the immigration inspector] for his condemnation, without permission to visit his home, see his family, or complete any unfinished business.[9]

This power to tear a man up by the roots is now conferred upon officials of the government, the same officials who prefer charges against him, and is extended from such definite facts as the race and birth of a Chinaman to such vague facts as the opinions and political affiliations of a European. Whatever the constitutional powers of the government, it ought not to deprive a man of liberty and happiness without being sure after a thorough and impartial investigation, such as a judge and jury in open court would afford, that the alien actually falls within a proscribed class. It is popular to defend the present arbitrary methods on the ground that he is only an alien; if he wants to acquire a home here, why does he not become naturalized? He cannot be naturalized for five years, and even after that time his omission ought not to make him an outlaw. He should not be dragooned into citizenship, and incidentally citizens acquired through pressure are not always desirable. A foreigner often has honest and even praiseworthy motives for retaining his old loyalties. He may desire to return to his birthplace in his old age after he has saved a competence by building roads and railways for us, or as in the case of most Russians in our midst before 1917, he may be waiting

[8] Fong Yue Ting v. U. S., 149 U. S. 698, 730 (1892).
[9] Dissenting opinion in same case, 759.

here with the hope that a tyranny at home will be overthrown. Surely, we do not reproach Americans who spend their lives in England or France without renouncing their allegiance. Why should we regard similar conduct by foreigners in this country as worse than crime, for even criminals would not receive such harsh and summary treatment? We have no business to act and talk as if we owed absolutely nothing to our unnaturalized immigrants. Most of them were brought in at the earnest desire of the very persons and corporations that are now loudly calling for more deportations. For years these foreigners have done our dirty work, and we might at least give them a jury trial before we throw them out neck and heels. Have we no confidence in our own institution? Every alien must expect to be expelled, if he furnishes legal cause, just as he must expect to be punished for an offense, but in each case we should be proud as citizens of a free land to furnish him the best legal machinery we can devise to ascertain whether or not the ground for governmental action really exists.

Let us now look more closely at the method which we actually employ to determine the political and economic views of an alien. Is it equivalent to a jury trial? Even that, I have tried to show, is a hazardous means for the investigation of another man's words and opinions, and often liable to err, but it is the best practicable means if we are going to inquire into those facts at all. What are the chances of error in the present deportation tribunals?

This can be best determined from a consideration of the actual practice as described by Judge Holt of the United States District Court for Southern New York: [10]

There are a number of officers called inspectors of immigration, connected with the office of the commissioner. Complaint that an alien is in this country in violation of law is usually made by one of these inspectors. The information upon which he bases the charge may have been obtained by himself upon

[10] Bosny *v.* Williams, 185 Fed. 598 (1911); see also Immigration Rules of May 1, 1917, Rule 22.

THE DEPORTATIONS 237

investigation, or may have been furnished to him by others. Frequently such information is furnished by the city police, or by enemies of the person charged, acting through malice or revenge. Affidavits are obtained and are sent by the inspector to the Secretary at Washington, who, if he thinks a proper case is made out, issues a warrant for the arrest of the persons charged. This warrant is usually intrusted for execution to the inspector who has made the charge, and he subsequently usually takes entire charge of the case. After the aliens have been taken to Ellis Island, they are held in seclusion and not permitted to consult counsel until they are first examined by the inspector, under oath, and their answers taken by a stenographer. After this preliminary inquisition has proceeded as far as the inspector wishes, the aliens are then informed that they are entitled to have counsel, and to give any evidence they wish in respect to the charge. Thereafter a further hearing is had before the inspector, at which further evidence may be given by him, and the aliens may appear by counsel and offer evidence in their own behalf. The inspector thereupon reports whether in his opinion guilt has been established, and the evidence taken and the inspector's finding are sent to the Secretary of Commerce and Labor at Washington, who thereupon makes an order either for the deportation or the release of the aliens. It is, of course, obvious that such a method of procedure disregards almost every fundamental principle established in England and this country for the protection of persons charged with an offense. The person arrested does not necessarily know who instigated the prosecution. He is held in seclusion, and is not permitted to consult counsel until he has been privately examined under oath. The whole proceeding is usually substantially in the control of one of the inspectors, who acts in it as informer, arresting officer, inquisitor, and judge. The Secretary who issues the order of arrest and the order of deportation is an administrative officer who sits hundreds of miles away, and never sees or hears the person proceeded against or the witnesses.

The proceedings are in secret. The public is excluded, so is the press, so are the alien's wife and children. His inability to speak English and the inspector's frequent inability to speak anything else make the record unsatisfactory, but the Secretary of Labor sees nothing else. Furthermore, this record is often made by the inspector himself, and he may stop it whenever he wishes, after a good case is made out. Like a policeman, like a district attorney, it is his business to get results. Unless the alien is represented by counsel there is some chance that matter in defense will not get on the record.[11] While he has a right to ask for counsel at such stage in the proceedings as the inspector shall deem proper, being defenseless until then, he is not, like a criminal, entitled to receive counsel at the expense of the government. Furthermore, the alien who does not speak English and is shut up on an island, often ignorant and out of funds, does not readily obtain a lawyer on his own initiative. Thus he may be rigorously cross-examined in the absence of counsel, not only on what he did and said, but on what he thinks. The proceedings are rarely reported in the newspapers, not being open, so that public opinion cannot easily be focussed on an unjust case. Once the alien is deported, all mistakes and wrongs are covered by the intervening ocean.

"If this," said Justice Brewer,[12] "be not a star chamber proceeding of the most stringent sort, what more is necessary to make it one?"

The alien has two slight possibilities of relief from a wrong decision of the inspector. The review by the Secretary of Labor has already been shown by Judge Holt to be inadequate, because the Secretary never sees the alien or the witnesses, but only the record, which was made up by the very person whose finding is attacked. Moreover, the Secretary of Labor determines and enforces the policy of the government in respect to deportations. Congress should refuse in so serious a matter to make a man final judge in his own cause. Secondly, the alien may in rare instances obtain a write of *habeas corpus*, which will bring his case before a United States judge. This remedy is very limited, for the conclusions and orders of the immigration officials can be attacked by judicial proceedings only if it is shown " that the proceedings were manifestly unfair, that the action of

[11] Low Wah Suey v. Backus, 225 U. S. 460 (1912), holds valid the rule denying counsel until after the preliminary hearing.
[12] U. S. v. Ju Toy, 198 U. S. 253, 268 (1905).

the executive officers was such as to prevent a fair investigation, or that there was a manifest abuse of the discretion committed to them by the statute;"[13] or if there was an error of law, for instance, in construing the statutory definition of some deportable class. In the absence of fraud, a finding of fact will be reversed only when there is a complete absence of evidence to justify it. So long as there is any evidence at all in its support, no matter how overwhelmingly this is outweighed by the testimony on behalf of the alien, a court cannot interfere.

The risks of grave injustice under this system are shown by a recent case.[14] A Canadian woman in northern New York, who had always earned her own living and owned several hundred dollars, part of it in local real estate, beside having well-to-do relatives, was ordered to be deported as a person "likely to become a public charge." The evidence showed that the alien had excited the jealousy of a married woman by receiving from her husband lessons in bicycle riding evenings, and it was suggested that the wife might sue this woman for alienation of his affections, and might in this suit take all her property and leave her without means of support. Also the woman might be prosecuted on a criminal charge, and eventually imprisoned at public expense. On these facts the immigration inspector arrested her and ordered her deportation, and his decision was affirmed by the Secretary of Labor. Obviously the whole case was framed up by a personal enemy, as many cases against radicals may have been framed up during this past winter. In this instance the alien was released by the court, because there was not a single fact to support the finding, but if there had been a scintilla of evidence the judge could have done nothing. Injustice of this kind may easily occur without any corruption on the part of the inspector if he is zealous in enforcing the deportation law and anxious to

[13] Low Wah Suey v. Backus, *supra*, 468; Gegiow v. Uhl, 239 U. S. 3.
[14] *Ex parte* Mitchell, 256 Fed. 229 (1919). See Post, Deportations Testimony, 80, 247, for other framed-up cases.

gratify the eagerness of his superior officers and satisfy the incessant demand of influential newspapers and organizations [15] for a high record of expulsions.

"In the administration of preventive justice," wrote James Madison, "the following principles have been held sacred: that some probable ground of suspicion be exhibited before some judicial authority, that it be supported by oath or affirmation; that the party may avoid being thrown into confinement, by finding pledges or sureties for his legal conduct sufficient in the judgment of some judicial authority, that he may have the benefit of a writ of habeas corpus, and thus obtain his release if wrongfully confined; and that he may at any time be discharged from his recognizance, or his confinement, and restored to his former liberty and rights, on the order of the proper judicial authority."

All these principles he declared to be violated by the Alien Act of 1798.[16] They are violated even more by the Alien Act of 1918. The hated statute of 1798 was a temporary measure called forth by impending war, and provided that the foreigner should first be served with a notice and given time to depart voluntarily. Only if he failed to do so was he arrested. Of this statute Madison said, "If a banishment of this sort be not a punishment, and among the severest of punishments, it will be difficult to imagine a doom to which the name can be applied." The Act of 1918 is a permanent measure, and provides for immediate arrest, confinement, and expulsion, without notice, or opportunity to close up one's affairs and embark freely. Even if such procedure has been declared constitutional, it is nevertheless dangerous that it can be inflicted with practically no judicial safeguards, "on mere suspicion, by the single will of an executive magistrate, on persons convicted of no prison offense against the laws of the land."

[15] See, for instance, the constant complaints that deportations are few, in the weekly letter issued by the President of the National Founders' Association, who has suggested that the entire administration of the law be transferred from the Secretary of Labor to the Attorney General. Such a transfer would probably involve sweeping changes in personnel among immigration inspectors.

[16] Act of June 25, 1798, c. 63; Madison's Report on the Virginia Resolutions, 4 Ell. Deb. (2 ed.) 581, 582.

III. *The Raids of January*, 1920

You may take my word for it, my dear Viceroy, that if we do not use this harsh weapon with the utmost care and scruple— *always, where the material is dubious, giving the suspected man the benefit of the doubt*—you may depend upon it, I say, that both you and I will be called to severe account, even by the people who are now applauding us (quite rightly) for vigor.—MORLEY, to Lord Minto, on deportation from India.

Such is the machinery which Attorney General Palmer has set in motion to bring thousands of radicals within the provisions of the Alien Act of 1918. Powerful as this machinery is, it is subjected by the law to three limitations in the interest of liberty. (1) The Act provides that arrest must be on a warrant signed by the Secretary of Labor, and the issue of the warrant is carefully regulated by the Immigration Rules.[17] (2) A house or a meeting-hall cannot be searched, and papers or other property cannot be seized, even with a search-warrant, for there is no law which authorizes the issue of a search-warrant in deportation proceedings.[18] (3) The alien must be given a fair admistra-

---

[17] Immigration Rules, 1917, Rule 22, Subd. 3. "*Application for warrant of arrest.* The application must state facts showing prima facie that the alien comes within one or more of the classes subject to deportation after entry, and . . . should be accompanied by some substantial supporting evidence. . . . If based upon statements of persons not sworn officers of the Government . . . the application should be accompanied by the affidavit of the person. . . . Telegraph application may be resorted to only in case of necessity, or when some substantial interest of the Government would be subserved thereby, and must state (a) that the usual written application is being forwarded by mail, and (b) the substance of the facts and proof therein contained. . . ."

[18] The subject of unreasonable searches and seizures will be discussed in the next chapter. There are some statements that the Fourth Amendment does not apply to deportation proceedings, Fong Yue Ting *v.* U. S., 149 U. S. 698, 730 (1893); *Re* Chin Wah, 182 Fed. 256 (1910), but the contrary has been held in a much cited case, U. S. *v.* Wong Quong Wong, 94 Fed. 832 (1899). See also Moy Wing Sun *v.* Prentis, 234 Fed. 24 (C. C. A. 1916). In Weeks *v.* U. S., 232 U. S. 392 (1914), Day, J., said of the Fourth Amendment: "This protection reaches all alike, whether accused of crime or not"; and in *Ex parte* Jackson, 96 U. S. 727 (1877), it was applied to administrative opening of the mails. It is inconceivable that the Amendment has no application to non-

tive trial, in accordance with the Rules. (4) The deportation laws apply only to aliens.

It is also some mitigation of the drastic features of this machinery that it has been entrusted by Congress, not to the Department of Justice which is engaged in the prosecution of crime, but to that Department which was created " to foster, promote, and develop the welfare of the wage earners of the United States," and is daily concerned with aiding millions of human beings, many of them poor, comparatively helpless, and unacquainted with our language and institutions. The Department of Justice may furnish legal advice or lend its agents for use under the control of the Department of Labor, but it has no more legal right or power to deal with the expulsion of aliens than has the Department of the Interior.

The raids of January, 1920, have been fully described in the opinion of Judge George W. Anderson in the Colyer case. This book will therefore only discuss briefly the extent to which the four principles of personal liberty just stated have been observed and the relative shares which the Departments of Justice and Labor have taken in these raids. My discussion is not based upon the evidence of aliens or journalists, however credible, but upon the statements of

criminal proceedings though of course the test of what is reasonable is different. *In re* Pacific Ry. Com'n, 32 Fed. 241, 251 (1887); I. C. C. *v.* Brimson, 154 U. S. 447, 478 (1894).

Moreover, searches and seizures without search-warrant violate the "due process" clause of the Fifth Amendment, except a few special cases like searching the *person* only of a man arrested for a *crime*. A warrant of arrest does not authorize search. And the Secretary of Labor has no power to issue search-warrants in immigration proceedings under any Act of Congress. Only a warrant issued by a court (under U. S. Comp. Stat., 1918, § 1239; Stern *v.* Remick, 164 Fed. 781) can make legal searches and seizures of the property of an alien not charged with crime, and no statute authorizes immigration officials to obtain a judicial search-warrant in the absence of judicial proceedings. No lawful search can be made in immigration proceedings with or without a search-warrant. Therefore, it seems probable that all the evidence seized in the recent raids cannot be used by the government, Silverthorne Lumber Co. *v.* U. S., 40 Sup. Ct. 182 (1920); and that actions for damages can be brought. Illegal searches and seizures were a ground for the release of an I.W.W. in *Ex parte* Jackson, 263 Fed. 110 (1920), and of Communists in the Colyer case.

THE DEPORTATIONS

sworn officials of the United States, and so far as possible upon the testimony of Attorney General Palmer.[19]

"Appreciating," he says, "that the criminal laws of the United States were not adequate to properly handle the radical situation, the Department of Justice held several conferences with the officials of the Department of Labor and came to an agreeable arrangement for the carrying out of the ' deportation statute.' " Whether the Secretary of Labor, William B. Wilson, and the Assistant Secretary, Louis F. Post, were informed of the " plans laid by the Department of Justice for the apprehension of members of the Communist Party and the Communist Labor Party," he does not state. The officials with whom he was in close co-operation were the third ranking officer, Mr. J. W. Abercrombie, a member of Mr. Palmer's Department detailed to serve as solicitor to the Department of Labor and vested with the powers of Acting Secretary when his superiors were absent or otherwise occupied, and Mr. A. Caminetti, the Commissioner General of Immigration, whose relations with Mr. Post have long been strained. Mr. Abercrombie signed 3,000 warrants for the arrest of persons alleged by affidavits of Mr. Palmer's agents to be members of the two Communist parties. Mr. Caminetti instructed the immigration officials that the aliens covered by the warrants would be arrested simultaneously by the Department of Justice and " held on local charges " until the officials had served the warrants that night or the following day. The agents would assist in serving warrants, perfecting detention arrangements, and providing evidence, but they could not legally conduct the deportation hearings, since this duty was delegated by statute to the immigration inspectors.

The character of the raids is best shown by the Instructions issued by Mr. Palmer's Bureau of Investigation to his

[19] Palmer Deportations Testimony; Post Deportations Testimony; testimony and instructions of government officials in Report upon the Illegal Practices of the United States Department of Justice, by 12 lawyers, Natl. Popular Govt. League, Wash., May, 1920; opinion of Judge G. W. Anderson in Colyer and Katzeff *v.* Skeffington, 265 Fed. 17 (cited hereafter as Colyer opinion). The only sentence based on an unofficial source is that on Detroit conditions.

Secret Service men throughout the country. Those in New England are reproduced in Judge Anderson's opinion. A slightly different form is reprinted on the front page of the *New York Times*, January 3, 1920:

INSTRUCTIONS

Our activities will be directed against the radical organizations, known as the Communist Party of America and the Communist Labor Party of America, also known as Communists.

The strike will be made promptly and simultaneously at 8:30 P.M. in all districts. The meeting places of the Communists in your territory, and the names and addresses of the officers and heads that you are to arrest, are on the attached lists.

You will also arrest all active members where found.

Particular efforts should be made to apprehend all the officers, irrespective of where they may be, and with respect to such officers, their residence should be searched and in every instance all literature, membership cards, records and correspondence are to be taken.

When a citizen is arrested as a communist, he must be present with the officers searching his home at the time of the search.

Meeting rooms should be thoroughly searched.

Locate and obtain the charter. All records, if not found in the meeting rooms, will probably be found in the home of the recording secretary or financial secretary, but in every instance, if possible, records should be found and taken.

All literature, books, papers, pictures on the walls of the meeting places, should be gathered together and tagged with tags which will be supplied you, with the name and address of the person by whom obtained and where obtained.

In searching meeting places, a thorough search should be made and the walls sounded.

It is an order of the Government that violence to those apprehended should be scrupulously avoided.

Immediately upon the apprehension of the alien, or citizen, search him thoroughly. If found in groups in a meeting room, they should be lined up against the wall and searched. Particular efforts should be made to obtain membership cards on the persons who are taken.

Make an absolute search of the individual. No valuables, such as jewelry and monies, to be taken away from those arrested.

After a search has been made of the person arrested you

THE DEPORTATIONS

will take all the evidence you have obtained from his person and place it in an envelope, which will be furnished you, placing the name, address, contents of the envelope, by whom taken and where on the outside of the envelope and deliver to me with the alien.

Everybody will remain on duty until relieved, without exception.

Flashlights, string, tags and envelopes should be carried, as per instructions.

In searching rooms of an alien pay particular attention to everything in the room and make a thorough search thereof.

You are also warned to take notice "that no violence is to be used."

You will communicate with me by telephone from your several districts, the number of the telephone herewith given.

Attached you will find a list of those to be apprehended in your district and you will also apprehend all those found arrested with these names at the time of the arrest, whom you find to be active members of the Communist party.

You are also instructed to use reasonable care and good judgment.

It is too early to write an account of the methods in which Mr. Palmer's agents carried out his Instructions, but I give the following authenticated facts.

First, aliens and citizens found in a Communist hall on the night of raids, whether they were members of the organization or not, were seized without any warrant whatever. In New England alone a hundred such persons were imprisoned for several days while the officials telegraphed for warrants to cover them, and hundreds more were not released for many hours. The Attorney General testifies on the nation-wide situation:

Where the aliens were assembled at their meeting places and an actual meeting of the Communist Party was in progress the agents of the Department of Justice did take into custody all aliens attending that meeting. It is quite likely that warrants had not been obtained for all such persons, but it is sufficient, it seems to me, that when an alien is apprehended in the commission of the unlawful act that the action of the government officer taking him into custody is warranted. Certainly it could be claimed that if the government officers had visited a meeting place and had permitted aliens found there for whom warrants had not been previously obtained to depart, that they had been derelict in their duty.

The Attorney General also states that when persons applied at the Hartford jail to see their friends who had been arrested at a Communist meeting, the visitors were properly arrested and locked up in the jail; for their coming to inquire was *prima facie* evidence of affiliation with the Communist Party.[20]

Mr. Palmer's contention is that his agents faced the same situation as a policeman who witnesses a robbery. If he goes to the station house for a warrant the offender will vanish. His agents "did the safe thing" in arresting every alien apparently a Communist. This analogy is clearly unsound. For many crimes a warrant is necessary to arrest, and a deportable alien is not a criminal at all. Neither he nor a citizen can be deprived of his liberty upon considerations of expediency which are not the law of the land. Congress makes that law, and has explicitly required that the alien shall be taken into custody " upon the warrant of the Secretary of Labor."

Secondly, the prisoners' property was overhauled and seized without search-warrants. The Chief of the Bureau of Investigation did direct his subordinates to apply to the local authorities for warrants " if you find it is absolutely necessary "; and the Attorney General states, " In every instance where practicable search-warrants were procured from either city authorities or the United States commissioner." He points to no law authorizing such warrants for papers, and none existed except possibly in states where Communists fall within anti-anarchy acts. Of course, warrants for the seizure of concealed weapons give no right to seize papers. No proof has been given by the government in the Colyer case or elsewhere that search-warrants were ob-

[20] Palmer Deportations Testimony, 69, 76, 115.

THE DEPORTATIONS 247

tained in these raids. Mr. Palmer also says, " In no instance can it be shown that any person or place was searched over the objection of the individual." Naturally an ignorant alien confronted by a posse of detectives at night would hesitate to object to anything. Moreover, Mr. Palmer's statement that consent was a prerequisite to search is contradicted by the peremptory language of the Instructions and the testimony of his agents. Except in the case of educated English-speaking aliens like the Colyers, there is no evidence that the agents paused before ransacking halls and houses for documentary evidence connected with Communism.

The justification urged is that this valuable evidence of membership would have been destroyed if not seized. Of course, no government has ever made an illegal search unless it expected to find something useful. If searches in deportation proceedings, with or without warrant, are necessary, they must be authorized by Congress and not by the Attorney General.

Thirdly, the hearings by the immigration inspectors were often unfair. This was in large measure due, not to the fault of the inspectors, but to the unprecedented pressure of work and the absence of adequate protection for the rights of the alien. For nearly a year before the raids aliens had been entitled to counsel throughout the deportation hearings. The old procedure described in this chapter, which deprived them of counsel during the important preliminary hearings, while not unconstitutional, was considered so harsh by Secretary Wilson that he abolished it. On December 29, 1919, just four days before the raids and during the Secretary's illness, the old harsh rule was revived. The Attorney General does not deny that this change was made through the efforts of the Department of Justice, and defends it on the ground that the examination of an alien, when under the advice of counsel, " got us nowhere." The fact remains that the Secretary of Labor had thought counsel desirable, and it was for him and not the Attorney General to fix the Immigration Rules. As soon as Mr. Wilson and Mr. Abercrombie (who had inadvertently approved the change without appreciating its effect) realized what was happening, they restored the right to counsel, but this was not until January 27, after most of the examinations were completed. Meanwhile, until the hearings were practically closed, the inspectors heard the evidence without the help of counsel for the defense, and on the other hand, for the first time in the experience of immigration officials (at least in New England), an agent of the Department of Justice was present through every hearing. The alien stood alone before an administrative official, confronted by a member of the force of detectives who had sworn out the warrant against him and accomplished his arrest. Thus the government after issuing warrants for the arrest of 3,000 persons suddenly repealed a rule so as to affect those specific persons and deprive them of rights which were guaranteed to them, not indeed by the Constitution, but by the existing law of the land.

The value of the evidence obtained in this way was also materially affected by the treatment which the aliens underwent before and during their trials. The police dragged many men out of their homes in the dead of night. The aliens, none of them under any criminal charge and many of them held without warrants, were taken on trains and through the streets in handcuffs and chains.[21] The prisoners were herded in vastly overcrowded quarters without sufficient clothing and food. For instance, the Mayor of Detroit described as "intolerable in a civilized city" conditions in the police "bull pen," a room 24 by 30 feet, where over a hundred men were kept for a week. Bail was often fixed at very high amounts; for instance, $10,000, although $500 is the normal sum specified in the Immigration Rules. The men arrested were separated for days from their wives and children, who were left without support by the government.

[21] Palmer Deportations Testimony, 115. On Detroit, Barkley, *infra* note 27. On Boston, Colyer opinion.

THE DEPORTATIONS

Instead, they were, Mr. Palmer assures us,[22] "looked after by the most prominent charitable organization of their own creed in their locality. It is no part of the Attorney General's duty to look after the families of the violators of our laws." The Supreme Court has declared repeatedly that aliens held for expulsion are not criminals.[23] This apology recalls the British General Dyer, the hero of Amritsar, who found shooting into a crowd a still more satisfactory way to get rid of sedition, and remarked that picking up the wounded was no affair of his—that was the business of the hospitals.

The men deported on the "Buford" were torn from their families, who still remain in America.

The public approval of these raids rests on a belief that all the thousands of men arrested were dangerous foreigners who advocated violence. Yet the daily press shows the eventual release for want of evidence of over a third of those seized. And a cursory glance at Mr. Palmer's Instructions shows that the character of an individual had absolutely nothing whatever to do with his arrest. The most harmless person was to be seized if suspected of membership in the specified political parties. And although there was no law authorizing the arrest of citizens, these instructions direct that all Communists shall be seized, expressly including citizens. Elsewhere it is ordered that if citizens are arrested "through error," they shall be referred to the local authorities. Thus United States officials would arrest American citizens for prosecution under the harsh state anti-anarchy acts.

That the President of the United States can have authorized these measures seems impossible. It is astonishing that the Attorney General and the Acting Secretary of Labor should have carried through the greatest executive restriction of personal liberty in the history of this country during the President's illness. Even so the British Cabinet took ad-

[22] See his circular letter in 110 *Nation* 190 (February 14, 1920).
[23] *E.g.*, Fong Yue Ting *v.* U. S., 149 U. S. 730 (1893).

vantage of the illness of their head, Lord Chatham, to make one of the worst onslaughts on freedom in modern England, the expulsion of Wilkes from the House of Commons in 1768. Macaulay's Second Essay on Chatham gives the facts.

> His colleagues for a time continued to entertain the expectation that his health would soon be restored, and that he would emerge from his retirement. But month followed month, and still he remained in mysterious seclusion. . . . They at length ceased to hope or to fear anything from him; and, though he was still nominally Prime Minister, took without scruple steps which they knew to be diametrically opposed to all his opinions and feelings.

The sequel to the raids made it plain that hardly a single alien then arrested by the Department of Justice would be deported. In the absence of the President, a sharp conflict between Mr. Palmer and the Department of Labor soon developed. Secretary Wilson released all the aliens imprisoned as members of the Communist Labor Party, holding that organization not to be within the deportation statute. Many of those arrested as members of the Communist Party were released by Assistant Secretary Post because their membership was not proved, and Judge Anderson in the Colyer case decided after an exhaustive survey of the New England raids that (1) many of the aliens who were ordered deported must be discharged for want of a fair trial; (2) even those who had a fair trial must be discharged because the Communist Party does not advocate " force and violence." If his decision is affirmed by the Supreme Court, nobody can be deported merely because of membership in either party. Consequently every alien seized in the raids must be released except the few who personally advocated the overthrow of the government by violence.

Meanwhile, when Mr. Abercrombie went away, Mr. Post had taken charge of deportation matters. He soon became convinced that many of the recommendations of the immigration inspectors and Mr. Caminetti for the deportation of

THE DEPORTATIONS

aliens were not in accordance with the evidence obtained at the hearings, and therefore canceled the warrants of arrest in these cases. This action aroused the indignation of Mr. Palmer and several members of the Immigration Committee of the House of Representatives. A House Resolution looking toward impeachment was referred to the Rules Committee, which heard the testimony of both Mr. Post and Mr. Palmer, but took no action before Congress adjourned.

Mr. Post pointed out that the power to determine whether an alien should be deported was vested by law in the Secretary of Labor and his deputies, and not in the Commissioner General of Immigration. The belief that the aliens discharged were dangerous revolutionists was derived from Mr. Caminetti's summaries, which were merely advisory, and not from the actual records of the hearings, which were often very different. It was Mr. Post's duty to decide each case upon the evidence and he had done so. When there was doubt as to the alien's guilt, the humanity of the situation might properly enter into his decision. Although deportation proceedings are not criminal in nature, he had drawn from the criminal law those principles which recognize the rights of the individual and especially his right to a fair decision whether or not he is guilty. The issue is, not whether those aliens who violate the law shall be deported, for he is deporting them, but whether those who have not violated the law shall be deported.

Mr. Palmer's position is this. While he has not " the slightest fear that any revolutionary movement can succeed in this country, even to the extent of seriously menacing our institutions," there was in 1919 a great deal of revolutionary agitation which led to several attacks on federal officials and other violence, and might easily have led to more. The best way to keep order was to attack the spreaders of agitation by means of the deportation statute. The raids caused a marked cessation of revolutionary activities, and the two organizations affected were completely broken by the Department of Justice. Now this same agitation has taken a new lease of life because of the decisions of Secretary Wilson and Mr. Post, which in Mr. Palmer's opinion are "neither based upon fact nor upon law."

Upon this position, which I have tried to state with absolute fairness, three comments may be made. First, it raises the fundamental issue discussed in the preceding chapter, how far violent acts can wisely be prevented by the suppression of violent talk. Secondly, the particular method of suppression used by the Attorney General was placed by law under the control of another Department, but the facts of the raids leave no doubt that the deportation machinery during the arrests and the hearings was very substantially directed and operated by the Department of Justice. If the Department of Labor has not properly administered the law, the duty to "care that the laws be faithfully executed" is vested, not in the Attorney General, but in the President. Finally, although it is undoubtedly true that the laws requiring warrants for arrest, forbidding searches, and allowing counsel make deportation more difficult, even in the case of dangerous revolutionists, every rule in the interest of personal liberty necessarily diminishes the efficiency of government. Mr. Palmer adopted the attitude of the men he denounced. Because the law hindered the result he wished to accomplish and thought desirable, he disregarded the law.

IV. *The Arrest of American Citizens for Deportation*

The American people ought to be startled out of their complacent acquiescence in these raids by the confinement of hundreds of their fellow-citizens in jails, without the slightest charge of crime or possibility of such charge under any law of the United States. The government actually contends that it has the right to issue so-called alien warrants, which state no evidence or facts whatever beyond a perfunctory repetition of clauses of the Deportation Act, and yet are the only substitute for an indictment in these proceedings, against any individuals, whether aliens or naturalized citizens or native-born citizens, arresting them whenever and wherever found, and holding them in custody until the question of citizenship is decided by the immigration authorities. It contends that a court has no jurisdiction to release an American citizen who has never been out of his native country from Deer Island or Ellis Island, or any other deportation jail, until the immigration official and the Secretary of Labor on appeal have denied his citizenship. Experience in the Chinese cases shows that these proceedings frequently last for many months. "It follows that on the theory now urged the right of native-born citizens to liberty, perhaps for months, lies at the mercy of the immigration authorities," and that even after the order of deportation is finally issued against the citizen, he cannot obtain the right from a court to remain in this country unless the proceedings were manifestly unfair or otherwise illegal.[24]

The case of Peter Frank, an American citizen of Swampscott, Massachusetts, is typical. The warrant of arrest, which he never saw, began, "Whereas from evidence submitted to me, it appears that the alien, Peter Frank, who landed at an unknown port on or about the 1st day of January, 1919," and went on to charge membership in the stereotyped words of the statute in six kinds of violent organizations, without naming a single one or describing it concretely. All the Boston warrants were in just this form. It was impossible for him to tell from it with what he was really charged. Moreover, no address or other identification of Frank was given, so that there was nothing to show that another man of the same name in another city was not intended. In his petition for *habeas corpus*, which was verified by the evidence, Frank states that he was born in Ohio and was always a citizen; that four days previously immigration officers broke into his house at one o'clock in the morning, arrested him, searched his house and carried off

[24] Peter Frank *v.* Henry J. Skeffington, Commissioner, unreported opinion of G. W. Anderson, J., (D. Mass., January 27, 1920).

papers, confined him in the Lynn police station and on Deer Island, refused to allow friends or counsel to visit him, and ejected from the immigration office the man who started judicial proceedings in his behalf. Nevertheless, Commissioner Skeffington still contended that Frank was an alien, and that the burden of proof was on him to establish citizenship. The only evidence which was offered to justify his confinement was a questionnaire, on which Frank had answered that he was born in Cincinnati and was not a member of either the Communist or Socialist party or any other organization, but the Shoe Workers' Union. At the end of this paper the government had stencilled, " I, the undersigned, not a citizen of the United States, on oath depose, etc.," and Frank had hastily signed without crossing out the " not." On this flimsy fact the immigration officials kept him five days in jail until against their will he was discharged by Judge George W. Anderson.

The Departments of Justice and Labor were baffled in this case, where there was absolutely no evidence that the prisoner was an alien, but they have not abandoned their main contention that the Secretary of Labor has absolute power, where citizenship turns upon a disputed fact like marriage, parentage, or place of birth, to confine a man who really is a citizen for months and then order him deported on a finding that he is not a citizen. And they are right that Congress has actually conferred this power, and that it makes no difference under the statute if the Secretary of Labor makes a mistake and classifies a man as an alien who is actually a citizen, for " the decision of the Secretary of Labor shall be final." The citizen is forbidden by Congress to appeal to the courts to correct the mistake of fact and prevent his banishment into places beyond the seas. It is, of course, possible that such a construction of this sentence would be held by the Supreme Court to conflict with the " due process " clause of the Constitution. It would seem that since the Constitution forbids an administrative official to deport any one but an alien without judicial proceedings, the Secretary is simply hauling himself up by his bootstraps when he decides that a citizen is within his jurisdiction and deportable. Nevertheless, the Supreme Court has already allowed him to make almost the same sort of decision under similar statutory language in United States *v.* Ju Toy.[25] That case permitted the Secretary to deport a Mongolian on a finding of fact that he was born in China, regardless of the decision of a court on *habeas corpus* that he was a native-born American citizen returning from a trip to China. On citizenship as on other questions, the Secretary can be reversed only if there is error of law or an absolute lack of evidence, or if the person to be deported does not receive a fair hearing.[26] It may be that the Ju Toy case will be limited not to apply to deportation after entry, but this cannot be predicted with any confidence. Enough has been said to indicate the possibility, under the present statutory and administrative machinery of deportation, of prolonged vexations for American citizens and even permanent exile.

It is all very well to say that only Communist citizens run this risk anyway, and that they and Chinese citizens have "no rights that a white man is bound to respect." The Frank case shows that the government officials were ready enough to confine a citizen who is not a Communist, and he was only one out of many in the recent raids.[27] Moreover, there is nothing in the Deportation Act of 1918 to limit the Secretary to Communists. As I shall show shortly, he may begin to break up other organizations by wholesale deportation of their members, both aliens and citizens whose citizenship is officially denied. Some native-born members of the American Federation of Labor may find a future Sec-

[25] 198 U. S. 253 (1905).

[26] *E.g.,* Chin Yow *v.* U. S., 208 U. S. 8 (1908). The Ju Toy case was held not to apply to deportations, Moy Suey *v.* U. S., 147 Fed. 697 (C. C. A., 1906); U. S. *v.* Low Hong, 261 Fed. 73 (C. C. A., 1919).

[27] F. R. Barkley, "Jailing Radicals in Detroit," 110 *Nation* 136 (January 31, 1920); Palmer Deportations Testimony, 109, 111; Colyer opinion.

retary of Labor ruling (1) that their association advocates the overthrow of the government by force and violence and (2) that they are aliens. So long as there is any evidence, however much outweighed, to support these two findings, the statute is plain, and allows them no remedy.

V. *A Review of the Actual Cases of Radicals Held for Deportation*

The public is therefore in error in assuming that only foreigners have been seized for deportation. It is also wrong in thinking that the aliens who have been arrested are all dangerous characters. Some of those expelled to Europe have undoubtedly been turbulent persons like Emma Goldman, but not all the persons who are held to come within the Deportation Act of 1918 are of the same sort. In order to make it plain just what kind of men the government wants to deport, I shall review the actual decisions relating to three types of radical aliens, Communists, Industrial Workers of the World, and anarchists.

(1) Communists—Guilt by Association and Government Spies

The Communist Labor Party and the Communist Party, which were the chief objective of the recent raids, seceded from the Socialist Party in September, 1919, taking with them several state Socialist organizations, and a very large number of left-wing Socialists.[28] Mr. Gordon Watkins, of the University of Illinois, reports the following estimates of the size of the three parties: Socialist Party after the secession, 39,000; Communist Labor Party, 10,000 to 30,000; Communist Party, 30,000 to 60,000, of whom 25,000 belong to foreign-language federations which are predominantly Russian in their constituency. The Secretary of Labor has ruled that all the aliens in the Communist Party are *ipso*

[28] Gordon S. Watkins, "The Present Status of Socialism in the United States," 124 *Atlantic Monthly* 821 (December, 1919).

THE DEPORTATIONS

facto liable to deportation under the Act of 1918, as members of or affiliated with an " organization that entertains a belief in, teaches or advocates the overthrow by force or violence of the government of the United States."[29] The Attorney General's Instructions evidently take the same view of the Communist Labor Party. Consequently, a card from either party found on any alien furnished the immigration officials with what they called " a perfect case." Nevertheless, Secretary Wilson took a different view of the Communist Labor Party in the Carl Miller case, and Mr. Post in the Truss case ruled that a card was not conclusive proof of membership. Judge Anderson in the Colyer case went still farther, and held that the Communist Party was not an organization within the Act of 1918.

These various decisions raise two questions: (*a*) When does an organization advocate force and violence? (*b*) if it does so, can all its members be justly subjected to painful consequences?

(*a*) The difficulties of the first question have already been pointed out in the preceding chapter, and the Program of the Communist Party affords a practical illustration thereof. Although this Program, which is reprinted in the *American Labor Year-Book* for 1919-20,[30] plainly intends that the proletariat shall " conquer and destroy the bourgeois parliamentary state " and substitute a very different political and economic system, there is not a word which expressly says that the conquest is to be by force and violence. Mr. Wilson, admitting that such a violent purpose is essential to bring the organization within the scope of the Act, finds it inferentially in various passages, which I give below with the omission of two that parallel the first. In the first place he relies on such statements as,

[29] *In re* Engelbert Preis, January 24, 1920, House Judiciary Hearings, 17. All the important administrative decisions are reprinted in House Immigration Hearings.

[30] Edited by Alexander Trachtenberg, published by Rand School of Social Science, N. Y., pp. 416-419. Also in House Judiciary Hearings, 78-80, which contains many other important documents relating to the two Communist parties.

"Participation in parliamentary campaigns, which in the general struggle of the proletariat is of secondary importance, is for the purpose of revolutionary propaganda only." The context, which he does not quote, qualifies the meaning of " revolutionary ":

> Parliamentary representatives of the Communist Party shall not introduce or support reform measures. Parliaments and political democracy shall be utilized to assist in organizing the working class against capitalism and the state. Parliamentary representatives shall consistently expose the oppressive class character of the capitalist state, using the legislative forum to interpret and emphasize the class struggle; they shall make clear how parliamentarism and parliamentary democracy deceive the workers; and they shall analyze the capitalist legislative proposals and reform palliatives as evasions of the issue and as of no fundamental significance to the working class.

The vital issue is plainly to determine what is the primary method which is meant to supersede political processes. Is it violence or is there some other alternative? The Program gives the answer, " The Communist Party shall make the great industrial struggle of the working class its major campaigns." Yet the Secretary decides that this primary method is violence, on the basis of the following extracts from the Party Manifesto:

> The conquest of the power of the state is accomplished by the mass power of the proletariat. Political mass strikes are a vital factor in developing this mass power, preparing the working class for the conquest of capitalism. The power of the proletariat lies fundamentally in its control of the industrial process. The mobilizing of this control against capitalism means the initial form of the revolutionary mass action that will conquer the power of the state.
>
> Mass action is industrial in its origin but it acquires political character as it develops fuller forms. Mass action, in the form of general political strikes and demonstrations, unites the energy and forces of the proletariat, brings proletarian mass pressure upon the bourgeois state. The more general and conscious mass action becomes, the more it antagonizes the bourgeois state, the more it becomes political mass action. Mass action is responsive

THE DEPORTATIONS

to life itself, the form of aggressive proletarian struggle under imperialism. Out of this struggle develops revolutionary mass action, the means for the proletarian conquest of power."

And then, making this violent purpose still more clear in his eyes, he gives this passage from the Manifesto of the Communist International, which the Communist Party is said to accept as a part of its policy:

The revolutionary era compels the proletariat to make use of the means of battle which will concentrate its entire energies, namely, mass action, with its logical resultant, direct conflict with the governmental machinery in open combat. All other methods, such as revolutionary use of bourgeois parliamentarism, will be of only secondary significance.

From these quotations and numerous other statements which he does not quote (and certainly nothing in the organic documents is more favorable to his view than the extracts reprinted by me):

" It is apparent," he says, " that the Communist party is not merely a political party seeking the control of affairs of state, but a revolutionary party seeking to conquer and destroy the state in open combat. And the only conclusion is that the Communist Party of America is an organization that believes in, teaches, and advocates the overthrow by force or violence of the government of the United States."

The last sentence is a complete *non sequitur*. The passages he quotes and the whole Program show that the combat is to be through the proletarian control over industry, which is to be used not merely to secure economic advantages but to put the government in such an uncomfortable position that it will give way to a new kind of government. He lays too much emphasis on the exact wording of the International Manifesto, for although applicants for membership in the Communist Party declare their adherence to the principles and tactics of the Communist International, they are not required to read its manifesto and so cannot be supposed to approve every word. And even if they do, " direct conflict with the governmental machinery in open combat " means lawlessness but not necessarily violent lawlessness. A continuation of the recent coal strike after the injunction would have been just such a conflict without any violence at all. The jargon of Socialism has always been full of such militant phraseology, which does not imply anything more than political and economic effort. " Revolutionary class struggle," " mass power," " mass action," mean big strikes for political ends. Such strikes like any strike might lead to violence, but Secretary Wilson as a former labor leader can hardly hold that advocacy of a strike is *per se* advocacy of force and violence. Objectionable as the purposes of the Communist Party are to all who have faith in our system of representative government and the possibility of progress through public opinion and the ballot, those purposes are not within the Deportation Act of 1918, for they are altogether compatible with the absence of force and violence. The general strike may be more effective against a government than an armed rebellion, and Congress can if it wants make advocacy of the general strike a ground for deportation, but it is not such a ground now. Secretary Wilson is wrong in assuming that non-political methods of overturning a government are necessarily criminal and violent methods. Francis Place, the tailor, overturned the government of England in 1832 and precipitated a revolution which the vote of the electorate had failed to accomplish, simply by posting placards urging the people to start a run on the banks. There is a middle method of political change between the ballot and the bomb, namely economic pressure, and that, however unwise or injurious in nature, is the method of the Communist Party. It advocates the overthrow of our government, but not by force or violence.

Undoubtedly there are men in the Communist Party who would use force to get rid of their opponents. Every party has such men. Billy Sunday preaches, " If I had my way

THE DEPORTATIONS

with these ornery wild-eyed Socialists and I.W.W.'s, I would stand them up before a firing squad and save space on our ships." Guy Empey tells his hearers to get rid of Bolsheviks; "the necessary implements can be obtained at any hardware store." The Republican Secretary of the State of Massachusetts would shoot Bolshevists and traitors every morning, at least in war time, and the next morning he would have a trial to see if they were guilty. But such men do not turn their party into a party of force and violence.

There is no sure test of what a party does advocate. The utterances of a leader may represent only his personal view and be rejected by his associates. Even platforms have never been taken very seriously in any party. The law has got itself into a bad mess by starting investigations into the opinions of associations, the vaguest kind of inquiry imaginable. And certainly the evidence adduced by Secretary Wilson, even if it can be construed as an encouragement of violence, is much more capable of a peaceful interpretation. Until he is sure that the violent construction is actually put upon the words by the members of the party, he is not justified in adopting an interpretation which makes possible the expulsion from their homes of thousands of workingmen in the United States.

The Communist Labor Party is also outside the scope of the Deportation Act. Its Program has the same talk about "the conquest of political power by the workers," "the class struggle," "action of the masses." It favors "the establishment of the Dictatorship of the Proletariat" by making "the great industrial battle its major campaigns, to show the value of the strike as a political weapon." [31] It is a revolutionary working-class party but there is nothing in its Platform or Program which advocates force or violence. As for the ruling of Assistant Attorney General Garvan that

[31] *Ibid.*, pp. 414-416. See Secretary Wilson's opinion in favor of Communist Labor Party, Post Deportations Testimony, 152. Contrast convictions of members under anti-anarchy acts of states.

the two Communist parties violate the Espionage Act because they are " pledged to fight any suggestion of military action by America against the Soviet Russians," [32] the widest construction of that convenient statute has never before extended it to prohibit opposition to war before war is declared.

(b) Even if Secretary Wilson is right in his ruling that some of the tenets of the Communist Party advocate force and violence, it does not necessarily follow that all its members are supporters of violence. It is true that persons joining the Communist Party sign a statement of allegiance to its platform, but this ought not to be taken as conclusive that they favor violence, especially as there is no express mention of violence in that document and the party had not then been declared illegal. The facts show that many persons are affiliated with this party for various innocent reasons. Some believe in peaceful industrial action as the only cure for social ills, some join because their friends do, others without being members of the party frequent its headquarters (and so may be held to be affiliated) to take lessons in physical geography or because the Communist restaurant has better meals at cheap prices than any other place. In Massachusetts, many persons are members of the Communist Party because they belonged to the local state Socialist organization when it seceded last September and turned Communist, and their year's Socialist membership had not yet expired. Many such men fall within Secretary Wilson's ruling just as much as the real revolutionists, very few of whom seem to have been caught. When hundreds were lined up together after the recent raids, the *Times* reported, " They were a tame, unterroristic looking crowd, and their appearance bore out the statements of operatives that not a man had tried to put up a fight." [33]

The idea that guilt is not necessarily personal, but can result from mere association is absolutely abhorrent to every

[32] *New York Times*, January 4, 1920.
[33] Quoted in 21 *New Republic* 232 (January 21, 1920).

THE DEPORTATIONS

American tradition or conception of criminal justice.[34] Therein it differs from the law of Germany. In 1878, after two attempts had been made upon the Emperor's life, Bismarck secured a law " against the generally dangerous efforts of Social Democracy," a party which then advocated the doctrine that the existing capitalistic society must be overthrown by forcible revolution. This law made men offenders, not for anything they individually did or said, but simply by reason of their membership in an association which aimed at the overthrow of the existing order of government or society. The party thrived and prospered under this law as never before. When it was repealed, the party became conservative.[35] Similar legislative measures were adopted in England during the hysteria of the French Revolution against associations which advocated universal manhood suffrage, although as May says, the few men who were really guilty of sedition and treason would have met with no sympathy among a loyal people. A statute was passed suppressing by name the " Societies of United Englishmen, United Scotchmen, United Britons, United Irishmen, and The London Corresponding Society " and enacting that any person who thereafter became or continued a member of any such society should be deemed guilty of an unlawful combination and confederacy and upon conviction might be transported for seven years.[36] Other societies were broken up by a general statute punishing any one concerned in taking oaths to engage in any " seditious purpose." This statute was used nearly forty years later to punish men for membership in a labor union.[37]

May's description of England in 1792 applies to this country in 1920, and should stand as a warning.[38]

---

[34] Alfred Bettman in Hearings before the Committee on Rules, 66th Cong., 2d Sess., on H. Res. 438, Wash., 1920, pp. 125-128.

[35] Ernst Freund, *The Police Power*, 513 note; 2 Stephen's *History of the Criminal Law* 395. Alfred Bettman, *supra*.

[36] 39 Geo. III, c. 79 (1799).

[37] 37 Geo. III, c. 123 (1797); 20 *Columbia L. Rev.* 234 note (February, 1920).

[38] 2 May's *Constitutional History of England*, 32, 33. Aliens are specifically discussed on 156 ff.

In ordinary times the insignificance of these societies would have caused contempt, rather than alarm; but as clubs and demagogues originally not very formidable had obtained a terrible ascendancy in France, they aroused apprehensions out of proportion to their real danger. . . . The Government gave too ready a credence to the reports of their agents; and invested the doings of a small knot of democrats, chiefly workingmen, with the dignity of a widespread conspiracy to overturn the constitution. Ruling over a free State, they learned to treat the people in the spirit of tyrants. Instead of relying upon the sober judgment of the country, they appealed to its fears, and in repressing seditious practices they were prepared to sacrifice liberty of opinion. Their policy, dictated by the circumstances of a time of strange and untried danger, was approved by the prevailing sentiment of their contemporaries, but has not been justified in an age of greater freedom by the maturer judgment of posterity.

Ireland is another country where the policy of guilt by association has been a favorite with the government. In 1825 the Catholic Association, which advocated the admission of Roman Catholics to full civil and political rights, was suppressed by an Act of Parliament declaring unlawful every society acting for more than fourteen days for the purpose of procuring the redress of grievances in church or state, and making membership thereafter a misdemeanor punishable by fine and imprisonment in the discretion of the court. The Catholic Association was dissolved, and its former members started a new society every fourteen days to do exactly the same things. When the statute expired after three years, the Catholic Association immediately revived. In 1829 it was suppressed again by name, but it had accomplished its object of securing Catholic Emancipation.[39] In 1881 the English Cabinet repeated this policy with what Morley, who ought to know, calls " about the most egregious failure in the whole history of exceptional law." Parnell's Land League was suppressed by proclamation under authority of a Coercion Act, and hundreds of suspects, including Parnell himself, were arrested and imprisoned, " but the only effect of these measures was largely to increase agrarian crime in

[39] 6 Geo. IV, c. 4 (1825); 10 Geo. IV, c. 1 (1829); 2 May, *ibid.*, 88-93.

THE DEPORTATIONS

Ireland and to strengthen the malign influence of the instigators to violence who had to some real extent been held in check by the imprisoned leaders." [40]

It is this policy of guilt by association which our government now proposes to imitate. The American policy has always been different. A man has not been visited with legal penalties because he had bad companions. He has not been imprisoned except for acts which he himself did or injurious words which he himself uttered, and he has not been expelled unless after investigation of his individual qualities he was found undesirable. The deportation clauses against radical organizations were practically a dead letter until these raids. Even with treason, the most dangerous crime of all, he is not guilty just because he associates with treasonable persons. Chief Justice Marshall held in the case of Aaron Burr that he must himself commit overt acts of treason.[41] Unless a man is a member of a conspiracy he is not responsible for the acts of others unless they are authorized by him. And no one contends that the two Communist parties are conspiracies. The Supreme Court has just handed down a decision squarely in point.[42] It held unanimously that the president and treasurer of the Philadelphia *Tageblatt* could not lawfully be convicted for items in its columns violating the Espionage Act, which were put in by their associates on the newspaper, since they were in no way responsible for the publications complained of. The same principle applies to the rank and file of the Communist parties.

The deportation statutes introduce the European principle that a man is known by the company he keeps and that guilt is not personal. This is an unprecedented and obnoxious feature of the various syndicalist statutes mentioned in the last chapter, and it is equally obnoxious as a ground for expulsion, which, as I have shown, is in all its practical

---

[40] 44 Vic., c. 4 (1881); 3 May, *ibid.*, 160; Morley's *Recollections*, II, 318.
[41] Beveridge's *Marshall*, III, c. 9.
[42] Schaefer *v.* U. S., 251 U. S. 468; see p. 94, *supra*.

effects equivalent to punishment of the severest kind. These membership clauses in the deportation statutes have never been construed by the Supreme Court, but even if it be held that the power of Congress over aliens is so extensive that expulsion for mere membership in an association without themselves expressing or even holding prohibited opinions is " due process of law " and a permissible abridgment of freedom of speech, nevertheless the clauses are drastic and dangerous.

It would be like some of the obnoxious statutes just mentioned for the Secretary of Labor to rule that the Communist Party is an outlawed organization, and that all aliens who *thereafter* join it or neglect to withdraw are liable to deportation. It is even harsher to expel them because they were members before the ruling. How many can fairly be supposed to have known until then that that party was within the statute? Its violent character was not so obvious that they can fairly be considered to have assumed the risk of such a severe penalty. To impose banishment on them without warning recalls Bentham's complaint that the criminal judges of his time gave laws to the poor just as a man makes laws for his dog. " When your dog does anything you want to break him of, you wait until he does it and then you beat him for it. That is the way you make laws for your dog," and that is the way we are making laws for our radical aliens.

The proposition that men who are personally dangerous must be vigorously dealt with is in no way affected by what I have said about these membership clauses of the deportation statute. Those clauses give administrative officials the right to expel men who are in themselves harmless, and if the free speech and due process clauses do not invalidate them, they are none the less unjust. Burke said in his Speech on the Conciliation of a certain rebellious people, when his opponents wanted a bill " with teeth in it," that you cannot draw an indictment against a whole nation. You cannot draw it against a whole party either. Those Republicans and Democrats who shout for the deportation or imprisonment of the entire Communist Party because of certain clauses in its platform might recover their sense of humor long enough to ask themselves if they ever endorsed every plank in their respective party platforms. Even Congressmen, party leaders, and Presidents have been known to disregard some such principles. Let us deport men for the injuries they do or, if we must, for what they say, but stop condemning them for the grandiose phrases of a party creed.

People seem to think high-handed acts a matter of indifference, so long as the men who suffer are Communists, like the Spanish woman who did not object to watching autos-da-fé because only heretics were burned.[43] But if the Secretary of Labor has final power to decide whether any organization advocates force or violence, if this is an administrative question of fact like an alien's having tuberculosis, then there is no logical reason for him to stop with the Communist parties. As we shall see in the next chapter, a very energetic attempt has been made to put the Socialist Party in the same category. The Non-Partisan League, the American Labor Party, the Committee of 48, have all been called forcible revolutionists. The Western Federation of Miners has been accused of violence. Nor is the American Federation of Labor exempt from such charges. The recent steel strike was frequently denounced as revolutionary, and there is no doubt that the Bridge and Structural Iron Workers have blown up many bridges and buildings.[44] Suppose not only that the law punishes individual members of these organizations who commit or even talk violence, but that a future Secretary of Labor shares the opinions of those who believe that the organizations themselves advocate force and violence. Deportations will follow for the purpose of driving these organizations out of existence.

[43] Ernst Freund in 21 *New Republic* 266 (January 28, 1920).
[44] Hoxie, *Trade-unionism in the United States,* passim.

And even if the wording of the present constitutions of these various bodies makes such a possibility very remote, some future change of language may easily bring any of them within the scope of the statute. Here a very sinister opportunity is afforded to the enemies of any radical organization, whether they be the Federal Government or a state government, unscrupulous employers or a detective agency proceeding on its own initiative, a conservative union or a rival political party. Spies can be sent into the councils of the organization in question, for the purpose of inducing the insertion of violent planks in its constitution. Once this is accomplished, all alien members of the organization are presented with the alternatives of immediate resignation or deportation; to say nothing of the fact that citizen members may face prosecution under a state syndicalism statute or perhaps under a future federal sedition statute like section 10 of the Graham Bill. These clauses in deportation and syndicalist statutes making mere membership a basis for severe penalties render it so easy to destroy any organization in the way I have suggested that the temptation may not be resisted in times of excitement. Indeed, it is believed by Judge Anderson that some of the extreme planks in the Communist Party Platform, to which Secretary Wilson points, may possibly have been inserted in this very manner.

The very existence of spies, whether or not they would thus influence statements of radical principles, is one of the worst evils of sedition legislation, whether directed toward prosecution or deportation. Espionage goes with an Espionage Act. Informers have been the inseparable accompaniment of government action against the expression of opinion since the delators of Tiberius.[45] The state cannot reach such crimes without them. It needs no great force of eavesdroppers to report murders and robberies. The overt act marks the offense, and if a detective is required at all it is either to chase the criminal, to ward off bomb-plots and assassinations, or to discover who is committing especially

[45] Merivale, *The Romans under the Empire*, c. 44.

ingenious thefts. But if political utterances are made criminal, secret police are indispensable to discover that the crime has been committed at all. That was why the original loose Anti-Anarchy Bill introduced in the Massachusetts legislature in 1919 was accompanied by a bill to establish a secret police.[46] The Attorney General was empowered to "make inquiry into any matters concerning the public safety," and for that purpose to employ "officers, agents, or deputies," whose names were known only to him and the governor, and to have at his disposal a fund from which disbursements could be made without audit. When the Anti-Anarchy Bill was made less sweeping, the Secret Police Bill became unnecessary and was dropped.

We do not need to go out of Anglo-Saxon countries to Russia for examples of this system in actual operation. The accounts of the historic English sedition trials are full of the employment of spies at the meetings of political societies. And the spy often passes over an almost imperceptible boundary into the *agent provocateur*, who instigates the utterances he reports, and then into the fabricator, who invents them. There was plenty of this in England, and the same kind of liar, Captain Zaneth of the North West Mounted Police, has just been exposed in Canada after convicting one of the Winnipeg strike leaders on a charge of seditious conspiracy.[47] This dirty business is the price a government must pay for the suppression of political crime. Are we willing to pay that price?

"The freedom of a country," writes the historian already quoted, "may be measured by its immunity from this baleful agency."[48] We have never had it before in the United States, but there is disquieting evidence that this inevitable machinery of sedition-hunters is already at work. At the end of the instructions which W. J. Flynn, Director of the

[46] Mass. Senate Bill No. 184 (January, 1919). This did not become law.

[47] J. A. Stevenson, "A Set-back for Reaction in Canada," 110 *Nation* 292 (March 6, 1920).

[48] 2 May, *ibid.*, 150.

Bureau of Investigation in the Department of Justice, issued, on August 12, 1919, "to all special agents and employees," ordering an investigation of the promotion of sedition and revolution, which should be particularly directed to aliens with a view of obtaining deportation cases, we find this enigmatic passage: [49]

Special agents will constantly keep in mind the necessity of preserving the cover of our confidential informants, and in no case shall they rely upon the testimony of such cover informants during deportation proceedings.

Who these "cover informants" were is disclosed by the *New York Times* [50] in its account of the raids on the Communists four months later:

For months Department of Justice men, dropping all other work, had concentrated on the Reds. Agents quietly infiltrated into the radical ranks, slipped casually into centers of agitation, and went to work, sometimes as cooks in remote mining colonies, sometimes as miners, again as steel workers, and, where the opportunity presented itself, as "agitators" of the wildest type. Although careful not to inspire, suggest, or aid the advancement of overt acts or propaganda, several of the agents, "under cover" men, managed to rise in the radical movement, and become, in at least one instance, the recognized leader of a district.

The Attorney General and his subordinates testify that the Department of Justice employs men who are or have recently been spies in outlawed organizations. One special agent, though never an under-cover informant in the Department, was a spy for the Lusk Committee a short time before as recording secretary of the Buffalo Communist local. The letter of instructions about the raids from Chief Burke of the Bureau of Investigation to his Boston agent,

[49] Investigation Activities of the Department of Justice, 34.
[50] January 3, 1920. For additional evidence as to the activities of these informants, see the testimony of Captain Swinburne Hale in Hearings before the Committee on Rules, *supra*, note 34; Colyer opinion; Palmer Deportations Testimony, 48, 87 ff., 199; Report upon Illegal Practices.

THE DEPORTATIONS

December 27, 1919, whatever its precise meaning, shows that United States employees were active and influential members of both Communist parties:

> If possible, you should arrange with your under-cover informants to have meetings of the Communist Party and the Communist Labor Party held on the night set. . . . This, of course, would facilitate the making of the arrests.

It is to be hoped that these men have been as " careful " as the *Times* reporter says, and that Mr. Palmer is right in denying his employment of *agents provocateurs*, but we would do well to recall one more warning from May:[51]

> The relations between the Government and its informers are of extreme delicacy. Not to profit by timely information were a crime; but to retain in Government pay, and to reward spies and informers, who consort with conspirators as their sworn accomplices, and encourage while they betray them in their crimes, is a practice for which no plea can be offered. No Government, indeed, can be supposed to have expressly instructed its spies to instigate the perpetration of crime; but to be unsuspected, every spy must be zealous in the cause which he pretends to have espoused; and his zeal in a criminal enterprise is a direct encouragement of crime. So odious is the character of a spy, that his ignominy is shared by his employers, against whom public feeling has never failed to pronounce itself, in proportion to the infamy of the agent, and the complicity of those whom he served.

When the litigation growing out of the Communist raids is over, and we can count how many men out of the many thousands arrested are actually deported, and determine how many of those deported are really bad, then only will it be possible to say whether it was worth while instead of deporting the conspicuously dangerous men to go through all this enormous expense, all this spying, arresting, and herding, to save the country from men who in ordinary peacetime conditions were advocating a revolution at some distant

[51] 2 May, *ibid.*, 151-2. See Graham Wallas, *Francis Place*, N. Y., 1919, 121.

and indefinite day through legislative and other propaganda and occasional future unspecified and improbable general strikes.

(2) Industrial Workers of the World

The Industrial Workers of the World have been classified differently from the two Communist parties. Both the Department of Justice and the Secretary of Labor have taken the position, contrary to some state decisions,[52] that the organization does not advocate the unlawful destruction of property. "Its constitution and by-laws have been adroitly drawn so as to avoid the possibility of construing it as teaching either anarchy or sabotage." Consequently, mere membership is not a ground for deportation.[53] It is evident that local immigration inspectors do not all agree with this view of the organization, for Secretary Wilson has released some aliens who after being carried from Oregon to Ellis Island, declared they joined the I.W.W. without realizing its principles.[54] The leaders, organizers, and distributers of literature, at any rate, are getting deported, and this action has been sustained by United States courts in Washington and Oregon on the ground that there is some evidence to justify the administrative order of expulsion.[55] One judge has cancelled the naturalization of an I.W.W. organizer, who at

[52] State *v.* Moilen, 140 Minn. 122 (1918); and the injunction mentioned on p. 193, *supra;* also State *v.* Lowery, 104 Wash. 520 (1918), which refused to admit in evidence the Report of the President's Mediation Commission.

[53] Investigation Activities, etc., 33; letter of W. B. Wilson to John E. Milholland, 110 *Nation* 327 (March 13, 1920).

[54] *New York Times,* March 18, 1919. See adverse editorial, March 19. Officials of the Department of Justice are reported, *ibid.,* February 11, as asserting that mere membership is enough, so that "it will be impossible for that organization to continue in existence." The Ellis Island I.W.W.'s would have been discharged by a judge if they had not been released.—Post Deportations Testimony, 207.

[55] *Ex parte* Bernat and Dixon, 255 Fed. 429 (1918); Guiney *v.* Bonham, 261 Fed. 582 (C. C. A., 1919); and see administrative decisions in "The Anarchist Deportations," 21 *New Republic* 96 (December 21, 1919); and Charles Recht, *American Deportation and Exclusion Laws. Cf.* U. S. *ex rel.* Grau *v.* Uhl, 262 Fed. 532 (1919).

THE DEPORTATIONS

the time he became a citizen approved of sabotage and indorsed the preamble and constitution of the organization.[56] The judge said that since the I.W.W. is "opposed to all forms of government, advocates lawlessness, and constructs its own morals, which are not in accord with those of well-ordered society," but are "adapted by design to the demoralization and degradation thereof," its adherents must *ipso facto* be guilty of fraud in declaring that they are attached to the principles of the United States constitution. Therefore, they cannot become citizens, and if they do, the right can be taken away and deportation follows. The Districts Courts go further than Secretary Wilson, since they denounce the organization itself and regard all members of the I.W.W. who understand and approve its tenets as barred from citizenship and within the Deportation Act, whether or not they have personally advocated violence. There is, of course, no question that many alien officers and members have preached sabotage, and are deportable.

It is unnecessary to repeat here what was said in the preceding chapter about the wisdom of coercion against the propagandist activities of the I.W.W., as distinct from the commission of sabotage and other violence, which of course must be vigorously punished. I will only add that the Department of Labor should be sure that the organization against which it employs this great power is fundamentally revolutionary and not at bottom a labor union. The use of deportation to break up unions, little as I sympathize with them, seems to me to be wholly wrong. It is said, for instance, that when the Chinese workers in New York chop suey restaurants organized a union and struck on New Year's Eve, 1918, the leaders were arrested for deportation.[57] The facts of another case are given in the decision of

---

[56] U. S. *v.* Swelgin, 254 Fed. 884 (1918).

[57] *American Labor Year-Book,* 1919-20, p. 113. *Ex parte* Jackson, 263 Fed. 110 (1920), Bourquin, J. The whole decision should be read. The attitude of the government toward labor unions outside the A. F. of L. is shown by the Attorney General's statement about the Amalgamated Clothing Workers, Palmer Deportations Testimony, 196, 197.

a United States judge, who discharged the alien held for deportation:

> From August, 1918, to February, 1919, the Butte Union of the Industrial Workers of the World was dissatisfied with working places, conditions, and wages in the mining industry, and to remedy them was discussing ways and means, including strike if necessary. In consequence, its hall and orderly meetings were several times raided and mobbed by employers' agents, and federal agents and soldiers duly officered, acting by federal authority and without warrant or process. The union members, men and women, many of them citizens, limited themselves to oral protests, though in the circumstances the inalienable right and law of self-defense justified resistance to the last dread extremity. There was no disorder save that of the raiders. These, mainly uniformed and armed, overawed, intimidated, and forcibly entered, broke, and destroyed property, searched persons, effects, and papers, arrested persons, seized papers and documents, cursed, insulted, beat, dispersed, and bayoneted union members by order of the commanding officer. They likewise entered petitioner's adjacent living apartment, insulted his wife, searched his person and effects, and seized his papers and documents, and in general, in a populous and orderly city, perpetrated a reign of terror, violence, and crime against citizen and alien alike, and whose only offense seems to have been peaceable insistence upon and exercise of a clear legal right.

This opens up dangerous possibilities of influence not only by employers but also by rival conservative unions to secure the annihilation of radical labor organizations through wholesale arrests and expulsions. I believe that the eventual disappearance of the I.W.W. is highly desirable, but Congress ought to consider carefully in the light of the English experience with the Irish Land League whether the deportation of all intelligent alien members is the best method to obtain that result.

The government ought not to be satisfied to base such drastic action merely on an examination of the literature of the organization by men who are unfamiliar with its economic background. An alternative plan for dealing with the very difficult problem of this organization would be a vigorous

THE DEPORTATIONS

suppression and punishment by state law of acts of sabotage, while the Federal Government before arresting or deporting any more members should ascertain the possibility of curing the causes of the revolutionary character of the I.W.W., such as the permanent presence of a large body of migratory labor, homeless, wifeless, jobless. The Department of Labor has at hand for purposes of consultation men who have studied the I.W.W. carefully and men who aroused the enthusiastic efforts of its members in war industries.[58] Such a conference might evolve a new and more satisfactory policy.

For example, deportation does not seem quite the right way to handle the case of John Meehan,[59] who was arrested in Everett, Washington, in May, 1917, for violation of a local anti-billboard law, and then ordered deported as an I.W.W. to England, from which he came twenty-four years ago. After eighteen months of incarceration he was landed, hatless, penniless, and with insufficient clothing, in England, where he has neither kith nor kin.

(3) Anarchists

Anarchists have long been subject to exclusion and expulsion. If the term be taken in the popular sense of supporters of bomb-throwing and assassination generally, the statute is undoubtedly constitutional, and has been so held by the Supreme Court[60] in sustaining the exclusion of an Englishman named Turner. The case possesses some literary interest, for one of his counsel was Edgar Lee Masters, whose acid-bitten portraits of life at Spoon River have indicated possibilities of improvement in American life.

It is well known, however, that anarchism has no necessary connection with violence. It really means the belief which opposes every kind of forcible government and favors the

[58] See Bibliography, on I.W.W.
[59] Charles Recht (counsel for Meehan), *American Deportation and Exclusion Laws,* p. 9.
[60] Turner *v.* Williams, 194 U. S. 279 (1904).

abolition of all coercion over the individual by the community.[61] Philosophical anarchists argue that most governmental action is required because of inequalities in property, and point to many activities of life where these inequalities do not operate and coercion has been found unnecessary. For example, if a number of friends are cruising on a sloop, they require no policeman to keep order or compel each person to do his allotted task. Mutual agreement and the desire to achieve praise and avoid blame from one's companions furnish sufficient incentive to right action. The anarchist looks forward to the time when life will be such a perpetual holiday, and hopes to convert all men to the same faith in human nature. While waiting and working for the millennium, he will, with rare exceptions, think it consistent with his theories to render obedience to existing laws, until they shall disappear forever. Kropotkin and Tolstoi in Russia, Herbert Spencer and Bertrand Russell in England, have at least been strongly influenced by this view that all government is evil. It is obvious that such men and many others have no desire to employ force to end force, but seek to attain their ideal system gradually and peacefully through discussion and education.

These philosophical anarchists caused much perplexity in the early days in this country, even to such a strong champion of soul-liberty as Roger Williams, who argued for their suppression in his celebrated letter of 1655 to the people of Providence: [62]

There goes many a ship to sea, with many hundred souls in one ship, whose weal and woe is common, and is a true picture of a commonwealth or a human combination or society. It hath fallen out sometimes that both Papists and Protestants, Jews and Turks, may be embarked in one ship; upon which supposal I affirm, that all the liberty of conscience that ever I pleaded for, turns upon these two hinges—that none of the Papists, Protestants, Jews, or Turks, be forced to come to the ship's prayers or worship, nor compelled from their own particular prayers or

[61] Bertrand Russell, *Proposed Roads to Freedom*, 32.
[62] Moses Coit Tyler, *History of American Literature*, II, 261.

THE DEPORTATIONS

worship, if they practise any. I further add, that I never denied that, notwithstanding this liberty, the commander of this ship ought to command the ship's course, yea, and also command that justice, peace, and sobriety, be kept and practised, both among the seamen and all the passengers. If any of the seamen refuse to perform their services or passengers to pay their freight; if any refuse to help, in person or purse, toward the common charges or defense; if any refuse to obey the common laws and orders of the ship, concerning their common peace or preservation; if any shall mutiny and rise up against their commanders and officers; if any should preach or write that there ought to be no commanders or officers, because all are equal in Christ, therefore no masters nor officers, no laws nor orders, nor corrections, nor punishments; —I say, I never denied, but in such cases, whatever is pretended, the commander or commanders may judge, resist, compel, and punish such trangressors, according to their deserts and merits. This, if seriously and honestly minded, may, if it so please the Father of Lights, let in some light to such as willingly shut not their eyes.

However, when government became stronger in this country and stood ready to punish any of these men who actually disobeyed the law, it was realized that they presented no danger merely because of their thought and teachings. Many Quakers in the Colonies refused to participate in government because of the New Testament teachings of non-resistance. A similar philosophy was held by many great Americans in the 1840's when as Emerson said, with a twinkle in his eye, every reading man went round with a draft of a new community in his waistcoat pocket. The famous settlements at Brook Farm and Fruitlands were peopled by just such persons.

The Deportation Act of 1918 undoubtedly applies to these peaceful disbelievers in organized government as well as to the bombers, and so did all the statutes since 1903, but the power of Congress to bar them out has never been upheld by the Supreme Court. In the decision just mentioned, which involved only the exclusion of a violent anarchist, Chief Justice Fuller said nothing at all about expulsion, but suggested in passing that Congress could exclude even innocent anarchists if it was of the opinion " that the *tendency* of the general exploitation of such views is so dangerous to the public weal that aliens who hold and advocate them would be undesirable additions to our population." On the other hand, Justice Brewer, in concurring, expressly refused to determine the right of an alien, if only a philosophical anarchist, " one who simply entertains and expresses the opinion that all government is a mistake, and that society would be better off without any." [63]

The public does not realize that it is men of this type as well as violent anarchists whom the government is now sending out of the country after long residence, during which they have necessarily remained aliens since the law forbids their naturalization. Take, for instance, the case of Frank R. Lopez, a Spaniard of the Ferrer school. This man has been in the United States seventeen years, belongs to the A. F. of L., is married, has a son born in this country, owns his own home, and has always been a law-abiding member of society. Yet he has been ordered deported to Spain because he held and expounded, in speech and writing, views which Judge Rogers of the Circuit Court of Appeals in New York expressly stated to be only philosophical anarchism and in no sense advocacy of a resort to force and revolution. Judge Rogers upheld the order of deportation because of the following testimony of Lopez [64] before the immigration inspector :

Q. Do you believe in or advocate the overthrow by violence or force of the government of the United States? A. No, sir.

[63] 194 U. S. 294, 296; italics mine.
[64] The testimony and opinion are from Lopez *v.* Howe, 259 Fed. 401 (C. C. A., 1919). See the opinion of Knox, J., below, quoted in 260 Fed. 485. The facts about the life of Lopez are stated by his counsel, Charles Recht, with additional extracts from his testimony, in *American Deportation and Exclusion Laws*, Boston, 1919, p. 9. The testimony is also reprinted in 21 *New Republic* 98 (December 24, 1919). See the letter in 21 *New Republic* 356 (February 18, 1920), which finds the case so " incredible " that it wrongfully accuses the magazine of withholding utterances by Lopez of an inflammatory nature. The decision in the Federal Reporter expressly rests on philosophical anarchism and denies any advocacy of violence.

THE DEPORTATIONS

Q. Any other government, Spanish, or Italian, or Mexican? A. No, sir; our ideals are founded on education.

Q. What are your ideals? A. Free thinking.

Q. Don't you believe in the power of authority? A. What do you mean?

Q. Organized government. Don't you think, if the President gives an order when Congress empowers him, that it should be obeyed? A. Yes; the orders should be obeyed.

Q. Do you believe in the propriety of assassination of public officials of the United States or any other government? A. No, sir; not only of officials, but of nobody. Everybody has a right to live.

Q. Do you believe in anarchy? A. What do you mean by anarchy?

Q. Well, it would be anarchy to fight against the laws of the United States, tear down buildings, blow them up. A. Anything else? I believe in anarchy, but it is not the way you explain it, or the way newspapers say anarchy is. Anarchy, the way newspapers explain it, assassinating women and children, dropping bombs, or anything like that, I don't believe in that. But I believe in teaching, educating, and telling the people to better their conditions. If you mean that, I am proud of being an anarchist. I am against killing and against destruction. We are to construct.

Q. How are you going to proceed to do this? A. We are not going to force our ideals on anybody's mind. We have conferences, we have lectures. The doors are open, and everybody is welcome.

Q. You try to get people through advertising means? A. Yes, for educational purposes.

Q. For the educational purposes of teaching them anarchy? A. To teach them anarchy the way we understand it, but not the way you understand it; the way many writers understand it.

Q. What writers? A. Tolstoi, Marx, Ferrer, Zola, Kropotkin, and many others.

Q. If you are ordered deported, do you want to be separated from your wife and boy, or would you desire to have them go with you to Spain? A. It's up to the government; I think it is an injustice; I have done nothing wrong; I call it an injustice; if a man is going to be punished for his thoughts and ideas, it is an injustice.

Unless the Supreme Court declares this construction of the statute unconstitutional, Lopez will be deported to Spain.

The expulsion of other men with just the same views has been sustained.[65] Judge Rogers emphasizes the point that Lopez had never become naturalized, overlooking the fact that if he had become a citizen our courts would take his naturalization papers away from him on the ground that they were obtained by fraud,[66] although it seems just as consistent for a man who believes that all government should eventually be abolished to swear allegiance honestly to the government of the United States as it is for a man to render obedience to a statute which he thinks ought to be repealed. Certainly the conduct and testimony of Lopez show that he would have made as good a citizen as most native-born Americans. Judge Rogers also says that Lopez is deported, not because he entertained these thoughts and ideas, but because he sought to instil them into the minds of others. However this may be in his case, the statute expressly authorizes men to be thrown out of this country after long residence for ideas which they have never expressed to a single person until they were subjected to an inquisition by the immigration inspector. Such a law suppresses not only freedom of speech but freedom of thought. The following entry added by the Inspector to the testimony of Louis Gyori, who has been ordered deported because he expects a revolution which will compel every one to work but will only come at some uncertain time when the majority want it, is very significant:[67]

Very careful and steady questioning was necessary to bring out the alien's beliefs, political and industrial.

VI. *The Deportations and the Bill of Rights*

Having thus shown that the deportation statute has been put into force against men who are in no way advocates

[65] *Ex parte* Pettine, 259 Fed. 733 (1919); see also 21 *New Republic* 98.
[66] U. S. *v.* Stuppiello, 260 Fed. 482 (1919).
[67] "The Anarchist Deportations," 21 *New Republic* 98 (December 24, 1919).

THE DEPORTATIONS

of violence, I will now return to the general question of the power of Congress to make laws excluding or expelling men from this country because of mere membership in societies which it considers objectionable or because of the holding or expression of peaceful ideas which it regards as having a bad political tendency. The constitutionality of such statutes is defended on two grounds.

First, it is said that the power of Congress to decide what aliens shall be admitted or shall remain in this country is unrestricted by the Constitution. One judge calls this power "well-nigh plenary in its absolutism."[68] Chief Justice Fuller suggests that if Congress can shut out all aliens, it can therefore shut out any group of aliens it pleases. Such a contention seems to me unsound. One might as well argue that because a Republican Congress can refuse to naturalize all aliens, therefore it can refuse to naturalize only those who express the intention of casting a Democratic vote at the next election. The First and Fifth Amendments in the Bill of Rights limit all the powers of Congress, including the power over the exclusion and expulsion of aliens.

Aliens are "persons" within the Fifth Amendment, whom Congress cannot deprive of liberty and property except "by due process of law," that is, by methods which are appropriate to the emergency. It cannot turn the aliens whom it wishes to deport loose in an open boat on the Atlantic, or carry them across the border into Mexico and leave them wandering the desert. No one would consider this a reasonable way of returning them to their own country. Moreover, the method of classifying aliens for deportation is as important as the manner of expulsion. If Congress has unlimited power to remove alien members of any group it chooses, all Roman Catholics, all Jews, all Russians, any class that happens to be unpopular at the moment, can be ousted no matter how long they have been in the United States. It has been repeatedly decided by the Supreme Court that the mere existence of a legislative power such as taxation, does

[68] *Ex parte* Pettine, *supra*.

not (under the "due process" clause) involve the right to exercise that power in a discriminatory manner against a group such as all red-headed men, who are selected arbitrarily without reasonable relation to the facts and the needs of society.[69] The discretion of Congress to determine the basis of classification must be very wide, but it is not unbounded. In particular, classification of the objects of any recognized Congressional power must not be used solely for the purpose of accomplishing a result prohibited by the First Amendment. Congress can tax all incomes, but an income tax of 50 per cent on Socialist college professors alone would be a convenient but unconstitutional way to suppress freedom of speech. Furthermore, it seems probable that the "due process" clause renders the power of Congress over the expulsion of aliens much narrower than the power to refuse them admission, because the deprivation of liberty and property is so much greater after an alien has once been admitted and become settled in this country. Many more individual interests claim protection. Congress could undoubtedly refuse admission to aliens with diseased eyes and could probably expel such aliens after several years' residence; possibly it could exclude aliens with blue eyes; but a law ordering all aliens with blue eyes to leave the country no matter how long they had been here would be clearly a violation of the Fifth Amendment.

The power over aliens must also be subject to the First Amendment, for that declares that "Congress shall make no law abridging the freedom of speech or of the press," and a deportation statute is a "law." Nevertheless, that Amendment does not mean to deny the government the power of self-preservation. Some opinions may be so dangerous to the nation that men holding them may be kept out or even expelled. In other words, we must determine the limits of freedom of speech in relation to deportation according to the principles laid down in the first chapter.

[69] Gulf, etc., Ry. *v.* Ellis, 165 U. S. 150, 165 (1897); Connolly *v.* Union Sewer Pipe Co., 184 U. S. 540, 560 (1902).

In this connection, I must consider the second argument in favor of the validity of these clauses against radicals in the Deportation Act. It is urged by Chief Justice Fuller in the Turner case [70] that the statute has nothing to do with freedom of speech.

It is, of course, true that if an alien is not permitted to enter this country, or, having entered contrary to law, is expelled, he is in fact cut off from worshiping or speaking or publishing or petitioning in the country, but that is merely because of his exclusion therefrom. He does not become one of the people to whom these things are secured by our Constitution by an attempt to enter forbidden by law.

This argument seems to me very questionable because it regards freedom of speech as purely the individual interest of the alien. We have seen in the first chapter that it is also a social interest of the community as a whole. Although the alien who is barred out may not be entitled to any claim under our Bill of Rights, persons already here are seriously affected if they are denied the privilege of listening to, and associating with a foreign thinker. Furthermore, the progress of the country as a whole may be gravely retarded. Truth is truth, whether it comes from a citizen or an alien, and the refusal to admit a wise foreigner, especially if there is a postal censorship on books, may simply result in our remaining ignorant. Massachusetts in the middle of the eighteenth century would have been unwilling to allow Bishop Berkeley to settle in her midst, but if Rhode Island had also refused to admit him, it would have impoverished American thought. Refusal to admit Bernard Shaw or Bertrand Russell in 1920 would operate in the same way. Roman Catholic citizens of the United States would surely be aggrieved by a law barring all future immigrants of that faith. Therefore, freedom of speech is necessarily affected by the exclusion of aliens for their opinions, and such exclusion is unconstitutional unless the social inter-

[70] See note 60.

est in the attainment of truth is outweighed in the balance by the other interests involved. The First Amendment does not read, " No citizen shall be deprived of freedom of speech." It prohibits all laws " abridging the freedom of speech or of the press."

What has been said applies still more forcibly to the expulsion of long-established aliens for their views and utterances. This has always been a favorite method of dealing with the heterodox. Almost all the wholesale deportations of history, just like Mr. Palmer's January raid, have been an effort to overcome " evil thinking." Spain expelled the Moors; England in the reign of Edward III banished fifteen thousand Jews; and Louis XIV in 1685 drove out the Huguenots from France. In 1891 President Harrison called the attention of Congress to the action of Russia, a friendly nation, in banishing thousands of Jews.[71] Although there are many precedents in history for the wholesale expulsion of Communists, they are not precedents which we should be proud to follow.

Therefore, the deportations may infringe the national policy expressed by the First Amendment, even if they do not transcend the extreme limits of constitutional power. It seems to me more profitable to leave the question of constitutionality to future judicial discussion, and simply outline the conflicting factors which determine the wisdom of the deportation of radical aliens to-day.

In favor of deportation are, first, the desire of society for order, which was considered in the last chapter, and besides this, the interest of the nation in keeping its population free from elements which are considered undesirable additions to our present and future stock. The same social need found expression in the Chinese Exclusion Acts. It is this second factor which makes the power of Congress over aliens so wide. The war power should, I have endeav-

---

[71] Moore's *Digest of International Law,* VI, 358; this has reference to Russian subjects. On American Jews expelled from Russia, see *ibid.,* IV, 111 ff.

THE DEPORTATIONS

ored to show, be used against utterances only to ward off dangerous acts, but this power over immigration is primarily directed to dangerous persons. It is concerned less with what men do than with what they are—whether they are diseased, crippled, of psychopathic inferiority, liable to become a public charge. The danger-test of the Schenck case still holds good, but in a new form. Congress may wisely act now, although there is " no clear and present danger " of violence, for " the substantive evil which Congress has the right to prevent " is in this problem the presence of persons who are so undesirable that they ought to be denied or deprived of an American domicile.

Undoubtedly, men may be undesirable and dangerous persons because of their ideas as well as physical and mental derangements. On the other hand, the need of society for truth and progress must come into play, and in determining who are undesirable we must be ever on our guard against applying the test of conjectural and remote tendencies. It is not at all the same provable question of fact as heart trouble or insanity.[72] For instance, much of the reasoning in the philosophical anarchist cases, which stigmatize the doctrine as " inimical to civilization," is purely speculative, and smacks of the eighteenth century sedition trials. And the organization clauses, in expelling men who are not undesirable themselves just because they have undesirable associates, carries the logic of national integrity one step beyond the standard of individual suitability for residence in America.

The record of philosophical anarchists shows that they are no more prone to disorder than any religious sect, and whatever we may think of their ultimate faith, they may be of great benefit in society, both for their constructive schemes of voluntary organization and for their pointed criticisms of the evils of existing governments. Let me offset the rea-

[72] See American School of Magnetic Healing *v.* McAnnulty, 187 U. S. 94 (1902), and the quotation from Justice Brandeis in the Pierce case, p. 105, *supra*.

soning of Roger Williams with another ship-parable (ships being rather appropriate in this chapter): [73]

"A sailor related to me," writes Benjamin Constant, "that he was once on board a vessel with a passenger who had frequently made the same voyage. This passenger pointed out to the captain a rock hidden beneath the waves, but the captain would not listen to him. On his insisting upon it, the captain had him thrown into the sea. This energetic measure put an end to all remonstrances, and nothing could be more touching than the unanimity that reigned on board, until, suddenly, the vessel touched the reef, and was wrecked. They had drowned the giver of the warning, but the reef remained."

Another reason against wholesale deportation for ideas is that we have a national reputation to live up to, which we should hesitate to sacrifice. We have drawn millions of workers to our soil, not merely by the material magnet of high wages, but by the great hope of freedom from all the tyranny of European empires. After priding ourselves for a century on being an asylum for the oppressed of all nations, we ought not suddenly to jump to the position that we are only an asylum for men who are no more radical than ourselves. Suppose monarchical England had taken such a position toward the Republican Mazzini or the anarchist Kropotkin. Sweden, next door to Bolshevik Russia, allows and even encourages by law extensive freedom of speech. Switzerland, with her small population, has harbored even bomb-throwers and Nicolai Lenine with perfect safety. But the United States with one hundred million inhabitants, four thousand miles away from the scenes of revolution, is urged to be afraid of a few thousand men like Lopez and the advocates of "mass action." We shall soon be in the shameful position of seeing political offenders from this country demanding asylum in the very lands from which men once fled to be free to think and talk on our shores.

The international consequences of the deportations are

[73] *Letters on England*, Louis Blanc, London, 1866, I, 438.

THE DEPORTATIONS

very serious. Not only are we erecting a Chinese wall to keep out ideas, but we are helping to increase the very unrest in Europe that we fear. Every one of sense, no matter what his opinion of the present government of Russia, believes that the restoration of order in that country is essential to the provisioning and the peace of Europe. We began this pacification of Russia by sending in Admiral Kolchak. We end by sending in Emma Goldman. The harm that she did during her thirty-four years in the United States was nothing beside the unrest and international irritation she is creating in Russia, where she has already organized the "Friends of American Freedom." A nuisance here, she is a heroine over there and one more element of instability in the Russian situation. Look at Larkin, whom the British deported from Ireland, where they could keep an eye on him. No single man has done more to stir up bad feeling against Great Britain in this country. What sort of an international house-cleaning are we going to have if each country grabs up turbulent persons and dumps them across the border upon its neighbor's land? I have no sympathy whatever with these extremists, but as a matter of expediency they may be doing far less harm when they talk to foreigners who are in this country under American inspiration than when they are sent with bitterness in their hearts to spread hatred against us in the very countries to which we must look for future immigrants.

Other international difficulties are bound to arise. If we make peace with the Soviet Government, how can we declare any one who endorses its political and economic theories an outlaw? Already the Secretary of Labor is proposing to decide whether that government advocates revolution so that he can deport Mr. Martens,[74] a job which seems more within the duties of the Secretary of State. Soon some one will suggest that the attempted assassination of Vis-

---

[74] "Martens and Our Foreign Policy," Lincoln Colcord, 110 *Nation* 324 (March 13, 1920). Palmer Deportations Testimony, 180, gives the case for deportation.

288   FREEDOM OF SPEECH

count French and the death of numerous English officials in Ireland is some evidence that Sinn Fein is an organization which "advocates the duty, necessity, or propriety of the unlawful killing of officers of an organized government because of their official character," and Secretary Wilson will have to pass on the deportation of President De Valera.

Think of the example which these recent raids have set to less orderly nations, this resorting to methods which we have repeatedly declared to be a violation of international law, when used against Americans abroad.[75] We can no longer take that position. If Mexico should conclude that certain Americans there had advocated a revolution in that country by force and violence, or a "clean-up" by the United States (by force), then it could seize our fellow-citizens from their beds at midnight, throw them into Black Holes like the Detroit bull-pen, separate them from their families, let their business go to pieces, turn their wives and children over to the local charities, and ship them in an army transport to New Orleans, knowing that every act would be supported by precedents of what has been done in

[75] *Cf.* with the January, 1920, raids, the following facts from Moore's *Digest of International Law*, IV, 108: "In May, 1898, F. Scandella, a citizen of the United States, engaged in the cattle and transportation business at Ciudad Bolivar, Venezuela, was suddenly arrested while walking in the streets of that city, and was thrown into prison, where he was denied communication with his family and friends. Next day he was taken under guard to a steamer, and was sent to the British island of Trinidad. His wife and five young children were left without funds; his cattle and mules were stolen; and his house, which was about three miles from town, was sacked. The authorities of the State of Bolivar alleged as the cause of his seizure and expulsion 'frequent denunciations' and 'well-founded suspicions' that he was 'plotting secretly against public order.' The United States minister interposed in the case, presenting testimonials as to Mr. Scandella's character and standing; and the President of the Republic intimated a desire to settle the case outside of diplomatic channels. Scandella was permitted to return to Venezuela; and early in July, 1898, the case was understood to have been adjusted on the basis of $1,600 in cash, American gold, and a promise of reimbursement for property taken or destroyed." Other examples of arbitrary expulsion are the Hollander case in Guatemala, *ibid.*, 102; and the Bluefields cases in Nicaragua, *ibid.*, 99. Several arbitrations on expulsion are contained in Moore's *Digest of International Arbitrations*, IV, c. LX.

THE DEPORTATIONS

this country last winter to the citizens of a government that was too weak to hit back.

Finally, in deciding whether radical deportations should be carried out further, we ought to consider two classes of people in this country—first, ourselves; secondly, all the aliens.

That deportations are very popular with American citizens is undeniable, far more so than the proposed federal sedition bills. How can we account for this astonishing desire to reverse our national policy? Besides the nervous effect of the war, the shock of the Russian Revolution, the unpreparedness for wide intellectual divergencies, of which I shall speak more fully in the next chapter, there is, I suspect, another element. Genuinely grateful as we all are in our thinking moments to our immigrant population, most of us have a hidden emotion which comes to the surface in a time of excitement, the wish that we did not have in our midst these foreigners who are so different from ourselves. The basis of dislike is normally unlikeness.[76] It is just the same feeling that led Dr. Johnson to say after the experience of a lifetime that most foreigners were fools. We are going through the old Know Nothing affair over again.

This instinct is normally controlled by a recognition of what immigration has done for the United States. It is not true that the aliens owe us everything and we owe them nothing. They have no vote, but they have hands and muscles. They have come here at our request, often at our earnest solicitation, to dig our sewers, cart our garbage, weave our cloth, build our roads and railways. And they have minds like ourselves. Absence of citizenship means the loss of the vote, but does it give us the moral right after a man is admitted to prescribe what he shall think, under penalty of banishment from his new home, and perhaps forcible return to the secret police from whom he fled? Doubt-

---

[76] "The Nervousness of the Jew," Dr. A. Myerson, 4 *Mental Hygiene* 65 (January, 1920); Bagehot elaborates the point in his essay on "The Metaphysical Basis of Toleration."

less, a policy of hands-off will result in the presence of a few dangerous agitators springing up in the great army of workers, but we should be willing to take the foam with the beer. This is not the first time that restless spirits, many of whom had been actually engaged in the labor wars of Europe, have carried the instinct of industrial strife and violence with them to their new country.[77] We have lived through it until this year in confident serenity. We have believed that the unrest brought from the other side of the ocean would eventually be dissipated by contact with American life. The radical shows the same change under a fostering environment as the Jew, who is rapidly becoming assimilated to his neighbors. " What persecution could not do through the centuries, toleration does in a generation." [78] The Bolshevist peasant in Russia, having acquired a bit of land, is already angering his rulers by his conservatism. In the same way a savings bank account, a steady job, and plenty of good-humored toleration and friendly help and encouragement, will bring into harmony with our ideals all but a few heated theorists who have been in our midst all through the war and ought not in peace to be such a menace to our national safety that we cannot counteract them by sound reasoning. Secretary Wilson would, if he had his own way, adopt this very method: [79]

I look upon any alien who comes to this country and advocates the use of force for the overthrow of our Government as being in exactly the same position as an invading enemy, and that it is no undue hardship to send him back to the country whence he came. Nevertheless, I would not deal with the subject matter in that way. In dealing with it during the period of the war the policy of the Department of Labor was to send high-class, intelligent working men, who had lived the lives and spoke the language of the workers themselves, into the places where working men congregate, carrying a counter-propaganda puncturing the

[77] See account of the Molly Maguires in Rhodes, *History of the United States*, VIII.
[78] Myerson, *op. cit*.
[79] Letter to John E. Milholland, reprinted in 110 *Nation* 326 (March 13, 1920).

fallacy of the philosophy of force as applied to democratic institutions. We believed we had successfully met the situation until Congress in its wisdom curtailed the appropriation that made it possible for us to carry on the work we had been doing.

VII. *Suggested Changes in Our Deportation Policy*

As an alternative to our present policy of deportations I would suggest a continuance of Secretary Wilson's plan for the first step. The last few years have taught us that the melting-pot will not entirely take care of itself. Just as the merits of free trade in goods are lessened if the normal processes of competition are checked by monopolies and dumping, so free trade in ideas requires that the barriers to the interchange of argument presented by illiteracy and foreign languages shall somehow be broken down.

Secondly, Congress should put into force the following recommendation from the Secretary of Labor: [80]

If lawfully admitted aliens are to be deported from the United States for any cause, in my judgment the deportation should be the result of judicial proceedings in the courts rather than through administrative action.

The Assistant Secretary made the same recommendation four years ago: [81]

In most cases administrative decisions must in the very nature of administration be made by subordinates; in all instances they must be made along hard and fast lines according to unelastic legislation designed to promote a governmental policy. Determinations regarding private rights by such decisions are mere incidents of administration. . . . Nothing in my official experience in the Department of Labor has impressed me more deeply than the conviction that fundamental personal rights should be more

---

[80] *Ibid.*
[81] "Administrative Decisions in Connection with Immigration," Louis F. Post, 10 *Am. Pol. Sci. Rev.* 260, 261 (1916). See Post Deportations Testimony, 239, 246 ff. An alternative method would be an independent administrative tribunal of three experts to sit in a purely judicial capacity upon all deportation cases, like the Commissioner of Patents in his field.

scrupulously guarded in immigration cases than is possible through administrative decisions made in the course of executive routine.

Thirdly, a conference might be held to include immigration officials, members of Congress, men who have come into contact with radical aliens on the President's Mediation Commission and in the conduct of war industries, and scholars like Brissenden who have studied revolutionary organizations. This conference should outline for the guidance of Congress a program for our future deportation policy. It would seem desirable to limit deportable aliens to men who are themselves personally objectionable on account of the advocacy of force.

Finally, the Secretary of Labor or the President should be given discretion whether or not to expel an alien who is within a deportable class. At the present time Assistant Secretary Post [82] shows that deportation must be automatic, no matter how cruel or unwise it may be. An imprisoned criminal may be pardoned by the President, but not even he can prevent an alien who comes under the statutes from being sent overseas.

I make these suggestions as an American, believing that we must depend on a large immigrant population for many years to come and that we all desire them to be loyal members of the community, devoted to our institutions whether or not they decide to abandon their allegiance to their old land. Men cannot be forced to love this country. They will love it rather because it does not employ force except against obviously wrongful overt acts. They will love it as the home of wise tolerance, of confidence in its own strength and freedom. Undoubtedly there is much discontent in certain groups of aliens at the present time. It has been accentuated by the excitement of the Russian Revolution, which must eventually subside. We are not likely to decrease this discontent by dragging men away from their families and either shipping them abroad or releasing them

[82] *Ibid.*

after many bitter days in prison. The relatives and friends of those deported will not have any increased love for our government. The raids have become a text for more agitators, who speak to men and women who now have a real reason for wanting to get rid of the existing form of government. It is not the soap-box orators, but Mr. Palmer with his horde of spies and midnight housebreakers, that have brought our government into hatred and contempt. Yet it is not too late to abandon this great error, recompensing the injured and adopting a fresh policy for the future. Let us limit punishment to overt acts. Let us trust an Anglo-Saxon jury trial to safeguard us even from aliens. Let us rely on tried American methods, and not upon the secret and summary processes of the last few months.

CHAPTER VI

JOHN WILKES, VICTOR BERGER, AND THE FIVE MEMBERS

If Charles wished to prosecute the five members, a bill against them should have been sent to a grand jury.—MACAULAY, *Essay on Hallam*.

IT is one of the unfortunate results of governmental action against freedom of speech that the persons who retain sufficient courage to come into conflict with the law are often of a heedless and aggressive character, which makes them unattractive and devoid of personal appeal. Too often we assume that such persistent trouble-makers are the only persons injured by a censorship or a sedition law, and conclude from the indiscreet and unreasonable qualities of their speech and writing that after all the loss to the world of thought has been very slight. Too often we forget the multitude of cautious and sensitive men, men with wives and children dependent upon them, men who abhor publicity, who prefer to keep silent in the hope of better days. We cannot know what is lost through the effect upon them of repression, for it is simply left unsaid.[1] The effort of the agitator is made for their sake as well as his own, and if he wins the gain to truth comes, not perhaps from his ideas but from theirs. The men and women mentioned in this book, whom reflection has made me consider victims of unwise and often illegal suppression, are not indeed political prisoners whose ideals I can share, as I might those of

[1] Tolstoy once wrote: "You would not believe how, from the very commencement of my activity, that horrible Censor question has tormented me! I wanted to write what I felt; but at the same time it occurred to me that what I wrote would not be permitted, and involuntarily I had to abandon the work. I abandoned, and went on abandoning, and meanwhile the years passed away."—GRAHAM WALLAS, *The Great Society*, 196.

Silvio Pellico or Grotius, and it may be that even after due allowance has been made for the natural blindness of a contemporary to the merit of their thinking, that only one or two among them, like Bertrand Russell, are men whose work has enduring worth. Yet the views and even the personal qualities of the victims of persecution have little relation to the justice of their cause. Few objects of intolerance have touched such a low level of thought and action, few have rendered more numerous and more valuable services to liberty than John Wilkes.

I. *John Wilkes*

In his person though he were the worst of men, I contend for the safety and security of the best.—LORD CHATHAM.

"That name," says Trevelyan, "which was seldom out of the mouths of our great-grandfathers for three weeks together, had been stained and blotted from the first." A rake and a prodigal, unfaithful to the wife whose fortune he looted for use in election briberies, lacking in genuine devotion to any political ideal, he nevertheless by sheer pluck and impudence led the fight to establish in the law of all English-speaking countries five great principles of freedom: the immunity of political criticism from prosecution; the publicity of legislative debates; the abolition of outlawry, which condemned a man in his absence; the protection of house and property from unreasonable searches and seizures; and the right of a duly elected representative of a constituency to sit in the legislature unless disqualified by law, no matter what personal objections his colleagues may have to his opinions and writings or to his previous convictions for sedition. So great were his achievements that he became a household word on this side of the Atlantic. One of the largest cities in Pennsylvania is named for him. Men called their children after him. One New England admirer had three sons, Wilkes, Pitt, and Liberty. In the eyes of our forefathers he was the most conspicuous combatant against the doctrine, so obnoxious to them, that men might be maltreated, imprisoned, exiled, disfranchised, for the supposedly evil tendencies of their political opinions. The preceding chapters have shown the gradual revival of that doctrine in our midst, first in war and now in peace, first against pacifists and pro-Germans, then against radical aliens, until finally the war with " evil-thinking " has brought us to the point of governmental action against radical citizens with a constantly diminishing standard of radicalism, and two of the great principles for which Wilkes fought amid the applause of our ancestors are in grave peril, freedom from unreasonable searches and seizures and the right of the people to choose their representatives.

II. *The Raids of 1763 and the Raids of 1919*

The poorest man may in his cottage bid defiance to all the forces of the Crown; it may be frail, its roof may shake, the wind may blow through it; the storm may enter, the rain may enter; but the King of England can not enter; all his forces dare not cross the threshold of that ruined tenement.—LORD CHATHAM.

On the 23rd of April, 1763, appeared No. 45 of the *North Briton*, commenting upon the king's speech and upon the unpopular peace recently concluded. It was conducted by Wilkes, who had played a large part through this newspaper in driving Lord Bute from office and now castigated his successor, George Grenville, of Stamp Act fame. Other journalists abused public men under such disguises as the use of initials, but the *North Briton* called them by name. The Ministry resolved to prosecute for libel, but it was unknown who was the libeler, since those responsible for the newspaper had kept their identity concealed. Lord Halifax, one of the Secretaries of State, issued what was then called a general warrant, directing four messengers to take a constable, search for the authors, printers, and publishers, and seize them when found, together with their papers.

WILKES AND HIS SUCCESSORS

No one having been charged, or even suspected—no evidence of crime having been offered—no one was named in this dread instrument. The offense only was pointed at, not the offender. The magistrate, who should have sought proofs of crime, deputed this office to his messengers. Armed with their roving commission, they set forth in quest of unknown offenders; and unable to take evidence, listened to rumors, idle tales, and curious guesses. They held in their hands the liberty of every man whom they were pleased to suspect. Nor were they triflers in their work. In three days, they arrested no less than forty-nine persons on suspicion, many as innocent as Lord Halifax himself.[2]

Among the number were Leach, a printer who had printed another number of the *North Briton*, whose papers were seized; and the publisher and printer of No. 45, with all their workmen. From them Wilkes was discovered to be the real offender, and he was carried off to the Secretaries of State. As soon as he was out of his house, the messengers returned to it and took entire possession, refusing admission to his friends. They sent for a blacksmith, who opened the drawers of his bureau. The messengers dumped his papers, including his will and pocket-book, into a sack, and went off with them without even taking an inventory. Wilkes brought an action, not against the messengers, but against the man higher up, the Under Secretary of State, who had personally superintended the execution of the warrant. Chief Justice Pratt, afterwards Lord Chancellor Camden, said of the warrant:[3]

If such a power is truly invested in a secretary of state, and he can delegate this power, it certainly may affect the person and property of every man in this kingdom, and is totally subversive of the liberty of the subject.

Wilkes recovered £1,000. Then he went still higher, and sued the Cabinet Minister who had issued the warrant, for false imprisonment, obtaining £4,000 damages. His asso-

---

[2] 2 May's *Constitutional History*, 125.
[3] Wilkes *v.* Wood, 19 How. St. Tr. 1167 (1763).

ciates brought similar actions. It is said that altogether these suits cost the Grenville Government £100,000.

This warrant was doubly illegal in failing to specify the persons to be arrested and in giving no authority to search and seize papers or other property. Another warrant, issued the previous year because of alleged libels in the *Monitor*, did specify the author, John Entinck, and directed that he be seized, " together with his books and papers." This warrant was more specific, but not sufficiently so to be legal, for it did not name the particular papers to be seized, but gave authority to the messengers to take all his books and papers. Entinck sued the messengers and recovered £300. Pratt said in this case:[4]

. . . If this point should be determined in favor of the jurisdiction, the secret cabinets and bureaus of every subject in this kingdom will be thrown open to the search and inspection of a messenger, whenever the secretary of state shall think fit to charge, or even to suspect, a person to be the author, printer, or publisher of a seditious libel.

The messenger, under this warrant, is commanded to seize the person described, and to bring him with his papers to be examined before the secretary of state. In consequence of this, the house must be searched; the lock and doors of every room, box, or trunk must be broken open; all the papers and books without exception, if the warrant be executed according to its tenor, must be seized and carried away; for it is observable, that nothing is left either to the discretion or to the humanity of the officer.

This power so assumed by the secretary of state is an execution upon all the party's papers, in the first instance. His house is rifled; his most valuable secrets are taken out of his possession, before the paper for which he is charged is found to be criminal by any competent jurisdiction, and before he is convicted either of writing, publishing, or being concerned in the paper. . . .

Papers are the owner's goods and chattels: they are his dearest property; and are so far from enduring a seizure, that they will hardly bear an inspection; and though the eye cannot by the laws of England be guilty of a trespass, yet where private papers are removed and carried away, the secret nature of those goods will be an aggravation of the trespass, and demand more considerable damages in that respect. Where is the law that gives

[4] Entinck *v.* Carrington, *ibid.*, 1029 (1765).

any magistrate such a power? I can safely answer, there is none; and therefore it is too much for us without such authority to pronounce a practice legal, which would be subversive of all the comforts of society. . . .

If suspicion at large should be a ground of search, especially in the case of libels, whose house would be safe?

The law of this case that search must be by warrant describing the property to be seized is embodied in the Constitution of the United States. " Can we doubt," asks Justice Bradley,[5] " that when the Fourth and Fifth Amendments were penned and adopted, the language of Lord Camden was relied on as expressing the true doctrine on the subject of searches and seizures, and as furnishing the true criteria of the reasonable and ' unreasonable ' character of such seizures? " We had our own grounds for opposing such arbitrary practices. The first of that long series of contests which led up to the American Revolution was the attack of James Otis upon the Boston Custom House officers who were searching for smuggled goods under general warrants. " Then and there," said John Adams, " the child Independence was born."

The Fourth Amendment reads thus:

The right of the people to be secure in their persons, houses, papers, and effects, against unreasonable searches and seizures, shall not be violated, and no warrants shall issue, but upon probable cause, supported by oath or affirmation and particularly describing the place to be searched, and the persons or things to be seized.

The United States Supreme Court has made repeated use of this Amendment[6] to prevent the use of evidence which has been seized without a search-warrant (even though under a warrant of arrest) or with a search-warrant which fails to specify the particular papers to be seized.

[5] See the full discussion of the historical background of the Fourth Amendment in Boyd *v.* U. S., *infra.*
[6] Boyd *v.* U. S., 116 U. S. 616 (1886); Weeks *v.* U. S., 232 U. S. 383 (1914); Silverthorne Lumber Co. *v.* U. S., 251 U. S. 385 (1920).

In Boyd *v.* United States, the federal customs officials, acting under a statute and with a warrant, compelled the defendant to produce an invoice which they believed would enable them to forfeit goods. The Supreme Court held that the evidence could not be used.

> Any compulsory discovery . . . compelling the production of his private books and papers, to convict him of crime, or to forfeit his property, is contrary to the principles of a free government. It is abhorrent to the instincts of an Englishman; it is abhorrent to the instincts of an American. It may suit the purposes of despotic power; but it cannot abide the pure atmosphere of political liberty and personal freedom.

In Weeks *v.* United States, Justice Day said of a seizure of papers before indictment:

> . . . This protection reaches all alike, whether accused of crime or not, and the duty of giving to it force and effect is obligatory upon all entrusted under our Federal system with the enforcement of the laws. The tendency of those who execute the criminal laws of the country to obtain conviction by means of unlawful seizures and enforced confessions, the latter often obtained after subjecting accused persons to unwarranted practices destructive of rights secured by the Federal Constitution, should find no sanction in the judgments of the courts which are charged at all times with the support of the Constitution and to which people of all conditions have a right to appeal for the maintenance of such fundamental rights.
>
> . . . The efforts of the courts and their officials to bring the guilty to punishment, praiseworthy as they are, are not to be aided by the sacrifice of those great principles established by years of endeavor and suffering which have resulted in their embodiment in the fundamental law of the land.

The most recent case is Silverthorne Lumber Co. *v.* United States, decided in January, 1920. After the officers of a corporation had been arrested, " representatives of the Department of Justice and the United States Marshal without a shadow of authority went to the office of their company and made a clean sweep of all the books, papers, and documents found there." Photographs and copies were made and the originals returned. Justice Holmes held that the seizure

WILKES AND HIS SUCCESSORS

was "an outrage," which prevented the government from making any use of the copies or even from obtaining a court order directing the corporation to produce the originals. Thus, under the federal law, an illegal search and seizure not only subjects the officials and other persons participating in the raid to civil actions for damages, such as were brought by Wilkes and his associates, but also prevents the government from making even the most indirect use by way of evidence of the purloined material.

It is, of course, necessary and legal that searches should sometimes be made for the detection of crime. For instance, the person of the man apprehended as a criminal can be searched without a warrant for a revolver or burglar's tools; and search-warrants can be obtained to look for stolen goods or articles which are retained in violation of revenue laws. These warrants have such very serious consequences that they can only be obtained for very urgent and satisfactory reasons, and the rules of law pertaining to them already mentioned in the discussion of Wilkes and soon to be stated, are of more than ordinary strictness, and must be carefully observed. Even duly authorized searches are so obnoxious in a liberty-loving country, that the law should, as Cooley points out, be very slow to extend them:[7]

> The power of the legislature to authorize a resort to this process is one which can properly be exercised only in extreme cases, and it is better oftentimes that crime should go unpunished than that the citizen should be liable to have his premises invaded, his desks broken open, his private books, letters, and papers exposed to prying curiosity, and to the misconstructions of ignorant and suspicious persons,—and all this under the direction of a mere ministerial officer, who brings with him such assistants as he pleases, and who will select them more often with reference to physical strength and courage than to their sensitive regard to the rights and feelings of others. To incline against the enactment of such laws is to incline to the side of safety. In principle they are objectionable; in the mode of execution they are necessarily odious; and they tend to invite abuse and to cover the commission of crime.

[7] *Constitutional Limitations*, 7 ed., 432.

Searches and seizures, whether valid or not, are like spies, the price that a nation pays for sedition laws, for these can only be enforced by prying methods. The Espionage Act is careful to include a title on search-warrants. Over thirty-five big raids by federal officials took place during the war, sometimes with proper warrants, sometimes without.[8] Since the armistice, the Espionage Act was used to close the *Seattle Union-Record*, until a court declared the action to be invalid.[9] The preceding chapter has shown the absence of search-warrants in the recent deportation round-ups, which should not only result in the release of most of the aliens, but subject the members of the Department of Justice, including Attorney General Palmer, to the same kind of civil actions which Wilkes sustained against Lord Halifax, the Secretary of State.

The best known instance of searches and seizures, is, however, the spectacular series of raids conducted in June, 1919, by a joint committee of the New York Senate and Assembly. Probing committees seem indigenous to New York. They had one in 1780 to detect and defeat conspiracies of Loyalists.[10] On March 26, 1919, the legislature adopted a joint resolution, which, after reciting that a large number of persons within the state were circulating propaganda calculated to overthrow the government of the state and nation, and that it was the duty of the legislature to learn the whole truth regarding these seditious activities and pass appropriate laws, appointed a committee of six " to investigate the scope, tendencies, and ramifications of such seditious activities, and to report the result of its investigation to the Legislature." The committee had power " to compel the attendance of witnesses and the production of books and

[8] Act of June 15, 1917, c. 30, Title XI. For a list of raids, see *War-time Prosecutions*, 38-40.
[9] Chapter II, note 114.
[10] Minutes of the Commissioners for Detecting and Defeating Conspiracies in the State of New York, ed. V. H. Patsits, N. Y., 1909. See also on anti-Loyalist legislation in New York, establishing test oaths, Cummings *v.* Missouri, 4 Wall. 277, *passim*.

papers," and was in general a legislative committee. In no sense was it a body for the prosecution of crime.[11]

There were in New York several headquarters of radical organizations which this Lusk Committee, so called because of its chairman, determined to investigate. If the officers of these organizations had been served with a *subpœna duces tecum*, the usual order to produce any books and papers that were wanted, which as just stated the Committee had power to issue, no reason has ever been shown to believe that such material would not have been forthcoming. Instead, the Committee proceeded to take out search-warrants and raid the organizations, one after another, throwing their entire offices into hopeless confusion. New York has not a constitutional provision, like the Fourth Amendment, but its Civil Rights Law enacts precisely the same words, and the Code of Criminal Procedure is very explicit. Also no person can be compelled in any criminal case to give evidence against himself.[12] It is possible that the federal rule against the use of illegally seized evidence does not prevail in New York,[13] but the test of what is illegal remains the same and renders liable to civil and criminal penalties and to the condemnation of all law-abiding persons any officials who conduct lawless and disorderly searches and seizures, especially when they act in the name of law and order.

It is true that the Lusk Committee obtained search-warrants for its raids, but this does not render the proceedings valid unless the warrants complied with the definite requirements of the law, which are as follows: (1) Property may be seized even though no crime has been committed, if it is held or concealed with the intent to use it as the means of committing a public offense, for example, infernal machines.[14]

---

[11] Concurrent Resolution, March 26, 1919.
[12] I Birdseye & Gilbert, Consol. Laws, 2d ed., 1079, § 8; Code of Criminal Procedure, §§ 791-813; N. Y. Cons., Art. I., § 6. See Boyd v. U. S., 116 U. S. 616, on self-incrimination in connection with searches.
[13] P. v. McDonald, 177 N. Y. App. Div. 806 (1917).
[14] Cooley, *op. cit.*, 431, doubts the validity of warrants for preventive purposes. However, the *N. Y. Code of Crim. Proc.*, § 792, is ex-

A man's privacy must not be invaded for the sole purpose of obtaining evidence against him, but only to obtain a dangerous instrument of past or future crimes. (2) The warrant is to be issued by a judicial officer, after a showing made before him under oath that there is probable cause for suspicion of a crime and the concealment of articles involved in it, which must be particularly described by the affidavit. (3) The magistrate must examine on oath the complainant and any witnesses he may produce, take written depositions subscribed by the witnesses, and satisfy himself that there is probable cause to believe the suspicion of crime is well founded. The suspicion itself is no ground for the warrant except as the facts justify it.[15] (4) The warrant must specify the place to be searched and the precise objects to be seized. Very great particularity is required, and not such blanket descriptions as "goods, wares and merchandises," or, as Entinck's case proved, "his books and papers." In other words, there must be a real exercise of discretion on the part of the judge or magistrate, and he must not be a mere rubber stamp for any government official who wants a hurry-up warrant to clean out somebody's house or office. (5) The warrant must command that the articles to be searched for be brought before the magistrate, to the end that, upon further examination into the facts, the goods, and the party in whose custody they were, may be disposed of according to law. And it is a fatal objection to such a warrant that it leaves the disposition of the articles to the searching officer, instead of enabling the judge to determine by investigation the truth of the complaint made. The property must be delivered in conformity with the war-

---

plicit. In some cases, preparation of the dangerous object might amount to a criminal attempt.

[15] Cooley, *op. cit.*, 429; *Code Cr. Proc.*, §§ 793 ff.; Gaynor, J. (afterwards Mayor), in Matter of Blum, 9 Misc. 571 (1894), in nullifying a warrant of arrest issued on information and belief: "Human liberty was never so cheap as that under our law. . . . It is important that crime should be punished, but far more important that arbitrary power should not be tolerated. The 'oath or affirmation' required is of facts." Comfort *v.* Fulton, 39 Barb. 56 (1861), *accord*.

WILKES AND HIS SUCCESSORS

rant, together with a detailed written inventory.[16] A hearing is then to be held, and if the grounds for the warrant fail, the property must be returned. (6) The magistrate must send the depositions, warrant, and inventory, to the court which has power to inquire through a grand jury into the offense in respect to which the warrant was issued. The New York statutes and decisions are explicit on all these matters, and make it a misdemeanor to procure a warrant maliciously and without probable cause, or for an officer to exceed his authority or exercise it with unnecessary severity.[17]

Let us consider how these requirements were observed in the various raids. The first was against the Bureau of the Representative of the Russian Socialist Soviet Republic in the United States,[18] which had been established in April, 1918, in the World Tower Building, by L. C. A. K. Martens, the as yet unrecognized " ambassador " of the Republic in the United States. An agent of the Committee made affidavit to a magistrate that he had picked up a typewritten document from the floor of the Bureau entitled " Groans from Omsk," apparently a call to the workingmen of Omsk to establish a Soviet form of government, and that the Bureau was " engaged in the distribution of literature calculated to stimulate revolutionary activities in this state." A search-warrant was then issued in blanket form authorizing the seizure of " All documents, circulars, and papers printed or typewritten, having to do with Socialist, Labor, Revolutionary, or Bolshevik activities; all books, letters, and papers pertaining to the activities of said Bureau, all circulars and literature of any sort, kind, or character; " in the words of the *Times*, " practically everything that might be construed as documentary evidence in the place." These were

---

[16] Cooley, 431; *Code Cr. Proc.*, §§ 797, 805 ff.

[17] Notes 12, 13, 15, 16, 19-20; Sanford *v.* Richardson, 176 N. Y. App. Div. 199 (1916).

[18] For a description of the Bureau's work, see *American Labor Year-Book*, 1919-20, 383-386. The raid is narrated in *New York Times*, June 13, 1919, and following days. See Bibliography.

to be brought forthwith before the magistrate at his office. On June 12, 1919, a squad of the State Constabulary took possession of the Bureau, excluded all persons in charge, and ransacked every drawer and cabinet for papers and other material, even breaking open the cash-box. Hundreds of books and pamphlets, Martens's private bank books, and all letters and other documents in the files were taken away in disorder, including more than a thousand letters of American business concerns relating to the shipment of merchandise to Russia. All these papers were taken on trucks, not to the magistrate, but to the office of the Lusk Committee in the Prince George Hotel, where it is charged that they were examined not only by members of the Committee, but by an agent of the British Secret Service, who shortly afterwards departed for England with the information that he had obtained. It is, of course, well known that Great Britain may soon resume business relations with Russia. This charge is denied by the Committee, and the investigation proposed by the Socialist Assemblymen lapsed upon their expulsion. Letters taken from the Bureau were read into the record of the Lusk Committee, and disclosed to the press, besides the names of a large number of persons on the mailing list of the Bureau, although there was nothing to indicate that they were in any way connected with its work, or sympathized with its aims. None of this material was ever delivered to the magistrate who issued the search-warrant or steps taken to institute criminal proceedings. The seized papers and books were merely used as the basis for the Committee's subsequent examination of Martens and his associates, in order to prepare a report to the legislature and provide fire-eating material for the newspapers.

The Appellate Division of the New York Supreme Court has declared:[19]

Under the broad provisions of the Fourth Amendment to the Federal Constitution and of our Bill of Rights, which is sub-

[19] Matter of Ehrich *v.* Root, 134 N. Y. App. Div. 432, 438 (1909).

WILKES AND HIS SUCCESSORS

stantially the same as that enacted in the other States of the Union, it has been held that the right to security of one's person, house, papers and effects against unreasonable searches and seizures extends as well to letters and sealed packages, and prohibits searches for property other than those to aid in the administration of the criminal law.

If it be urged that the Lusk Committee was acting to obtain evidence as the basis of a criminal prosecution against this Bureau and its affairs, the proceeding was still more invalid, because it would compel persons to give evidence against themselves contrary to the New York Constitution. That the legislature intended by a mere joint resolution to confer upon a committee " a power far in excess of that conferred upon any tribunal or official—a power so extreme as to be despotic in its character " is unthinkable. The same court has said that the right against unnecessary searches and seizures and the right against self-incrimination are " the complements of each other, directed against the different ways by which a man's immunity from giving evidence against himself may be violated." [20]

No inquisitorial officer should be permitted, of his own volition, arbitrarily and without any check or safeguards upon the rights of the citizen, to compel him to produce and submit to his scrutinizing gaze all his books and papers of the most private and confidential character. . . . Nor is it any answer to say that this examination is not sought in any criminal proceedings. In the absence of a full and complete statute of indemnity, a person should not be compelled, when acting as a witness in any investigation, to give evidence which may tend to imperil his constitutional privilege. . . . Compulsory process to produce such papers, not in a judicial proceeding, but before a commissioner of inquiry is as subversive of " all the comforts of society " as their seizure under the general warrant.

If any business man will consider what it would mean to have a number of men breaking into his office with such

---

[20] Matter of Foster, 139 N. Y. App. Div. 769 (1910). See also *Ex parte* Clarke, 126 Cal. 235 (1899).

a blanket warrant and close his business for a day, turn all his letter files into confusion, and carry off some of his most important correspondence for disclosure to outsiders, he will see what is the possible result of encouraging lawlessness of this kind. We are disposed to pardon raids of this sort because they are against radicals. We ought to remember that the same methods may be used by any other investigating committee, for instance, for the purpose of learning why prices are high, in which case they might be employed against any wholesale or retail establishment.

The Lusk Committee next raided the Rand School, on East Fifteenth Street, near Fifth Avenue, a Socialist and Labor college, established in 1906, and having over 5,000 registered students. Its methods are those of any other institution of higher education, and its work is stated by its Director to fall into two parts, " that which offers opportunities for the general public to study Socialism and related subjects, that which gives Socialists such systematic instruction and training as may render them more efficient workers in and for the Socialist Party, the Trade Unions and the Co-operatives." [21] It also conducts a large reference library and reading room, containing several thousand volumes, pamphlets, and periodicals, open to the public without charge, and a book store, doing a large mail-order business, chiefly, though by no means exclusively, in books and pamphlets relating to social and labor questions. It is supported partly from this store and its moderate tuition fees and partly by private contributions. Except for the fact that its owner, the American Socialist Society, had been convicted under the Espionage Act for publishing Scott Nearing's *Great Madness*,[22] it had never come in conflict with the law.

On June 21, agents of the Committee appeared with ten

---

[21] *American Labor Year-Book* 1919-20, pp. 206-8, 109-112. The raid is narrated in *New York Times,* June 22, 1919, and following days. See Bibliography.

[22] See Appendix II and page 27, *supra.*

state troopers and forty ex-members of the American Protective League (now disbanded by the Department of Justice), carrying another blanket warrant, authorizing the seizure of "All publications, documents, books, circulars, letters, typewritten or printed matter having to do with Anarchists, Socialists advocating violence, revolutionary or Bolshevist activities, and all books, letters, and papers pertaining to the activities or business carried on in said offices, and all circulars and letters of any sort, kind, or character." This was obtained on affidavit that certain books and pamphlets which the informant purchased in the public book shop on the ground floor contained "revolutionary, seditious, and obscene statements." A number of the raiders carried arms. They proceeded to ransack all the rooms on the ground floor of the school and load the papers into trucks, which as before were not taken to the magistrate, but to the headquarters of the Lusk Committee. Two days later the raiders returned to the school with a new warrant obtained on affidavit that three persons had been heard to say at the school, "It is a good thing they haven't opened the big safe on the third floor." Safe experts were directed to drill a hole in the three-ton safe and open it. The raiders then removed all the correspondence, check stubs, accounts, and minutes of the meetings of the American Socialist Society. The Director of the school drew the attention of the state troopers to the fact that these papers clearly fell outside the warrant. He replied, "Oh, that ain't what we're after. We want to get at the source of the financial support of the Rand School." The Committee, without having any one from the Rand School to explain the papers and the purposes of the school, immediately gave all kinds of prejudicial reports to the press throughout the country. It will be recalled that the function of the Committee was to report to the Legislature. The Attorney General began an action to dissolve the charter of the Rand School, which was ignominiously dropped at the first sign of a fight. He could not even produce a *prima facie* case.

Mr. Samuel Untermyer, who, though not a Socialist, undertook the school's case without pay, wrote to Senator Lusk:

There is a library connected with the Rand School, which conducts also a book store for the sale of books and periodicals. Its printed catalogue, which I have now seen for the first time, embraces thousands of books, mainly classics and economics, among which, it appears, you have discovered one periodical and two or three books from which you have extracted and published occasional sentences containing discussions on birth control, revolutionary changes in government, and the like. You have deliberately attempted to distort these few instances in the public prints so as to create the false impression that this is the general character of the teachings of the School, when in point of fact the School appears to be an educational institution of an unusually high order, with courses of studies taught by some of the most eminent professors in the country, most of them holding positions in the great universities of the country.

The New York Public Library and probably every other great public library and book store has on its shelves hundred of books of the character you condemn to every one that the Rand book store or library contains. Why not seize their property and blow open their safes, under an improvidently granted warrant and try to close their doors? . . . You might with equal justification have raided any book store in New York City.

These searches were illegal: (1) the affidavit stated no probable cause of use of the papers for crime, but only the court's rumors and suspicions of something objectionable; (2) the complainant was not examined by the magistrate, who took no pains to satisfy himself of a valid cause for search; (3) the warrant did not particularly state the articles to be seized, but was as bad as that against Entinck, or worse; (4) a large portion of the correspondence and other papers seized could not possibly be instruments of crime; (5) the papers were not taken to the magistrate; (6) the whole affair had no connection with any criminal proceeding, but was half legislative investigation and half advertising.

Massachusetts has a constitutional provision in its Bill of

WILKES AND HIS SUCCESSORS

Rights [23] like the federal Fourth Amendment, requiring the same particular description of the articles to be seized. Nevertheless, the district attorney of Middlesex County raided a book-bindery in Cambridge and carried off forty-five hundred red-bound copies of *The Proletarian Revolution in Russia*, by N. Lenine and Leon Trotsky, a collection of documents on recent events, by virtue of a warrant authorizing the seizure of obscene literature. In Boston, the police raided a Communist hall with a warrant setting up that firearms were illegally on the premises,[24] but as the *Boston Herald* naïvely put it, " they had accurate information which made it possible for them to seize the *papers* they sought almost as soon as they entered the hall." If they could seize papers on such a warrant, they could enter a house and take silverware. And this in the state where James Otis denounced general warrants as " the worst instrument of arbitrary power, the most destructive of English liberty and the fundamental principles of law, that ever was found in an English law book," since they placed " the liberty of every man in the hands of every petty officer."

III. *The Exclusion of Wilkes from the House of Commons*

Dr. Johnson: " Is there not a law, Sir, against exporting the current coin of the realm? "

Wilkes: " Yes, Sir: but might not the House of Commons, in case of real evident necessity, order our own current coin to be sent into our own colonies? "

Dr. Johnson: " Sure, Sir, *you* don't think a resolution of the House of Commons equal to *the law of the land?*

Wilkes: " God forbid, Sir."

We now return to a second great principle established by Wilkes. The Grenville Government, which found him such an expensive opponent, brought an information against him

---

[23] Part First, Art. XIV. 3d District Court, E. Middlesex, No. 2972, Nov. 12, 1919. The court found there was no obscenity and the books were returned.

[24] *Boston Herald*, December 18, 1919; italics mine. Gun warrants are authorized by Mass. Laws, 1919, c. 179.

for seditious libel on account of what would now be considered an ordinary political editorial. He was a member of the House of Commons. The House ordered the newspaper to be burned by the common hangman and summoned Wilkes to attend for further proceedings. Meanwhile the government encouraged bullies to make way with him. Forced into a duel, he fled to France. Evidence was taken of his being the author and publisher of the *North Briton*, No. 45, and he was expelled for the seditious libel published during his term as member of Parliament. May considers that this expulsion was legal, but precipitate and vindictive, for Wilkes was about to be tried for his offense, and the House might at least have waited for his conviction, instead of prejudging his cause and anticipating his legal punishment.[25] Later he was convicted in his absence, and outlawed for contumacy.

Four years went by, the general election of 1768 was approaching, and he returned from exile to stand for Parliament. After a defeat in the City of London, he presented himself as a candidate for Middlesex. The working people allowed no man to travel to the polls without a paper in his hat inscribed, "Number 45. Wilkes and Liberty!" Convict and outlaw as Wilkes was, his vote was overwhelming.

After his election, Wilkes surrendered himself into custody, and went to jail. Lord Mansfield reversed the outlawry, and Wilkes was sentenced, on the original charge of seditious libel, to nearly two years in prison. Obviously, the King should have pardoned him. His sentence was unwarranted, and its remission would have relegated him, as Trevelyan puts it, " to an obscurity whence, but for the infatuation of his enemies, he would never have emerged." A feeble speaker, he would have been negligible; in the words of Junius, " a silent senator, and hardly supporting the eloquence of a weekly newspaper." But the King and the Cabinet were his implacable enemies and he was left in prison. And, then going back forty years to the precedent

[25] 1 May, *Constitutional History*, 312.

of a member who had been expelled for forgery, the House of Commons declared Wilkes's seat to be vacant by a vote of two hundred and nineteen to one hundred and thirty-seven.

A new election was held, and though still in prison, he was re-elected. The House next day voted that, having been expelled, he was incapable of serving in Parliament. A third election followed with the same result. Burke told his fellow members that Wilkes had grown great by their folly, and Townshend reminded his hearers "that a heavy account would some day be exacted from them if they continued to postpone all useful legislation for the sake of a frivolous and interminable squabble." But the election was declared null and void without a division. An opponent was produced for the fourth election in one Luttrell, who drew one vote to Wilkes's four, but was declared by the House of Commons to be member for Middlesex, after a debate in which even George Grenville rallied to the support of his old enemy, Wilkes, with such vehemence that when he sat down he spat blood, shortening his life to diminish the majority against the lawfully elected candidate. Blackstone tried to show that Wilkes was disqualified by common law, but was confuted by a passage in the early editions of his *Commentaries*, which he carefully altered in the edition of 1773 and which said that every British subject not in certain specified classes was " eligible of common right." The majority was forced to rely on precedents from the Great Civil War, when the majority expelled the minority and was itself expelled in turn, until the House of Commons was reduced to forty-six members. Luttrell's election was confirmed, against the petition of the Middlesex electors, and the King prorogued Parliament.

Burke expounded the principle involved in Wilkes's exclusion in his *Thoughts on the Present Discontents*. The only check on arbitrary power is the presence here and there on the benches of members endowed with a " spirit of independence carried to some degree of enthusiasm, an inquisitive character to discover, and a bold one to display, every corruption and every error of government." Such qualities are distasteful to those in power, and Wilkes was the example chosen to discourage others, just as the arrest of five members by Charles I, if successfully conducted, would have stifled liberty as effectually as the execution of fifty. The question was whether the people or the government should select the legislature. The leading Whigs stood behind Burke, and denounced the position, that a resolution of any branch of the legislature could " make, alter, suspend, abrogate, or annihilate the law of the land."

Of all the statements of the cause of Wilkes, that of Burke in debate has the greatest value for our own time:

> Accumulative crimes are things unknown to the courts below. In those courts two bad things will not make one capital offense. This is a serving up like cooks. Some will eat of one dish, and some of another, so that there will not be a fragment left. Some will like the strong solid roast-beef of the blasphemous libel. One honorable member could not bear to see Christianity abused, because it was part of the common law of England. This is substantial roast-beef reasoning. One gentleman said he meant Mr. Wilkes's petition to be the ground of expulsion; another, the message from the House of Lords. " I come into this resolution," says a fourth, " because of his censure upon the conduct of a great magistrate." " In times of danger," says a fifth, " I am afraid of doing anything that will shake the government." These charges are all brought together to form an accumulated offense, which may extend to the expulsion of every other member of this House. This law, as it is now laid down, is that any member who, at any time, has been guilty of writing a libel will never be free from punishment. Is any man, when he takes up his pen, certain that the day may not come when he may wish to be a member of Parliament? This, sir, will put a last hand to the liberty of the press.

It was not until his fourth election had been annulled that Wilkes left prison. The persecution of the government had turned him from an obscure member of Parliament into a man of national prominence. As Junius said, " The rays

WILKES AND HIS SUCCESSORS 315

of the Royal indignation, collected upon him, served only to illuminate, and could not consume." The people, unable to send him to Parliament, made him Alderman and then Lord Mayor of London, while Luttrell voted with the majority in the Commons. At the next general election in 1774, he was returned for Middlesex and allowed to take his seat, since Massachusetts was causing too much trouble to encourage a stirring up of old grievances at home. Thereafter, he sat without interruption, while the men who had expelled him brought the nation into its lowest humiliation. In 1782 the resolution of 1769 declaring him incapable of election was expunged from the records " as being subversive of the rights of the whole body of electors of this kingdom."

IV. *The Exclusion of Victor L. Berger from the House of Representatives*

The most prominent person convicted under the Espionage Act, with the exception of Debs, was Victor L. Berger. He was born in Austria in 1860, came to this country in 1878, and was a founder of the Socialist Party in the United States, editor of the *Milwaukee Leader*, and member of Congress, 1911-1913, the first Socialist to serve in Washington. The left-wing Socialists have always regarded him as a bourgeois member of the party. Before we entered the European War, he gave vigorous expression to the orthodox Socialist views about war, and employed many of the arguments in favor of American neutrality which were used at that time by non-Socialists, for instance, in the key-note speech of Governor Glynn at the Democratic National Convention of 1916 and in the President's note of December 18, 1916, to all the belligerents, asking them to state their terms of peace. Unlike the great majority of Americans, Berger and other Socialists did not consider the German submarine campaign of February, 1917, a sufficient reason for changing their minds, but maintained that war was justified only in case of invasion. He was a member of the resolutions committee of the Socialist Convention at St. Louis and signed the Proclamation and War Program of April 14, 1917, which has already been mentioned.[26] It branded the declaration of war as a crime against the people of the United States and the nations of the world, and stated that in all modern history there had been no war more unjustifiable. Mr. Roosevelt called these planks "treason to the United States."[27] Berger published this platform in the *Milwaukee Leader*, and poured out a stream of editorials, articles, and cartoons, denouncing the war policies of the government. He did not, however, urge any one to resist the draft, and indeed advised one Socialist conscientious objector to put on the uniform. Berger testified that several men in his immediate family volunteered, although his opposition would have prevented them from doing so. It is, of course, well known that the record of Wisconsin and Milwaukee in the war was very high, and while Berger can take no credit for this, it tends to disprove that opposition to war produces violations of the draft act or other war laws.[28]

In September, 1917, the *Leader* was deprived of its second-class mailing privilege for the future by a blanket order of the Postmaster General, and relief was subsequently denied by the courts.[29] The newspaper thus lost a daily circulation of approximately 15,000 subscribers. All first-class mail addressed to the *Leader* was returned to the sender. The District of Columbia Court of Appeals said of the articles on which the exclusion was based, and in this opinion the House of Representatives committee afterwards concurred:

No one can read them without becoming convinced that they were printed in a spirit of hostility to our own government and in a spirit of sympathy for the Central Powers; that through

---

[26] P. 162, *supra*.
[27] *Berger Hearings*, I, 72.
[28] *Ibid.*, II, 460; I, 323; I, 166.
[29] U. S. *ex. rel.* Milwaukee Social Democrat Pub. Co. *v.* Burleson, 258 Fed. 282 (1919). The full record is in *Berger Hearings*, I, 503 ff.

WILKES AND HIS SUCCESSORS

them, appellant sought to hinder and embarrass the government in the prosecution of the war.

The reader can determine the general character of the *Milwaukee Leader* from the passages abstracted in a later paragraph, and decide for himself whether the judicial and legislative comments quoted in this chapter are correct in concluding that Berger wanted to aid Germany. My own opinion is that they err in confusing opposition to the war with wishing the enemy to win. Whether Berger was within the terms of the Espionage Act or not, I find in his writings no desire that the militarism and autocracy of Germany should triumph, but rather a series of extremely bitter and cynical attacks upon what seemed to him the Junkerism and selfishness of all the governments on both sides of the war. They indicate that he wanted the war to end at once because in the absence of invasion he sincerely believed it unnecessary and a crushing burden upon the workers of America. I say this although I thoroughly detest the attitude of Berger. I can understand the abhorrence of Debs for a law which compels a man to kill fellow-workers because their rulers quarrel, and recognize that he speaks from the heart even while I disagree with him. But for Berger the war seems only an impersonal step in an economic argument. His is not the position of the man who has weighed the good and bad reasons and motives which are inextricably mingled in war as in most human actions, and finding that the bad outweigh the good, calls for peace despite the ideals which he recognizes behind the war. Berger ignores the good, and sets forth only meanness. He sneers at the possibility of noble purposes in the conflict, and nowhere utters a word of praise or sympathy for those who gave up home and life with the desire that the world should not be made an armed camp and that oppressed nations should be free from military domination.

Despite all this, the fundamental question remains, whether it is for the advantage of government by public opinion and popular election that just because most of us consider a person's views detestable, he should be thrown into prison and American citizens should be denied the right to be represented by the man of their choice.

In February, 1918, Berger was indicted with four other Socialists for conspiracy under the Espionage Act. The indictment was brought in Chicago, because the defendants were alleged to have agreed there for the issue of publications in various places. The overt acts which Berger himself was said to have committed consisted of five editorials in the *Leader*, which were in substance as follows: (1) We were in the war because the Allies were at the end of their rope, and their obligations would otherwise be worthless; continued fighting would maintain the existing high prices of munition stocks; war meant absolute freedom from labor troubles, since strikes would be put down as treason; the plutocracy and its government in Washington would be enabled to establish autocracy as a war necessity; war would be a wonderful chance to establish a large permanent army; the commercial rivalry of Germany would be ended. The submarines, Belgium, invasion, and democracy had nothing to do with it. (2) There are many men driven insane at the front. (3) Young men do not talk as if they considered it an honor to be drafted. (4) Only big business men and their satellites are enthusiastic over the war, but they do not fight. (5) The Bible contains many passages which are opposed to war and must therefore be considered as treasonable.

Shortly before the indictment, Berger was nominated for the United States Senate on a Socialist platform announcing that if elected he would work for a speedy, general, democratic, and permanent peace without forcible annexations and punitive indemnities; an immediate armistice and peace conference; the withdrawal of American troops from Europe and their use to secure this country from invasion; confiscation of war profits; and safeguards to prevent panic or unemployment when demobilization should take place. War would ruin the country and could be ended by electing men pledged to end it.³⁰ He was defeated, but in spite of the charges pending against him received over 100,000 votes.

In November, 1918, before the trial began, he was elected to Congress from the fifth district of Wisconsin, polling 17,920 votes against 12,450 for the Democratic candidate and 10,678 for the Republican. In December, he was put on trial before Judge Kenesaw Mountain Landis, who several years ago imposed a fine of $29,000,000 on the Standard Oil Company, which was afterwards set aside. Judge Landis sentenced Berger and the other defendants to twenty years imprisonment. An appeal to the Circuit Court of Appeals is still pending, and the defendants were released on bail.³¹

When Berger presented himself to the House of Representatives to be sworn in, it was charged that he was ineligible, and the question was referred to a special committee, which reported ³² for reasons hereafter stated that he was not entitled to take the oath of office or hold a seat as Representative. At the same time the candidate with the next highest number of votes, Joseph P. Carney, had claimed the seat, on the ground that since Berger was ineligible those persons who had voted for him should be considered to have deliberately thrown away their ballots—in the words of an English judge, just as if they had voted "for the man in the moon." ³³ Although this is the English law, and a Wisconsin decision had reached the same result where the leading candidate was known at the time of the election to be dead,³⁴ the Congressional practice is otherwise, and holds

---

³⁰ *Berger Hearings*, I, 340.

³¹ Volume II of *Berger Hearings* contains the full record of the trial. The charge is also in Bull. Dept. Just., No. 186. Comment from the Socialist side is in *American Labor Year-Book*, 1919-20, pp. 97-100, and the *Socialist Review*, February, 1920. O'Brian speaks of "the dignity and fairness" which characterized the work of the court. 52 Rep. N. Y. Bar Assn. 310 (1919).

³² House of Representatives, 66th Cong., 1st Sess., Ho. Cal. No. 91, Rep. No. 413, hereafter called Berger Report.

³³ Lord Campbell, C. J., in Regina *v.* Coaks, 3 E. & B. 249, 254 (1854).

³⁴ Beresford-Hope *v.* Lady Sandhurst, 23 Q. B. D. 79 (1889). Women were allowed to vote for County Councillor and were supposed to be eligible to hold the office. The highest candidate was a woman. The

that electors ought not to be disfranchised in such a fashion, especially when they supposed the leading candidate to be eligible.[35] It would be absurdly harsh to presume that those who voted for Berger in November knew that he was disqualified, just because a jury convicted him the following January. Consequently, Carney gained nothing by his contest, but on November 11, 1919, the House of Representatives with only one dissenting member, Voigt of Wisconsin, declared Berger's seat vacant.[36]

The Governor of Wisconsin ordered a special election on December 19, 1919. The Republicans and Democrats nominated a fusion candidate, H. H. Bodenstab, and the German paper, the *Herold*, appealed to all German-Americans to support their compatriot against Berger. The Socialist vote was increased by nearly 8,000 over the first election, Berger receiving 25,802 ballots to 19,800 for his opponent. On January 10, 1920, the House again refused to seat him. This time, six Representatives voted in his favor, including Floor Manager James R. Mann, who said during the debate:

Mr. Berger has been elected anew to the House by a majority of those who vote in his district and to me the question is whether we shall maintain inviolate the representative form of government where people who desire changes in the fundamental or other laws of the land shall have the right to be represented on the floor of this House, when they control a majority of the votes in a Congressional district.

I do not share the views of Mr. Berger, but I am willing to meet his views in an argument before the people rather than to say we shall deny him the opportunity to be heard when selected by the people in the legal form and invite them, in effect, to resort to violence.

Has it come to the point that a man who believes certain things cannot be heard? His people, his constituents, desire him to represent them. It is not our duty to select a representative from

court seated the highest male candidate. State *ex rel.* Bancroft *v.* Frear, 144 Wis. 79 (1910).

[35] Smith *v.* Brown, 1 Hinds' Precedents 448; *Re* Abbott, 1 *ibid.* 478. *Accord*, P. *ex rel.* Furman *v.* Clute, 50 N. Y. 451 (1872).

[36] The debates on the two exclusions are in *New York Times*, November 12, 1919, January 11, 1920.

this Congressional district. That is the duty of the people back at home. We cannot take the attitude of refusing to permit the voice of the people of a district to be heard by their own selection with safety to the future of the country.

Berger afterwards stated that he was accused of calling the late war a capitalist war, and that the President had said the same thing at St. Louis on September 5, 1919, when he declared:

> Why, my fellow citizens, is there any man here or woman who does not know that the seed of war in the modern world is industrial and commercial rivalry? This war was a commercial and industrial war. It was not a political war.

Within an hour after Berger was unseated, the Socialist committee in Milwaukee announced his renomination for a third contest. However, he has not yet equalled the record of Wilkes, for the Governor of Wisconsin has decided that another special election would be too expensive. Meanwhile, Berger has been forbidden to speak in several cities, including that founded by Roger Williams, and Jersey City forcibly ran him out of town. Whatever the legal merits of his case in the courts and Congress, his enemies like those of Wilkes have adopted against him the very methods that vastly increase his influence.

The question whether a person who is duly elected to either branch of Congress is rendered ineligible because during a war he expressed opinions opposed to its continuance and the methods by which it was waged is full of difficulties. It is sometimes supposed that the clause in the Constitution,[37] " Each House shall be the Judge of the Elections, Returns, and Qualifications of its own Members," gives a majority the unlimited right to exclude any one. The problem is less simple than that. Each house is to act as

---

[37] U. S. Cons., Art. 1, § 5. That this a judicial proceeding, to be decided in accordance with legal principles as established by precedents, cases of Abbott, 1 Hinds' Prec. 478; Lorimer, in Webb and Pierce, Senate Election Cases, 1061; and page 340, *infra.*

"judge," that is, it must decide the facts by applying to them rules of law, and must not proceed arbitrarily. For instance, the majority has no right to exclude the minority by a new Pride's Purge. It is undoubtedly true that if the House of Representatives should exclude a man on some whimsical ground, no appeal would lie from its action. Neither is there any appeal from the Supreme Court, but for this very reason it feels a grave responsibility to decide according to law. In the same way, the House has only the power to decide whether the man received the proper number of votes and satisfies the qualifications established by law, and it ought not to create new requirements for a particular case any more than a criminal judge ought to invent new crimes.

What then are the lawful qualifications for membership in the House of Representatives? The authorities disclose two divergent views. The first is, that the Constitution contains all the qualifications, and that if a district elects a man who conforms to its requirements, he must be seated, no matter how unfit he is considered by the rest of the House. His unfitness is not a reason for exclusion by a majority vote, but may if continuing in character justify his expulsion by a two-thirds vote. The second view holds that additional tests may be imposed by statute or possibly in accordance with established usage to cover obvious cases of unfitness, such as conviction of crime. Since the committee report in the Berger case held that he should be unseated, even under the first view, we can postpone the controversy whether his conviction was a bar, until after discussing his eligibility under the terms of the Constitution.

The original requirements are threefold: [38]

> No Person shall be a Representative who shall not have attained to the Age of twenty-five Years, and been seven Years a Citizen of the United States, and who shall not, when elected, be an Inhabitant of that State in which he shall be chosen.

[38] U. S. Cons., Art. I, § 2.

WILKES AND HIS SUCCESSORS

Berger satisfied all these. However, the committee reported that he was excluded by a fourth qualification, enacted in 1868 by section 3 of the Fourteenth Amendment:

> No person shall be a Senator or Representative in Congress, or elector of President and Vice President, or hold any office, civil or military, under the United States, or under any State, who, having previously taken an oath, as a member of Congress, or as an officer of the United States, or as a member of any State legislature, or as an executive or judicial officer of any State, to support the Constitution of the United States, shall have engaged in insurrection or rebellion against the same, or given aid or comfort to the enemies thereof. But Congress may by a vote of two-thirds of each House, remove such disability.

At the outset the committee decided not to be governed by the action of the judge and jury at Chicago, but to review all the evidence at that trial, the proceedings about the exclusion of the *Leader* from the mails, and the fresh testimony introduced at the hearings. The conclusions of fact were as follows: [39]

> After a careful consideration of all the evidence, in the opinion of your committee the admitted acts, writings, and declarations of Victor L. Berger and of the men with whom he was associated in the management and control of the Socialist Party from the time of the entrance of this country into the war until their indictment by a Federal grand jury, giving such acts and the language of the writings and declarations their ordinary everyday meaning and without considering any other evidence, clearly establishes a conscious, deliberate and continuing purpose and intent to obstruct, hinder, and embarrass the Government of the United States in the prosecution of the war and thus to give aid and comfort to the enemies of our country. The writings and activities of Mr. Berger and his associates could have had no other purpose. That Victor L. Berger was disloyal to the United States of America and did give aid and comfort to its enemies at a time when its existence as a free and independent Nation was at stake there can not be the slightest doubt.

Even if Berger's guilt under the Espionage Act be considered as established, three replies are conceivable to the

[39] *Berger Report*, 7.

proposition that such guilt renders him ineligible under the Fourteenth Amendment. (1) This provision may relate to the Civil War only, like section 4 of the same Amendment about pensions and Confederate debts. Since section 1, forbidding states to deprive citizens of the United States of life, liberty, or property without due process of law, has been construed to protect much more than the rights of emancipated slaves, the committee rejected this argument. (2) Early in the Spanish War, in order to cement good feeling between North and South, both houses by the necessary two-thirds vote adopted a blanket resolution, "that the disability imposed by section three . . . heretofore incurred is hereby removed." [40] The committee held that this could not apply to a subsequent disability. (3) Berger's violation of the Espionage Act was not a bar under the Fourteenth Amendment because it did not amount to treason. This is a very important point and it is an odd commentary on legislative justice that every one involved in the Berger case, except Representative Mann, overlooked it completely and assumed that " aid and comfort to the enemy " was synonymous with guilt under the Espionage Act. Of course, this phrase is often employed loosely in conversation and Congressional debates to include all sorts of language that is considered disloyal in war time, but legally these words have a technical significance, and they are used in a statute or in the Fourteenth Amendment in the same sense as in the clause of the Constitution defining treason.[41] Therefore, the

[40] Act, June 6, 1898, c. 389.
[41] Art. III, § 3: "Treason against the United States, shall consist only in levying War against them, or in adhering to their Enemies, giving them Aid and Comfort." The omission of any mention of adherence in the Fourteenth Amendment is immaterial. Judge Leavitt said in 1861 (1 Bond 611): "The words in the definition, *adhering to their enemies,* seem to have no special significance, as the substance is found in the words which follow—*giving them aid and comfort.*" Judge Learned Hand said in U. S. *v.* Robinson, 259 Fed. 685, 690 (1919): "The words 'adhering' must be taken as defined by the phrase 'giving aid and comfort.'" The U. S. Supreme Court has reached the same result in construing the Captured and Abandoned Property Act of March 12, 1863 (12 Stat. L. 820), which allowed the owner of any captured property to reclaim its value from the United States, on proof

acts of aid and comfort which would disqualify Berger from serving in Congress under the Amendment (if section three is still in force) must be of the same general character with those necessary to convict him of treason.

Was Berger guilty of treason? In answering this question, we must not be misled by colloquial usage. Mr. Roosevelt denounced the St. Louis Socialist platform as "treason," and "traitor" is a heart-warming conversational epithet for any one who wants a war stopped, but lawyers and legislators must be less vague in accusing a man of a crime that is punishable with death. Chief Justice Marshall said long ago [42] that treason should not be extended by construction to doubtful cases, and there has never been a decision that talking against a war is treason. If it were, Vallandigham, Milligan, and the other Copperheads would surely have been prosecuted for this crime. The few writers [43] who assert that the Espionage Act of 1917 created no new crimes, but that causing insubordination in the armed forces and obstructing enlistment are also treason,[44] are forced to rely on one or two sweeping judicial definitions, like Lord Reading's charge in the trial of Sir Roger Casement, that it is giving aid and comfort to the enemy to do any act which tends to strengthen them or tends to weaken the power of one's own country to resist.[45] So broad a statement would if taken

---

that he had "never given aid or comfort to the present rebellion." In Young v. U. S., 97 U. S. 39, 62 (1877), the Court held, through Chief Justice Waite, that although a British claimant could not commit treason since he owed no allegiance, "the acts of aid and comfort which will defeat a suit must be of the same general character with those necessary to convict of treason. . . . It is sufficient if he has done that which would have made him a traitor if he had owed allegiance to the United States."

[42] *Ex parte* Bollman and Swartwout, 4 Cranch 77, 127 (1807).

[43] Charles Warren, "What Is Giving Aid and Comfort to the Enemy," 27 Y. L. J. 331 (1918); Thomas F. Carroll, 17 *Mich. L. Rev.* 660 (1918).

[44] If so, the treason statute would have rendered the Espionage Act unnecessary. Instead the treason statute proved well-nigh useless during the war. See p. 41, *supra*.

[45] Rex v. Casement [1917], 1 K. B. 98, 133. Warren, *op cit.*, quotes other judges. They plainly refer to language used to cause men to join the enemy and participate in his operations. Such words form an

literally revive all the evils of constructive treason, but it must be limited with reference to the particular facts which the jury were considering. Casement had issued a proclamation to Irish prisoners in Germany urging them to form a regiment in the German army.[46] The use of words in an attempt to gain recruits for the enemy is absolutely different from telling your fellow-citizens that they ought to stop fighting. It may be that the latter is so dangerous that it must be punished, but only as sedition, which consists of *words* creating disaffection. Treason requires overt *acts* of direct assistance to the enemy. The distinction is fundamental. It is inconceivable that the trivial utterances which were held criminal under the Espionage Act because of their bad tendency and the supposed intention to hinder the war were already subject under the treason statute to a death penalty.

This distinction is clearly brought out by the kind of conduct which has been held to be " giving aid and comfort to the enemy," [47] for example, furnishing money, troops or arms, saltpeter for gunpowder, steamers for blockade running, delivering up deserters and prisoners, and actually joining the enemy in person. Contrast these acts, which advance the cause of the enemy by their immediate effect, with newspaper articles attacking the war, which may encourage the enemy but do not promote his success in any

element in acts of direct aid. These judges are not speaking of expressions of opinion about the injustice of a war, even if intended to deter men from enlisting in one's own army. *Cf.* note 49.

[46] It is doubtful if even this would be treason in this country, inasmuch as no one was persuaded to enlist. Respublica *v.* Roberts, 1 Dall. 39 (Pa. 1778). But see U. S. *v.* Robinson, 259 Fed. 685, 690, on unsuccessful attempts to aid. This point in the Casement trial received no attention from the Court of Appeal, which was entirely occupied with the question whether treason could be committed outside England, answered in the affirmative. It is interesting to Americans to find that one of the authorities relied on was a legal opinion rendered in 1775 that certain persons in New Hampshire could be prosecuted for treason.

[47] Carlisle *v.* U. S., 16 Wall. 147 (1872); U. S. *v.* Fricke, 259 Fed. 673 (1919); Young *v.* U. S., 97 U. S. 39 (1878); U. S. *v.* Hodges, 2 Wheel. Cr. 477 (1815); King *v.* Ahlers [1915] 1 K. B. 616. For other examples see Warren, *op. cit.*, especially on p. 347 a.

tangible or measurable way. The result is indirect and purely mental. It is true that words do sometimes constitute treason, as when a letter is sent to the enemy containing military information, or even a wireless message.[48] Here language has all the qualities of action, because it furnishes the enemy with something he can use. It is treason if he be given a gun to batter down a fort or a photograph of its plan or a written description. That the last is in words is immaterial. But if words are used in a speech demanding immediate peace, this is not assistance by acts at all, and furnishes the enemy with nothing but emotions of dubious value. Judges have frequently declared that expressions of opinion are not treason.[49] It is interesting to note that even in the excitement of the Civil War, when Congress was passing on the qualifications of members under the much broader terms of the Test Oath Act of 1862, soon to be more fully discussed, a line was usually (though not always) drawn between language adverse to the North, even though clearly intended to embarrass the conduct of the war, and definite acts of assistance to the South, such as participation in an ordinance of secession or the offer of a military invention to Jefferson Davis. In the Berger case, however, the committee did not consider at all whether he was guilty of acts of treason. There is nothing in the record to show any aid to Germany except by the indirect, intangible method of creating a body of opinion opposed to the continuance of the war. And this is a risk which a nation governed by public opinion must take, which ours has taken by guarantying freedom of speech. To call it treason is contrary not only to the First Amendment but to the law of treason. Therefore, Berger did not in any legal sense give aid and comfort to the enemy, and

---

[48] U. S. *v.* Robinson, 259 Fed. 685 (1919) (invisible ink); U. S. *v.* Werner, 247 Fed. 708. See Warren, *op. cit.*

[49] Charges to Grand Jury, 5 Blatchf. 549, 550 (1861): "Words, oral, written, or printed, however treasonable, seditious or criminal of themselves, do not constitute an overt act of treason within the definition of the crime"; *accord,* 1 Bond 609, 612 (1861); 2 Sprague 292, 294 (1863).

he was not barred from the House of Representatives by the Fourteenth Amendment.

Consequently, if Berger's exclusion is to be justified, it can only be on the second theory already mentioned, that the House of Representatives had power to impose qualifications not mentioned in the Constitution. The instances of additional qualifications mentioned in the *Berger Report* were imposed by statutes like the Test Oath Act of 1862 or the Edmunds Act abolishing polygamy. No such statute applies to Berger, so that he could only be barred if additional requirements can be based on unwritten law or the will of a single branch of the legislature. This question will be examined at length in connection with the New York Socialists. It will be seen that there is some authority that a man who has been convicted of crime *after* his election to the legislature should not be allowed to occupy his seat, but that there is a sharp disagreement whether he should be excluded or expelled.[50] The reason for declaring the seat vacant is that his constituents should have the opportunity to reconsider their votes if they were cast in ignorance of a fact which so materially affects his fitness for the office. This argument supports the first exclusion of Berger, but not the second, for the overwhelming vote received by him at the second election, after his conviction, made it clear that the electorate considered guilt under the Espionage Act no disqualification for their representative in Congress. The Wilkes case established the principle that such a decisive expression of opinion given with full knowledge of the offense of sedition should not afterwards be overridden by one branch of the legislature. Indeed, the House of Representatives went one step farther than the House of Commons, for Wilkes when disqualified was in prison and wholly incapable of serving, but Berger was out on bail pending an appeal. His conviction might be reversed and he was capable of taking his seat. An Ameri-

---

[50] See p. 344, *infra*. *Berger Report,* p. 10, says that the power of expulsion is limited to causes arising out of the conduct of a member after his induction into office.

WILKES AND HIS SUCCESSORS

can precedent is Matthew Lyon, who was elected to Congress by voters who had full knowledge of his prosecution under the Sedition Act of 1798. He was allowed to qualify, and when he was subsequently convicted and imprisoned the House of Representatives by a close vote refused to expel him.[51] The Wilkes and Lyon cases are opposed to the belief of some persons that sedition is more of a disqualification than other crimes because it involves a breach of allegiance. On the contrary, the opinion of the voters about a conviction for a political crime is entitled to peculiar respect. Such crimes do not usually arise from an individual malevolence, as do murder and robbery, but from political, economic, or ethical views which are shared by a group, for instance, of pacifists or Socialists, and which are considered dangerous because they clash with the will of the majority. The election of such a criminal is in effect an approval of these views by the voters of his district, so that the legislature by excluding or expelling him denies expression to a political, economic, or ethical theory which is held by a considerable mass of the electorate. The tide of public opinion with regard to disloyal utterances is very likely to vary with time and locality. The penalty affixed by the statute sufficiently guards against their dangerous consequences in the emergency of war. If an additional penalty not included in the law is imposed by one branch of the legislature after hostilities have ceased, the result is to block changes in public opinion, whereas the theory of democratic government is that such changes shall find an immediate and ready expression through the ballot.

Lincoln's principle [52] that the nation must be able to protect itself in war against utterances which actually cause insubordination and obstruct the raising of armies may justify some of the Espionage Act convictions, but his policy was absolutely opposed to the annexation of political disqualifications when the emergency had passed. Berger's utterances were far less dangerous in their tendency

[51] 2 Hinds' Precedents 850. [52] P. 117, *supra*.

than those expressed by many persons who took office unmolested during the Civil War. A large number of Democrats were elected to Congress in 1864 on a platform drafted by the notorious Vallandigham, which declared the war a failure.[53] The reasoning of the Berger committee would have allowed the Republican majority in Congress to exclude the Democratic minority. Apart from the fact of conviction, the conduct of these men furnishes a close analogy to Berger, much closer than the persons excluded under the Test Oath Act, most of whom had committed treason, while a few others came from Border States and had definitely identified themselves with the South. The Mexican War affords more honorable precedents for the principle that men who oppose a war in public discussion should afterwards be sworn in at the National Capitol without question. Daniel Webster said at a public meeting in 1847: " We are, in my opinion, in a most unnecessary and therefore a most unjustifiable war." Henry Clay asked: " Must we blindly continue the conflict, without any visible object, or any prospect of a definite termination? . . . It is the privilege of the people in their primary assemblies, and of every private citizen, however humble, to express an opinion in regard to the purposes for which the war should be continued." Charles Sumner outdid Berger in vituperation: " The Mexican War is an enormity born of slavery. . . Base in object, atrocious in beginning, immoral in all its influences, vainly prodigal of treasure and life; it is a war of infamy which must blot the pages of our history."[54] The additional element of conviction in the Berger case should be limited in its effect to the statutory penalty and should not overthrow the principle recognized in the cases just mentioned and many others, that variations of public opinion with respect to a war, especially if it is past, should be allowed to reflect themselves in the national legislature with-

[53] J. F. Rhodes, *History of the United States*, IV, 522 ff.
[54] *Berger Hearings*, I, 712, 713. On the War of 1812, see Beveridge's *Marshall*, IV, c. I.

WILKES AND HIS SUCCESSORS

out interference. It is significant that all the Entente powers, except Japan, have admitted to their legislatures without any hesitation Socialists who opposed the war as vigorously as Berger, with the same intention to bring it to an immediate close. Indeed, some of the Italian Socialists were elected while serving prison sentences for their militant anti-war activities.[55]

Therefore, although Berger's statements in the *Milwaukee Leader*, before the committee, and in Congress at the time of his exclusion, entitle him to no personal sympathy, nevertheless the twofold denial of his seat was, apart from all questions of legality, a great mistake and a wrong to the voters of the fifth district of Wisconsin.

The action of the House of Representatives has, however, still more serious and far-reaching aspects. If it had been based simply on Berger's conviction its effect would be limited to men who have been actually convicted under the Espionage Act, although if such were its ground, it would have been desirable to follow the view of the minority member of the committee, Mr. Rodenberg, and suspend legislative action until the final result of the prosecution had been reached by the Circuit Court of Appeals. The great evil of the case is that the House of Representatives and its committee assumed the power to go behind the conviction, and expressed the view that without any conviction at all Berger could be deprived of his seat because of his opposition to the war. The chairman of the committee, Mr. Dallinger, said in the debate upon the first exclusion:

The one and only issue in this case is that of Americanism. It is whether a man who in 1911 took an oath as a member of the House to support the Constitution of the United States and who, when this country declared war against the Imperial German Government, became the head and front of an organized conspiracy to hinder, obstruct, and embarrass the Government in its fight for existence, should be admitted to membership in this

[55] *Socialist Review*, February, 1920, p. 159.

House simply because a constituency in one of our States has seen fit to give him a plurality of its vote.

This issue is far broader than the question of a conviction for a violation of a particular statute by a court in Chicago, an appeal from which may be set aside by a higher court on technical grounds, and your committee is convinced upon all the facts and upon all the precedents in this House that Victor L. Berger should be excluded from membership, and that the question should be determined by the House here and now. In our opinion the House expects it; the men who fought for their country in the great war expect it; the entire country expects it.

Therefore, while the precise legal ground of the Berger exclusion was the Fourteenth Amendment, the case gave public currency to the broad proposition that "disloyalty" during a war would bar a duly elected representative. Thus long after a war was over, a legislature could without any previous judicial condemnation conduct an inquiry into the mental state of a man during the war and the tendency of his utterances to discourage the national cause, just the kind of investigation which is shown in my second chapter to have proved so vague and unsatisfactory in the hands of an impartial judge and jury and which was justified if at all only by the great necessities and dangers of the war. Furthermore, the conduct for which Berger was convicted and excluded was said by him and regarded by many of his opponents to be that of the Socialist Party generally, so that if conviction were an immaterial factor as Mr. Dallinger said, Berger's ineligibility could naturally be extended to any Socialist. Thus the popular impressions created by the Berger case paved the way for one of the most astonishing episodes in American political life.

V. *The Five Socialist Members of the New York Assembly*

Then stood there up one in the council, a Pharisee, named Gamaliel, a doctor of the law, had in reputation among all the people, and said unto them: "Ye men of Israel, take heed to yourselves what ye intend to do as touching these men. Refrain from these men and let them alone: for if this counsel or this work be of men, it will come to nought; but if it be of God, ye can not overthrow it; lest haply ye be found even to fight against God."—*The Acts of the Apostles.*

On January 7, 1920, just before the second exclusion of Berger, and while the front pages of the press were still full of the great conspiracy which would have overthrown the nation had it not been for the New Year's round-up of four thousand left-wing radicals, the New York Legislature opened its session. Among the members of the Assembly or lower house were five Socialists, Claessens, Solomon, Waldman, De Witt, and Orr. The Socialist Party of New York was a legally recognized party under the Election Law,[56] so that its candidates had as much right on the ballot as Democrats or Republicans. All these Socialists except De Witt had previously served in the Assembly. The opposition of the party to the war had aroused no objection to its representatives at any time during the conflict, even when ten of them took their seats at Albany just before the Spring Drive of 1918. And on this day, in 1920, the five members took office without interference, swearing that they would support the Constitution of the United States and that of New York, and discharge the duties of their office to the best of their ability, and that they had not influenced votes by bribe or promise. The New York fundamental law prescribes this oath and makes it all-sufficient:[57]

No other oath, declaration or test shall be required as a qualification for any office of public trust.

They occupied their seats and entered into all the business of the day, participating in the organization of the House and voting for Speaker and other officers. These proceedings occupied upwards of two hours.

[56] Sec. 3 (9) "The term 'party' means any political organization which at the last preceding election for governor polled at least fifteen thousand votes for governor." The Socialist candidate in 1918 received over 120,000.
[57] N. Y. Const., Art. XIII, § 1.

Suddenly the newly-elected Speaker, without notice or motion, directed the Sergeant-at-Arms to present the five Socialist members before the bar of the House.[58] The surprised men were paraded down into the well of the Assembly chamber in front of the Speaker's rostrum, in full view of their fellow members and hundreds of guests, who crowded the galleries and the floor to witness the ceremonies of the opening day. There they were lined up with the Sergeant-at-Arms on guard, while the Speaker addressed them:

> You are seeking seats in this body, you who have been elected on a platform that is absolutely inimical to the best interests of the State of New York and of the United States.

He then declared that the Socialist Party was not truly a political party, but a subversive and unpatriotic organization, and informed them that if the House should adopt a resolution declaring their places vacant they would be given an opportunity to appear before a tribunal to prove their rights to a seat in the Assembly.

A resolution [59] drafted by the Attorney General in his capacity as counsel for the Lusk Committee was presented. This did not even recite that the members were charged with certain offenses, but stated facts as if already proved, an Alice-in-Wonderland performance of "sentence first—verdict afterwards." It declared that they were members of the Socialist Party of America, which adhered to the revolutionary forces of Soviet Russia and endorsed the principles of the Communist International of Moscow, and this was pledged to the forcible and violent overthrow of all organized governments. They agreed to be guided by the party constitution and platform, and could be expelled from the party for disobeying the instructions of the Executive Committee, which might include aliens. The party by its St. Louis platform had opposed the war, and thereby stamped itself and all its members with an inimical attitude to the

[58] *Briefs*, and *New York Times*, January 8, 1920.
[59] *Record*, p. 367.

best interests of New York and the United States. These
five members had subscribed to its principles and its aims
and purposes against the government. They had been connected with an organization convicted of a violation of the
Espionage Act. Therefore, it concluded, they were denied
seats in the Assembly " pending determination of their qualifications and eligibility to their respective seats"; and the
investigation of their qualifications and eligibility was referred to the Committee on Judiciary. The roll-call was
then taken and the five Socialists were called upon to vote
as members. After the passage of the Resolution they were
hustled by the Sergeant-at-Arms out of the chamber, where
their seats remained vacant for the remainder of the session, to the disfranchisement of sixty thousand voters of
the City of New York.

In one of those magnificent decisions whereby the Supreme
Court of the United States in former years fortified the
civil liberties wrested from authority by the long struggles
of the seventeenth and eighteenth centuries and proclaimed
in the American Bill of Rights, Justice Bradley warned us
that illegitimate and unconstitutional practices get their
first footing by silent approaches and slight deviations from
legal modes of procedure.[60] Since the 15th day of June,
1917, the nation had been led on by its panic-stricken fear
of adverse opinion to abandon one national tradition after
another. Every unheeded prediction of the handful of liberals was more than fulfilled. The Espionage Act was
only to punish interference with recruiting and military discipline. It was used against all prominent opposition to
the war. Every one agreed that freedom of speech meant
the absence of previous administrative restraint on political
discussion—and the Postmaster General was allowed to establish a whimsical censorship of the political press and
maintain it long after the last American soldier had been
demobilized. Suppression was said to be only a war measure. The states prolonged it into peace, and the Attorney

[60] Boyd *v.* U. S., 116 U. S. 616, 635 (1885).

General of the United States begged Congress to imitate them. Radical aliens were put under control, and a similar law was demanded for radical citizens. One by one, the right of freedom of speech, the right of assembly, the right to petition, the right to protection against unreasonable searches and seizures, the right against arbitrary arrest, the right to a fair trial, the hatred of spies, the principle that guilt is personal, the principle that punishment should bear some proportion to the offense, had been sacrificed and ignored. Here and there a solitary and despised protest—the rest was silence. And now the waves of hysteria dashed against the very foundation of American life, the right of the people to elect their own rulers. Berger was excluded after he was convicted of crime, but these men were excluded without any conviction, without any crime, without any trial, from the offices which they had taken with all the qualifications and formalities prescribed by the fundamental law. At last the leaders of thought were awakened to the realization that a government cannot be saved, is not worth saving, at the cost of its own principles.

The successor of Jefferson had taken no step to stop the encroachments on freedom of speech, had signed his name to both Espionage Acts, had allowed his officers without a reproach to censor and raid and arrest as they chose. It was reserved for the Republican presidential candidate at the election of 1916 to become the champion of Anglo-Saxon liberties. Charles Evans Hughes, leader of the American bar, former Governor of New York, former Justice of the Supreme Court, within forty-eight hours of the Albany imbroglio, wrote Speaker Sweet that it was absolutely opposed to the fundamental principles of our government for a majority to undertake to deny representation to the minority through the men who had been elected by a ballot lawfully cast.[61]

If there was anything against these men as individuals, if they were deemed to be guilty of criminal offenses, they should have

[61] *New York Times,* January 10, 1920; Sweet's reply, January 11.

been charged accordingly. But I understand that the action is not directed against these five elected members as individuals but that the proceeding is virtually an attempt to indict a political party and to deny it representation in the Legislature. This is not, in my judgment, American government.

Are Socialists unconvicted of crime, to be denied the ballot? If Socialists are permitted to vote, are they not permitted to vote for their own candidates? If their candidates are elected and are men against whom, as individuals, charges of disqualifying offenses cannot be laid, are they not entitled to their seats? . . .

I understand that it is said that the Socialists constitute a combination to overthrow the Government. The answer is plain. If public officers or private citizens have any evidence that any individuals, or group of individuals, are plotting revolution and seeking by violent measures to change our Government, let the evidence be laid before the proper authorities and swift action be taken for the protection of the community. Let every resource of inquiry, of pursuit, of prosecution be employed to ferret out and punish the guilty according to our laws. But I count it a most serious mistake to proceed, not against individuals charged with violation of law, but against masses of our citizens combined for political action, by denying them the only resource of peaceful government; that is, action by the ballot box and through duly elected representatives in legislative bodies.

Speaker Sweet, after consultation with the Lusk Committee, replied that the Socialists were not expelled, but merely subjected to an investigation by the body which was charged by the Constitution with the authority to inquire into the fitness of those who seek seats in the Assembly. The question presented squarely was whether the different organizations which they sought to represent in the legislature advocated methods and employed tactics to overthrow our form of government, which would justify their exclusion from participating in legislative proceedings. He thus characterized the proceeding, as did the Attorney General of New York,[62] not as an inquiry into the personal unfitness of these men or into the overt acts of any one, but into the opinions and words of whole groups. Finally he stated that criticism of the Assembly action without full

[62] *Ibid.*, January 9.

knowledge of the facts gave aid and comfort to those elements of our society which seek the destruction of our institutions.

Nevertheless, criticism poured in, not only from Socialists and labor unions, but from large conservative groups like the National Security League. The New York Board of Aldermen refused to follow the example of the Assembly as to its Socialist members. For once the *Tribune* and the *Review* stood shoulder to shoulder with the *New Republic* and the *Nation*, and outdid them in the vigor of their condemnation. The Bar Association of the City of New York adopted resolutions offered by Governor Hughes, opposing any attempt to exclude legislators because of their affiliation with any political party, when they are seeking by constitutional and legal methods to bring about any change in the Constitution and laws. The Association appointed a committee of non-Socialists to appear before the Judiciary Committee of the Assembly and safeguard the principles of representative government.[63] No action could have done more to strengthen the confidence of workingmen in the public spirit of the bar.

The Assembly paid no more attention to these protests than the House of Commons to the remonstrances of Burke and the voters of England on behalf of Wilkes. The Assembly was past saving, but the nation was saved. The American people, long bedrugged by propaganda, were shaken out of their nightmare of revolution. The red terror became ridiculous on the lips of Speaker Sweet. A legislature trembling before five men—the long-lost American sense of humor revived and people began to laugh. That broke the spell. The light of day beat in not only upon the Assembly, but upon Congress and the Department of Justice. Never again did the hysteria of the past year return. The raids of January 2d were flood-tide, and with Governor Hughes' letter on the 9th, the ebb set in. Then followed the opposition of the conservative press and sober

[63] *New York Post*, January 14.

WILKES AND HIS SUCCESSORS

speakers to the pending federal sedition bills, the disclosures in the Colyer trial of the illegal character of the New Year's round-up, the decision of Secretary Wilson legalizing the Communist Labor Party, the wholesale cancellation of deportation warrants. The American people owe a lasting debt of gratitude to the New York Assembly.

But there was no return to sanity in Albany. On January 20th the investigation of the five members began before the Judiciary Committee, which was appointed by the Speaker who had taken such a definite stand against them. At the outset the Bar Association committee appeared, with Mr. Hughes as its chairman, but was not allowed to participate in the proceedings. Before withdrawing it filed a brief and these recommendations: [64]

> That the Judiciary Committee at once report to the Assembly that there is no question properly before the Judiciary Committee of any disqualification on the part of these members; that no charges against these members of any constitutional disqualification, or of any misconduct in office or of any violation of law on their part have been properly made, that the members under suspension should at once be restored to the privileges of their seats and that if it be desired to present any charges against them of any violation of law, such charges should be properly formulated, and that until such charges, properly laid, have been established by proof, after due opportunity to be heard, these members shall enjoy all the privileges of their seats in recognition of their own rights and of the rights of their constituencies.

This position is conclusively established by the Bar Association in its brief.[65] After the respondents had taken the constitutional oath of office, and in the absence of any personal misconduct during their term, they became entitled to participate in all proceedings of the Assembly until they were actually ousted. This has always been the practice in Congress, even on charges of bribery; for instance, Senator Lorimer participated in all the proceedings of the Senate until he was finally disqualified, and Senator Truman

[64] *Record*, p. 6; *Socialist Brief*, p. 7.
[65] Pages 8-20.

FREEDOM OF SPEECH

H. Newberry of Michigan, who has been actually convicted of corrupt practices, still retains his seat and will continue to do so even during any investigation that may be made of his conduct by the Senate. The issue of free speech, however, is less concerned with the unwarranted method of the proceedings against the five members than with the question whether there was any legal cause to deprive them of their seats by any method whatever.

The opening clause of the New York Constitution provides that no member of this state shall be disfranchised unless by the law of the land, or the judgment of his peers. Like the United States Constitution, it makes each House "the judge of the elections, returns and qualifications of its own members,"[66] but it imposes the restriction already mentioned that no declaration, test or oath shall be imposed except that specified. Certain offices are a disqualification,[67] but even the right to vote is not a requisite for eligibility.[68] The power to expel is conferred by statute.[69] The power to suspend is not given by Constitution or statute. Although this was an inquiry into qualifications and not an expulsion, yet since the method is immaterial it is desirable to review the cases of both exclusion and expulsion to determine whether a Legislature, especially in the absence of any disqualifying statute, can lawfully unseat a member for opinions and affiliations without overt acts.

The analysis of the law on this question is peculiarly difficult. The judicial precedents are necessarily few and indirect in their bearing, for the courts have uniformly denied that they have any power to review either legislative expulsions or legislative decisions on the qualifications of members.[70] The house in making decisions on qualifications

[66] Art. III, § 10.
[67] Art. III, § 8.
[68] Barker *v.* People, 3 Cow. 686, 703 (1824); Cooley, *Constitutional Limitations,* 7th ed., 894 note.
[69] Legislative Law, § 3. "Each house has the power to expel any of its members after the report of a committee to inquire into the charges against him shall have been made."
[70] Hiss *v.* Bartlett, 3 Gray (Mass.) 468 (1855); French *v.* Senate,

WILKES AND HIS SUCCESSORS

and in other election cases acts in a judicial capacity, in spite of the doctrine of the separation of powers, and such controversies do not fall within the general judicial power vested in the courts, since the constitutions expressly confer jurisdiction upon the legislative chamber in question. However, judges have sometimes been called upon to discuss whether anybody has power to add to the constitutional requirements for eligibility. Justice Story, in denying that the states can impose additional tests for a member of Congress, for example, that he shall reside in the district which elects him, writes: [71]

It would seem but fair reasoning, upon the plainest principles of interpretation, that when the Constitution established certain qualifications as necessary for office, it meant to exclude all others as prerequisites. From the very nature of such a provision, the affirmation of these qualifications would seem to imply a negative of all others.

There is much force in his position, that the power to judge "qualifications" means only constitutional qualifications, but it does present difficulties, especially when the constitutional requirements for eligibility are so meagerly stated as in New York. Can insanity be made a bar, or is it only a ground for expulsion after admission? Were women eligible to Congress, before they were allowed to vote, inasmuch as they were not specifically excluded? Or were they under a common law ineligibility, which had to be read into the Constitution? [72] At all events, some judges have been willing to admit that in some instances the requirements of the Constitution may be added to, but only within narrow limits. (1) Additional qualifications can be imposed only by law; that is, by a statute enacted by both houses of the legislature, and signed by the governor. The body which

---

146 Cal. 604 (1905); P. *ex rel.* Hatzel *v.* Hall, 80 N. Y. 117, 122 (1880); P. *v.* Mahaney, 13 Mich. 482, 492 (1865).

[71] 1 Story on the Constitution, § 625; Congress has always refused to recognize these state limitations as valid. 1 Hinds' Prec. 381, 384, 387.

[72] "Eligibility of Women for Public Office," 33 *Harv. L. Rev.* 295 (1919).

judges the qualifications of its members cannot itself legally create new qualifications any more than the Supreme Court of the United States can legally create new income taxes. One house cannot make the law, and eligibility is fixed by law.[73] (2) The highest court of the state of New York has decided that the legislature under its power to punish crimes can pass a valid statute, making conviction for duelling a disqualification for the legislature, but said through Chancellor Sanford:[74]

> Eligibility . . . belongs equally, to all persons whomsoever, not excluded by the constitution. I therefore conceive it to be entirely clear, that the legislature can not establish arbitrary exclusions from office, or any general regulation requiring qualifications, which the constitution has not required. If, for example, it should be enacted by law, that all physicians, or all persons of a particular religious sect, should be ineligible to public trusts; . . . any such regulation, would be an infringement of the constitution; and it would be so, because, should it prevail, it would be in effect, an alteration of the constitution itself. . . . *There may be an exclusion by law, in punishment for crimes; but in no other manner, and for no other cause.*

(3) In New York and other states which have constitutions forbidding any other " oath, declaration, or test " except that specified, this prohibits not merely new forms of test oaths, but all arbitrary requirements as a qualification for voting or office-holding, particularly those based on opinions and party affiliations, and it makes no difference that these requirements are imposed by statute. Thus, the New York Court of Appeals has held a statute unconstitutional which required voters to swear that they had never borne arms against the United States, given aid to the enemy, deserted, or evaded the draft.[75] It has also invalidated a statute

---

[73] Barker *v.* People, 3 Cow. 686, 707 (1824); P. *ex rel.* Bush *v.* Thornton, 25 Hun 456, 463 (1881).

[74] Barker *v.* People, 3 Cow. 686, 703, 704, 707. The italics are mine.

[75] Green *v.* Shumway, 39 N. Y. 418 (1868); Goetcheus *v.* Matthewson, 61 N. Y. 420 (1875). Similar disqualifications for preaching, teaching, or practising law have been declared invalid under the U. S. Constitution. Cummings *v.* Missouri, 4 Wall. 277 (1866); *Ex parte* Garland, 4 Wall. 333.

which made all persons except members of the two leading political parties ineligible for the Albany police commission. Judge O'Brien declared: [76]

> The legislature of this state has no power to enact a law which proscribes any class of citizens as ineligible to hold public office on account of political belief or party affiliations.

Clearly, all these cases render the unseating of the five Socialists illegal. They were not made ineligible by any law, but by the fiat of the Assembly alone. They had not been convicted of crime, and they were guilty of no crime which was a statutory bar to office. And they were proscribed for their political beliefs and party affiliations.

Let us now turn to the legislative precedents and see how far they agree with the judicial discussion. At the outset, the reader must be warned that these precedents rarely afford a satisfactory formulation of the principle on which the house acted, which can be automatically applied in subsequent cases after the manner of court decisions. A legislature is not by nature a judicial body. Its members are chosen and organized for carrying out policies, and not, like judges, for the sole purpose of thinking together. When they are called upon to perform judicial duties in trying impeachments and charges of bribery, the most earnest efforts to attain impartiality hardly prevent them from being swayed by party motives, and their debates lack the training and the restraints which mold the words of judges. The Lorimer case brought out these qualities of a legislative trial, and a few years ago the New York Senate refused to expel two members for corrupt practices, who were subsequently tried and convicted for the same offense. Moreover, the basis of a legislative discussion is often obscure because of

---

[76] Rathbone *v.* Wirth, 150 N. Y. 459, 485 (1896), and see cases cited from other states. (Some of the judges rested the invalidity of the statute on other clauses of the N. Y. Constitution.) The legislature may of course impose requirements which relate directly to fitness for the particular office, *e.g.*, that only physicians are eligible to the board of health. Rogers *v.* Common Council, 123 N. Y. 173, 184 (1890).

the number of persons who join in the debate. Sometimes the only certain fact is that the member was or was not unseated. It is significant that the Wilkes case led Parliament to delegate the trial of controverted elections to a tribunal of judges.[77] The Berger and Socialist cases might well lead us to consider establishing a preliminary investigation by judges instead of by a legislative committee and thus obtaining the benefit of a trained judicial opinion as the basis of the action of the house.[78]

The English legislative precedents show that Parliament has no control over the eligibility of candidates but simply administers the laws defining their qualifications. One house of Parliament cannot create a disability unknown to the law. This was established by the Wilkes case and by that of Charles Bradlaugh, who was at first debarred and expelled from the House of Commons on the ground that as an agnostic he could not conscientiously take the oath, but was eventually on re-election sworn in without objection, and the resolution debarring him was expunged from the journals. On the other hand, each house has power to suspend or expel by way of punishment. Members have been suspended for disregarding the authority of the chair or obstructing business. They have been expelled for crimes and other disgraceful acts which render them unfit for a seat and which if not so punished would bring discredit on Parliament. Lord Campbell thinks even an offense before election is cause for expulsion if conviction follows election, for there might be a presumption that his constituents would not have elected a person guilty of such misconduct, and it might be fair to give them an opportunity of determining whether they would still have him for a representative. Expulsion is not a disqualification if the member be re-elected. Except for

---

[77] May, *Parliamentary Practice*, 12 ed., 581.

[78] This plan is already in force in Pennsylvania. *Re* McNeill, 111 Pa. St. 235 (1885). The legislature could not completely delegate the decision of such contests. S. *v.* Gilmore, 20 Kan. 551 (1878); Dalton *v.* S. *ex rel.* Richardson, 43 Oh. St. 652, 680 (1885). The Presidential Electoral Commission of 1877 affords an analogy.

WILKES AND HIS SUCCESSORS

Wilkes and Bradlaugh, no person has been expelled in modern times for conduct involving the expression of opinions, and both these expulsions were officially declared to be wrong and expunged.[79]

The Congressional precedents also afford no support for the contention of the New York Assembly that duly elected legislators can be disqualified or expelled for disloyal opinions which have not been made a bar by law. There is no authority that a house will go into the question of the moral fitness of a member to occupy a seat. Where would such an inquiry stop, and what standards could be fixed? Each house undoubtedly has the right to expel a member for actual crimes committed after his induction to office, but it is settled that it cannot punish him for an offense committed before his election, and even Lord Campbell's view of the effect of conviction after election is opposed by the case already mentioned of Matthew Lyon, imprisoned under the Sedition Act of 1798. This disposes of the half-hearted contention that the New York Socialists had violated the Espionage Act during the war.[80]

At the outbreak of the Civil War several Southern Senators and Representatives were expelled for their treasonable conduct in remaining permanently absent from their Congressional duties and either taking up arms against the

---

[79] May, *op. cit.*, 59-62, 153-156, 187. He does not discuss the question whether a member can be expelled for an offense committed before his election. 1 Story on the Constitution, § 838, says the power is not limited to offenses during the particular session. Lord Campbell's opinion is in his *Life of Lord Camden, Lord Chancellors,* (1846 ed.) V, 276.

[80] *Berger Report,* 10; opinion by Speaker Cannon in 3 Hinds' Prec. 1157; 2 *ibid.* 829-860, 1 *ibid.* 521, for cases. But see arguments contra, 1 *ibid.* 437, 524. Apparently no one has been expelled from Congress for crimes, except those against the Government, but several men have resigned. There is some doubt whether a member can be expelled for crimes unrelated to his office. See the majority and minority reports in the Roberts case. 1 Hind's Prec. 523. The House refused to expel Herbert of California in 1857, who was charged with homicide, and Harris of Maryland in 1865, though convicted of aiding the rebellion (probably before election), and Cannon of Utah in 1875, though a polygamist. 1 Hinds' Prec. 500. For the Espionage Act charge, see *Assembly Outline,* 75. No evidence is given.

government or entering the Confederate lines and actively participating in the rebellion.[81] On the other hand, both houses refused to expel members from border states who had committed no overt acts, but had vigorously opposed by speeches the prosecution of the war by the North.[82] Among these were Representative Long of Ohio, who declared himself in favor of recognizing the independence of the Confederacy, Representative Harris of Maryland, who said, " I hope you will never subjugate the South," and Senator Powell of Kentucky. Powell presided at a large Southern States' Rights convention in Kentucky in June, 1861, which urged the recall of the Northern armies and the recognition of the Confederacy and endorsed the action of the Governor in refusing to furnish troops to subjugate the South and forbidding both sides to invade Kentucky. In September, 1861, he was a delegate to a second convention, which adopted resolutions drafted by a committee of which he was a member, proclaiming the neutrality of Kentucky and refusing aid by money, taxation, or loans to " a cause so hopeless as the military subjugation of the Confederate States." The Committee on the Judiciary reported against expulsion, and its chairman, Senator Trumbull of Illinois, whose loyalty no man can question, stated in debate that though the resolutions were downright opposition to the constituted authorities of the government and wholly unjustifiable, and though the neutrality of Kentucky did favor the cause of the rebellion, yet when that neutrality was abandoned Powell had discharged his duties to the government at Washington; " and no man is to be expelled from this body because he disagrees with others in opinion." The resolution of expulsion was overwhelmingly defeated.

The Assembly relies on the case of Senator Bright of Indiana, who was expelled by a bare two-thirds for writing a letter to Jefferson Davis, bringing a military invention to

[81] 2 Hinds' Prec. 812, 813, 822-826. See also the expulsion of Senator Blount in 1797 for trying to alienate the Creek Indians from the resident Government officials, 2 *ibid.* 813.

[82] 2 *ibid.* 803, 827.

WILKES AND HIS SUCCESSORS

his attention. It is true that some language used in the debate about other utterances of Bright implied a power to expel merely for disloyal opinions, but his conduct was treasonable aid to the enemy if the requisite intent existed, and Senator Trumbull in moving his expulsion based it squarely on the ground of treason.[83] Therefore, this and all the other expulsion cases draw the line between overt acts identifying the legislator with the enemy and opposition to war by words. A legislator can be expelled only for criminal or otherwise disgraceful conduct subsequent to his election, and not for disloyal language or for affiliations with political groups, even if like the Kentucky neutrals they oppose the government without, however, joining its enemies.

The Congressional precedents on the unseating of members because they are not qualified are still more important, since the action of the New York Assembly, though often called an expulsion, was really an adjudication of ineligibility and not an expulsion for misconduct. A review of these precedents reveals two sharply conflicting views. The first accords with Story's opinion that no addition can be made to the constitutional requirements.[84] The Constitution gives the people the inalienable right to choose any one they please who has the qualifications named. An insane man cannot take his seat if he lacks the mental capacity to take the constitutional oath. Bribery and corrupt practices connected with the election prevent him from being duly elected, for fraud vitiates all transactions, and an unseating on this ground, as in the Lorimer case,[85] is not a disqualification for

[83] 2 *ibid.* 821; see extracts from debates omitted by Hinds in *Assembly Outline*, 83, and *Socialist Brief*, 110.

[84] The fullest discussion of both views is in the minority report in the Roberts case, 1 Hinds' Prec. 518 (unseated). See also Stark, 1 *ibid.* 433 (seated); Smith v. Brown, 1 *ibid.* 441 (unseated); McKee v. Young, 1 *ibid.* 451 (unseated); Thomas, 1 *ibid.* 466 (unseated); Maxwell v. Cannon, 1 *ibid.* 493 (seated); Campbell v. Cannon, 1 *ibid.* 500 (unseated); Smoot, 1 *ibid.* 561 (seated); discussion by House Committee, 1 *ibid.* 591; *Berger Hearings and Report* (unseated). Among those presenting the first view are Littlefield of Maine, 1 *ibid.* 537; Senator Knox, 1 *ibid.* 587; Senator Reverdy Johnson, 1 *ibid.* 489.

[85] Webb and Pierce, Senate Election Cases, 1002. But see P. *ex rel.* Bush v. Thornton, 25 Hun 456 (1881).

crime, but a decision that no valid election has taken place. Crime as such is no bar, except treason by virtue of the Fourteenth Amendment. Representative government relies on the judgment of the people to pick fit men, not on the wisdom of a House of Congress or any other select group. In the improbable event that a district should elect a convicted murderer, he can act so long as he is at large. If the general welfare requires that this be made impossible, then the Constitution should be amended. A power in the legislature to add new qualifications is equivalent to a power to change those prescribed by the fundamental law. If it can add crime or disloyal acts as bars, it can add profiteering as well. There is no line to be drawn, once it is allowed to cross the constitutional limits. It can turn our democracy into an oligarchy by imposing high property qualifications, or into a dictatorship of the proletariat by declaring ineligible all persons deriving income from rents and invested capital.

The second view allows some additions to be made to the constitutional qualifications. Otherwise, the great leaders of the Confederacy might have been seated before the Fourteenth Amendment, or Brigham Young could have been elected and his forty wives have occupied the gallery to see him sworn in. Is a man to be brought from a felon's cell to the floor of the Senate? Suppose a representative just before he is sworn in should create some outrageous disturbance in the House; if he cannot be disqualified, will it be necessary to go through the rigmarole of first swearing him in, and then expelling him? The duty of each chamber to preserve the nation and carry on business is said not to be sufficiently safeguarded if the constitutional requirements are exclusive of all others.

The view forbidding all additions seems to me the sounder in the United States Government, and still more obligatory under the New York Constitution, with its clause against other tests. It must be conceded, nevertheless, that notwithstanding the ability of the men who have taken this position,

WILKES AND HIS SUCCESSORS

it has frequently been rejected in Congressional practice, and is also opposed to the opinion of the New York Court, rendered however before the adoption of the test clause just mentioned, that conviction for crime could be made a bar by statute.[86] Yet even if the second view be accepted, the range of new qualifications has been so closely limited by Congress that neither of the two views furnishes the slightest support for the proceedings of the New York Assembly.

In the first place, the Congressional precedents agree with the Wilkes case and the judicial decisions that qualifications must be established by law, and that the resolution of one house of Congress cannot make law. When Representative Connor of Texas was charged with having cruelly whipped negro soldiers under his command and bribing them not to testify against him before a military court, Garfield asked if anything in the Constitution and laws of the United States forbade that a moral monster should be elected to Congress. Connor was sworn.[87] The House also refused to inquire into a charge of seduction, and the Senate into one of embezzlement.[88] All the exclusions which have occurred were for offenses which had expressly been made a disqualification by Act of Congress.[89]

The most important of these statutes was enacted in July, 1862. In January of that year the Senate had decided that Stark of Oregon was entitled to take his seat, although he had made disloyal speeches. Senator Harris of New York, the Chairman of the Judiciary Committee, denied in debate that the Senate ought to be the ultimate judge of a man's fitness or was competent to reject him upon any view it

---

[86] See p. 342, *supra*.
[87] Grafton *v.* Connor, 1 Hinds' Prec. 488.
[88] Acklen, 1 *ibid.* 489; Roach, 1 *ibid.* 570.
[89] Besides the statutes mentioned, Act of February 26, 1853, c. 81, 10 Stat. at L. 171, disqualifies any member convicted of receiving bribes for discharging an official function. B. F. Whittemore of South Carolina resigned to avoid expulsion for sale of West Point appointments, was at once re-elected, and disqualified. 1 Hinds' Prec. 487. The case cannot be supported. See 1 *ibid.* 540 for a vigorous attack on this case.

might take of his moral, intellectual, or political capacity.[90] It was not until the passage of the Test Oath Act,[91] obliging men to swear before admission to office that they had never borne arms against the United States, given aid, countenance, counsel, or encouragement to the enemy, or yielded a voluntary support to any pretended government, that persons were excluded for disloyal conduct. Such an Act is of course impossible under the New York Constitutional prohibition of additional oaths and tests. And it is noteworthy that although the terms of this statute included much more than treason, the ironclad oath was not used to bar members for personal disloyalty or passive sympathy with the rebellion, or speeches denouncing the war as an abolition war and opposing any further aid toward its prosecution.[92] One man was excluded who had sent food to a Confederate camp, brought a gun, and pointed out a house where a Union soldier was hiding, telling the Southerners to go and get him, a clear case of treason.[93] The most extreme case was John Young Brown, who was disqualified for a letter to the press, saying that Kentucky would not furnish a man or a dollar to aid Lincoln in his unholy war against the South, that an invading Northern army would be resisted to the death, and that any Kentuckian joining it ought to be and would be shot down before he left the state.[94] This is the only instance of disqualification from Congress for utterances without overt acts. Thus, even in the heat of the

[90] 1 Hinds' Prec. 433. *The Assembly Outline,* 82, erroneously cites this case as authority for the exclusion of the Socialists; besides that of Smoot, who was also seated. The only other authorities cited are the case of Roberts, a polygamist disqualified by statute, and Bright expelled for treason, and a Virginia vote of 1619 excluding men who denied they were subject to the government of Virginia. The Assembly Brief cites several cases under the Test Oath Act; and several instances of expulsion. The principles of these cases are discussed in the text.

[91] Act of July 2, 1862, c. 128, 12 Stat. at L. 502.

[92] Kentucky Members, 1 Hinds' Prec., 441; Symes *v.* Trimble, 1 *ibid.* 459.

[93] McKee *v.* Young, Rowell Dig. Election Cases H. R., 222. Hinds does not state the facts fully. Senator Thomas of Maryland was disqualified for aiding his son to enter the Confederate army. 1 Hinds' Prec. 466.

[94] Smith *v.* Brown, 1 Hinds' Prec. 444.

Civil War, disloyalty was not a bar to an elected member of Congress, until it was expressly made so by a statute, and not then unless it was evidenced by actual aid to the enemy or words of acute virulence.

Some doubt was cast upon the validity of the Test Oath Act, and in 1868 it was virtually superseded by section three of the Fourteenth Amendment,[95] on which rightly or wrongly the exclusion of Berger was based.

The Church of Jesus Christ of Latter-day Saints is a much more closely knit and powerful organization than the Socialist Party and instead of being legalized by statute has frequently been made the object of adverse legislation. Consequently, the decisions upon the admission of Mormons to Congress are much in point. The constitutional question was not squarely raised while Utah was still a territory because each house was held to have complete control over the eligibility of Delegates, who were distinguished from Representatives. Nevertheless, the decisions at that time make the distinction which I have emphasized between overt acts and mere opinions.[96] In 1868 the election of Hooper was contested on the ground that he represented the institution of polygamy and a community hostile to the other portions of the United States and was disqualified by a secret oath. The House Committee reported that Mormonism was antagonistic to the United States but had never organized rebellion or sedition against the supreme authority of the Union, or committed treason by any overt act. Hooper was accordingly seated. On the other hand, a Delegate who was himself a polygamist was unseated. Even in this case a strong minority protested against the assumption by the House of the arbitrary power to inquire into the moral fitness of candidates, and asked whether if it was a bar for a Delegate to live with four women who were married to him, it would also be a bar if three of them were not.

---

[95] P. 323, *supra*. See Reverdy Johnson in 1 Hinds' Prec. 469.
[96] McGrorty *v.* Hooper, 1 Hind's Prec. 490; Maxwell *v.* Cannon, 1 *ibid.* 493; Campbell *v.* Cannon, 1 *ibid.* 500.

After the admission of Utah as a state, the issue became acute. The Edmunds Act of 1882 had disqualified any polygamist, whether convicted or not, from office under the United States.[97] Brigham H. Roberts, a convicted polygamist, who was still living with three wives, was elected Representative in 1898, and was finally unseated after a thorough discussion from both points of view of the question whether Congress or the House could add qualifications to those specified in the Constitution.[98] The majority relied to a large extent on his ineligibility under the Edmunds Act, so that the case supports the principle already stated, that if any disqualification can be added to the Constitution, it must be created by law. The minority in an opinion by Representative Littlefield of Maine, and De Armond of Missouri, which has been approved by Chief Justice Cullen of New York,[99] contended that Congress could not add any qualification to the Constitution, especially if it did not satisfy the test of Chancellor Sanford[100] that it must be based upon a conviction of crime. The minority declared that Roberts should not be disqualified but expelled, not for any offense prior to his election but because he was continuing to commit the crime of polygamy. Inasmuch as the vote for unseating him was more than two-thirds, the method of removal became academic. At all events the decision is no authority for the case of the New York Socialists, because it rested upon a statute and upon an alleged breach of the compact which Utah had made on entering the Union to abandon polygamy forever, and furthermore it involved overt criminal acts and not opinions or party affiliations.

This distinction is clearly brought out by the refusal of

[97] Act, March 22, 1882, c. 47, § 8; 22 Stat. at L. 31. This was held in the Roberts case to apply to members of Congress.

[98] 1 Hind's Prec. 518-560.

[99] Dissenting opinion, P. v. Ahearn, 196 N. Y. 221, 252 (1909): "No lawyer can read the clear and forceful minority report of Messrs. Littlefield and De Armond without at least doubting the correctness of this decision."

[100] P. 342, *supra*.

the Senate in 1904 to exclude or expel Reed Smoot.[101] He was not himself a polygamist or otherwise disqualified by statute, and had personally opposed polygamy in Utah, but he was one of the twelve apostles who together with the first president ruled over the Mormon hierarchy, and as a body encouraged the continuance of polygamous cohabitation (at least in long-standing marriages) and controlled the political affairs of Utah. According to the majority of the Committee, Mr. Smoot came there, "not as the accredited representative of the State of Utah, but as the choice of the hierarchy which controls the church and has usurped the functions of the State."[102] Nevertheless, the Senate refused to look beyond the question of his personal guilt of crime or disbar him for the political and ethical purposes of the organization to which he belonged. A powerful argument for the prevailing view was made in debate by Senator Knox of Pennsylvania, who pointed out that the Constitutional disqualifications do not in any way involve the moral qualities of a man. They relate to facts outside the realm of ethical consideration and are requirements of fact easily established. As to all matters affecting a man's moral or mental fitness the states are to be the judges, in the first instance, subject to the power of the Senate to reverse their judgment by a two-thirds vote of expulsion when an offense or offensive status extends into the period of service; and such a question can only be raised after a Senator has taken his seat. It is hardly proper to adopt a rule of constitutional construction based upon the theory that states will send criminals or idiots to the Senate. This position limits the effect of the Test Oath cases and relegates them to the status of consequences of the extraordinary situation following the Civil War.

And finally the precedents in the New York Assembly

[101] 1 Hinds' Prec. 561-590. *Socialist Brief*, 116. The majority of the committee recommended disqualification but the Senate adopted the minority view, which did not however dispute the political power of the hierarchy or its attitude toward polygamy.

[102] 1 *ibid.* 587.

itself are inconsistent with its recent action.[103] In 1906 it refused to disqualify a member for fraudulent practices in connection with a nomination. In 1917 it refused to oust another on the ground that he was not a resident of the district which he had been elected to represent. And in 1918 Lucas E. Decker, who was found to have failed to register for the selective draft and lied to excuse himself, was not excluded. The committee reported that the circumstances were matters of public record while Decker was a candidate for election, and that "in order to remove a member of the Assembly from office, under the Constitution, some question involving the election or returns is necessary before the Assembly has jurisdiction in the premises, or further, that the person so elected must be entirely disqualified under the Constitution, or by his conduct in the house must disqualify himself." The committee's report was adopted and Decker declared entitled to his seat by a unanimous vote.

Consequently, the principle is indubitably established, by judicial and legislative precedents, that the power to add qualifications to those fixed by the Constitution, if it exist at all, extends at the most to overt acts which have been made a bar by statute. And in New York State in view of the test clause in the Constitution and the decision of Chancellor Sanford, it is doubtful if even a statute could impose any other bar than conviction for crime. No such statute existed in the case of the New York Socialists. They were convicted of no crime, they were not even charged with any crime except a vague and unsubstantiated allegation of violation of the Espionage Act.[104] The action of the As-

---

[103] *Socialist Brief,* 104-109.

[104] *Assembly Outline,* 75. The subsequent Assembly Brief reached me too late for extended comment upon its argument (64-76, 195) that the Constitution, by requiring an oath to support it, also impliedly requires an "inner state of mind" and so makes "disloyalty" or membership in a "disloyal organization" a disqualification for taking the oath, which the Assembly is authorized to investigate. The dangers of such a vague disqualification are obvious and no precedent exists for this doctrine. Even in the exasperations and exacerbations of politics after the Civil

sembly must be characterized as a flagrant usurpation of power, only to be found in that government of which Senator Root,[105] who had good reason to know, said that for forty years it had been about as representative and responsible as the government of Venezuela.

The conduct of the investigation was thoroughly in harmony with its illegality. It was not based on any definite charges nor was it even limited to the accusations in the Resolution of January 7th. The affair had all the characteristics of an accumulative crime as described by Burke in the Wilkes case.[106] Whenever the Attorney General or his associate counsel thought of some new offense with which the Socialist Party could be taxed, it was lugged into the case and made a fresh reason for exclusion. The Resolution was construed as a roving commission to the Judiciary Committee, to find as many objectionable opinions of the Socialist Party as possible, on the theory that twenty-seven bad grounds[107] for exclusion might be rolled together and make one good ground. Inasmuch as there was no demarcation of counts in this rag-bag and ever-reopened indictment, no single fact had to be proved to the satisfaction of a majority of the Assembly. One member could vote to exclude the five Socialists because he thought they were as guilty under the Espionage Act as the three men who were convicted at Syracuse;[108] another because he considered Socialism threatened the family; a third to protect the church; a fourth, because Socialists sought to set up a

---

War Congress only refused the Test Oath to men found to have committed *in the past* the very acts which the oath denied. When the Constitution requires a solemn oath *as to the future*, it leaves the guarantee of its performance, not to the speculations of other human beings, but to the strongest sanctions of conscience and religion. *Cf.* note 112.

[105] Quoted in 40 Rep. Am. Bar. Assn. 365 (1915).

[106] P. 314, *supra*.

[107] See a list of these charges in *Socialist Brief*, 10; also the report of the Committee, *New York Times*, March 31.

[108] See p. 115, *supra*. The whole of Judge Garvin's opinion in the Syracuse case was read into the *Record*, p. 492, and reprinted in *Assembly Outline*, 75. No facts or other reasons than this are given to establish the guilt of the five members under the Act.

Soviet in the United States; some one else, because he disliked the vote of Claessens against the military training of boys. Others might object on the ground that the party fostered the claims of conscientious objectors or worked for the repeal of the draft or opposed the conscription of labor or voted against large military appropriations. The range was large and every member could find a reason of his own. It was the Wilkes case over again: [109]

> The very enumeration of so many grounds of expulsion implied their separate weakness and insufficiency; while it was designed to attract the support of members, influenced by different reasons for their votes.

Few legal documents furnish more delightful reading than the *Outline*, as it is called, of " the case of the Assembly against the five Socialist Assemblymen,"—the title is a significant comment on the impartiality of a tribunal which constitutes itself both judge and prosecutor. This makes it clearer than ever that the Socialists were not excluded for any personal unfitness but for the supposed principles of the party. Against Orr and De Witt as individuals, nothing whatever is said. Claessens and Waldman are charged with intemperate speeches, which " breathe in every word the spirit of treason and revolution with thinly veiled phrases to escape the prosecutions of the federal agents." In other words, because they spoke so as not to violate the Espionage Act, that makes it all the worse. Also Claessens is guilty of teaching at the Rand School. That is an institution which circulates the decrees of Soviet Russia, and has been convicted of publishing Nearing's *Great Madness*. Also one of his fellow-instructors was imprisoned for leading raids on churches. Obviously, Claessens " stands for the overthrow of our government." And Solomon at least has committed overt acts of undoubted enormity.

In 1692 the chief accusers of the Salem witches were a club of young girls who sent more than one old woman to her death by telling how they had seen her drink their blood

[109] May's *Constitutional History*, I, 316.

WILKES AND HIS SUCCESSORS

or cause a yellow bird to sit on the minister's hat where it hung on a peg in the pulpit.[110] In 1920 Ellen Chivers, a stenographer just under eighteen years old, testified that three years before when she was barely fifteen, she heard Solomon make a speech in Brooklyn, with an American flag and a red flag flying on his stand.[111] A detachment of soldiers rode up recruiting and asked to borrow his platform. She heard Solomon reply, " Lend you my platform? Can you borrow my platform? Huh; the gutter is good enough for you." They spoke from their jitney and went on. Nor was this the worst. A band of music came by on a trolley-car, stopped about three minutes, and struck up the " Star-Spangled Banner." And then in her presence and in the presence, she declared, of two policemen, " Mr. Solomon turned up his coat collar, put down his hat, and pulled it over his eyes, spit on the American flag and sat down." And the police did nothing.

The spy who is regularly employed by the government was brought into undesired publicity by the Colyer trial. The voluntary informer is also a recurrent feature of all prosecutions for opinion since the day of Titus Oates and beyond. This girl was a member of the American Anti-Socialist League and had attended weekly meetings for two years before she testified. She had not mentioned these incidents to any member of that society or to her sister or to any one else, until after the investigation began, when she wrote to Speaker Sweet, because she thought " it was the duty of any American to take the stand against one who has committed treason against their country." The two policemen on the spot afterwards swore that no such disloyal acts occurred. The Attorney General's brief reprints without question the testimony of Ellen Chivers.

Another group of charges was presented to appeal to Assemblymen who were not entirely convinced by Miss

[110] Palfrey, *History of New England*, IV, 102; Hutchinson, *History of the Province of Massachusetts Bay*, II, 27.
[111] *Assembly Outline*, 71; *Record*, 705-723, for Chivers' testimony.

Chivers and to attack the Socialists who could not be accused of such open disloyalty. Candidates of the Socialist Party were said to be bound by certain pledges, which might conceivably operate to ruin the country, and were so inconsistent with their constitutional oath as to make it false. First, the National Socialist Constitution provides that Socialist office-holders who vote to appropriate money for military or naval purposes shall be expelled from the party. The New York Constitution makes it the duty of the Legislature to maintain a minimum militia of 10,000 men. Therefore they have disqualified themselves to take the oath to support this Constitution. Even if this oath were not obligatory, they have made themselves ineligible by promising to take a course which if supported by a majority of the Assembly would destroy the entire military organization of the state and tend to expose state and nation to destruction from its enemies without and within. The state's right of self-defense gives it the right to exclude such traitors. Their intention to disregard the constitutional provision about the minimum militia is shown by their opposition in previous sessions to laws giving extra pay for the National Guard and pay while in federal service, also to laws for the expulsion of alien enemies from teaching in the public schools, punishing the desecration of the flag, establishing military training for boys, and conscripting labor. The Attorney General neglected to add that they also voted against the establishment of the Lusk Committee.

The Socialists replied that the Constitution was paramount. Inconsistent party pledges were rejected by virtue of their oath as Assemblymen. The National Party platform naturally failed to consider the militia requirement of a particular state, and they were ready to carry out whatever duty that requirement imposed. However, until some one knew better what it meant, other members of the Assembly had no right to define this duty for them [112] or say

[112] That constitutional duties must be interpreted by the person obligated under the sanction of his official oath, Ops. of the Justices,

that it included extravagant appropriations to maintain far more than the constitutional minimum of 10,000 men. If a question of maintaining that minimum were presented, they would do so. They were not obliged to vote extras or conscript boys.

Still more flimsy is the charge that the Socialist legislators were to vote as a unit and obey the wishes of the party organization. This promise, the Republican Attorney General gravely explains, must not " be confused with party action in caucus where party men uniformly reserve the right to withdraw if a proposed measure violates their conscience or their patriotism or is not with party issues." [113] And then a few days later the Republicans proposed to displace Floor Manager Adler because he voted against the unseating of the five members. Nothing can be more touching than the indignation which the bare possibility of political control by outsiders inspired in the henchmen of New York's " invisible government ": [114]

> It makes no difference what name you give, whether you call it Fenton or Conkling or Cornell or Arthur or Platt, or by the names of men now living. The ruler of the state during the greater part of the forty years of my acquaintance with the state government has not been any man authorized by the constitution or by the law.

The meat of the *Outline* is the portrayal of the iniquities of Socialism. This is a very different affair from the body of economic principles which is attacked by Carver, Taussig, and other economists, none of whom was summoned as an expert by the prosecution. The *Outline* conceives it as " a Revolutionary Party, having the single purpose of destroy-

---

56 N. H. 576 (1875); Andrew Jackson, in United States Bank veto, quoted by W. M. Evarts, *Arguments and Speeches*, I, 445.

[113] *Assembly Outline*, 13. *Cf.* Bryce, *Am. Commonwealth*, 3 ed., I, c. XIX, p. 204. See Hillquit's remarks on the Roman augurs' wink. *Socialist Brief*, p. 22. I omit to discuss the charge that the Socialists were required to resign if they violated the party platform, as this was a dead-letter.

[114] Elihu Root, *Addresses on Government and Citizenship*, p. 202 (at the N. Y. Const. Conv. of 1915).

ing our institutions and government and substituting the Russian-Soviet government, . . . an anti-national party whose allegiance is given to the Internationale and not to the United States." Its purposes, mass action and the general strike, are treasonable. For its crimes the five members are responsible, and more than that, for the acts of any other person in that party, whether or not he belongs to their particular faction. As Mr. Stanchfield, for the prosecution, openly stated: [115]

> The whole theory of this investigation rests upon the proposition that the Socialist Party, of which the five members under investigation are confessedly, concededly members, has embarked upon a program that calls for the overthrow of our form of government, some assert by constitutional means, others by violence. Now, assuming that that program is the basic charge under investigation, then my argument runs along this line: That every pamphlet, every declaration, every speech, every statement of every men who is affiliated with or belongs to that party, not necessarily in a technical sense of belonging to it, but everybody who upholds those claims, who supports those principles, who stands upon that platform, is bound by the speeches, the sentiments, the writings, the books, the publications of every other man affiliated with that association, whether they were present at the time when it was made or they were uttered, or whether they were absent.

No person who has followed with any intelligence the proceedings of the Socialist Party at the conventions of September, 1919, or May, 1920, can doubt that that party is as much divided into factions as any other. Nevertheless, the five members were held responsible on Stanchfield's principle, not merely for the statements in the party platform but for the Debs speech at Canton, Ohio, statements in the Moscow manifesto, extracts from a book in Yiddish published by the Jewish Socialist Federation of America, all the articles contributed to the *American Socialist*, for everything that was said by speakers at meetings at which one of the assemblymen was present as well as for statements made in a letter

[115] *Record*, 335.

WILKES AND HIS SUCCESSORS 361

by an organization to which he was bitterly opposed. This was guilt by association with a vengeance.

And finally the Attorney General corrects one member of the Committee in his misapprehension of thinking that the duty to disqualify for disloyalty rests with the people of the district. This, he says, misconceives the representative as an officer of the district and not of the state, and he shows the gravity of the error by an extract from Burke's "Speech to the Sheriffs of Bristol":

You choose a member indeed; but when you have chosen him, he is not a member of Bristol, but he is a member of *Parliament*.

"Thoughts on the Present Discontents" had been more to the point. And, quoting more political scripture, he warns the Committee in Madison's words against that sectionalism which leads state legislators to sacrifice the comprehensive and permanent interest of the state to the particular and separate views of the counties or districts where they reside.

When such testimony and arguments were admitted, the result was a foregone conclusion. The Committee recommended expulsion, the Assembly characteristically waited until April 1st, which was too late for a re-election, and then disregarding the maiden speech of Theodore Roosevelt, who, with all his inherited abhorrence of Socialism and pacifism, refused to condemn the Socialist Party as a conspiracy for a state of mind, expelled the five members by an overwhelming vote.[116] The Legislature proceeded to enact the bills drafted by the triumphant Lusk Committee, which not only throttle the Rand School, but exclude from the definition of a party under the Election Law any organization which advocates:

Principles, doctrines, or policies that tend, if carried into effect, to the destruction, subversion or endangering of the existing governments of the United States and of the State of New

[116] *New York Times,* April 1st and 2nd.

York, and of the rights, privileges and institutions secured under such constitutions.[117]

Any person who is a member of such organization is made ineligible for public office. And then leaving the governor's welfare bills untouched the New York Legislature adjourned, and Speaker Sweet proclaimed the session "a victory for undivided Americanism."

Surely this event ought to free us from the tyranny of this word, which seems like some magic helmet to render the true qualities of the wearer invisible to those around him. The men who use the ideals of the founders of our Republic, not as an inspiration for high-minded action on their own part but as a test by which they may condemn and imprison and disfranchise their fellow-citizens, are as unpardonable as the persecutors who used the teachings of the Gospels to send men to the stake in this world and hell-fire in the next. Years ago William Graham Sumner commented:

> Who dares say that he is not "American"? Who dares repudiate what is declared to be Americanism? It follows that if anything is base and bogus it is always labeled American. If a thing is to be recommended which cannot be justified it is put under "Americanism" .... Then we see what Americanism and patriotism are. They are the duty laid upon us all to applaud, follow and obey whatever a ruling clique of newspapers or politicians chooses to say or wants to do.[118]

The absurdity to which our greatest state has descended in its frantic desire to suppress disloyalty cannot be entirely explained by the fear of Bolshevism, because the danger of that is far greater in European countries, which have large groups of Socialists in their legislatures unmolested. Nor is it entirely due to the activities of organizations like the Lusk Committee. Something more is needed to account for the statement of the *New York Times* that the expulsion of the Socialists was as clearly and demon-

---

[117] 2 *Review*, 422. Governor Smith vetoed all the Lusk bills in a stinging message.
[118] *Folkways*, p. 177.

strably a measure of national defense as the declaration of war again Germany.[119]   Speaker Sweet and his associates would not have acted as they did had they not been assured of wide support, especially in the country districts. Much of the panic-stricken dread of Socialism is due to the sentiment that we must have unanimity of thought in this country. The surprising uniformity of American life has long excited attention from foreign observers.[120] Until recently we have had only a middle class without any proletariat or large group of extremely wealthy men. Since the issues of the Civil War died away, whatever few fundamental differences in opinion have existed have rarely coincided with party lines. A French writer in his biography of President Wilson remarks that a foreigner on coming to this country does not understand our political parties. In Europe every party has a platform which represents a definite policy, like monarchy, clericalism, Socialism. He finds nothing of the kind here. Why do we have two parties when they do not differ? Halévy explains that the Republican and Democratic parties are like two great department stores, such as the *Bon Marché* and the *Louvre*. Both sell very much the same things. Some people go entirely to one, some go entirely to the other, some go first to one and then to the other. They are there because they have always been there.[121] But now a new party has entered the field which has real issues, vital one way or the other to all of us and hence the antagonism of its opponents is immediate and bitter. When it shows signs of gaining real strength then there is an energetic effort to stamp it out, which likes to base itself on patriotism and self-preservation.

It is not by such methods that the nation can be saved from the evil tendencies of any doctrine. The great strength of our argument against violent-talking radicals in the past has been that we could say to them: " It is true that in the

[119] Editorial of April 2nd.
[120] See Bryce's *American Commonwealth*, II, c. CXII.
[121] Daniel Halévy, *Le Président Wilson*, Paris, 1918, p. 109.

countries that you came from you naturally resorted to violence because you had no vote and could not abolish the abuses to which you objected. It is not so in this country. If you want a change, go and vote for it, vote for men who have promised to bring it to pass." The New York Assembly has deprived us of this argument in the state where the left wing is strongest. It has appealed to force as the normal method for settling conflicts between ideas. It has disregarded the counsel of its wisest men to take that of the Lusk Committee, whose whole existence has been a violation of constitutional rights. It has disfranchised 60,000 American citizens on the basis of a caricature of Socialism and the testimony of Ellen Chivers. It has repudiated government by representation and substituted government by misrepresentation.

CHAPTER VII
FREEDOM AND INITIATIVE IN THE SCHOOLS

The *Liberty* is likely to survive longer than anything else that I have written, because it is a kind of philosophic text-book of a single truth, which the changes progressively taking place in modern society tend to bring out into ever stronger relief: the importance, to man and society, of a large variety in types of character, and of giving full freedom to human nature to expand itself in innumerable and conflicting directions.—JOHN STUART MILL, *Autobiography*.

The state which refrains from fighting revolutionary doctrines by force except in times of clear and present danger is not helpless, for besides abolishing some causes of discontent, it can employ education to establish among its citizens faith in progress through law. If, however, the advocates of revolution by violence should share in the control of education, the state would seem to be surrendering its last stronghold. Such a possibility is indicated to many by the presence of radicals among public school teachers. The situation is complicated by factors which lie outside the province of this book, like the claim of teachers to participate in deciding the dismissal of one of their number. Questions of the fitness of some particular teacher to teach, instead of being settled purely on their merits, have become storm-centers of conflict for employees, trade-unions, and the press. On one side, some teachers who are dismissed for good reasons are believed by their friends to be ousted for political or economic views. On the other side, the authorities assert that any one who holds certain views is *ipso facto* unfit to teach. For example, Dr. John L. Tildsley, while Associate Superintendent of Schools in New York, declared,[1] " that men or women who are *Marxian Socialists*, who believe in

[1] The Public and the Schools, May 17, 1919, Public Education Assn., N. Y.

365

the Communist Manifesto, have no right to be in the school system because such teachers believe in the overturn by force of those elements on which our civilization is based." The student of freedom of speech is concerned with the comparative redness of these proscribed views, and with the question whether a teacher is to be dismissed for merely believing in them or only if he expresses them to his classes. The following reflections grow out of the New York controversy, but merely endeavor to suggest some controlling principles. Since the problem does not involve the legal questions which have received attention in previous chapters, it may be helpful, at the cost of some repetition, to restate in non-technical language the main conclusions of this book.

When I heard Dr. Tildsley say he believed in freedom of speech I felt glad that we stood in the same position. But when he went on and said no one who favored Marxian Socialism should teach in the schools, it seemed to me a little like a character in James Russell Lowell, a gentleman of the *Biglow Papers*, who said: "I du believe in Freedom's cause, Ez fur away as Payris is." Or something like the Irishman who inquired of his friend, "What is this Socialism that I hear so much about?" Mike said, "Why, Pat, don't you know what that is? If you had a million dollars, you would give me half, wouldn't you?" "Sure, I would!" "Well, that's Socialism." Pat said, "That is a grand thing! Tell me some more about it." "Well," replied Mike, "If you had ten dollars, you would give me half, wouldn't you?" "I would not! I've got ten dollars!"

We all believe in freedom of speech, but the question is, do we believe in it when it is disagreeable to us? After all, if freedom of speech means anything, it means a willingness to stand and let people say things with which we disagree, and which do weary us considerably. A good deal of the public discussion on the matter turns on the use of the word "rights." Those who want to speak freely insist on the right of freedom of speech; and, on the other hand, those who wish to restrict speakers talk of the right of the government to carry on war and the right of the government to maintain order, and there we have a deadlock. Each side says it is in the right, and that does not bring us anywhere at all. I think we will do well to get away from this word "right" entirely, and look at it from another point of view, not from the legal point of view, but simply from the point of view of the individual human being who wants to speak and the great group of human beings which constitute the society in which he speaks. That is, we have his individual interests and the interests of society at large.

First, we have the individual interest in freedom of speech. "Good," as Emerson says, "does not mean good to eat and good to wear." It means to live our own lives as fully as we can and to bear witness to the truth for which we came into the world. I did intend at this point to quote from *Jean-Christophe*, by Romain Rolland, but this is one of the proscribed books for recommending which to his pupils a teacher was dismissed from the New York high schools, and so I will refrain. But instead, I will take a book which was written three thousand years ago, which is fairly safe—the *Apology of Socrates:*

If in acquitting me you should say: "We will not put faith this time, O Socrates, in your accusers, but will let you go, on the condition, however, that you no longer spend your time in this search nor in the pursuit of wisdom, and that if you are caught doing either again you shall die "—if, I say, you were to release me on these conditions, I should say to you: " Athenians, I love and cherish you, but shall obey the God rather than you; and as long as I draw breath and have the strength, I shall never cease to follow philosophy and to exhort and persuade any one of you whom I happen to meet. For this, be assured, the God commands; and I believe that there has never been a greater good in the state than this my service to the God; for I do nothing but go about persuading you, both young and old, not to let your first thought be for your body or your possessions, nor to care for anything so earnestly as for your soul." And, Athenians, I should go on to say: "Either hearken to my accusers or not, and either acquit me or not; but understand that I shall never act differently, even if I have to die for it many times."

That is the individual interest in free speech. Over against that we have to set the social interests—the interest in the safeguarding of the government and the nation from foreign attack, the interest in order, without which all our individual interests would be lost, the interest in moral and decent living, and the interest in the training of the young, which is the main thing that we have to consider here. As between that individual interest and those social interests, it seems easy to conclude that the individual interest should always give way; that, as is often said, freedom of speech means liberty, not license; that we must not advocate anything that is wrong, anything which interferes with the social interests in order, and so on. But we have to remember that not only do we have the social interest in order, and in the education of the young, and in morals, but that freedom of speech is itself a social interest; that one of the purposes for which society exists just as much as for the maintenance of order is the discovery and the spread of truth.

Another member of the Lowell family, now President of Harvard, said in his report to the Corporation on the subject of freedom of speech, which every Harvard professor can regard as a Magna Charta:

Education has proved, and probably no one would now deny, that knowledge can advance, or at least can advance most rapidly, only by means of an unfettered search for truth on the part of those who devote their lives to seeking it in their respective fields, and by complete freedom in imparting to their pupils the truth that they have found. This has become an axiom in higher education, in spite of the fact that a searcher may discover error instead of truth, and be misled, and mislead others, thereby. We believe that if enough light is let in, the real relations of things will soon be seen, and they can be seen in no other way.

We cannot be sure that any statement is either wholly true or wholly false. We cannot separate the truth at once. We have to leave the separation on the whole to time. Any subject may have some bad features, but we must let the wheat grow with the tares until the time comes when the crop is ripe, and we can decide between them. If what is

FREEDOM AND INITIATIVE IN SCHOOLS 369

said does dangerously and directly interfere with those other social interests in order and in education of the young, then speech must be restrained. But until that time comes— and we ought to be sure that it has come—we should be very careful how we interfere. Because it is by the contest of argument that the truth is found. Argument on one side and argument on the other is the best way that we have on earth to bring about truth. Once force is thrown into the scale, once the pressure of government is used on one side or the other, it becomes simply a matter of chance on which side it is used, and then the natural ability to decide the matter by argument is altogether gone. I say it is just a matter of chance. For instance, force here is to be thrown against Marxian Socialism, a doctrine with which I do not at all agree; but, in North Dakota it is to be thrown on the side of something that comes pretty near Marxian Socialism. Under a populist régime in Kansas the State issued textbooks that had to be used in the schools, which devoted more time to the " crime of '73," by which free silver was abolished, than to the Civil War. It just depends on what government you have. The administration in Washington is now publishing textbooks for use in the schools.[2] When we have a Republican administration we may have a different kind of textbook. Therein lies the difficulty with Dr. Tildsley's argument that teachers must teach and think according to the decision of a majority in Congress. It is true that a majority decision is the best way of determining how the government shall act, but it is not the best way of deciding what is right. We have to act on the decision of the majority, but the minority are not thereby precluded from doubting the wisdom of the decision, and it may eventually be that they will again become the majority and will put an end to that particular measure.

If the majority of Congress declares war, the minority must realize that we are at war, but they are not necessarily

[2] "A Case of Federal Propaganda in our Public Schools," Natl. Industrial Conference Board, Feb., 1919.

bound to believe that the war is right, and why should they not endeavor to stop it by argument when they believe that it has gone far enough? Once again, we have got to balance the interests in this matter—the public interest in the discovery of truth against the public interest in the education of the young and protection against invasion. And it is very necessary that the balancing should be done by people who realize the importance of freedom of speech. Freedom of speech ought to weigh very heavily in the scale.

It is all very well to say that religious views should be free; that scientific investigation should be free; but that political opinion cannot be free, because that is dangerous; that Marxian Socialism is so dangerous that it cannot be free. Three centuries ago, people felt just as strongly about religious views and about scientific investigation as they do now about political investigation. They felt just as sure that any view which was not in accord with the orthodox religion would unsettle the very foundations of morality, and that consequently no one should teach in the schools who was not an orthodox Christian. And they felt just as sure about scientific investigation; that if a man said the earth went around the sun, he should not be trusted anywhere. If they felt so strongly about it then, and were wrong, how can we be sure that we are right if we feel the same way about political investigation? On that we must have just as much freedom of investigation as in the old days was necessary for scientific discoveries. It is easy enough to think that everything that is different from ourselves must necessarily be dangerous. It is easy to believe that political ideas which are different from our own must necessarily advocate the use of force. We say, how could Socialism come into existence except by violence, because it is so objectionable. I do not believe in it, and hope it will not come into existence. But I do not see why it may not be adopted by popular suffrage, the same as other ideas. We ought not to assume it can only win by violence, simply because it differs from our views. In the old days they used

FREEDOM AND INITIATIVE IN SCHOOLS

to get rid of objectionable persons on the ground that they would overthrow society. They got rid of Socrates by saying he was a corrupter of the youth. They got rid of Jesus by saying he planned to upset the Roman state, and they said it is more expedient that one man should die than that the people should perish. It is more expedient, now, that one man should be put in prison or lose his job—it is just the same argument we use—than that the people should perish. But let us be sure that the people, after all, are going to perish.

In war time, the problem is perhaps peculiar. Everybody is very much occupied. We haven't time to think things over, and people will say, " We don't care what sort of war it is. My country, right or wrong. Let us go ahead." It is something like the colored man who went with his son to rob a hen coop, and sent his son inside. The boy turned and stuck his head out of the door and said, " Father, am dis right? " And the father said, " Dat am a great moral question. We will argue it out at home dis evening. You get busy and hand out dem chickens."

I think this war was right, but the people who opposed it, who were wrong this time, may be right next time, as they were right in the Mexican War. They may be right next time, and we ought to be careful how we require every person who teaches in the schools to support every war that is going on. But now we have peace. We cannot postpone the discussion of problems until the " war " is over. We shall have to meet them as they arise. Dr. Tildsley spoke of our being under the spell of words. There is one word we are all under the spell of at the present time, and that is, Americanism. What does it mean? We are afraid of something. We were afraid of Germany, but we got over that. What is it we are scared about now? We are scared of Russia. Why? Is it because Russia has a different political system from ours? She had a different political system under the Czar, and we were perfectly willing to discuss his system. Is it because the people have a tremendous control there? We have been perfectly willing to discuss the initiative and the referendum for years. Is it because they have a restrictive franchise there? We have a restrictive franchise in certain states where half the adult population is not allowed to vote. In Rhode Island, where I used to live, the men who are most scared of Bolshevism are the men who are most ready to keep the property franchise under which people who have less than $134 cannot vote for many important offices. What we are really scared of is not something political; it is economic. We are afraid of a system which takes property from the people who have inherited it or who have earned it, and that is an economic question. It is not Americanism against something else. It is simply a choice of two economic systems, and we have got to have that controversy discussed if we are going to decide it rightly.

If Americanism means anything, it means free speech, right from the start. The Pilgrims came to Massachusetts to get it, and Roger Williams left Massachusetts, not only because he had his own religious views but because he attacked property rights in land not purchased from the Indians. Thomas Jefferson is usually considered a good American, but he said things about the desirability of rebellion that would make us all shudder. Alexander Hamilton argued for free speech here in New York, and James Russell Lowell called the Mexican War murder. The abolitionists, men whom we all honor to-day, believed in Americanism— freedom to criticise the government of their day and the institutions of property of their day, which included a tremendous form of property—the property in negro slaves. I believe in private property myself, but because I believe in it I want to know why it ought to be supported.

And now, for the problem as it affects teachers. There are two views of teaching. One regards teaching as a sort of handing out canned goods to the pupils, so much canned goods, so much knowledge. Well, if it is a canned goods business, we may need a Pure Food Law to make sure the

FREEDOM AND INITIATIVE IN SCHOOLS 373

children get the right brand of "corn." But this is not the real theory. That was held by President Gilman of Johns Hopkins, when he took Professor Gildersleeve into a bare room and said, "Now, radiate." We have got to have the kind of teachers that radiate. For that we not only need contented teachers, but we must have teachers who think for themselves.

In a pamphlet issued in the New York school controversy, the "Reply of the Superintendents," is a statement that teachers should be obedient, and to support it a quotation about the sort of obedience that is necessary in the army and navy. Of course, teachers to some extent have to obey, but the kind of obedience we ought to get from them is far from the kind they get in the army and navy. In an autocracy, they might get along without teachers of independence. But this country has to be run by the people in it, and they are the people who are taught in the schools; and if the teachers cannot think for themselves, the pupils cannot think for themselves. They cannot discuss merely the questions of the past. They must discuss the critical problems of the present time if they are to solve them.

In England there is a leisure class to carry on the government. We cannot depend on that. Now, to what branch of citizens should we turn more for help in these matters than the teachers? And there is no class of people who are more injured by repression than teachers. If you say to any other man that he must not express his ideas on political questions, he can at least devote himself to his job, but if you confine the teacher in his thinking, what do you leave him? That is his job, to think.

People say that the teacher is employed by the government, and ought to agree with the government which pays him. The courts are just as much a part of the government as the schools—more so, for we have private schools, but we do not have private courts. Do we say that every one in the court must agree with the government? Do we say that the judges must always decide in favor of the government? Not at all! They often decide against it. We retain lawyers to defend criminals whom the government accuses. It is even suggested we should have one lawyer to do so all the time. Progressive manufacturing corporations employ men just to criticise the products of the corporation and see how they can be better made. The teacher may be serving the state even while he criticises it.

Of course, we have special considerations in the schools. We have this social interest in favor of the education of children. We cannot let everything be said in the schools that we might let be said outside. A teacher might be allowed to stand on his head at home, but not in school. In the same way there is much he ought not to do there in the way of free speech. If he taught that all boys and girls at sixteen were of a proper age to marry, he certainly ought to lose his position. He must adapt his discussion to the maturity of the pupils before him. And we certainly can require concentration on his subject; we can require judgment; we ought to demand of a teacher that he should be a master of his subject and a man of sound common sense.

But, on the other hand, you cannot control the mind of an expert. You cannot stand over Galileo and say "Use your telescope, but do not find that the earth goes around the sun." You cannot stand over Pasteur and say, "Investigate spontaneous generation, but do not discover that spontaneous generation exists." You cannot stand over a man that deals with economics and say, "Find out that economics exists according to this or that system"; or, if he deals with history, say to him, "Find out that the men who are in power in Russia are a gang of thugs." If he finds it out, all right; but you cannot force him to do so, and you cannot force him to teach lies. Outside of the classroom he should be even more free. There he is a citizen, and as the New York Constitution says, every citizen may safely speak, write, and publish his sentiments on all subjects, being responsible for the abuse of that right; and no law shall be passed to restrain or abridge the liberty of speech or of the press.

… FREEDOM AND INITIATIVE IN SCHOOLS 375

Be sure that the right is abused. Be sure that freedom of speech weighs much in the scale. I think if every board which had to pass on the removal of a teacher would first read Milton's *Areopagitica* and Mill on *Liberty*, that some of the decisions would be very different; because they would see that, after all, freedom of speech is just as important as the maintenance of order.

Why are we so worried? Why are we so scared? Have we no confidence in the arguments that can be used against these radical ideas? Parents argue on the other side, and we have with us the army and the police, and everybody who has a savings bank account or a life insurance policy. After all, the dangers of rebellion are not very great, unless our case is very weak, and I do not think it is.

Finally, repression will produce just the kind of spirit in the teachers that we want to get rid of—that is, the revolutionary spirit. The French experience in this matter has been very instructive.[3] There the government threw its force against religion. Teachers were dismissed because they went to church. Teachers were dismissed for attacking the Prefect of their department. The state held a general inquisition into the opinions of all the teachers, a cabinet minister saying, "The government will not surrender the right to know the attitude of its servants toward the public." And they even had a law that government officials, including teachers, should wear a cheerful countenance on national holidays. What was the result? The teachers of France, although by birth, by training, by disposition affiliated with the middle class rather than the working class, have formed a revolutionary trade-union and affiliated themselves with the syndicalist organizations of France.

It is all very well to say that we ought to be loyal to the state. What do we mean by the state? After all, it comes right straight down to the government that we deal with, and the government comes down to the men that we deal with, which means the educational authorities, and those who have power to put us in prison, and if those men do not

[3] H. J. Laski, *Authority in the Modern State*, c. V.

stand for the best things we stand for,—for the development of mind and spirit and the search for truth, we begin to wonder whether, after all, that government ought to endure, and whether we do not want a government which will stand for the things that we believe in. So it becomes important that the men who constitute the government, who, after all, are really the state, should stand for these things. We cannot love the state as a mystical unity, when that unity as we actually face it prevents us from living a true human life. So that, in order to make people loyal to the state, you must make the state a sort of thing that they want to be loyal to.

We have got to take risks. Of course, it is not perfectly safe to allow teachers to be free. There ought to be this balancing of youth against truth. But there are plenty of risks that we take in life. We let our children go on the street although they may be run over by automobiles and trolley cars. We do not keep them home until they are twenty-one years of age. In the same way, we might like to leave them until a little later before we discuss some of these economic problems, but then they are out at work, and it is too late. We have got to take them when we can get them. And even if an occasional teacher does speak very radically, that does not mean that high school students will believe all he says. If we go back to the time when we were sixteen, we remember the keenness with which we discussed those problems. We did not take everything the teacher said for granted, and the more he said, the more we were likely to oppose him.

We cannot lead sterilized lives. Think of the chances America took by allowing people with very little education to vote, and yet that is a risk we are ready to run. Democracy is not a water-tight compartment. It is a great adventure, and in order to prepare people for that adventure we have to teach them to think for themselves on the problems they will have to face when they grow up. It is not simply teaching them the ideals of the day,—we must train them to make the ideals of to-morrow.

APPENDIX I

BIBLIOGRAPHY ON FREEDOM OF SPEECH

Note: This Bibliography is far from a complete list of even the modern material in the English language. No Continental literature is included and information about religious liberty must be sought elsewhere. The purpose is to cover only the topics of the book.

A. General and Historical (Chapter I)

The legal meaning of freedom of speech cannot properly be determined without a knowledge of the political and philosophical basis of such freedom. Four writings on this problem may be mentioned as invaluable: Plato's *Apology of Socrates;* Milton's *Areopagitica;* the second chapter of Mill, *On Liberty;* and Walter Bagehot's essay, "The Metaphysical Basis of Toleration." The second chapter of J. F. Stephen, *Liberty, Equality, Fraternity,* has an important critique on Mill. See, also, J. B. Bury, *A History of Freedom of Thought,* the first and last chapters; Grote, *Plato,* Chap. VI; Graham Wallas, *The Great Society,* 195-98. The relation of freedom of thought to political progress is discussed by same, "The Price of Intolerance," 125 *Atlantic* 116 (January, 1920); H. J. Laski, *Authority in the Modern State,* passim; same, "The Temper of the Present Time," 21 *New Republic* 335 (February 18, 1920). Francis Hackett, "The Invisible Censor," 21 *New Republic* 11 (December 3, 1919), sketches the psychology of suppression. For a caustic point of view, see Fabian Franklin, "Some Free Speech Delusions," 2 *Unpopular Rev.* 223 (October, 1914). The difficulties of the problem as seen from actual experience on both sides are presented in Viscount Morley's *Recollections.*

By far the best textbook on this and the other civil rights is Cooley, *Constitutional Limitations,* 7th ed.; Dicey, *The Law of the Constitution,* 8th ed., Chaps. VI and VII gives the English law of freedom of speech and assembly.

The best discussion of the legal meaning of "Freedom of the Press in the United States" will be found in an article under that name by Henry Schofield, in 9 *Publications of the American Sociological Society* 67 (1914). This volume is devoted entirely to "Freedom of Communication," and contains several valuable papers on different aspects of the problem. Other general legal articles are: "The Jurisdiction of the United States over Seditious Libel," H. W. Biklé, 41 *Am. L. Reg.* (N. S.) 1 (1902); "Restrictions on the Freedom of the Press," 16 *Harv. L. Rev.* 55 (1902); "Free Speech and Free Press in Relation to the Police Power of the State," P. L. Edwards, 58 *Cent. L. J.* 383 (1904); "Freedom of Speech and of the Press," 65 *Univ. of Pa. L. Rev.* 170 (1916); Joseph R. Long, "The Freedom of the Press," 5 *Va. L. Rev.* 225 (1918). Freedom of speech is discussed by Dean Pound as an interest of the individual in his "Interests of Personality," 28 *Harv. L. Rev.* 445, 453 (1915); and as an alleged bar to injunctions of libel in his "Equitable Relief against Defamation and Injuries to Personality," 29 *Harv. L. Rev.* 640, 648 (1916). For the technique of political trials, see Robert Ferrari, "Political Crime and Criminal Evidence," 3 *Minn. L. Rev.* 365 (1919); "Political Crime," 20 *Col. L. Rev.* 308 (1920); "The Trial of Political Criminals Here and Abroad," 66 *Dial* 647 (June 28, 1919). Much useful material is collected in the writings of Theodore Schroeder, of which a bibliography by N. E. Sankey-Jones is published by the New York Free Speech League, 1919. Recent articles by him are "A Psychologic Study of Judicial Opinions," 6 *Cal. L. Rev.* 89 (1918); "Political Crimes Defined," 18 *Mich. L. Rev.* 30 (1919).

Origins of the First Amendment:

The history of freedom of speech in America has not yet been fully investigated, but Clyde A. Duniway, *The Development of Freedom of the Press in Massachusetts*, Cambridge, Harvard University Press, 1906, is extremely useful for the Colonial period. Max Farrand, *Records of the Federal Convention,* gives material on the proposed free speech clause, II, 334, 340, 341, 545; III, 122, 256, 290, 595, 599, 609. The state debates on this clause are in *Elliot's Debates* (2d ed., 1836), I, 359, 360, 362, 369, 371, 375; II, 424, 511, 537; III, 411, 414, 415, 431, 551; IV, 159, 175, 209, 301, 302. J. B. McMaster and F. D. Stone, *Pennsylvania and the Federal Convention, 1787-1788,* Hist. Soc. of Penn., 1888, has contemporary press discussion.

English History and Law:

Much light is thrown on the problem by sedition trials in England, before our Revolution and during the French Revolution. The best account of these is in T. Erskine May, 2 *Constitutional History of England*, 2d ed., 1912, Chaps. IX-X, summarized by Charles A. Beard in 16 *New Republic* 350 October 19, 1918). See, also, 2 Stephen, *History of the Criminal Law,* Chap. XXIV; Graham Wallas, *Life of Francis Place*, N. Y., 1919; Philip A. Brown, *The French Revolution in English History,* London, 1918; G. O. Trevelyan, *The Early History of Charles James Fox,* relates Wilkes and Junius controversies. See bibliography in J. F. Rhodes, *History of the United States*, IV, 233 note.

For the modern law: F. M. Anderson, "The Law of Sedition in the British Empire," *House Judiciary Hearings,* p. 273; H. J. Laski, "The Fundamental Law in England, 31 *Harv. L. Rev.* 296 (1917). Canada: A. V. Thomas, "Quoting Isaiah in Winnipeg," 110 *Nation* 850 (January 3, 1920); J. A. Stevenson, "A Set-back for Reaction in Canada," 110 *ibid.* 292 (March 6).

Sedition Act of 1798:

Frank Maloy Anderson, "The Enforcement of the Alien and Sedition Laws," Ann. Rep. Am. Hist. Assn. (1912) 115; same, "Contemporary Opinion of the Virginia and Kentucky Resolutions," 5 *Am. Hist. Rev.* 45 (1900); Albert J. Beveridge, *Life of John Marshall*, vols. II and III, *passim*, is vivid and collects much contemporary material. The four reported prosecutions are in Wharton's *State Trials*, —Lyon, 333 (1798); Cooper, 659 (1800); Haswell, 684 (1800); Callender, 688 (1800). Wharton, 23, narrates the events leading up to these statutes; see, also, Channing and other standard histories. For references to the Sedition Act in Jefferson's letters, see the edition of Paul Leicester Ford, VII, 245: "The object of that [the bill] is the suppression of the whig presses;" VII, 246; VII, 266, on unconstitutionality; VII, 283, "The alien and sedition laws are working hard;"

APPENDICES 379

VII, 289, 311, 336, 350, 354, 355, 356, on popular opposition to the acts; VII, 367, 371, 483, on continuation of Sedition Law by Congress; VIII, 54, 56 ff., 308 ff., on unconstitutionality and pardons; IX, 456, on dismissal of prosecutions. Madison's Report on the Virginia Resolutions is reprinted in *Elliot's Debates*.

Reference Books:

Soule's *Lawyer's Reference Manual*, for abbreviations of legal reports.

New York Times Index, issued quarterly, is very valuable for finding press accounts of prosecutions, etc.

B. The War (Chapters II and III)

Important decisions under the U. S. Espionage Act are printed in the Federal (Fed.) and United States Supreme Court Reports (U. S.). The latter are in public and university libraries. The Bulletins of the Department of Justice on the Interpretation of War Statutes (cited herein as Bull. Dept. Just.), Nos. 1-204, contain many charges not otherwise reported. Appendix II, *infra*, tells where all reported prosecutions can be found. Supreme Court records and briefs are in the Harvard Law School Library. The cases before July, 1918, are collected by Walter Nelles, *Espionage Act Cases, with Certain Others on Related Points*, Natl. Civil Liberties Bureau, N. Y. This has some state cases, and gives a careful analysis of the decisions. The Bureau has also published *War-time Prosecutions and Mob Violence*, involving the rights of free speech, free press, and peaceful assemblage (from April 1, 1917, to March 1, 1919), containing an annotated list of prosecutions, convictions, exclusions from the mail, etc. It has prepared in MSS. "A Memorandum Concerning Political Prisoners Within the Jurisdiction of the Department of Justice in 1919," for the Attorney General; and "Memorandum to the President of the United States as to Persons Imprisoned for Violation of the War Laws" (copies in Harvard Law School Library).

The enforcement of the Espionage Act and similar statutes is officially summarized in the Reports of the Attorney General for 1917, 1918, and 1919, with lists of prosecutions and results, and circulars issued to district attorneys. See, also "Suggestions of Attorney-General Gregory to Executive Committee in Relation to the Department of Justice," 4 *Am. Bar. Assn. J.* 305 (1918). An invaluable account of the war work of the Department is, John Lord O'Brian, "Civil Liberty in War-time," 52 *Rep. N. Y. Bar Assn.* 275 (1919). A military view of censorship is "The Proper Relations between the Army and the Press in War," Army War College, November, 1915.

The American Labor Year-Book, 1919-20, Rand School, N. Y., narrates several prosecutions in detail.

The issues involved in the current decisions are presented in nontechnical form by these articles: "Freedom of Speech," Z. Chafee, Jr., 17 *New Republic*, 66 (November 16, 1918); Ralph Barton Perry in a book review, 7 *Yale Rev.* 670 (April, 1918); "The Supreme Court vs. the Supreme Court," 22 *New Republic* 235 (April 21, 1920).

Legal Articles on the War:

"Freedom of Speech and of the Press," W. R. Vance, 2 *Minn. L. Rev.* 239 (1918); "The Espionage Act Cases," 32 *Harv. L. Rev.* 417

(1919); "Threats to Take the Life of the President," 32 *Harv. L. Rev.* 724 (1919); "The Vital Importance of a Liberal Construction of the Espionage Act," Alexander H. Robbins, 87 *Cent. L. J.* 145 (1918); "Sufficiency of Indictments under the Espionage Act," 87 *Cent. L. J.* 400 (1918). The Espionage Act is one of the topics covered by Judge Charles M. Hough, "Law in War Time—1917," 31 *Harv. L. Rev.* 692, 696 (1918). Thomas F. Carroll, "Freedom of Speech and of the Press in War Time," 17 *Mich. L. Rev.* 621 (1919); Z. Chafee, Jr., "Freedom of Speech in War Time," 32 *Harv. L. Rev.* 932 (1919).

Treason:

Charles Warren, "What Is Giving Aid and Comfort to the Enemy?", 27 *Yale L. Rev.* 331 (1918).

Post-office:

"Federal Interference with the Freedom of the Press," Lindsay Rogers, 23 *Yale L. J.* 559 (1914), substantially reprinted as Chapter IV of his *Postal Power of Congress*, Baltimore, John Hopkins Press, 1916; R. E. Cushman, "National Police Power under the Postal Clause of the Constitution," 4 *Minn. L. Rev.* 402 (1920); William Hard, "Mr. Burleson, Espionagent," 19 *New Republic* 42 (May 10, 1919), and "Mr. Burleson, Section 481½ B," 19 *New Republic* 76 (May 17, 1919); "Burleson and the Call," 22 *New Republic* 157 (January 7, 1920); "The Call," 1 *Review* 652 (December 13, 1919). For examples of war censorship and legal discussion of Title XII of the Espionage Act, Carroll, *op. cit.*, in 17 *Mich. L. Rev.* 629.

Particular Cases under the Espionage Act and State War Acts:

Abrams (Chapter III):

The principal sources are the *Transcript of Record*, Supreme Court of the United States, October Term, 1919, No. 316, Jacob Abrams *et al.*, Plaintiffs-in-Error, *v.* The United States; the two briefs; and the opinions of the court in 40 Sup. Ct. Rep. 17 (1919), also reprinted in "The Espionage Act Interpreted," 20 *New Republic* 377 (November 26, 1919). Transcript and briefs are in the library of the Law School of Harvard University. It has not been thought necessary to give references to the *Record* except for significant passages. Some information about the trial not contained in the *Record* is taken from current issues of the *New York Times* and the *New York Call*, or from personal conversation and correspondence; the sources of such unofficial data are indicated in every instance, and have been carefully checked from the Stenographic Minutes of the trial, in the U. S. Attorney's office, N. Y., where they were very kindly placed at my disposal. See also Palmer Deportations Testimony, 173.

For criticism of the trial, see the pamphlet, *Sentenced to Twenty Years Prison*, published by the Political Prisoners Defense and Relief Committee, New York, 1919; "Our Ferocious Sentences," 107 *Nation* 504 (November 2, 1918).

Comment in support of the majority opinion of the Supreme Court will be found in a note, "The Espionage Act and the Limits of Legal Toleration," 33 *Harv. L. Rev.* 442 (January, 1910); and in articles, "Justice Holmes's Dissent," 1 *Review* 636 (December 6, 1919); John H. Wigmore, "Freedom of Speech and Freedom of Thuggery," 14 *Ill. L. Rev.* 539. The minority opinion is supported by a note, "Free Speech in Time of Peace," in 29 *Yale L. J.* 337 (January, 1920); and

14 *Ill. L. Rev.* 601; and articles "The Call to Toleration," 20 *New Republic* 360 (November 26, 1919), "What Is Left of Free Speech," Gerard C. Henderson, 21 *New Republic* 50 (December 10, 1919).

Berger (see under Legislative Exclusion).

Debs:
David Karnsner, *Debs, his Authorized Life and Letters from Woodstock Prison to Atlanta*, N. Y., 1919. Reviewed by Harry Salpeter, "Martyr or Felon?", 110 *Nation* 520 (April 17, 1920). Scott Nearing, "The Debs Decision," Rand School, N. Y., 1919, contains Debs' addresses at Canton and in the court-room. "The Law of the Debs Case and Freedom of Speech," 19 *New Republic* 13 (May 3, 1919); followed by correspondence, *ibid.*, 151 (May 31). "The Trial of Eugene Debs," Max Eastman, *The Liberator* (November, 1918), gives another defendant's impression.

I. W. W. (see under Radical Activities).

Nearing:
Scott Nearing, "The Great Madness: a Victory for the American Plutocracy," Rand School, N. Y., 1917.

O'Hare:
"The Conviction of Kate Richards O'Hare and North Dakota Politics," Natl. Civil Liberties Bureau, N. Y.; "The Kate O'Hare Booklets," published by Frank P. O'Hare, St. Louis.

Syracuse Socialist Case of 1920 (Steene, Hotze, and Preston): 21 *New Republic* 302 (February 11, 1920); "Bringing the Constitution into Disrepute," *ibid.* 330 (February 18, 1920).

Townley:
C. R. Johnson, "The Conviction of Townley," 20 *New Republic* 18 (August 6, 1919); Judson King, "The Prosecution of Mr. Townley," 109 *Nation* 143 (August 2, 1919); "The Trial of Townley and Gilbert," 1 *Review* (July 26, 1919). An impartial account of the Non-Partisan League is Arthur Ruhl, "The North Dakota Idea," *Atlantic Monthly* (May, 1919).

C. Radical Activities in the United States and Peace-time Restrictions upon Freedom of Speech (Chapters IV and V)

Backgrounds:
All consideration of governmental activity against radicalism should be preceded by an inquiry into the nature and purposes of the various radical movements, which must be carefully kept distinct. Bertrand Russell, *Proposed Roads to Freedom: Socialism, Anarchism and Syndicalism*, N. Y., 1919, is a fair-minded survey though opposed to the present system. Among books on Russia are E. H. Wilcox, *Russia's Ruin; Russian-American Relations,* ed. Cumming and Pettit. See, also, under I.W.W., *infra.*

On anarchy legislation of the past and similar problems, Ernst Freund, *The Police Power*, §§ 471-484. F. T. Hill, *Famous Battles of the Law*, narrates the Chicago affair of 1886. Concrete data on the handling of radical meetings before the war are furnished by Arthur Woods, *Policeman and Public*, New Haven, 1919; and J. F. Rhodes, *History of the United States*, Vol. VIII, N. Y., 1919. The work of the New York Bomb Squad is told by Tunney and Hollister in *Throttled,* Boston, 1919.

Blasphemy:
Austin W. Scott, "The Legality of Atheism," 31 *Harv. L. Rev.* 289 (1917).

Sex topics:
Theodore Schroeder, *Obscene Literature and Constitutional Law,* N. Y., 1911, and other writings by him; J. C. Ruppenthal "Criminal Statutes on Birth Control," 10 *J. Cr. L. & Crim.* 48 (1919); and see P. v. Byrne, 163 N. Y. Supp. 680, 682.

Moving-picture Censorship:
Amy Woods, "Boston and the 'Movie' Censorship," 44 *Survey* 108 (April 17, 1920).

Strikes and Labor Troubles:
The ability of freedom of speech to withstand such strains has not been sufficiently studied. William Hard has written a series of articles on Passaic: "America in Passaic," 22 *New Republic* 182 (April 7, 1920); "Learn from Passaic," 22 *ibid.* 213 (April 14); "They Must Have Espionage," 22 *ibid.* 248 (April 21). On the Steel Strike, see S. Adele Shaw, "The Makings for Revolution," 20 *ibid.* 52 (August 13, 1919); W. Z. Foster, *The Great Steel Strike;* The Interchurch Report on the Steel Strike of 1919.

Proposed Federal Sedition Bills and National Conditions:
Four official reports have been published, which are valuable not only in relation to this topic, but also for information about deportations, state legislation, radical activities, and the work of the Department of Justice. These are: (1) *Bolshevik Propaganda, Hearings before a Subcommittee of the Committee on the Judiciary,* United States Senate, Sixty-fifth Congress, Third Session and thereafter, pursuant to Senate Resolutions 439 and 469 Washington, 1919. This is the report of the Overman Committee, and contains the testimony of Raymond Robins and others on Russian internal affairs. Cited as Bolshevik Propaganda in this book.

(2) Investigation Activities of the Department of Justice, Letter from the Attorney General transmitting in Response to a Senate Resolution of October 17, 1919, a Report on the Activities of the Bureau of Investigation of the Department of Justice against Persons advising Anarchy, Sedition, and the Forcible Overthrow of the Government, Sen. Doc. No. 153, 66th Cong., 1st Sess., Wash., 1919. Cited as Investigation Activities in this book.

(3) Rule Making in Order the Consideration of S. 3317, Hearings before the Committee on Rules, House of Representatives, 66th Cong., 2d Sess., on H. Res. 438, Wash., 1920. Cited as House Rules Hearings in this book.

(4) Sedition, Hearing before the Committee on the Judiciary, House of Representatives, 66th Cong., 2d Sess., on S. 3317, H. R. 10650 and 12041, Serial 16, February 4 and 6, 1920. Wash., 1920. This contains official publications of the Communist parties, etc. Cited as House Judiciary Hearings in this book.

See also copies of the various bills and the proposed amendments;

also House Judiciary Report submitting Graham Bill, H. R. Report No. 542, 66th Cong., 2d Sess.; also Reports listed under *Deportations.*

Among articles in periodicals on these bills and the "red hysteria," are: Frank I. Cobb, "The Press and Public Opinion," 21 *New Republic* 144 (December 31, 1919); Z. Chafee, Jr., "Legislation Against Anarchy" (Overman Bill), 19 *ibid.* 379 (July 23, 1919); "A New Alien and Sedition Law," 20 *ibid.* 366 (November 26, 1919); Swinburne Hale, "The 'Force and Violence' Joker," 21 *ibid.* 231 (January 21, 1920); "The Red Hysteria" (Harvard Liberal Club Dinner), 21 *ibid.* 249 (January 28); William Hard, "Perhaps the Turn of the Tide" (House Rules hearings on Graham Bill), 21 *ibid.* 313 (February 11); "What Is Attorney General Palmer Doing?" (circular letter by him), 110 *Nation* 190 (February 14); "The Issue of Free Speech," 1 *Review* 634 (December 6, 1919); "Mock-Hysteria," 2 *Review* 43 (January 17, 1920); "What Shall We Do with the Direct Actionist?", 89 *Cent. L. J.* 313 (1919); Walter Lippman and Z. Chafee, Jr., "Free Speech and Free Press as Factors in International Affairs," League of Free Nations Bulletin, March, 1920.

State Sedition and Syndicalism Laws:

"Criminal Syndicalism," 20 *Colum. L. Rev.* 232 (1920); letter in 110 *Nation* 202 (February 14, 1920). *California,* Perry L. Edwards, "Criminal Syndicalism—Back-firing Against Industrial Unrest by the Legislature of California," 89 *Cent. L. J.* 336 (1919); "The Conviction of Anita Whitney," Clare Shipman, 110 *Nation* 365 (March 20, 1920). *Connecticut,* "'The Most Brainiest Man,'" 110 *ibid.* 510 (April 17). *Massachusetts,* Z. Chafee, Jr., "Warns of Anti-Anarchy Bill," *Boston Sunday Advertiser,* April 13, 1919. *New Jersey,* H. E. Cory, "The Intellectuals and the Wage Workers," N. Y., 1919 (p. 208 on Boyd case). *New York,* Swinburne Hale, "Criminal Anarchy," 21 *New Republic* 270 (January 28, 1920); [McAdoo decision against Gitlow and Larkin], House Judiciary Hearings, p. 155; A. Giovannitti, "Commercialism on Trial," *Liberator,* March, 1920 (Gitlow trial). *Oregon,* "American by Decree" (foreign language press), 22 *New Republic* 262 (April 28, 1920).

See U. S. official reports, *supra,* and Appendix V, *infra.*

Industrial Workers of the World:

There are two studies by scholars. Paul Frederick Brissenden: *The I.W.W.: A Study of American Syndicalism.* Colum. Univ. Studies in History, etc., vol. 83, 2d ed., N. Y., 1920. Carleton H. Parker: "The I.W.W.," *Atlantic Monthly,* 651 (November, 1917), reprinted in his *The Casual Laborer and Other Essays,* N. Y., 1920.

For the Chicago trial, see U. S., v. W. D. Haywood *et al.* Bull. Dept. Just., No. 175; Evidence and Cross-Examination of W. D. Haywood [in same]; Evidence and Cross-Examination of J. T. (Red) Doran [in same]; Indictment [in same], I.W.W. Pub. Bureau, Chicago.; "The Truth about the I.W.W.", Natl. Civil Liberties Bureau, N. Y.; "The Persecution of the Radical Labor Movement in the United States." N. Y. Defense Committee of the I.W.W., N. Y.

The Sacramento trial is discussed in "Ol' Rags and Bottles," 108 *Nation* 114 (January 25, 1919); *American Labor Year-Book,* 1919-20, 100 and 107, has accounts of Chicago and Sacramento trials.

For the Washington situation, see [Washington Injunction Against Membership in the I.W.W.], 109 *Nation* 843 *(January* 3, 1920);

Jerrold Owen: "Centralia," *American Legion Weekly*, December 12, 1919; Anna Louise Strong, "Centralia: An Unfinished Story," 110 *Nation* 508 (April 17, 1920); E. M., "Centralia," 22 *New Republic* 217 (April 14, 1920). Ole Hanson, *Americanism vs. Bolshevism*.

Deportation of Aliens (Chapter V):

The best review of the procedure is by Assistant Secretary of Labor Louis F. Post, "Administrative Decisions in Connection with Immigration," 10 *Am. Pol. Sci. Rev.* 251 (1916). Recent legal articles: Howard L. Bevis, "The Deportation of Aliens," 62 *U. of Pa. L. Rev.* 97 (1920); "Deportation of Seditious Aliens," 23 *Law Notes* (N. Y.) 64 (1919); "Deportation of Aliens who Advocate the Overthrow of Government by Force," 89 *Cent. L. J.* 369 (1919). John Lord O'Brian, "The Menace of Administrative Law," address to Maryland Bar Association; June, 1920.

Original sources: The administrative hearings are largely buried in the files of the immigration officials. A few cases are extracted in Charles Recht, "American Deportation and Exclusion Laws," League for Democratic Control, Boston, 1919, and "The Anarchist Deportations," 21 *New Republic*, 96 (December 24, 1919). The whole procedure in the Communist raids is exhaustively shown by the record in Katzeff v. Skeffington (Colyer case) in the United States District Court in Boston. The *Federal Reporter* contains several recent decisions on the deportation of radicals. The decision of Secretary of Labor Wilson on the Communist Party is in *House Judiciary Hearings* (p. 17), which also gives the platform, manifesto, etc., of this and the Communist Labor Party. Much of the same material with a history of the creation of the two parties is also accessible in *American Labor Year-Book*, 1919-20. Part of the decision of Assistant Secretary Post on the raid cases is in "On Behalf of Louis F. Post," 22 *New Republic* 264 (April 28, 1920). The most valuable document in the raids is Judge Anderson's decision in the Colyer case, in the *Federal Reporter*, 265 Fed. 17.

The history of left-wing Socialism is also narrated by an impartial observer, Gordon S. Watkins, "The Present Status of Socialism in the United States," 124 *Atlantic* 821 (December, 1919); and in H. W. Laidler, "Socialism in Thought and Action."

Congressional reports of especial value, 66th Congress, 2d Session, 1920: (1) Three pamphlets of Hearings before a Subcommittee of the House Committee on Immigration and Naturalization, "Communist and Anarchist Deportation Cases," "I.W.W. Deportation Cases," "Communist Labor Party Deportation Cases," all cited herein as *House Immigration Hearings*. These contain many administrative decisions, but not the complete records. (2) "Investigation of Administration of Louis F. Post, Assistant Secretary of Labor, in the Matter of Deportation of Aliens, Hearings before the Committee on Rules, etc., on H. Res. 522," 2 parts; cited herein as *Post Deportations Testimony*. (3) "Attorney General A. Mitchell Palmer on charges made against the Department of Justice by Louis F. Post and others, Hearings before the Committee on Rules, etc.," Part I; cited herein as *Palmer Deportations Testimony*.

Much important testimony from the Colyer case, including the official instructions, is in the pamphlet, "To the American People. Report upon the Illegal Practices of the United States Department of Justice," by 12 lawyers, National Popular Government League, Washington, May, 1920; cited herein as *Illegal Practices*.

APPENDICES

Popular articles on the "Buford" and the January raids are: "The Deportation," 1 *Review* 695 (December 27, 1919); "The Raid on the Reds," 2 *Review* 22 (January 10, 1920); "Deporting a Political Party," 21 *New Republic* 186 (January 14, 1920). Ernst Freund, "Burning Heretics," 21 *ibid*. 266 (January 28, 1920); "A Federal Judge Speaks Up" (Bourquin, J., in *Re* Jackson), 22 *ibid*. 135 (March 31); "Deportations and the Law," 110 *Nation* 131 (January 31); F. R. Barkley, "Jailing Radicals in Detroit," 110 *ibid*. 136; F. C. Howe, "Lynch Law and the Immigrant Alien," 110 *ibid*. 194 (February 14); "Another Man Without a Country," 110 *ibid*. 289 (March 6); Lincoln Colcord, "Martens and Our Foreign Policy" (correspondence of Secretary Wilson and John E. Milholland), 110 *ibid*. 324 (March 13); Winthrop D. Lane, "The Buford Widows," 43 *Survey* 391 (January 10); "Aliens and Sedition in the New Year," 43 *ibid*. 422 (January 13); Sidney Howard, "The Colyer Trial Opens," 44 *Survey* 105 (April 17). See, also, some of the articles on the red hysteria, etc.

Accounts of the New England raids from the point of view of the aliens are, "The Soviet of Deer Island, Boston Harbor, January-February, 1920, by One of the Members," Boston Branch of Am. Civil Liberties Union; "Deported via Deer Island," MSS. report prepared for the Bureau.

Searches and Seizures (Chapters V and VI):
"The Case of the Rand School," published by the School, N. Y., 1919; "The Truth about the Lusk Committee," Nation Press, N. Y., 1920; "Whose Home Will Be Safe?", 19 *New Republic* 303 (July 9, 1919); Anna L. Strong, "A Newspaper Confiscated—and Returned," 109 *Nation* 738 (December 13, 1919).

D. POWER OF A LEGISLATURE TO EXCLUDE OR EXPEL FOR OPINIONS
(CHAPTER VI)

For the English law, T. Erskine May, *Parliamentary Practice*, 12th ed., London, 1917; same, *Constitutional History of England*, vol. I, for Wilkes, and also G. O. Trevelyan, *Early History of Charles James Fox*, and Macaulay's second *Essay on Chatham*. Justin McCarthy, *History of Our Own Times*, vol. III, for Bradlaugh.

For Congress, Asher Hinds, *Precedents of the House of Representatives of the United States*, Washington, 1907. This contains many Senate cases. See, also, Webb & Pierce, Compilation of Senate Election Cases, 1789-1913, Washington, 1913. Other Congressional compilations may be useful. Massachusetts cases are collected by Cushing, Loring, and Russell; New York, by Armstrong.

Berger:
Victor L. Berger, Hearings before the Special Committee appointed under the Authority of House Resolution No. 6 concerning the Right of Victor L. Berger to be Sworn in as a Member of the Sixty-sixth Congress, 2 vols., Wash., 1919. (These contain records of the prosecution and *Milwaukee Leader* case.) Cited herein as *Berger Hearings*.

Ho. Cal. No. 91, 66th Cong., 1st Sess., Report No. 413, Case of Victor L. Berger of Wisconsin. Cited herein as *Berger Report*.

"Victor L. Berger," *Socialist Review*, (February, 1920); "The Berger Victory," 109 *Nation* 820 (December 27, 1919); for account of the trial from the side of the defense, *American Labor Year-Book*, 1919-20, 97-100.

New York Socialists:
The record of the investigation was printed by the Assembly. Briefs include, Brief of Special Committee appointed by the Association of the Bar of the City of New York (January 20, 1920); Outline of the Evidence taken before the Judiciary Committee to and including February 5, 1920, with a discussion of some conclusions to be drawn therefrom [against Socialists and signed by Attorney-General and associate counsel]; Brief for the Socialist Assemblymen, March 15, 1920; Brief for the Judiciary Committee, March 24, 1920.

Articles in periodicals (all in 1920): "The Issues in the Fight at Albany," 2 *Review* 121 (February 7); "Hillquit on the Socialist Programme," 2 *Review* 193 (February 28); "Governor Smith's Opportunity," 2 *Review* 421 (April 24); "Speaker Sweet Does His Bit," 22 *New Republic* 210 (January 21); "The Mob in High Places," 22 *New Republic* 279 (February 4); "Up to the Voters," 22 *New Republic* 200 (April 14) [Lusk Bills]; 22 *New Republic* 171 (April 7); "Minority Rights at Albany," 110 *Nation* 288 (March 6); Lewis S. Gannett, "The Socialists' Trial at Albany: A Summary," 110 *Nation* 361 (March 20); Loula D. Lasker, "Back in the Districts: What New York Assemblymen's Constituents Are Thinking," 53 *Survey* 767 (March 20); Robert Minor, "Dissolving the Duma at Albany," *Liberator* (March 20).

E. Schools

Henry R. Linville, John L. Tildsley, and Z. Chafee, Jr., "The Schools and the Issue of Freedom," in leaflets, "The Public and the Schools," published by Public School Education Assn., N. Y., May 3, 17, 24, 1919. Various pamphlets have been issued on both sides of the controversies in New York and Washington, and several articles printed in the *Nation*.

APPENDIX II

INDEX OF REPORTED CASES UNDER THE ESPIONAGE ACTS OF 1917 AND 1918

This index is meant to include all Espionage Act cases involving freedom of speech which are contained in the following reports, abbreviated as shown:

Bulletins of the Department of Justice on the Interpretation of War Statutes (B);

Federal Reporter (F), containing cases in the Circuit Court of Appeals, and occasionally in the District Courts;

United States Reports (U. S.), containing Supreme Court decisions;

One case is officially reported only in Report of the Attorney General for 1918 (A), which gives facts of many more.

Some recent Supreme Court cases are in the Supreme Court Reporter (Sup.).

A few cases are from Nelles, Espionage Act Cases (N).

So far as practicable I have indexed not only the defendant who gives his name to the case but every defendant. This seemed undesirable in the cases of the 93 I.W.W.'s in the Haywood case and the 27 Socialists in the Baltzer case. Consequently, while there are 184 persons indexed below, 118 more should be added to give the total number of persons whose prosecutions are reported, making 302 in all. Besides these many Espionage Act cases have never been reported. Notes of these are in *War-time Prosecutions and Mob Violence*, which contains the facts of many others. The total number of persons convicted is reported as 877, with 285 cases still pending on June 30, 1919. The Attorney General's Reports for 1918 and 1919 show that there were 988 cases commenced in 1917-18, and 968 in 1918-19. Out of these 1,956 cases only a small fraction are reported anywhere. In each instance I have given the defendant's name, the state where he was prosecuted (omitting United States Districts within a state), a reference to the report, the result of the case, and the sentence.

Abbreviations are:

C., conviction.

Acq, acquittal.

Acq d., acquittal directed.

Ind., indictment.

Aff., affirmed by Circuit Court of Appeals or Supreme Court.

Rev., reversed by Circuit Court of Appeals or Supreme Court.

An asterisk shows that the sentence has been shortened by the President, and the length of the commuted sentence or date of its expiration is added. It is possible that some commutations have been omitted. Information as to convictions, sentences, pardons, etc., if not contained in the reports, has been obtained from *War-time Prosecutions*; *New York Times*, May 9, 1919; and from the Attorney General's Report for 1919.

387

I. PROSECUTIONS UNDER TITLE I, SECTIONS 3 AND 4, AND TITLE XII

Abrams, J.	N. Y.	250 U. S. 616	C. 20 yrs., aff.
Albers, H.	Oregon	B. 191; 263 F. 27	C. Aff.
American Socialist Society	N. Y.	B. 129, 252 F. 223; B. 192; B. 198	C. Fine $3,000
Anderson, O.	S. D.	264 F. 75	C. Aff.
Ault, E. B.	Wash.	263 F. 798, 800	Ind. bad
Baer, Elizabeth	Pa.	B. 43; B. 194, 249 U. S. 47	C. Aff.
Balbas, *sub* Capo			
Baltzer, E., and 26 others	S. D.	B. 3; 248 U. S. 593	C. 1-2 yrs. Rev. on confession of error
Bentall, J. O.	Minn.	B. 180, 262 F. 744	C. 5 yrs. Rev.
Berger, V. L.	Illinois	B. 186	C. 20 yrs.
Binder, L.	N. Y.	B. 117, B. 126	C.
Blodgett, D. T.	Iowa	N. 48	C. 20 yrs.
Bold, F. W.	Oregon	B. 183	
Bosco, P.	W. Vir.	B. 71	C. 10 yrs. (*2 yrs.)
Bouldin, G. W. (negro)	Texas	261 F. 674	C. Aff.
Boutin, A.	N. Y.	251 F. 313	Ind. good
Brackett, W. A.	Mo.	B. 170	C. $150
Brenne, R.	Ohio	B. 199	Acq. d.
Brinton, J. W.	N. D.	B. 132	
Buessel, T.	Conn.	B. 131	C. 10 yrs. (*4/1/19)
Bunyard, C. D.	Mo.	B. 168	C. $200
Capers, H.	Okla.	B. 74	
Capo, V. Balbas	Porto Rico	B. 30, B. 37, 257 F. 17	C. 8 yrs. $4,000. Rev.
Carlson, J. A.	Wash.	B. 185	C. 5 yrs. Rev.
Casey, J. E.	Wash.	B. 78	C. Rev.
Caughman, J. M.	S. C.	258 F. 434	C. 10 yrs. Rev.
Cecca, G. de	N. Y.	B. 119; 258 F. 855	
Coldwell, J. M.	R. I.	B. 158; B. 201, 256 F. 805; 250 U. S. 661 (memo.)	C. 3 yrs. Aff.
Creo, A.	N. Y.	245 F. 878, 888; B. 15; B. 52; 40 Sup. 205	C. Aff.

Curran, W. C.	N.Y.	B. 140	
Darkow, M.	Pa.	248 F. 290; B. 181, 254 F. 135; 40 Sup. 259. See B. 42	C. 5 yrs. Aff.
Deason, T.	Texas	254 F. 259	C. Aff. 1½ yrs. (*1 yr.)
Debs, E. V.	Ohio	B. 155; B. 196, 249 U. S. 211	C. 10 yrs. Aff.
Deilman, C. S.	N.Y.	245 F. 878, 888; B. 15; B. 52; 40 Sup. 205	C. Aff.
Dembowski, J.	Mich.	252 F. 894	Ind. bad
Denson, W. A.	Ala.	B. 142	Acq.
Dodge, W.	N.Y.	B. 202; 258 F. 300; 250 U. S. 660 (memo.)	
Doe, P. B.	Colo.	B. 55; 253 F. 903	C. 6 yrs. Aff.
Doll, C.	S. D.	B. 5; B. 163, 253 F. 646	C. 1½ yrs. Aff. (*5/8/19)
Eastman, M.	N.Y.	252 F. 232	C. Rev.
Elmer, W. P.	Mo.	B. 171; 260 F. 646	2 mistrials
Enfield, O. E.	Okla.	261 F. 141	C. $1,000. Rev.
Engdahl, J. L.	Illinois	B. 186	C. Rev.
Equi, Marie	Oregon	B. 172; 261 F. 53	C. 20 yrs.
Feltman, H.	Ky.	264 F. 1	C. 3 yrs. $500. Aff.
Fisher, G. H.	N.Y.	B. 119; 258 F. 855	C. Aff.
Fontana, J.	N. D.	B. 148; 262 F. 283	C. 20 yrs. Rev.
Foster, L.	Wash.	B. 78	C. Rev.
Frerichs, H.	Neb.	B. 85	C. 5 yrs.
Frohwerk, J.	Mo.	B. 128; 248 U. S. 540; B. 197, 249 U. S. 204	C. 10 yrs. Aff. (*1 yr.)
Germer, A.	Illinois	B. 186	C. 20 yrs.
Gneiser, G. A.	W. V.	B. 71	
Goldsmith, C. H.	Ala.	B. 133	
Goldstein, R.	Cal.	258 F. 908. See B. 33	C. 10 yrs. $5,000. Aff. (*3 yrs.)
Graham, J. I.	Tenn.	B. 120	C. Rev.
Granzow, F. A.	Iowa	261 F. 172	Acq. d.
Groeschl	Ky.	N. 3	C. Rev.
Grubl, F.	S. D.	264 F. 44	

APPENDICES

Guggolz, J. C.	Cal.	262 F. 764	C. Rev.
Hall, J. K.	S. C.	256 F. 748, B. 189	C. Rev.
Hall, V.	Mont.	248 F. 150	Acq. d.
Hamm, E.	Cal.	261 F. 907	C. Aff.
Harper, S. J.	La.	B. 76	Acq.
Harshfield, J.	Neb.	260 F. 659	C. Rev.
Haywood, W. D., and 92 others	Illinois	B. 175	C. 16 for 20 yrs. 33 for 10 yrs. 30 for 5 yrs. 12 for 1 yr. 2 for 10 days. Aff.
Head, W. J.	S. D.	248 U. S. 593	C. 3 yrs. $500. Rev. on confession of error Ind. bad
Henning, J.	Wis.	B. 184	
Henricksen, H. M.	Neb.	B. 86	
Herman, E.	Wash.	B. 109; 257 F. 601	C. 10 yrs. Aff.
Heynacher, W.	S. D.	257 F. 61	C. 5 yrs. Aff. (*1 yr.)
Hicks, W. M.	Okla.	B. 160	C. 20 yrs. (*5 yrs.)
Hickson, F. C.	S. C.	258 F. 867	C. Rev.
Hitchcock, A. L.	Ohio	B. 122	C. 10 yrs. (*2 yrs.)
Hitt, O.	Colo.	B. 53	Acq.
Hodges, W.	Wash.	B. 78	C. 5 yrs. Rev.
Hotze, W.	N. Y.	263 F. 130	C. 1½ yrs.
Howenstine, F. P.	Cal.	263 F. 1	C. Aff.
Huhn, W.	Wyo.	B. 58	Mistrial; case dismissed
Hundelshausen, H. v.	N. J.	B. 130, 251 F. 946; B. 156	C. 3 yrs., $5,000. Rev.
Kammann, C. H.	Illinois	259 F. 192	Mistrial; case dismissed
Katzler, W. von	N. J.	B. 130, 251 F. 946; B. 156	C. 5 yrs.
Kaufman, W. H.	Wash.	B. 134	C. Aff.
Kennedy, I.	Cal.	263 F. 1	C. 2 yrs. Aff. (*5/8/19)
Kirchner, H. E.	W. V.	B. 69; B. 174, 255 F. 301	Acq. d.
Koenig, H. C.	Mo.	B. 123, 166	C. 10 yrs. Rev. on confession of error
Kornmann, C.	S. D.	B. 89; 248 U. S. 594	

Krafft, F.	N. J.	B. 6, 84; 249 F. 919; 247 U. S. 520	C. 5 yrs., $1,000 Aff. (*4/1/19)
Kruse, J. H.	Ky.	264 F. 1	C. Aff.
Kruse, W. F.	Illinois	B. 186	C. 20 yrs.
Kumpula, E.	Oregon	261 F. 49	C. Rev.
Lachowsky, H.	N. Y.	250 U. S. 616	C. 20 yrs. Aff.
Lemke, H.	Pa.	248 F. 290; B. 181, 254 F. 135; 40 Sup. 259. See B. 42	
Lipman, S.	N. Y.	250 U. S. 616	C. 2 yrs. Aff.
Listman, G. B.	Wash.	263 F. 798, 800	C. 20 yrs. Aff.
Lockhart, A. P.	Tenn.	264 F. 14	Ind. bad
McMillan, A. H.	N. Y.	B. 119; 258 F. 855	C. Aff.
Mackley, H. G.	Vt.	B. 83	C. 20 yrs. Rev.
Magon, R. F.	Cal.	260 F. 811	C. 15 yrs. (*3 yrs.)
Mamaux, J.	Ohio	264 F. 816	C. 20 yrs. Aff.
Martin, F. A.	Wash.	B. 78	C. Aff.
Martin, R. J.	N. Y.	B. 119; 258 F. 855	C. 5 yrs. Rev.
Martin, W. E.	Ky.	B. 157	C. 20 yrs. Rev.
Mayer, F.	Ky.	B. 146, 252 F. 868	Acq. d.
Mead, W. E.	Wash.	B. 103; 257 F. 639	C. 5 yrs. Aff.
Miller, J. A.	Colo.	B. 104	C. 2 yrs. (*1 yr.)
Mills, W. T.	N. D.	B. 204	Acq. d.
Mullen, P.	Wash.	B. 78	C. 5 yrs. Rev.
Nagler, L. B.	Wis.	B. 127, 252 F. 217	Ind. good, C.
Nearing, S.	N. Y.	B. 129, 252 F. 223; B. 192; B. 198	Acq.
Nelson, C.	N. Y.	245 F. 878, 888; B. 15; B. 52; 40 Sup. 205	
O'Hare, Kate R.	N. D.	B. 49; B. 165, 253 F. 588	C. Aff.
Olivereau, Louise	Wash.	B. 40	C. 5 yrs. Aff. (*5/29/20)
Pape, T. B.	Illinois	B. 151, 253 F. 270	C. 10 yrs.
Partan, A. J.	Oregon	261 F. 515	Ind. bad
Perry	Wash.	B. 78	C. Aff.
Peterson, J. A.	Minn.	A. 52	C. 5 yrs. Rev.
Phelan, J. B.	Wash.	B. 78	C. 4 yrs.
			C. 5 yrs. Rev.

392 APPENDICES

Pierce, C. H.	N. Y.	245 F. 878, 888; B. 15; B. 52; 40 Sup.	C. Aff.
Preston, F. L.	N. Y.	263 F. 130	C. 1½ yrs.
Prieth, B.	N. J.	B. 130, 251 F. 946; B. 156	Mistrial; case dismissed
Prieth, E. S.	N. J.	B. 130, 251 F. 946; B. 156	Mistrial; case dismissed
Prober, G. See Abrams	N. Y.		Acq.
Pundt, G.	Neb.	B. 82	
Ramp, F.	Oregon	B. 66	C. 5 yrs., $1,000. Aff.
Reitz, E.	S. D.	257 F. 731	C. Aff.
Reivo, W. N.	Oregon	261 F. 515	C. Aff.
Rhuberg, J.	Oregon	B. 94; B. 107; 255 Fed. 865	C. 15 yrs. Aff.
Rivera, F.	Cal.	260 F. 811	C. 20 yrs. Rev.
Robison, L. H.	N. Y.	B. 119; 258 F. 855	C. 3 yrs. Aff. (*5/8/19)
Rosansky, H.	N. Y.	250 U. S. 616	Ind. bad
Rust, F. A.	Wash.	263 F. 798, 800	C. 20 yrs. Rev.
Rutherford, J. F.	N. Y.	B. 119; 258 F. 855	C. 2 yrs., $500. Rev.
Sandberg, A.	Ariz.	257 F. 643	
Sandvick, H.	Alaska	B. 113	
Schaefer, P.	Pa.	248 F. 290; B. 181, 254 F. 135; 40 Sup. 259. See B. 42	C. 1 yr. Rev.
Schenck, C. T.	Pa.	B. 43; B. 194, 249 U. S. 47	C. Aff.
Schoberg, C. B.	Ky.	B. 149; 264 F. 1	C. Aff.
Schulze, C. G.	Cal.	253 F. 377; 259 F. 189	C. Aff.
Schumann, W.	Iowa	258 F. 233; 250 U. S. 66 (memo.)	C. Aff.
Schutte, B. H.	N. D.	252 F. 212	Ind. bad
Seattle Union-Record Pub. Co.	Wash.	263 F. 798, 800	Ind. bad
Seebach, J. C.	Minn.	262 F. 885	C. Aff.
Shaffer, F.	Wash.	B. 125; B. 190, 255 F. 886	C. 2½ yrs. Aff. (*1 yr.)
Shidler, A.	Nev.	257 F. 620	C. 2 yrs. $100. Aff.
Shilter, K.	Cal.	257 F. 724	C. Aff.
Spillner, C.	Hawaii	B. 145	C. 16 yrs. (*3 yrs.)
Steene, C. W.	N. Y.	263 F. 130	C. 1½ yrs. Aff.
Steimer, Molly	N. Y.	250 U. S. 616	C. 15 yrs. Aff.
Stenzel, B.	Iowa	261 F. 161	C. 1½ yrs., $300. Rev.
Stephens, E. A.	Cal.	261 F. 590	C. Aff.

APPENDICES

Stephens, F.	Del.	B. 116, 121	Acq.
Stilson, J. V.	Pa.	B. 177; 40 Sup. 28	C. 3 yrs. Aff.
Stokes, Rose P.	Mo.	B. 106; 264 F. 18	C. 10 yrs. Rev.
Strong, Anna L.	Wash.	263 F. 798, 800	Ind. bad
Sugarman, A. L.	Minn.	B. 12; 245 Fed. 604; B. 195, 249	
		U. S. 182	
Sukys, J.	Pa.	B. 177; 40 Sup. 28	C. 3 yrs. Aff.
Sykes, J.	Cal.	264 F. 945	C. 3 mos. Aff.
Tanner, W. B.	Colo.	B. 56	C. Aff.
Taubert, G. H.	N. H.	B. 108	Acq.
Tucker, I. S. J.	Illinois	B. 186	C. 3 yrs. (*1½ yrs.)
Van Armburgh, W. E.	N. Y.	B. 119; 258 F. 855	C. 20 yrs.
Vevig, T.	Alaska	B. 162	C. 20 yrs. Rev.
Vogel, P.	Pa.	248 F. 290; B. 181, 254 F. 135; 40	
		Sup. 259. See B. 42	C. 1 yr. Rev.
Von Bank, H.	N. D.	B. 164, 258 F. 641	C. Rev.
Waechter, H.	N. J.	B. 130, 251 F. 946; B. 156	Mistrial; case dismissed
Waldron, C. H.	Vt.	B. 79	C. 15 yrs. (*4/1/19)
Wallace, D. H.	Iowa	B. 4	C. 20 yrs., went insane and died in jail
Wehmeyer, W. F.	Mo.	B. 176	C. $1,000
Weinsberg, C. H.	Mo.	B. 123	Acq.
Weist, A.	Pa.	B. 169	C., $200
Werner, L.		248 F. 290; B. 181, 254 F. 135; 40	
		Sup. 259. See B. 42	
Wessels, G.	Tex.	262 F. 389	C. 5 yrs. Aff.
White, J. A. G.	Ohio	263 F. 17	C. Aff.
Whitney, A. G.	N. Y.	N. 55	C. Aff.
Williams, L. E.	Colo.	B. 118	No. ind.
Wimmer, P.	Ky.	264 F. 11	C. Aff.
Windmueller, D.	Alaska	B. 112	C. 1 yr, $250 (*1 yr.)
Wishek, J. H.	N. D.	B. 153	
Wolf, J. H.	S. D.	B. 81; 259 F. 388	C. 5 yrs., $1,000. Rev.
Woodworth, C. H.	N. Y.	B. 119; 258 F. 855	C. 20 yrs. Rev.

Youngman, P. G.	Ala.	B. 137	Acq.
Zademack, C. F.	Ohio	B. 143	C. 5 yrs. (*1½ yrs.)
Zimmerman, J.	Ind.	N. 10	Acq. d.
Zittel, J.	Wash.	B. 90	

II. SEIZURE OF MOTION PICTURE FILM UNDER TITLE XI

U. S. v. Motion Picture Film, "The Spirit of '76"	Cal.	B. 33, 252 F. 946	Upheld

III. EXCLUSIONS FROM THE MAILS UNDER TITLE XII

Masses Pub. Co. v. Patten	N. Y.	244 Fed. 535; 245 F. 102; B. 7, 246 Fed. 24 B. 26	Injunction refused for Aug. issue Injunction refused for Sept. issue
Jeffersonian Pub. Co. v. West	Ga.	245 Fed. 585	Injunction refused
U. S. ex rel. Milwaukee Soc. Dem. Pub. Co. v. Burleson	D. C.	258 F. 282; 255 U. S. 407	Mandamus refused, as to present and future issues

APPENDIX III

TEXT AND CONSTRUCTION OF THE ESPIONAGE ACT OF 1918

Title I, § 3, as amended, reads as follows (Act of May 16, 1918, c. 75, § 1, *U. S. Comp. Stat.*, 1918, § 10212 c). The italicized words punish language for remote tendencies: *Cf.* the Sedition Act of 1798.

"Whoever, *when the United States is at war,* shall willfully make or convey false reports or false statements with intent to interfere with the operation or success of the military or naval forces of the United States, or to promote the success of its enemies, or shall willfully make or convey false reports or false statements, or say or do anything except by way of bona fide and *not disloyal* advice to an investor or investors, with intent to obstruct the sale by the United States of bonds or other securities of the United States or the making of loans by or to the United States, and whoever, when the United States is at war, shall willfully cause, or attempt to cause, or incite or attempt to incite, insubordination, disloyalty, mutiny, or refusal of duty, in the military or naval forces of the United States, or shall willfully obstruct or attempt to obstruct the recruiting or enlistment service of the United States, and whoever, when the United States is at war, shall willfully utter, print, write, or publish any *disloyal, profane, scurrilous, or abusive language about the form of government of the United States, or the Constitution of the United States, or the military or naval forces of the United States, or the flag of the United States, or the uniform of the Army or Navy of the United States, or any language intended to bring the form of government of the United States, or the Constitution of the United States, or the military or naval forces of the United States, or the flag of the United States, or the uniform of the Army or Navy of the United States into contempt, scorn, contumely, or disrepute,* or shall willfully utter, print, write, or publish any language intended to incite, provoke, or encourage resistance to the United States, or to promote the cause of its enemies, or shall willfully display the flag of any foreign enemy, or shall willfully by utterance, writing, printing, publication, or language spoken, urge, incite, or advocate any curtailment of production in this country of any thing or things, product or products, necessary or essential to the prosecution of the war in which the United States may be engaged, with intent by such curtailment to cripple or hinder the United States in the prosecution of the war, and whoever shall willfully advocate, teach, defend, or *suggest* the doing of any of the acts or things in this section enumerated, and whoever shall *by word or act support or favor the cause of any country with which the United States is at war or by word or act oppose the cause of the United States therein,* shall be punished by a fine of not more than $10,000 or imprisonment for not more than twenty years, or both: Provided, That any employee or official of the United States Government who commits any *disloyal* act or utters any *unpatriotic or disloyal language,* or who, in an *abusive and violent manner criticizes the Army or Navy or the flag of the United States* shall be at once dismissed from the service. Any such employee shall be dismissed by the head of the department in which the employee may be engaged, and any such official shall be dismissed by the authority having power to appoint a successor to the dismissed official."

The conspiracy, harboring, and search-warrant sections of the Act of 1917 apply to the section just quoted; and also the mail provisions, which were amended on May 16, 1918, by the addition of a section authorizing the Postmaster General, "upon evidence satisfactory to him that any person or concern is using the mails" in violation of the Espionage Act, to have all mail of every kind addressed to that person or concern returned to the sender. (Act, May 16, 1918, c. 75, § 2; *U. S. Comp. Stat.*, 1918, § 10401 d. See Carroll, in 17 *Mich. L. Rev.* 689.)

Cases involving the new crimes created by the Espionage Act of 1918, reported in the *Bulletins of the Department of Justice on the Interpretation of War Statutes*, the *Federal Reporter*, and the *U. S. Reports*, through 1919, are as follows:

(1) Obstruction of war loans. United States *v.* Bold, *Bull.* 183 (Ore., Wolverton, J.); United States *v.* Brackett, *Bull.* 170 (E. D. Mo., Munger, J.); Kumpula *v.* United States, 261 Fed. 49 (C. C. A. 9th, 1919, per Hunt, J.); Hall *v.* United States, 256 Fed. 748, *Bull.* 189 (C. C. A. 4th, 1919, per Pritchard, J.).

(2) Disloyal, etc. language about form of government of United States. Abrams *v.* United States, 40 Sup. Ct. Rep. 17 (1919) (Clarke, J.; Holmes, J., dissenting.)

(3) Language intended to defame form of government. Abrams *v.* United States, *supra*.

(4) Disloyal, etc. language about military or naval forces. United States *v.* Buessel, *Bull.* 131 (Conn., 1918, Howe, J.); United States *v.* Curran, *Bull.* 140 (S. D. N. Y., 1918, L. Hand, J.); United States *v.* Martin, *Bull.* 157 (E. D. Tenn., 1918, Sanford, J.; criticism of President's military policy is within this clause since he is commander-in-chief of army and navy); United States *v.* Equi, *Bull.* 172 (Ore., 1918, Bean, J.); Partan *v.* United States, 261 Fed. 515 (C. C. A. 9th, 1919, per Hunt, J.).

(5) Language intended to defame the military or naval forces. United States *v.* Equi, *supra;* United States *v.* Vevig, *Bull.* 162 (Alaska, 1918, Bunnell, J.); Partan *v.* United States, *supra*.

(6) Disloyal, etc. language about flag. United States *v.* Buessel, *supra*.

(7) Language intended to defame the flag. United States *v.* Equi, *supra*.

(8) Language intended to incite, etc. resistance to United States or promote cause of enemies. United States *v.* Zademack, *Bull.* 143 (N. D. Oh., 1918, Westenhaver, J.); United States *v.* Debs, *Bull.* 155 (N. D. Oh., 1918, Westenhaver, J.); United States *v.* Martin, *supra;* United States *v.* Weist, *Bull.* 169 (E. D. Mo., 1918, Munger, J.); United States *v.* Equi, *supra;* United States *v.* Carlson, *Bull.* 185 (W. D. Wash., 1918, Neterer, J.); United States *v.* Albers, *Bull.* 191 (Ore., 1919, Wolverton, J.); United States *v.* Dodge, *Bull.* 202 (W. D. N. Y., 1919, Hazel, J.); 258 Fed. 300 (C. C. A. 2d, 1919, Rogers, J.); certiorari denied, 250 U. S. 660, 40 Sup. Ct. Rep. 10 (1919); Abrams *v.* United States, *supra;* Kumpula *v.* United States, *supra*.

(9) Language urging curtailment of production of war materials. United States *v.* Carlson, *supra;* Abrams *v.* United States, *supra*.

(10) Favor cause of enemies or oppose that of United States. United States *v.* Buessel, *supra;* United States *v.* Zademack, *supra;* United States *v.* Schoberg, *Bull.* 149 (E. D. Ky., 1918, Cochran, J.);

APPENDICES

United States v. Bunyard, *Bull.* 168 (E. D. Mo., 1918, Munger, J.); United States v. Weist, *supra;* United States v. Bold, *supra;* United States v. Albers, *supra;* United States v. Dodge, *supra;* Schulze v. United States, 259 Fed. 189 (C. C. A. 9th, 1919, per Gilbert, J.); United States v. Brackett, *supra;* Kumpula v. United States, *supra.*

See also recent cases in Appendix II: Ault, Listman, Lockhart, Rust, Seattle etc. Co., Strong, Mamaux, Wimmer.

APPENDIX IV

NORMAL LAW OF FOUR JURISDICTIONS AGAINST ACTUAL OR THREATENED VIOLENCE

(See page 165)

Massachusetts: Treason, R. L. (1902) c. 206; murder or attempt to murder, c. 207; destruction of property by explosives, or attempt thereto, c. 208 §§ 85, 86; indirect participation in a crime, c. 215, § 3; attempts to commit any crime, c. 215 § 6; solicitation of another to commit a crime is punishable under this section, Commonwealth v. Peaslee, 177 Mass. 267, and also at common law, Commonwealth v. Flagg, 135 Mass. 545, quoted in the text.

New York: Treason, Penal Law (1909), §§ 2380-2383; murder, §§ 1044 ff.; damage to building by explosive, § 1420; manufacture, storing, or shipping of explosives, § 1894; attempt to injure building without damage, § 1895; indirect participation or attempt to commit any crime, §§ 2, 260-262; solicitation of another to commit a crime is probably punishable under this section, People v. Strauss, 100 Misc. 661, and also at common law; any act seriously disturbing the person or property of another, or seriously disturbing the public peace, § 43; this includes advocacy of revolution and assassination, People v. Most, 171 N. Y. 423. The N. Y. anarchy act is discussed in the body of the book.

Washington: Treason, Remington's Code (1915), §§ 2317-2319; murder, §§ 2392 ff.; damage by explosives, or placing them, §§ 2652, 2653; unlawful making, storing, or shipping explosives, §§ 2403, 2504, 2506; indirect participation in any crime, § 2260; attempts toward any crime, § 2264; solicitation of another is punishable under this section, State v. George, 79 Wash. 262, and also at common law. The Wash. syndicalism and sedition acts are discussed in the body of the book.

District of Columbia: Treason, punishable under general Federal law; murder, Code, § 798; placing explosives near buildings or discharging them, §§ 825 a, 885; indirect participation in crime, § 908; attempts, § 906; solicitation is probably a common law offense punishable under § 910.

APPENDIX V

STATE WAR AND PEACE STATUTES AFFECTING FREEDOM OF SPEECH

(Note: As some of the statutes have varying penalties, in order to avoid confusion only the punishment for the most serious offense is mentioned, which will indicate the relative severity of these laws. Fines may operate as a term of imprisonment if the defendant is obliged to work them out when too poor to pay. An asterisk shows that this particular statute has been discussed in a reference listed in the Bibliography. The cases listed are only the appellate court decisions under the statutes; many prosecutions never reach such a court. Each decision given affirms a conviction by the trial court unless otherwise described. "Reversed" means that a conviction was reversed on appeal. The list ends with the year 1921.)

PART I

Statutes against Opposition to War. (See p. 110 of text.)

Alaska Laws, 1917, c. 60 (utter any seditious matter or tending to excite discontent, etc.; fair and honest criticism excepted.) 1 yr. or $1,000.

Florida Laws, 1917, c. 7392, No. 134 (persuading or publicly attempting to persuade a person not to enlist in war or when "our foreign relations tend to indicate an impending war or state of war"). Misdemeanor.

Hawaii Laws, 1918 sp., Act 19 ("language calculated or tending to discourage or prevent the vigorous prosecution of the war"; "disrespect to any flag of the United States"; "contemptuous or abusive language about any allied nation or its flag or uniform"; also peace clauses). 1 yr., $1,000.

Iowa (See sedition statute, part II; no express war provision, but opposition punished in:)

State v. Gibson, 174 N. W. 34 (1919).

Louisiana Laws, 1917 sp., No. 10 (like Minn., 1917). 3 mos.-1 yr., $100-$500.

Laws, 1918, No. 138 (like contempt part of Espionage Act of 1918). 5 yrs., $50-$5,000.
(See sedition statute, part II.)

Minnesota Laws, 1917, c. 463 (see text; repealed by next statute). 1 yr., $100-$500.

400 APPENDICES

> State v. Holm, 139 Minn. 267; L. R. A. 1918C 304 (1918).
> State v. Spartz, 140 Minn. 203 (quashed).
> State v. Freerks, 140 Minn. 349.
> State v. Townley, 140 Minn. 413 (quashed).
> State v. Kaercher, 141 Minn. 186 (ind. good).
> State v. Luker, 169 N. W. 700 (1918).
> State v. Hartung, 169 N. W. 712 (1918) (dissent).
> State v. Gilbert, 169 N. W. 790; 254 U. S. 325.
> State v. Martin, 169 N. W. 792 (dissent).
> State v. Deike, 172 N. W. 777 (1919 reversed).
> State v. Gilbert, 171 N. W. 798 (ind. good).
> State v. Townley, 171 N. W. 930 (ind. good).
> State v. Rempel, 172 N. W. 919 (reversed).
> State v. Ludemann, 172 N. W. 887 (reversed).
> State v. Rempel, 172 N. W. 888 (reversed).
> State v. Randall, 173 N. W. 425 (reversed).
> State v. Hartung, 179 N. W. 646 (1920 reversed.)
> State v. Townley, 182 N. W. 773; 42 Sup. Ct. 54 (1921).

Laws, 1919, c. 93 (practically all of U. S. Act of 1918, except obstructing enlistment). 20 yrs., $20,000.

Montana   Laws, 1918 sp., c. 11 (model for U. S. Act of 1918). 1-20 yrs., $200-$20,000.

> State v. Kahn, 182 Pac. 107 (1919).
> State v. Griffith, 184 Pac. 219 (1919) (reversed).
> State v. Wolf, 185 Pac. 556 (quashed).
> State v. Wyman, 186 Pac. 1.
> State v. Smith, 188 Pac. 644 (1920 reversed).
> State v. Brooks, 188 Pac. 942 (reversed).
> State v. Smith, 190 Pac. 107 (reversed)).
> *Ex parte* Starr, 263 Fed. 145 (habeas corpus denied).
> State v. Diedtman, 190 Pac. 117 (reversed).
> State v. Dunn, 190 Pac. 121 (reversed).
> State v. Smith, 194 Pac. 131 (reversed).
> State v. Fowler, 196 Pac. 992; 197 Pac. 847 (1921).
> State v. Schaffer, 197 Pac. 986.
> State v. McGlynn, 199 Pac. 708 (reversed).

Laws, 1919, c. 77 (copies U. S. Act of 1917 for war, and rest of U. S. Act of 1918 for all times). 1-20 yrs., $200-$20,000.

Nebraska   Laws, 1918 sp., c. 5 (very wide; punishes concealment of knowledge that sedition has been committed; also any violation of U. S. Act of 1917). 20 yrs., $10,000.

APPENDICES

	Gerdes *v.* State, 175 N. W. 606 (1919) (reversed).
New Jersey	Laws, 1918, c. 36 (like Minn., 1917). 7 yrs., $100-$2,000.
	(See sedition statute, part II.)
Texas	Laws, 1918 (4th Called Sess.), c. 8 (like La.). 2-25 yrs.
	Ex parte Acker, 212 S. W. 500 (1919). Fromme *v.* State, 212 S. W. 501 (reversed). Meyer *v.* State, 212 S. W. 504. *Ex parte* Meckel, 220 S. W. 81 (1920, held unconstitutional). Schellenger *v.* State, 222 S. W. 246 (reversed).
Wisconsin	Laws, 1918 sp., c. 13 (like Minn., 1917). 1 yr., $1,000.

(Note: In addition to the sedition statutes mentioned, several states during the period of hostilities passed criminal syndicalism laws, see part II—Arizona, Idaho, Minnesota, Montana, South Dakota.)

Part II

Statutes not Limited to War. (See pp. 180-194 of text.)

A. *Red Flags and Other Insignia:*

Alabama	Laws, 1919, No. 83. 10 yrs., $500-$5,000.
Arizona	Laws, 1919, c. 11. 6 mos., $100-$300.
Arkansas	Laws, 1919, c. 512, sec. 2. 6 mos., $1,000.
California	Laws, 1919, p. 142. Felony. Los Angeles Red Flag Ordinance. *Ex parte* Hartman, 188 Pac. 548 (1920, held unconstitutional).
Colorado	Laws, 1919, c. 171. 1-10 yrs.
Connecticut	Public Acts, 1919, c. 35. 6 mos., $200. New Haven Red Flag Ordinance (1919), 29 *Yale L. Journ.* 108.
Delaware	Laws, 1919, c. 231. 15 yrs., $2,000.
Idaho	Laws, 1919, c. 96. 1-10 yrs., $1,000.
Illinois	Laws, 1919, p. 420, sec. 265 f. 1-10 yrs.
Indiana	Laws, 1919, c. 125 (preamble referring to Russia). 5 yrs., $5,000.
Iowa	Laws, 1919, c. 199. 6 mos., $1,000.
Kansas	Laws, 1919, c. 184. 18 mos.-3 yrs.

APPENDICES

Kentucky	Laws, 1920, c. 100, sec. 10. 21 yrs., $10,000.
Massachusetts	Laws, 1913, c. 678, sec. 2 (repealed by Laws, 1915, c. 255). 6 mos., $100.
	Comm. v. Karvonen, 219 Mass. 30 (1914).
Michigan	Laws, 1919, No. 104. 5 yrs., $1,000.
Minnesota	Laws, 1919, c. 46. Felony.
Montana	Laws, 1919, c. 25. 1-5 yrs., $500.
Nebraska	Laws, 1919, c. 208. 5 yrs., $1,000.
New Jersey	Laws, 1919, c. 78. 15 yrs., $2,000.
New Mexico	Laws, 1919, c. 33. 6 mos., $100.
New York	Laws, 1919, c. 409. Misdemeanor.
Ohio	Laws, 1919, p. 57, $100.
Oklahoma	Laws, 1919, c. 133. 10 yrs., $1,000.
Oregon	Laws, 1919, c. 35. 10 yrs., $1,000.
Rhode Island	Laws, 1919, c. 1771, sec. 1. 10 yrs., $10,000.
South Dakota	Laws, 1919, c. 191. 30 days, $100.
Utah	Laws, 1919, c. 129. 1-10 yrs., $1,000.
Vermont	Laws, 1919, c. 195. 6 mos., $200.
Washington	Laws, 1919, c. 181. Felony.
West Virginia	Laws, 1919, c. 24, sec. 2. 1 yr., $100-$500 (first offense); 1-5 yrs. (second offense).
Wisconsin	Laws, 1919, c. 369. $10-$100 (30 days on default).

B. *Statutes Against Incitement to Specific Acts of Violence:*

(Note: The grouping adopted below is necessarily somewhat arbitrary. Groups B-E run into one another, and the line between sedition and syndicalism is not always clear.)

* *Massachusetts*	Laws, 1919, c. 191. 3 yrs., $1,000.
* *New Jersey*	Laws, 1908, c. 278. High misdemeanor.
	State v. Boyd, 86 N. J. L. 75; 87 N. J. L. 328 (1915).
	State v. Quinlan, 86 N. J. L. 120; 87 N. J. L. 333 (1915; with dissenting opinion).
	State v. Scott, 86 N. J. L. 133 (1914) (reversal).
Vermont	Laws, 1919, No. 194 (like Mass., but has "indirectly"). 3 yrs., $1,000.

APPENDICES

C. *Statutes Against Incitement to Crime Generally:*

Indiana — Laws, 1919, c. 125, sec. 2 (includes advocacy of revolution by "general cessation of industry"). 5 yrs., $5,000.

Washington — Laws, 1909, c. 249, sec. 312. Gross misdemeanor.

> State v. Fox, 71 Wash. 185 (1912).
> Fox v. Washington, 236 U. S. 273 (1915).

Wyoming — Laws, 1919, c. 76. 5 yrs., $5,000.

D. *Statutes Against Criminal Anarchy:*

* *New York* — Laws, 1902, c. 371. 10 yrs., $5,000:

> Von Gerichten v. Seitz, 94 App. Div. 130 (1904).
> Re Lithuanian Workers' Literature Society, 196 App. Div. 262 (1921, amendment of charter refused).
> People v. Gitlow, 111 Misc. 641; 195 App. Div. 773.
> People v. Kalnin, 189 N. Y. Supp. 359 (search).
> People v. Ferguson, 192 N. Y. Supp. 24 (1922).

Washington — Laws, 1909, c. 249, secs. 311, 314-316. 10 yrs., $5,000.
State v. Lowery, 104 Wash. 520 (1918).

E. *Peace-Time Sedition Statutes:*

Arkansas — Laws, 1919, c. 512 ("propaganda which tends to overthrow the present form of government by any violence or unlawful means"). 6 mos., $10-$1,000.

* *Connecticut* — Public Acts, 1919, c. 191 (public advocacy of "any measure, doctrine, proposal or propaganda intended to injuriously affect the government" of U. S. or Conn.). 3 yrs., $1,000.

Public Acts, 1919, c. 312 ("abusive, disloyal, scurrilous matter about form of government of U. S., military forces, etc., or matter intended to bring them into contempt, or which creates or fosters opposition to organized government"). 5 yrs., $500.

> State v. Sinchuk, 115 Atl. 33 (1921).

Hawaii — Laws, 1918 sp., Act 19 (like contempt part of Espionage Act of 1918; also war clauses and peace clauses). 1-10 yrs., $100-$1,000.

Illinois — Laws, 1919, p. 420, adding to Criminal Code secs. 265 a-g (advocacy of reformation or overthrow of present representative form of government by violence or other unlawful means; issuing books, etc.; membership in society, etc.) 1-10 yrs.

APPENDICES

Iowa — Laws, 1917, c. 372 (exciting or attempting to excite insurrection or sedition, advocating subversion or destruction by force of Ia. or U. S. government; attempting to excite hostility or opposition to them; membership in association, etc.). 20 yrs., $1,000-$10,000.

> State *v.* Gibson, 174 N. W. 34 (1919).

Kentucky — Laws, 1920, c. 100 (very sweeping). 21 yrs., $10,000.

Louisiana — Laws, 1917 sp., No. 24 (like Ia.). 20 yrs., $10,000.

Montana — Laws, 1919, c. 77 (like war-time statute, *supra,* and U. S. Espionage Act of 1918). 1-20 yrs., $200-$20,000.

New Hampshire — Laws, 1919, c. 155 (advocating overthrow of government or interference with any public or private right whatever by force; any act which *tends* to encourage violation of law). 10 yrs., $5,000. Injunction provision.

New Jersey — Laws, 1918, c. 44 (like Ia.). 20 yrs., $10,000.

> State *v.* Tachin, 106 Atl. 145 (1919), 108 Atl. 318 (dissent); 254 U. S. 662.
> State *v.* Gabriel, 112 Atl. 611 (1921, reversed, sec. 3 unconstitutional).
> See Colgan *v.* Sullivan, 109 Atl. 568 (1920).

Laws, 1920, c. 235 (encouraging hostility to the government). High misdemeanor.

New Mexico — Laws, 1919, c. 140 (any act in opposition to the organized government). 1-10 yrs., $200-$1,000.
> State *v.* Diamond, 202 Pac. 988 (1921, held unconstitutional).

New York — Laws, 1917, vol. 2, c. 416 (removal of officers, civil service employees, and teachers for treasonable or seditious acts or utterances).

Laws, 1918, vol. 2, c. 246 (elimination of school textbooks containing seditious or disloyal matter).

Laws, 1921, c. 666 (public school teachers must obtain certificate of loyalty; none issued to advocates of "a form of government other than the government of the U. S. or of this state").

Laws, 1921, c. 667 (all private schools must obtain license from state; none issued if instruction includes teaching of doctrine "that organized governments shall be overthrown by force, violence, or unlawful means"). 60 days, $100. Injunction provision.

APPENDICES

Pennsylvania — Laws, 1919, No. 275 (any publication, utterance, or conduct which *tends* to cause any outbreak of violence, to encourage conduct with a view of overthrowing by force or show or threat of force the government of U. S. or Pa., to encourage any overt act with a view of bringing them into hatred or contempt, or to incite harm to officials or public property, etc. *Cf.* Palmer federal bill). 20 yrs., $100-$10,000.

Rhode Island — Laws, 1919, c. 1771 (language intended to incite "a disregard of the Constitution or laws"). 10 yrs., $10,000.

West Virginia — Laws, 1919, c. 24 (see text). 1 yr., $100-$500 (first offense); 1-5 yrs. (second offense).

Criminal Syndicalism Statutes (substantially of a uniform type, unless otherwise noted):

Alaska — Laws, 1919, c. 6. 10 yrs., $5,000.

Arizona — Laws, 1918 sp., c. 13 (special wording). 10 yrs., $5,000. Message of Governor Hunt, refusing to sign this Act, *ibid.* 49; Senate and House Resolutions denouncing the I.W.W., *ibid.* 55, 67.

* *California* — Laws, 1919, c. 188. 1-14 yrs.

> *Ex parte* McDermott, 183 Pac. 437 (1919).
>
> Whitney *v.* Superior Court, 187 Pac. 12 (1920).
> People *v.* Malley, 194 Pac. 48.
> People *v.* Lesse, 199 Pac. 46 (1921).
> People *v.* Steelik, 33 Cal. App. Dec. 594; 203 Pac. 78 (1921).
> People *v.* Taylor, 34 Cal. App. Dec. 414; 203 Pac. 85.
> People *v.* Wieler, 204 Pac. 410 (reversed).

Hawaii — Laws, 1919, c. 186. 10 yrs., $5,000.

Idaho — Laws, 1917, c. 145. 10 yrs., $5,000.

Iowa — Laws, 1919, c. 382. 10 yrs., $5,000.

Kansas — Laws, 1920, c. 37. (Adds "or for profit.") 1-10 yrs., $1,000.
State *v.* Berquist, 199 Pac. 101 (1921, quashed).

Michigan — Laws, 1919, No. 255. 10 yrs., $5,000.

Minnesota — Laws, 1917, c. 215. 10 yrs., $5,000.
State *v.* Moilen, 167 N. W. 345 (1918); 1 A. L. R. 331.
State *v.* Worker's Socialist Pub. Co., 185 W. W. 931 (1921, partly reversed).

Montana — Laws, 1918 sp., c. 7. 1-5 yrs., $200-$1,000.

Nebraska	Laws, 1919, c. 261. (Adds "or for profit.") 1-10 yrs., $1,000.
Nevada	Laws, 1919, c. 22. 10 yrs., $5,000.
Ohio	Laws, 1919, p. 189. 10 yrs., $5,000.
Oklahoma	Laws, 1919, c. 70. (Adds "or for profit.") 10 yrs., $5,000.
Oregon	Laws, 1919, c. 12. (Adds "or for profit.") 1-10 yrs., $1,000. (Amended, Laws, 1921, c. 34.) State v. Laundy, 204 Pac. 958 (1922, reversed).
South Dakota	Laws, 1918, c. 38. 1-25 yrs., $1,000-$10,000.
Utah	Laws, 1919, c. 127. 1-5 yrs., $200-$1,000.
Washington	Laws, 1919, c. 3. 10 yrs., $5,000. (Repealed by the following act.) Laws, 1919, c. 174 (special wording, favoring "crime, sedition, violence, intimidation or injury" as a means of change). Felony. State v. Hennessy, 195 Pac. 211 (1921). State v. Brown, 195 Pac. 218. State v. Hestings, 196 Pac. 13. State v. Hemhelter, 196 Pac. 581. State v. Shoemaker, 196 Pac. 1066. State v. Gibson, 197 Pac. 611 (reversed). State v. Flogarus, 197 Pac. 612. State v. Pico, 199 Pac. 289. State v. Payne, 200 Pac. 314. State v. McLennen, 200 Pac. 319 (reversed). State v. Pettilla, 200 Pac. 332 (reversed). State v. Passila, 201 Pac. 295. State v. Aspelin, 203 Pac. 964 (1922, reversed). Laws, 1919, c. 173 (special wording, favoring sabotage). Felony. State v. Kowalchuk, 200 Pac. 333 (1921). Spokane Syndicalism Ordinance, 1921. Spokane v. Grady, 195 Pac. 1043 (1921, ind. good).

INDEX OF CASES

NOTE: Prosecutions are indexed by the name of the accused, whether conducted by the King (Rex), the Queen (Regina), the United States, or a state (People, Commonwealth, Respublica). All other cases are indexed by the plaintiff's name. Important prosecutions and election cases are also in the General Index. Many federal and state prosecutions not discussed in this book are indexed in Appendices II and V.

Abbott, *Re*, 320 *n*., 321 *n*.
Abrams *v*. U. S., 120-160; see General Index.
Acklen Election Case, 349 *n*.
Ahearn, P. *v*., 352 *n*.
Ahlers, R. *v*., 326 *n*.
Albers, U. S. *v*., 57 *n*., 59 *n*.
American School of Magnetic Heating *v*. McAnnulty, 105 *n*., 285 *n*.
American Socialist Society *v*. U. S., 27 and *n*., 308, 356.
Aso, U. S. *v*., 167, 168 and *n*., 173.
Atchison etc. Ry. *v*. Brown, 11 *n*.
August *v*. U. S., 149 *n*.
Ault, U. S. *v*., 115 *n*.

Bailey *v*. Alabama, 36 *n*.
Baker, U. S. *v*., 101 *n*.
Baltzer, U. S. *v*., 64, 65 and *n*., 88 *n*.
Bancroft *v*. Frear, 320 *n*.
Barker, P. *v*., 340 *n*., 342 *n*.
Beatty *v*. Gillbanks, 183 and *n*.
Beresford-Hope *v*. Lady Sandhurst, 319 *n*.
Berger Election Case, 315-332; see General Index.
Bernat and Dixon, *Ex parte*, 272 *n*.
Billingsley *v*. U. S., 166 *n*.
Blanding, C. *v*., 8 *n*., 24 *n*.
Blodgett, U. S. *v*., 62, 64.
Blount, Expulsion Case, 346 *n*.
Blum, Matter of, 304 *n*.
Bollman and Swartwout, *Ex parte*, 325 *n*.
Bosny *v*. Williams, 236 and *n*.
Boutin, U. S. *v*., 57 *n*.
Boyd, S. *v*., 192 *n*.

Boyd *v*. U. S., 299, 300, 303 *n*., 335 *n*.
Bradlaugh Election Case, 344
Bright Expulsion Case, 346, 347, 350 *n*.
Brinton, U. S. *v*., 83.
Bryant *v*. U. S., 40 *n*.
Buessel, U. S. *v*., 128 *n*.
Burman, P. *v*., 183 *n*.
Bush, P. *ex rel.*, *v*. Thornton, 342 *n*., 347 *n*.
Butler *v*. Perry, 36 *n*.

Campbell *v*. Cannon, 347 *n*., 351 *n*.
Cannon, Election and Expulsion Cases, 345 *n*., 347 *n*., 351 and *n*.
Carlisle *v*. U. S., 326 *n*.
Casement, R. *v*., 325, 326.
Chandler, S. *v*., 31 *n*.
Charges to Grand Jury, 327 *n*.
Chin Wah, *Re*, 241 *n*.
Chin Yow *v*. U. S., 255 *n*.
Clap, C. *v*., 24 *n*.
Clark, S. *v*., 151 *n*.
Clark, U. S. *v*., 215 and *n*.
Clarke, *Ex parte*, 307 *n*.
Claudius *v*. Davie, 7 *n*.
Cobbett, Trial of, 8 *n*.
Coaks, R. *v*., 319 *n*.
Coldwell, U. S. *v*., 9 *n*.
Colyer and Katzeff *v*. Skeffington, 242-249, 257, 270 and *n*., 271, 339.
Comfort *v*. Fulton, 304 *n*.
Connolly *v*. Union Sewer Pipe Co., 282 *n*.
Cowan *v*. Fairbrother, 12 *n*.
Croswell, P. *v*., 30 and *n*.
Cummings *v*. Missouri, 302 *n*., 342 *n*.

407

INDEX OF CASES

Curran, U. S. v., 128 n.
Cuthell, R. v., 58 and n.

Dailey v. Superior Court, 61 n.
Dalton, S. v., 344 n.
Danbury Hatters' Case, 53 n.
Darmer, U. S. v., 110 n.
Darwin, S. v., 112 n.
Davidson v. New Orleans, 16 n.
Dean of St. Asaph, R. v., 8 n., 9 n.
Debs v. U. S., 90-93; see General Index.
Dennie, Resp. v., 8 n.
Denson, U. S. v., 57 n., 59 n.
Dobbs' Case, 150 n.
Doe v. U. S., 60, 67.
Drakard, R. v., 27, 28.

Eastman, P. v., 171 n.
Eastman, U. S. v., 85 n., 86, 126.
Ehrich v. Root, 306 n.
Eisner v. Macomber, 106 n.
Entinck v. Carrington, 298 n., 304.
Equi, U. S. v., 33 n., 128 n.

Flagg, C. v., 165.
Fong Yue Ting v. U. S., 235 n., 241 n., 249 n.
Fontana, U. S. v., 48 n.
Foster, Matter of, 307 n.
Fox, S. v., 188 n.
Fox v. Spicer, 42 n.
Fox v. Washington, 188 n.
Fraina v. U. S., 13 n., 59 and n.
Frank v. Skeffington, 252-254.
Freerks, S. v., 57 n.
French v. Senate, 340 n.
Fricke, U. S. v., 41 n., 326 n.
Frishman, C. v., 182-185.
Frohwerk v. U. S., 15, 16 and n., 88 n., 90.
Furman, P. ex. rel., v. Clute, 320 n.

Garland, Ex parte, 342 n.
Gegiow v. Uhl, 239 n.
Gibson, S. v., 111 n.
Gillow, R. v., 150 n.
Gilmore, S. v., 344 n.
Goetcheus v. Matthewson, 342 n.
Goldman, U. S. v., 13 n., 41 n., 126.
Goldsmith, U. S. v., 57 n., 59 n.
Goldstein v. U. S., 10 n., 60, 61.
Gompers v. Bucks Stove and Range Co., 53 n.
Gompers v. U. S., 32 n.

Grafton v. Connor, 349 n.
Granzow, U. S. v., 57 n.
Grau, U. S. ex rel., v. Uhl, 272 n.
Green v. Shumway, 342 n.
Guiney v. Bonham, 272 n.
Gulf etc. Ry. v. Ellis, 282 n.

Haffer, P. v., 172 n.
Hall, U. S. v., 59 n.
Halliday, R. v., 42 n.
Halter v. Nebraska, 112 n.
Harris Expulsion Case, 345 n., 346.
Harrison, Ex parte, 11 n.
Harshfield v. U. S., 59 and n., 93 n.
Hatzel v. Hall, 341 n.
Haywood, U. S. v., 85 n., 87 n., 163.
Head v. U. S., 88 n.
Henning, U. S. v. 48 n.
Herbert Expulsion Case, 345 n.
Hiss v. Bartlett, 340 n.
Hitchcock, U. S. v., 57 n.
Hodges, U. S. v., 326 n.
Holm, S. v., 111 n.
Houston v. Moore, 112 n.
Hunt, R. v., 27, 28, 68.
Hurtado v. California, 36 n.

I. C. C. v. Brimson, 242 n.

Jackson, Ex parte, (Fed.), 242 n., 273 n., 274. [241 n.,
Jackson, Ex parte, (U. S.), 108 n.
Ju Toy, U. S. v., 238 n., 255 and n.

Kammann v. U. S., 93 n.
Kansas v. Colorado, 34 n.
Karvonen, C. v., 186 n., 187 n.
Kaufman, U. S. v., 57 n.
Kentucky v. Dennison, 191 n.
Kentucky Members Election Case, 350 n.
Kirchner, U. S. v., 57 n.
Konkel v. S., 112 n.
Krafft, U. S. v., 57 n.
Kramer, U. S. v., 110 n.
Kumpula v. U. S., 83 and n.

Listman, U. S. v., 115 n.
Loewe v. Lawlor, 53 n.
Lopez v. Howe, 278-280.
Louthan v. C., 11 n.
Lowery, S. v., 272 n.
Low Hong, U. S. v., 255 n.
Low Wah Suey v. Backus, 238 n., 239 n.
Ludemann, S. v., 60 n.

INDEX OF CASES 409

Lynch, P. v., 111 n.
Lyon Expulsion Case, 329, 345.

McClure, S. v., 7 n.
McCulloch v. Maryland, 34 n.
McDonald, P. v., 303 n.
McGrorty v. Hooper, 351 n.
McKee, S. v., 11 n.
McKee v. Young, 347 n., 350 n.
McNeill, Re, 344 n.
Magon v. U. S., 214 n.
Mahaney, P. v., 341 n.
Mamaux v. U. S., 80 n.
Martin, U. S. v., 128 n.
Masses Publishing Co. v. Patten, 46-56; see General Index.
Maxwell v. Cannon, 347 n., 351 n.
Meckel, Ex parte, 111 n., 192 n.
Merryman, Ex parte, 34 n., 81 n.
Metcalf, S. ex rel., v. Dist. Ct., 11 n.
Miller, In re, 257, 261 n., 339.
Miller, U. S. v., 57 n.
Milligan, Ex parte, 33 and n., 42 n., 69 n., 81 n., 96 n., 113, 116, 117 n., 325.
Milwaukee Social Dem. Pub. Co. v. Burleson, 316 n.
Mitchell, Ex parte, 239 n.
Moilen, S. v., 192 n., 272 n.
Molyneux, P. v., 85 n.
Moore, U. S. v., 150 n.
Most, P. v., 205, 206.
Most, R. v., 205 n.
Moy Suey v. U. S., 255 n.
Moy Wing Sun v. Prentis, 241 n.
Muir, R. v., 28, 146 n.
Mutual Film Co. v. Industrial Commn., 10 n.

Nagler, U. S. v., 57 n.
Neagle, Re, 200.
Nearing, U. S. v., 27, 53 n., 55 n., 85 n., 125.
Nesin, P. v., 110 n.
New Yorker Staats-Zeitung v. Nolan, 110 n.
Nishimura Ekiu v. U. S., 230 n.
Norman v. Mathews, 42 n.

Ogletree v. S., 150 n.
O'Hare, U. S. v., 83, 162.
Orear v. U. S., 40 n.
Oswald, Resp. v., 8 n.

Pacific Ry. Com'n, In re, 242 n.
Palmer, R. v., 28.

Pape, U. S. v., 59 and 60 n.
Patterson v. Colorado, 9 n.
Peaslee, C. v., 53, 89.
Pembliton, R. v., 150 n.
Pettine, Ex parte, 280 n., 281 n.
Phillips, U. S. v., 13 n., 41 n., 79 n., 126.
Pierce, S. v., 11 n.
Pierce, U. S. v., 13 n., 94 and n., 101-106, 134, 135 n., 285 n.
Pioneer Press Co., S. v., 12 n.
Powell Expulsion Case, 346.
Preis, In re, 257, 261.
Printing Co., S. v., 12 n.
Public Clearing House v. Coyne, 108 n.

Quinlan, S. v., 189 n.

Ragan, S., ex rel., v. Junkin, 11 n.
Rathbone v. Wirth, 343 n.
Reeder, U. S. v., 41 n.
Roach Election Case, 349 n.
Roberts Election Case, 345 n., 347 n., 350 n., 352 and n.
Roberts v. People, 150 n.
Roberts, Resp. v., 326 n.
Robertson v. Baldwin, 7 n., 36 n.
Robinson, U. S. v., 41 n., 324 n., 326 n., 327 n.
Rogers v. Common Council, 343 n.
Rogers, U. S. v., 166 n.
Ronnfeldt v. Phillips, 119 n.
Russell, Bertrand, R. v., 2, 42 n., 59 and n.

St. Louis etc. Ry. v. Griffin, 11 n.
Samson v. Columbia, 110 n.
Sandberg, U. S. v., 57 n., 59 n.
Sanford v. Richardson, 305 n.
Schaefer v. U. S., 85, 87, 94-101, 106, 218 n., 265 and n.
Schenck v. U. S., 9 n., 16 n., 88-93; see General Index.
Schoberg, U. S. v., 38 n., 59 n.
Schurmann v. U. S., 110 n.
Scott, S. v., 189 n.
Selective Draft Law Cases, 7 n., 40 n.
Shaffer, U. S. v., 57 n.
Shelley's Case, 38.
Silverthorne Lumber Co. v. U. S., 242 n., 299 n., 300.
Skuy v. U. S., 149 n.
Smith v. Brown, 320 n., 347 n., 350 n.

INDEX OF CASES

Smoot Election Case, 347 n., 352, 353.
Socialists Election Case, 332-364.
Spirit of '76, U. S. v., 10, 38 n., 43, 60, 61.
Star v. Brush, 110 n.
Star Opera v. Hylan, 110 n., 183 n.
Stark Election Case, 347 n., 349, 350 and n.
Starr, *Ex parte*, 113 n.
Steene, U. S. v., 116 n.
Stephens, U. S. v., 51 n.
Stern v. Remick, 242 n.
Stilson v. U. S., 93 and n.
Stokes, U. S. v., 13 n., 28 n., 58, 59, 67, 87 n., 92, 118, 119.
Strong, U. S. v., 115 n.
Stuppiello, U. S. v., 280 n.
Sugarman v. U. S., 88 n., 89, 90.
Sultan v. Star Co., 110 n.
Swelgin, U. S. v., 272 and 273 n.
Swift v. U. S., 53 n.
Symes v. Trimble, 350 n.

Tachin, S. v., 111 n., 112 n., 192 n.
Taubert, U. S. v., 81 n.
Thomas Election Case, 347 n., 350 n.
Toledo Newspaper Co. v. U. S., 12 and n.
Townley; see General Index.
Truss, *In re*, 257.
Turner v. Williams, 275, 277, 278, 283.

U. S. Steel Corp., U. S. v., 106 n.

Vallandigham, *Ex parte*, 117 n., 325.

Van Lonkhuyzen v. Daily News, 110 n.
Vegelahn v. Guntner, 53 n.
Von Bank, U. S. v., 57 n.
Von Gerichten v. Seitz, 188 n.

Waldman Election Case, 332-364.
Waldron, U. S. v., 61, 62.
Wallace, U. S. v., 13 n., 62.
Wallace v. Georgia Ry., 11 n.
Weeks v. U. S., 241 n., 299 n., 300.
Weems v. U. S., 148 n.
Weinsberg, U. S. v., 57 n.
Weist, U. S. v., 57 n.
Wells v. U. S., 41 n., 168 and n., 173.
Werner, U. S. v., 41 n., 327 n.; see Schaefer v. U. S.
Wheeler, U. S. v., 45 n.
Whitaker, P. v., 110 n.
White, U. S. v., 57 n.
Whittemore Election Case, 349 n.
Wiborg v. U. S., 149 n.
Wilkes v. Wood, 297 n.
Wilkes Election Case, 311-315, 328, 356.
Wishek, U. S. v., 48 n.
Wong Quong Wong, U. S. v., 241 n.
Workingmen's Co-operation Publishing Association, U. S. *ex rel.*, v. Burleson, 115 n.
Wursterbarth, U. S. v., 109, 110 n.

Young, U. S. v., 325 n., 326 n.

Zenger trial, 23 and n.
Zimmerman, U. S. v., 82.

GENERAL INDEX

NOTE: The Index of Cases should also be consulted for prosecutions, etc., since only a few of the most important are listed in this index.

ABERCROMBIE, J. W., Solicitor of the Department of Labor, 243, 248, 249, 258.
ABOLITIONISTS, 3, 209, 210, 372.
ABRAMS, Jacob, 123-126, 131, 138 n., 141, 142, 148; trial and decision, 9 n., 22 n., 46, 68, 85 n., 93, 94, 100, 106, 116; chapter III., 120-160, 202, 207, 215, 216, 220.
ADAMS, John, 2, 210, 299; on assassination, 223.
ADDISON, Judge, 21 n.
ADMINISTRATIVE LAW, conclusiveness of the decisions of officials: post-office, 45, 54, 106-109, 199, 233, 234; deportations, 232-240, 254-256, 291, 292; treaty funds and Land Office, 233; taxation, 233; danger of wide range of administrative discretion in criminal statutes, 75.
Agents provocateurs, 269-271.
AGITATORS, value for liberty, 294, 295.
ALDRICH, Edgar, Judge, 81.
Alice in Wonderland, 232, 334.
ALIEN LAW OF 1798, 1, 162; text summarized, 29; compared with contemporary deportations, 109, 240.
ALIENS, denaturalization of, see same; deportation of, 109, 110, 229-293; value to U. S., 227, 236, 289, 293; reasons for not becoming naturalized, 235, 236.
ALTERCATIONS, language in, prosecuted, 59 and n., 68.
AMERICAN FEDERATION OF LABOR, 193, 198, 255, 267, 272 n., 278.
AMERICAN LABOR PARTY, 267.
American Labor Year-Book, 257, 273 n., 305 n., 308 n., 319 n.
AMERICAN PROTECTIVE LEAGUE, 71, 308.

AMERICAN REVOLUTION, 2, 9, 17, 21, 24, 46, 203, 209, 299, 326 n.; censorship of moving pictures, 10, 60, 61.
AMERICAN SOCIALIST SOCIETY, Rand School, 308-310; prosecution, 27 and n., 308, 356.
AMERICANISM, 178, 227, 331, 362, 372.
AMIDON, C. F., Judge, 46, 48 n., 56, 76, 83.
AMNESTY, after Civil War, 2; after World War, 116, 117, 118 and n.
ANARCHISTS, 2, 83, 97, 223, 309; in Abrams case, 123, 142-147, 159; past outrages, 164, 165; regulation of explosives, 168, 169; state statutes against criminal anarchy, 187-194; anarchy acts generally, 163-228 *passim;* extradition, 191 n.; deportations of violent anarchists, 275; of philosophical anarchists, 275-280, 285.
ANDERSON, A. B., Judge (Ind.), 82.
ANDERSON, F. M., on Sedition Law of 1798, 78 n., 81 n.
ANDERSON, G. W., Judge (Mass.), 70 n., 194 n., 242-250, 253-257, 268.
ANGELL, W. F., on Caillaux trial, 136 n.
ANSELL, S. T., General, on militia, 111 n.
ANTIN, Mary, 82.
ANTONELLI, Etienne, *La Russie Bolcheviste*, 132 n.
ANTONY, funeral oration, 55, 214.
ARIETE, EL, anarchistic society, 167, 168, 173, 174.
ARIZONA, Bisbee deportations, 45; syndicate law, 190.

GENERAL INDEX

ARMY, criticism of flogging in, 27, 28, 68; abuse of uniform, crime, 45, 114, 115; criticism of incompetent general by troops, 50. See CONSCRIPTION; WAR.

Army and the Press, Relation Between, 98, 99.

ARRESTS, without warrant, in Civil War, 116, 117; under Espionage Act, 123, 159; in deportation proceedings, 237, 241 and *n.*, 243-246, 248; of citizens for deportation, 242, 244, 245, 249, 252-256; general warrants, 296, 297.

ART, and freedom of speech, 17, 31, 32, 175. See CENSORSHIP.

ASSASSINATION, 52, 163-169 *passim*, 173, 175, 196, 198, 199, 205 *passim*, 230, 231, 263, 268.

ASSEMBLY, right of, 5, 7 *n.*, 50; in war, 57, 58; in peace, 172, 177, 178, 180, 182-185, 205, 206; permits for use of streets, 15, 180, 182, 183; red flag laws, 180-187.

ASSOCIATION, guilt by, 112, 113, 192, 193, 230, 231 and *n.*, 250, 257, 262-268, 281, 285, 336, 337, 360, 361.

ASSOCIATIONS, to suppress sedition, 71, 72, 357.

ATHEISTS, 2, 172 *n.*, 196 and *n.*

ATTEMPTS, criminal, 304 *n.*; relation to freedom of speech, 25, 165, 173; to Espionage Act, 51-53, 88, 89, 155; attempts to obstruct recruiting, 41, 44, 46; in federal crimes, 166, 201.

ATTORNEY GENERAL, alleged Star-Spangled Banner prosecutions, 102, 103; supervision over judges, 84, 85; no control over deportations, 242, 252. See GREGORY; PALMER; JUSTICE, DEPARTMENT OF.

AUDIENCE, character of, as affecting criminality of utterances, 57-61, 206.

BAGEHOT, Walter, 34, 140 *n.*, 197, 207, 289 *n.*

BAIL, under Espionage Act, 46; in deportations, 248.

BAKUNIN, 221.

BALDWIN, Roger, 193 *n.*

BARKLEY, F. R., 248 *n.*, 255 *n.*

BEALE, Joseph H., on criminal attempts, 51 *nn.*

BEAN, R. S., Judge, 33 *n.*

BEARD, imprisonment for wearing long, 172, 183.

BECKSTROM, J. W., prosecution, 102 *n.*

BEECHER, Edw., *Alton Riots*, 3 *n.*

BELGIUM, 63.

BENTHAM, J., 266.

BERGER, Victor L., *Milwaukee Leader*, 64, 107, 315-318, 323; prosecution, 79, 101, 162, 318, 319, 323, 331; exclusion from Congress, 201, 315-332, 333, 336.

BERKMAN, A., 47.

BERRI, Duc de, 175.

BETTMAN, Alfred, 73, 125 *n.*, 167, 262 *n.*, 263 *n.*

BEVERIDGE, A. J., *Life of Marshall*, 11 *n.*, 22, 23 *n.*, 65 *n.*, 81 *n.*, 211 *n.*, 265 *n.*, 330 *n.*

Bible, 110, 332, 333; prosecution for quoting, 218. See JESUS.

BIKLÉ, H. W., on sedition law, 199 *n.*, 204 *n.*

BILLBOARD-POSTERS, indecent, 10.

BILL OF RIGHTS, adopted by U. S., 4; important for interpreting as well as invalidating statutes, 4-6; comparison with European constitutions, 5 and *n.*; subject to implied exceptions, 7; apply in war, 33, 34, 42 *n.*, 86 and *n.*; do not crystallize antiquity, 35, 36; deportation, 281-291; miscellaneous references, 3, 228.

BISBEE DEPORTATIONS, 45.

BISHOP, on intent, 150 *n.*

BISMARCK, sedition legislation, 263.

BLACK, Jeremiah, 69, 113.

BLACKSTONE, William, 9, 31 *n.*; definition of freedom of speech, 8-12, 19, 21, 22 *n.*, 23 *n.*, 31, 32, 108, 199; on incitement, 53; on Wilkes, 313.

BLANC, Louis, 286 *n.*

BLASPHEMY, 14, 170, 172.

BLEDSOE, B. F., Judge, 10, 38.

BOLSHEVISTS, in U. S., 2, 60-120 *passim*, 124, 168, 185, 196, 197, 219, 261, 309; Overman Committee, 134, 135, 164. See RUSSIA.

BOMBS, 163-169 *passim*, 196, 212, 268.

GENERAL INDEX

BONDS. See LIBERTY BONDS.
Books, danger of suppression under federal sedition law, 220-224; Rand School, 308-310.
BORAH, Senator, 37 n.
BOSTON, 182-186, 191, 311.
BOURQUIN, G. M., Judge, 59 n., 273 n., 274.
BRADLAUGH, Charles, exclusion case, 344.
BRADLEY, Joseph, Justice, 299, 335.
BRANDEIS, L. D., Justice, 53 n., 85, 89, 94-106, 148, 202, 218, 285 n.
BRAXFIELD, Lord, 87, 146 n., 210.
BREACH OF THE PEACE, acts causing, not protected by free speech clauses, 24, 25; punishment of language as, 74 and n., 102 n., 110 n., 111, 171, 172, 205, 208.
BREWER, Justice, 278.
BRIGHT, John, 104, 117.
BRISSENDEN, Paul, 292.
BROOK FARM, 177, 277.
BROWN, Philip A., *French Revolution in English History,* 28 n., 146 n.
BRYCE, James, 6 n., 363 n.
Buford, 230, 249.
BUREAU OF INVESTIGATION, 164, 195, 243-247, 269-271. See JUSTICE, DEPARTMENT OF.
BURKE, Edmund, 266, 313, 314, 338, 355, 361.
BURLESON, A. R., Postmaster General, 107, 108, 109 n., 115, 199, 229, 335.
BURNSIDE, Ambrose E., General, suppression of newspapers, 116.
BURR, Aaron, 201, 265.
BYRON, 52.

CAFFEY, F. Z., U. S. Attorney, 126.
CAILLAUX, Mme., trial, 136 n.
CALIFORNIA, syndicalism prosecution, 190 n.; Oriental question, 209.
CALLENDER, prosecution under Act of 1798, 78 n.
CAMBRIDGE, raids, 311.
CAMDEN, Lord, 297, 298.
CAMINETTI, A., Commissioner General of Immigration, 243, 251.
CAMPBELL, Lord, 344.
CANADA, free speech in, 42, 218, 269.
CARROLL, T. F., on war laws, 42 n., 325 n.
CARTOONS, Opper, 52; in *Masses,* 46.
CASEMENT, Sir Roger, treason prosecution, 325, 326.
CENSORSHIP, press, 8-12, 19, 21, 23 n., 25, 32, 38, 42 and n., 179, 180; in Russia, 176, 294 n.; billboards, 10; moving pictures, 10, 61 n., 179, 203 n.; theater, 172, 175; mails, see POST-OFFICE, telegraph, 109 n.; of military information, 10, 98, 99; by municipalities, 110 n., 190, 191; foreign-language press, see same; *Ex post facto* censorship of books, 190, 220-224.
CENTRALIA SHOOTINGS, 115, 163, 197, 212.
CHAMBERLAIN, Senator, sedition bill, 41, 42.
CHASE, Samuel, Justice, 80.
CHASE, S. P., Chief Justice, 33 n.
CHATHAM, Lord, 250, 295, 296.
CHESTERFIELD, Lord, 52.
Chicago Times, suppression, 116 and 117 n.
CHINESE, exclusion of, 230 ff., 255, 273.
CHIVERS, Ellen, testifies against Socialist assemblymen, 357, 358, 364.
CIBBER, Colley, 175.
CITIZENS, American, arrests for deportation, see ARRESTS; in foreign countries, 288 and n.
CIVIL RELIEF ACT, SOLDIERS' AND SAILORS', 112.
CIVIL WAR, American, 2, 363; opposition to, 41, 46, 81, 90, 116, 117; treason cases, 324; legislation exclusions, 325-330, 345-353.
CLARKE, J. H., Justice, 87, 94, 129, 139, 140-142, 148-159, 215, 216.
CLAESSENS, August, N. Y. Socialist assemblyman, 333, 356.
CLAY, Henry, 330.
CLAYTON, H. D., Judge, in Abrams trial, 28 n., 86 n., chapter III., 125-148.
COBDEN, Richard, 117.
COKE, Edward, 19.
COLLEGES, expulsion of pacifist student, 110 n.

GENERAL INDEX

Collier's Weekly, on telegraph censorship, 109 n.

Columbia Law Review, 192 n., 263 n.

COLUMBIA UNIVERSITY, expels pacifist student, 110 n.

COLYER CASE, deportations, 242-250, 257, 268, 270 and n., 271, 339, 357.

COMMON LAW, not embodied in constitutional definition of free speech, 14, 22-24, 170; of crimes not adopted in U. S. courts, 22.

COMMUNISTS, 52, 139, 172, 177, 188, 223, 365; raids, 230, 242-272; under Espionage Act, 261; Communist Labor Party, 243 *ff.,* 250, 256, 257, 261 and n., 262, 339; Communist Party of America, 243, 250; origin, 256, 262, 268; program and Secretary Wilson's decision, 256-262; proof of membership in, 231 n., 250, 257, 262-268; spies in, 268-272; Communist International, 259, 260, 334.

COMMUTATIONS, of Espionage Act sentences, 73, 86 n. See PARDONS.

CONFEDERACY, control of the press, 117 and n.

CONGRESS, 116; freedom of debates, 3; criticism of, punished under Sedition Act of 1798, 29, 204; under Espionage Act, 62-64, 102 *ff.,* 129; declaration of war against Germany, 40; used as evidence in prosecutions, 57, 103 *ff.;* freedom of discussion for elections, 62-65, 329-331; sedition bills, 194-199; House Rules hearings, 198, 250-252; House Judiciary Committee, 197; House Immigration Committee, 251; repays fines of 1798, 30, 157; Continental Congress, 17; Confederate Congress, 117 n. See UNITED STATES STATUTES; SEDITION BILLS; ESPIONAGE ACT; DEPORTATIONS; LEGISLATIVE EXCLUSIONS (Berger, Test Oath Act, etc.).

CONNECTICUT, Bridgeport strike, 153; sedition prosecution, 190 n.; Hartford deportations, 246.

CONSCIENTIOUS OBJECTORS, discussion of, 2, 47, 59, 86.

CONSCRIPTION, military, violation of, 40, 144, 145; constitutionality, 7, 35, 40; criminal to discuss, 57, 62, 88; advocacy of resistance to draft, 40, 41, 53, 57, 88-90, 200; discussion opposing draft, 25, 57, 62, 64, 65, 86, 102; in *Masses* case, 46-56; opposing re-election of Congressmen who voted for, 62; urging rearrangement of quotas, 64, 65; men of draft age held within armed forces, 57, 58, 64; efficiency of draft organization, 40, 64; slacker round-up, 107, 108; in peace, 35, 115, 358.

CONSERVATIVES, benefit from freedom of speech, 3; some advocate violence, 260, 261.

CONSPIRACY, at common law, 92, 110 n.; under United States Criminal Code, in war, 40-42, 46, 81 n., 90, 101, 148 n., 168, 173; in peace, 166-169, 173, 196, 205, 206, 213; does not cover injurious conduct of single person, 41, 50, 90, 167, 196; under Espionage Act, 43, 45, 124, 265.

CONSTANT, Benj., 286.

CONSTITUTION, see various topics, e.g., SPEECH, FREEDOM OF; also UNITED STATES CONSTITUTION, and the names of states; and BILLS OF RIGHTS.

CONSTRUCTIVE MEASURES, proposed by writer, for opposition to war, 41, 46; for anarchy and violence, 165-169; for I. W. W., 274, 275; for revolutionary aliens generally, 289-293.

CONTEMPT PROCEEDINGS, 8, 11 n., 12 n., 15.

CONTINENTAL CONGRESS, address to people of Quebec, 17.

CONVENTIONS, political, prohibition of, invalidated by free speech clause, 11 n.

CONVERSATIONS, prosecuted, 59 and n.

COOLEY, Thomas M., on freedom of speech, 11, 13, 14, 48, 219 n.; on searches and seizures, 301, 303 n., 304 n., 305 n.; on legislative eligibility, 340 n.

GENERAL INDEX 415

COPPERHEADS, 41, 325.
CORRUPT PRACTICES, statute void under free speech clause, 11 n.
CORY, H. E., N. J. sedition law, 189 n.
COURTS MARTIAL, for sedition, 33 n., 42.
CREEL, George, 108.
CRIMES, relation to free speech clauses, 14, 15, 16; normal law of, 164-180.
CRUEL AND UNUSUAL PUNISHMENT, excessive sentences as, 148 n.
CRUELTY, charges against officials, 145, 146, 159, 189 n., 247, 248.
CUDGEL, liberty of the, 18.
CULLEN, Chief Justice, on exclusion for opinions, 352.

DALLINGER, F. W., Representative, on Berger case, 331, 332.
DARWIN, Charles, 32.
DAVIS, David, Justice, 33 n.
DAY, Justice, 241 n., 300.
DE ARMOND, Representative, 352 and n.
DE WITT, S. A., N. Y. Socialist assemblyman, 333, 356.
DEBS, E. V., prosecution, 16, 22 n., 79, 85-93 *passim*, 100, 117, 124, 162, 212, 317, 360.
DECLARATION OF INDEPENDENCE, 60, 209, 223.
DEFAMATION. See LIBEL.
DEFENSE OF THE REALM ACT. See GREAT BRITAIN.
DENATURALIZATION, of Pro-Germans, 109, 110; under sedition bills, 198; of I. W. W., 272, 273; of philosophical anarchist, 280.
DEPORTATIONS, Bisbee, 45; from Russia, 176; of Americans from other countries, 288 and n.; from England, 263 n.; in history of persecution, 284; of aliens in U. S., 229-293; Act of 1798, 29, 109, 240; effect of economic views of judges, 81; punishment for sedition, 198; federal power, 200, 230, 284; Statute of 1918, 109, 110; text, 230, 231, 240; of 1920, 230 n., 231 n.; administrative machinery, 232-240, 291, 292; raids of January, 1920, 230, 241-254, 292, 293; Palmer-Post controversy, 250-252; arrest of citizens, 242, 244, 245, 249, 252-256; Communists, 256-272; Wilson decision on Communist Party, 257 ff., 268; on Communist Labor Party, 261; proof of membership in proscribed associations, 231 n., 250, 257, 262-268, 281, 285; use of spies, 268-272; I. W. W., 272-275; violent and philosophical anarchists, 276-280; effect of due process clause and First Amendment, 280-291; wisdom, 284-291; danger of international difficulties, 287 ff.; constructive measures suggested, 289-293; need of pardoning powers, 292.
DETROIT, deportations, 243 n., 248, 255 n., 288.
DICEY, A. V., 5 n., 76 and n., 183 n.
DICKENS, Charles, 140.
DICTAGRAPH, used to prosecute for conversations, 59 n.
DISORDERLY CONDUCT, pacifism punished as, 74 and n., 102 n., 110 n. See BREACH OF THE PEACE.
DISQUE, Colonel, 113, 163.
DISTRICT ATTORNEYS, United States. See PROSECUTING OFFICIALS.
DISTRICT COURTS, UNITED STATES, administration of Espionage Act, 46-87; juries in, 78-80.
DOE, J. P., prosecution, 60, 67.
DORR WAR, 164.
DRAFT. See CONSCRIPTION.
DREYFUS, Alfred, 115, 136.
DUE PROCESS OF LAW, involves balancing, 35, 38; in deportation proceedings, 232, 241, 242 n., 254, 255, 280-285.
DUGUIT, Leon, on the state, 109.
DUMA, 176.
DUNIWAY, C. A., *Freedom of the Press in Mass.*, 19 n., 23 n., 24 n.

EASTMAN, Max, 79, 85 n., 86, 126. See *Masses*.
EGYPT, 108.
EIGHTEENTH AMENDMENT. See PROHIBITION.
ELECTORAL COLLEGE, 114.
ELLENBOROUGH, Lord, 28, 68.
ELLIOT'S DEBATES, cited, 5 n., 19 n., 20 n., 21 n., 211 n., 240 n.
EMERSON, 277, 367.

GENERAL INDEX

EMPEY, Guy, 261.
ENGLAND. See GREAT BRITAIN.
ENLISTMENT, voluntary, interference with, 41, 43, 53, 57, 169.
ENTINCK, John, raid on, 298, 304.
ERSKINE, Thomas, 19, 23.
ESMEIN, A., 175 n.
ESPIONAGE ACT, 40-160.

Act of 1917: origin and text, 40-43; a military statute, 48 and n., 50, 51, 73; construction generally, 43, 44, 57, 58, 69, 216, 218, 335, in Masses case, 46-56, in prosecutions, 56-66, by Supreme Court, 1, 15-17, 57, 65, 87-106, 265; false statements, 51, 56, 57, 94-106, 134, 135, 218; insubordination and recruiting, 57 ff.

Act of 1918: origin, 43-46; summarized, 44, 45; text and digest of cases, 395-398; construction generally, 51, 113 ff., by prosecuting attorneys, 74-76, by employers, 74, in Abrams case, 120-160, by Supreme Court, 116, 141, 148-160; Constitution and government clauses, 114, 128, 129; army and navy clauses, 114, 115; munitions clause, 127, 129, 130, 137-144, 149-153; resistance to U. S., 127, 129, 137, 141, 149, 153 n., 215, 216; opposing cause of U. S., 114.

Human machinery of Act, 66-87, public feeling, 70-73, prosecuting officials, 73-76, juries, 76-80, judges, 80-87; sentences, 58-62, 87 and n., 147, 148, 159, 220; constitutionality, 12 and n., 15, 16, 32, 47, 48, 88, 89, 114-116, 128, 129, 154; relation to state war statutes, 110-113; use of Act against radicals, 77, 81 ff., 162, against actual incitement to violation of draft law, 57, 88-90, after armistice, 113-116, 229, 261, 302, 335; comparison, with Sedition Act of 1798, 56, 128, with Civil War, 41, 46, 116, 117, with Defense of the Realm Act, 118 and n.; inadequate and evil results of Act, 46, 100, 118, 119, 335, 336; effect in future wars, 46, 64, 113-119; repeal essential, 93, 159, 160.

Conspiracy section, 43, 45, 124; misprision section, 43, 45; search warrants, 43, 45, 302; postal powers, 43, 45, see POST-OFFICE; non-sedition parts of Act, 6, 43; deportation, 23 n.

Relation of Act to law of attempts and solicitation, 49, 51-53, 88, 89, 155; intention in prosecutions, 54-56, 63-68, 86; proved by utterances outside indictment, 58, 67, 85 and n., 140-142, and before U. S. entered War, 67; in Abrams case, 127 ff., 139-145; truth usually no defense, 56, 115.

Relation of Act to peace-time sedition statutes, 197, 216; to treason, 325-328.

Effect on legislative exclusion, 323-335 passim, 345, 354-356.

Alphabetical index of cases, 387-395.

EVARTS, W. M., 229, 359 n.
EVIDENCE, questions of, in war cases, utterances outside indictment, 58, 67, 68, 85 and n.; self-incrimination, 69; law and fact, 101-106; Robins testimony in Abrams case, 132-137.
EXILE, as punishment for sedition, 109, 110, 157, 176, 197, 198. See DEPORTATIONS; DENATURALIZATION.
EXPLOSIONS, 163-169 passim.
EXPRESS, as substitute for mails, 109 and n.
EXTRADITION, of political criminals, 191 and n., 286.

FACT, questions of, 101-106.
FEDERALIST JUDGES, 8, 9, 21, 22, 31, 78, 80, 81.
FEDERALIST PARTY, wrecked by Sedition Act of 1798, 30, 116.
FERRARI, Robert, on political trials, 85 n., 136 n.
FERRER, 278, 279.
FIELD, Stephen, Justice, 96 n., 235.
FIFTH AMENDMENT, in war, 33 and n., 42 n., 299. See DUE PROCESS OF LAW.
Finished Mystery, pamphlet, 101.

GENERAL INDEX 417

FIRST AMENDMENT. See SPEECH, FREEDOM OF.
FISH, Hamilton, on intervention, 160 n.
FLAG, United States, 185, 187; abuse of, 45, 171, 185.
FLAG, RED, 180-187.
FLETCHER, Henry J., on war powers, 33 n.
FLOGGING, in army, criticism of, 27, 28, 68.
FLYNN, E. G., I. W. W., 189 n.
"FORCE AND VIOLENCE," legislation punishing advocacy of, 139, 140, 194; constitutionality, 198-207; wisdom, 207-228, 231; in deportation statute, 257-262.
FORD, an I. W. W., 163.
FOREIGN LANGUAGE PRESS, in war, 90, 94 ff., 10o n., 110 n.; in peace, 195, 199.
FORTY-EIGHT, COMMITTEE OF, 184, 267.
FOUR-MINUTE MEN, 64, 74.
FOURTEENTH AMENDMENT, 35, 38, 323-328.
FOURTH AMENDMENT. See SEARCHES AND SEIZURES.
Fox, Charles James, 23, 174.
FOX'S LIBEL ACT, 9, 23, 25, 27, 29, 39, 69.
FRANCE, threatened war of 1798, 29; Rhine policy, 64; Restoration sedition laws, 175; attacks on, suppressed in U. S., 108; Dreyfus affair, 115, 136; teachers, 375. See FRENCH REVOLUTION.
FRANK, Peter, citizen arrested for deportation, 252-254.
FRANKLIN, Benjamin, 18, 21.
FREEDOM. See *sub* ASSEMBLY, PERSON, PRESS, SEAS, SPEECH, etc.
Freeman's Journal and Catholic Register, excluded from mails, 108.
FRENCH REVOLUTION, 109, 221; French trials, 26; effect on English sedition trials, 13, 27, 28, 77, 87, 118, 157, 158, 175, 263, 264; effect in U. S., 29, 162.
FREUND, Ernst, 92, 175 n., 206, 207, 211 n., 263 n., 267.
FROHWERK, prosecution, 15, 16 and n., 88 n., 90.

FUGITIVE SLAVE LAW, 114, 209, 210.
FULLER, M. W., Chief Justice, 277, 283 *passim.*
FURNEAUX, Philip, *Letters to Blackstone,* 31 n.

Gaelic American, excluded from mails, 108.
GALSWORTHY, John, 10.
GARRISON, W. L., 209, 210.
GARVAN, Assistant Attorney General, 261, 262.
GAYNOR, Wm. J., on searches, 304 n.
GEIGER, Judge, 48 n.
GEORGE III., sedition under, 312. See GREAT BRITAIN.
GEORGE, Lloyd, 117.
GERMAN OPERA, prohibited, 110 n., 183 n.
GERMANY, treaty with, 2; opposition to war with, 6, 40-119, 317 ff.; propaganda by, 42, 70; submarine warfare, 57, 60; invasion of Belgium, 63; spies, 6, exaggerated reports, 70-72; connection with Russian Revolution, 132 and chapter III *passim;* laws against associations, 263. See PRO-GERMANS.
GILBERT, W. S., quoted by Judge Clayton, 134.
GILMAN, President, 372, 373.
GITLOW, Benjamin, prosecution, 188.
GOETHE, 52.
GOLDMAN, Emma, 13 n., 41 n., 47, 56, 126, 177, 200, 256, 287.
GOLDSTEIN, prosecution, 10 n., 60, 61.
GOMPERS, Samuel, 108.
GRAHAM BILL, 197, 198, 203, 268.
GRANT, U. S., 2.
GRAY, Horace, Justice, 234.
GRAY, John Chipman, on rights and interests, 36 n.
GREAT BRITAIN, sedition trials, 22, 23, 26-29, 118, 146 n., 157, 175, 210, 211, 216; informers and anti-sedition associations, 72; Defense of the Realm Act in World War, 42 and n., 58, 118 n.; other wars, 104, 117; Combination Acts, 192; treason, 201-203; Reform Bill, 260; laws against seditious associations,

263, 264; expulsion of aliens, 263 n.; spies, 269-271; Wilkes, 295-299, 311-315; other Parliamentary cases, 344; effect of English law on Federalist judges, 8, 9, 21, 22; criticism of England suppressed under Espionage Act, 10, 60, 61, 108; British Secret Service and Lusk Committee, 306.

GREGORY, Thomas W., Attorney General, on war laws, 40, 43, 44, 54, 65; on propaganda, 176; requests amendment of Espionage Act, 43, 44; on baseless spy rumors, 72; circulars to district attorneys, 74-76; on slacker round-up, 107, 108. See ATTORNEY GENERAL.

GRENVILLE, George, 296, 298, 311, 313.

GUESTS, prosecute host for sedition, 59.

GUILT BY ASSOCIATION. See ASSOCIATION.

GYORI, Louis, philosophical anarchist deported, 280.

HABEAS CORPUS, right to, 3, 69, 95 and n., 238, 239, 240, 253, 255. See COLYER CASE.

HALE, Swinburne, 270 n.

HALÉVY, D., on American political parties, 363.

HALIFAX, Lord, 296, 297, 302.

HAMERSLEY, Judge, 12.

HAMILTON, Alexander, 2, 15; definition of free speech, 3 and n., 4 n., 30 and n., 372; rejected for Espionage Act, 44.

HAMILTON, Andrew, 19, 23 n. See ZENGER.

HAND, Augustus, Judge, 86, 126.

HAND, Learned, Judge, 15, 17, 125, 128 n., 194, 324 n.; interpretation of freedom of speech in *Masses* case, 46-56, 63, 69, 76 n., 88, 89, 107, 174, 216.

HANSON, Ole, 115 n., 193 n.

HARPER, Saml. N., 186 n.

HARRISON, Benjamin, 284.

HARTFORD, deportations, 246.

HARTFORD CONVENTION, 97.

HARVARD, red flag, 187; dismissal of Loring, 209; Russian library, 221; academic freedom, 368.

Harvard Law Review, unsigned notes, 42 n., 51 n., 54 n., 57 n., 76 n., 82 n., 83 n., 128 n., 150 n., 156 n., 202 n., 214 n.

HARVARD LIBERAL CLUB, 194 n., 226 n.

HAYWOOD, W. D., prosecution, 85 n., 87 n., 163.

HAZEL, Judge, 167, 168 and n.

HEARST, W. R., 52; newspapers in the war, 110 n.

HENRY, Patrick, 60, 205.

HIGGINS, Henry B., on conciliation courts, 192 n.

HOBBES, Thomas, 13.

HOLMES, O. W., Justice, on freedom of speech, 9, 15, 16, 22, 88-93, 94, 101, 120, 148 n., 148-159, 188, 194, 197, 226; on socialism, 82; on searches, 300; 32, 37, 53.

HOLT, Judge, 236, 237, 238.

HOLT, Lord, 211.

HOUGH, Judge, 13 n., 54 n., 55, 108 n., 119.

HOXIE, 267 n.

HUGHES, Charles E., 2, 189, 332, 333, 336-339.

HUMAN MACHINERY, for enforcing statutes: Espionage Act, 66-87; peace-time sedition laws, 207-219; deportations, 231-240, 291-293.

HUNT, Governor, 190.

HUNT, Leigh, prosecution, 27, 28, 68.

HUTCHINSON, Chief Justice, on freedom of speech, 23 n.; on witches, 356 n.

HYDE, C. C., on Czecho-Slovaks, 131 n.

HYLAN, Mayor, 110 n., 183 n., 190, 191.

HYMNS, military imagery in, 140.

IDAHO, syndicalism law, 190.

IHERING, von, on rights and interests, 35 n.

Illegal Practices of the United States Department of Justice, pamphlet, 243 n., 270 n.

ILLINOIS, Alton riots, 3; Haymarket murders, 165; sedition statute, 191.

IMMIGRATION OFFICIALS, hearings. See DEPORTATIONS.

INCITEMENT. See SOLICITATION.

GENERAL INDEX 419

INDECENT PUBLICATIONS. See OBSCENITY.

INDIA, discussion of, suppressed in U. S., 108; sedition in, 66, 212, 241, 249.

INDUSTRIAL WORKERS OF THE WORLD (I. W. W.), Bisbee deportations, 45; Chicago trial, 85 n., 87 n., 163; Sacramento trial, 87 n.; other federal prosecutions, 77, 83; attitude toward war, 81, 162, 163; state war prosecutions, 110, 113; peace prosecutions, 189 n., 190-193; Centralia, 164, 212; economic causes, 193; injunction against, 193; raids upon, 212, 242 n., 260, 271; deportations, 242 n., 272-275; denaturalization, 272, 273; constructive measures suggested, 274, 275.

INJUNCTION, of libels, 8; against exclusion from mails, 47, 48; against coal strike, 82, 260.

INTENTION, doctrine of constructive, 26, 28-30, 54-56, 67, 97, 134-136; in Sedition Law of 1798, 29; in Espionage Act, see same.

INTERESTS, principle of social and individual, 34-38, 170, 179, 180, 284, 366 ff.

INTERNATIONAL, COMMUNIST, 259, 260, 334, 360.

IOWA, war sedition act, 111 n.

IRELAND, 186, 287; discussion of, in war, suppressed in U. S., 108, 134, 154; suppression in, 212, 264, 265; status under our deportation statute, 287, 288.

Irish World, excluded from mails, 108.

ISAIAH, prosecution for quoting, 218.

I. W. W. See INDUSTRIAL WORKERS OF THE WORLD.

JEFFERSON, Thomas, 17, 18, 21, 30, 31, 56, 66, 67, 108, 161, 162, 217, 227, 336; on revolution, 323, 372.

JEFFREYS, Judge, 213.

JENKINS, cause of war, 114.

JESUS, 362, 370; a crime to quote against war, 57, 61, 62; called anarchist, 146 and n.; Sermon on the Mount, 55, 119.

JEWS, 82, 83, 108, 126, 281, 284, 289 n., 290.

JOHNSON, Reverdy, Senator, on legislative exclusion, 347 n., 351 n.

JOHNSON, Samuel, 10 n., 118 n., 172 n., 175 n., 289, 311.

JU TOY, deportation, 238 n., 255 and n.

JUDGES, effect of free speech clauses on, 5; Federalist, 8, 9, 21, 22, 31, 78, 80, 81; function in libel and petition prosecutions, 19, 22-28, 29, 85, 86; interpretation of Espionage Act, in *Masses* case, 46-56; in other cases, 56-66, 81, 87, 91, 96, 100; under Sedition Act of 1798, 80, 81; attitude toward radicals, 81-84, 146-148, 158, 159, 185; supervision by Department of Justice, 84, 85; sentences, 86, 87; Abrams case, 125 ff.; jesting with prisoners, 146-148; unfitness to determine bad intention and bad tendency, 213-219.

JUNIUS, 23, 312, 314.

JURY, right to, grouped with freedom of speech, 3, 4, 17; function in libel and sedition prosecutions, 19, 22-28, 29, 85, 86, 91-93, 96-100; not a sure guarantee of free speech because of unfitness to determine bad tendency and bad intention, 24-28, 49, 52, 66-69, 76, 92, 93, 158, 213-219; and affected by popular hysteria, voluntary informers, and antisedition societies, 70-72; in Espionage Act trials, 73, 76-80, 91, 98, 99, 103 ff., 132-136 and ff.; importance of methods of selection, 26, 77-79; under Sedition Act of 1798, 78 and n.; age and occupation, 79, 80; divergent opinions of same writing, 26, 27; denied in post-office exclusion proceedings, 158, 199; in deportation proceedings, 158, 232-240.

JUSTICE, DEPARTMENT OF, 202, 309; administration of Espionage Act, 73-76, 90, 112, 113, 124-126, 229, 261, 262, 302; recommendations for reduction of sentences, 73, 87 n.; policy toward radicals, 164, 195-197, 229; enforcement

GENERAL INDEX

of state sedition laws, 229, 249; of deportation statute, 229, 240 n., 241-252, 272-274, 293, 338, 339; *Illegal Activities* pamphlet, 243 n.; Silverthorne raid, 300, 301; civil liability, 302; instructions to agents, 243-247, 249, 257; employment of spies, 268-272.

KANSAS, red flag law, 181 n.; schools, 369.
Kansas City Star, 118.
KENYON, Lord, 13, 58, 213.
KIMBALL, Day, on Abrams case, 156-158.
KNITTING, discouragement of, criminal, 57.
KNOX, Judge, 278 n.
KNOX, P. C., Senator, on legislative exclusion, 347 n., 353.
KOHLER, on construction of fundamental statutes, 31, 32 n.
KROPOTKIN, 276, 279, 287.

LABOR, DEPARTMENT OF, exclusion and deportation of aliens, 232-293; no other Department has control of deportations, 242, 252. See DEPORTATIONS; WILSON, W. B.; POST.
LABOR, SECRETARY OF, 232-293 *passim;* conclusiveness of decisions in deportation cases, 232-240, 254-256, 291, 292.
LABOR UNIONS, 11 n., 53, 192, 193, 263, 267, 268, 273 and n., 274, 308. See STRIKES; INDUSTRIAL WORKERS OF THE WORLD.
LACHOWSKY, H., prosecution, 124, 126, 143 n., 144, 147 n., 148. See ABRAMS.
LA FOLLETTE, R. M., Senator, 36, 95, 98.
LANGTRY, Secretary, 261.
LANSING, Robert, 60.
LARKIN, James, 287.
LASKI, F., 109 n.
LASKI, H. J., 42 n., 109 n., 375 n.
LATZKO, *Men in War,* excluded from the mails, 107.
LEAVITT, Judge, 324 n.
LEGISLATIVE DEBATES, freedom of speech in, 3.
LEGISLATIVE EXCLUSIONS, 311-364; Russia, 176; Wilkes, 311-315;

Berger, 315-332; eligibility of next highest candidate, 319, 320; grounds of disqualification, 321 *ff.;* in U. S. Constitution, 321, Fourteenth Amendment, 323 *ff.,* 348, guilt of treason, 324 *ff.,* opposition to war as disqualification, 328 *ff.;* N. Y. Socialists, 332-364; original proceedings, 332 *ff.;* protests, 335 *ff.;* Judiciary Committee sits, 339 *ff.;* power to suspend, 339, 340; power to disqualify on grounds not stated in the constitution, 321, 322, 328-332, 340 *ff.,* 347 *ff.,* judicial precedents, 340-343; legislative precedents, 343-354, in England, 344, expulsions from Congress, 345 *ff.,* disqualifications in Congress, 349 *ff.,* under Test Oath Act, 328, 330, 349-351, 353, Mormons, 348, 351 *ff.,* in New York, 354; disqualification for probability of breach of oath, 354 n.; charges against Socialists, 355; testimony, 356-361; the vote, 361; conclusions, 362-364.
LENINE, N., 107, 135, 147, 286, 311.
LETTERS, prosecutions based on, 57-60 *passim,* 118.
LEVER ACT, 148 n.; coal-strike injunction, 82, 153.
LIBEL, criminal and seditious, 4 n., 8, 9, 14, 15, 19-32, 52, 170-172; truth as defense, 4 n., 19, 22-25, 29, 30 n.; functions of judge and jury, same; injunction of, 8; civil actions, 12-18, 32; privilege and fair comment, 15, 32, 104; libel in war controversy, 110 n.; on the dead, 172. See SEDITION; Fox.
Liberator, 79 n.
LIBERTY, of the person, press, speech, etc. See PERSON, PRESS, SPEECH, etc.
LIBERTY BONDS, effect of campaigns on discussion, 7, 74; interference with sales, 44, 45, 53 n., 57, 64, 65, 81, 107, 169; refusal to buy prosecuted, 59, 60.
LICENSE AND LIBERTY, theory of freedom of speech, 12-16, 210, 211.

GENERAL INDEX 421

LINCOLN, Abraham, 46, 116, 117, 224, 329; on revolution, 223.

LIPMAN, S., prosecution, 123, 126, 138, 140, 141, 142, 143 n., 145, 147, 147 n., 148. See ABRAMS.

LIPPMANN, Walter, 67 n.

LITTLEFIELD, Charles, Representative, 347 n., 352 and n.

LOANS, as cause of war with Germany, 102-106. See MORGAN; LIBERTY BONDS.

LOPEZ, F. R., philosophical anarchist deported, 278-280, 286.

LORIMER, Wm., Senator, exclusion case, 339, 343, 347.

LOVEJOY, E. P., 3.

LOWELL, A. L., on academic freedom, 368.

LOWELL, JAMES RUSSELL, 16, 97, 104, 116, 202, 366, 372.

LOYALISTS, British, 2, 302 and n.

LOYD, W. H., 23 n.

LUDENDORFF, 6.

LUSK COMMITTEE, 203, 204, 270, 302-310, 334, 337, 358, 361-364.

LYON, Matthew, expulsion case, 329, 345.

McKELLAR, Senator, 198.

McKENNA, Justice, 94-98, 148 n.

McKINLEY, William, 52, 165, 187, 205, 230.

McMASTER, J. B., 19 n.

MACAULAY, T. B., 19 n., 66 and n., 203, 250, 294.

MADISON, James, 15, 19-22, 211, 240, 361.

MAGNA CHARTA, abandoned in war, 119.

MAINE, Sir Henry, 69.

MAILS. See POST-OFFICE.

MAITLAND, F. W., 22.

MANN, J. R., Representative, on Berger, 320, 324.

MANSFIELD, Lord, 8, 23, 310.

MARSHALL, John, 3, 22 n., 34 n., 200, 201, 211 n., 265, 325.

MARSHALS, United States, 78, 80.

MARTENS, L. C. A. K., 287, 305-308.

MARTIAL LAW, for opponents of war, 33 n., 41, 42, 116, 117; for discussion in army, 50.

MARTIN, Luther, 17.

MARX, 221, 223, 279, 365 ff.

MARYLAND, demands federal free speech clause, 4, 19.

MASSACHUSETTS, 283, 315; constitution, free speech clause, 4 and n.; Blackstonian decision, 8; restriction of press by stamp tax, 19 n.; colonial sedition law, 23 n.; libel statute, 24 n.; Roxbury Riots, 182-186, 212; red flag law, 186, 187; anarchy act, 189, 190, 204, 212, 269; Boston ordinance, 191; deportations, 248 n., see COLYER CASE; Secretary Langtry, 261; raids, 310, 311.

Masses, exclusion from mails, 9 n., 46-56, 107, 108 n., 118, 119, 125, 154, 174, 175 n., 194, 205 n., 207, 214, 216. See EASTMAN.

MASTERS, Edgar L., 275.

MAY, J. W., on intent, 150 n.

MAY, T. E., on English sedition, 22 n., 23 n., 28 n., 72 and n., 77, 263 n., 264 n., 265 n., 269 n., 271 n., 297 n.; on exclusion from Parliament, 312, 344 n., 345 n., 356.

MAY DAY RIOTS. See RIOTS.

MAYER, J. M., Judge, 13 n., 27 n., 40, 54 n., 79 n., 125.

MAZZINI, 286.

MEEHAN, John, I. W. W., 275.

MEETINGS. See ASSEMBLY.

MERCHANT VESSELS, sinking of, 57, 60.

MERIVALE, on Tiberius, 268 n.

MEXICO, possible war with, 114, 133; opposition in U. S., in 1846, 16, 64, 104, 116, 330; possible deportation of Americans, 288.

Mikado, quoted by Judge Clayton, 134.

MILITARY INTELLIGENCE POLICE, 123, 124, 145, 146, 159.

MILITIA, compulsory training constitutional, 35; state and federal control, 111 and n.

MILL, John Stuart, 32, 50, 157, 197, 205, 219 n., 365, 375.

MILLER, Justice, 16 n.

MILLER, S. L., Asst. U. S. Attorney, 126.

MILLIGAN, 33 and n., 42 n., 69 n., 81 n., 96 n., 113, 116, 117 n., 325.

MILTON, John, 1, 32, 197, 375.

Milwaukee Leader, 64; exclusion from mails, 107, 315-317, 323, 331.

MINNESOTA, safety commission, 33; war sedition act, 57, 77, 85 n., 110-113, 162.

MINORITIES, legal rights should be upheld, 2, 3, 156, 157, 294.

MISDIRECTION, unexcepted, 149 n.

MISSISSIPPI, constitution, free speech clause, 4 n.

MOB VIOLENCE, 44, 45, 46, 212; incitement to, 50, 260, 261.

MONTANA, war sedition law, 44, 113 n.; peace sedition law, 190, 191.

MOONEY, Thomas, 163.

MOORE, J. B., *Digest of International Law*, cited, 160 n., 191 n., 284 n., 288 n.; *Digest of International Arbitrations*, 288 n.

MORGAN, J. P., 81 n., 102, 104.

MORLEY, John, 66, 117, 159 n., 212, 241, 264, 265 n.

MORMONS, exclusion from Congress, 348, 351-353.

MORTON, Chief Justice, 165.

MOST, Johann, 205, 206.

MOTHERS, discouragement of, in war, criminal, 58, 103.

MOVING PICTURES, censorship and prosecutions, 10, 43, 60, 61 and n., 179, 203 n.

MUIR, prosecution, 28, 146 n.

MUNICIPAL CORPORATIONS, censorship of press, 110 n.; prohibition of German opera, 110 n., 183 n.; of meetings, 182-186, 190, 191.

MUNITION FACTORIES, limiting wartime discussion, 7, 58.

MUNITIONS, curtailment of production, 45, 65, 127-153 *passim*, 152 n., 163; see ESPIONAGE ACT; criticism of defective munitions prosecuted, 62.

MYERSON, A., 289, 290.

NAPOLEON, propaganda in England, 27.

Nation, excluded from mails, 107; editorials, 132 n., 190 n., 193 n., 338.

NATIONAL FOUNDERS' ASSOCIATION, 240 n.

NATIONAL GUARD. See MILITIA.

NATIONAL POPULAR GOVERNMENT LEAGUE, 243 n.

NATIONAL SECURITY LEAGUE, 338.

NATURALIZATION, compulsory undesirable, 235, 236; forbidden to anarchists, 278, 280; limits on power, 281. See DENATURALIZATION.

NAVY, abuse of, crime, 45, 114, 115. See SIMS.

NEARING, Scott, prosecution, 27, 53 n., 55 n., 85 n., 125, 308, 356.

NEGROES, freedom of speech and, 175, 184, 195, 203, 204.

NELLES, Walter, *Espionage Act cases*, 82 n., 83 n., 86 n., 110 n.

NEW HAMPSHIRE, constitution, free speech clause, 4 n.

NEW JERSEY, war sedition law, 111 n., 112 n.; Plainfield regulation of meetings, 184; anarchy act, 189 and n., 190, 204; Berger, 321.

New Republic, editorials, 116 n., 132 n., 272 n., 278 n., 280 n., 338.

NEW YORK:
State. Constitution on free speech, 4 n., 21 n., 24 n., 30 n., 374; demands U. S. clause, 4; libel statute, 24 n.; Croswell case, 30 and n.; red flag law, 180; criminal anarchy statute, 187, 188, 216; Loyalist investigation, 302 and n.; law of searches and seizures, 303-310. See LUSK COMMITTEE; LEGISLATIVE EXCLUSIONS (N. Y. Socialists).
City. Slacker round-up, 107, 108; federal juries, 79; radical meetings, 177-179; Hylan ordinances, 110 n., 183 n., 190, 191; Socialist aldermen, 338; school situation, 365 *ff*.

NEW YORK BAR ASSOCIATION, of City, 189 n., 338-340.

New York Call, excluded from mails, 115, 229.

New York Times, Current History of the War, 130 n.; editorial on Abrams case, 146 n.; article on anarchistic press, 222; editorial on I. W. W., 272 n.; on N. Y. Socialist assemblymen, 362.

New York Tribune, on Socialist assemblymen, 338.

GENERAL INDEX

New York World, telegrams censored, 109 n.

NEWBERRY, T. H., Senator, 337, 338.

NEWSPAPERS, restraint in war, 10, 46-59, 90, 94 ff., 106-109, 110 n., 116; effect of exclusion from mail, 107, 199, 234; effect of publication of facts of sedition trials, 119, 222; revolutionary press, 164, 195, 213, 222; conspiracy to compel handling of distasteful newspaper, 110 n.; opposition to sedition bills, 198, 338. See FOREIGN-LANGUAGE PRESS; *Milwaukee Leader*.

NEWTON, Attorney General of N. Y., 309, 334, 337, 355, 357, 361.

NON-PARTISAN LEAGUE, 77, 78, 81, 83, 85 n., 110-113, 162, 267, 369.

NORTH CAROLINA, discussion of federal free speech clause, 5 n.

NOTICE, constructive, 103, 104.

Nude and the Prudes, 188.

NUISANCES, relation to freedom of speech, 52, 171, 205.

OATES, Titus, 357.

O'BRIAN, J. L., 40, 41, 44 n., 46 n., 70-77 *passim*, 107, 108, 112, 113, 231 n., 319 n.

O'BRIEN, Judge, 343.

OBSCENITY, 10, 14, 15, 52, 170-172, 188, 214, 234, 311.

OFFICIALS. See UNITED STATES OFFICIALS.

O'HARE, Kate R., prosecution, 83, 162.

Official Record of the Rebellion, cited, 117 n.

OPERA. See GERMAN OPERA.

OPPER, cartoonist, 52.

ORDER, social interest in, limits freedom of speech, 34, 170, 179, 284, 366, 368.

ORR, Samuel, N. Y. Socialist assemblyman, 333, 356.

OTIS, James, 210, 299, 311.

OVERMAN, Senator, 181, 182; Bill, 197; Committee, 134, 135, 197.

PACIFISTS, 2, 26, 37, 46, 64, 68, 70, 73, 102 ff., 106, 224, 296, 317, 329; expulsion from college, 110 n.

PALESTINE, 108.

PALFREY, J. G., on Salem witches, 357 n.

PALMER, A. Mitchell, U. S. Attorney General, enforcement of Espionage Act after armistice, 115, 229, 302; house bombed, 163, 197; recommends federal sedition bill, 167, 195-198, 203, 207 ff., 335; on federal conspiracy statute, 167-169; does not fear revolution, 196, 251; recommends and enforces state sedition laws, 195, 229, 249; enforces deportation statute, 196, 229, 230, 241-252, 257, 274, 283, 293, 302; controversy with Post, 250-252; on spies, 270-272; on independent labor unions, 273 n.

PALMER, Joseph, 172.

PALMER, T. Fyshe, prosecution, 28.

PARDONS, in Espionage Act cases, 61, 62 n., 73; impossible in deportation cases, 292. See COMMUTATIONS; AMNESTY.

PARKER, Carleton, 162, 163.

PARLIAMENT. See GREAT BRITAIN.

PARNELL, C. S., 264.

PARTIES, in America, 267, 363.

PECK, Jared, 65 n.

PENNSYLVANIA, constitution, free speech clause, 4 and n., 18, 24 n.; discussion of federal free speech clause, 19 n.

Pennsylvania and the Federal Constitution, 19 n., 23 n.

PERSECUTION, Justice Holmes on, 155, 156. See RELIGION.

PERSON, liberty of, 17; searches of, 242 n., 301. See ARRESTS.

PETITION, right of, 5, 7 n.; Baltzer case, 64, 65, 116.

Philadelphia Tageblatt, 94, 101. See SCHAEFER.

PHILLIPS, prosecution, 13 n., 41 n., 79 n., 126.

PHILLIPS, Wendell, 209.

PIERCE, prosecution, 13 n., 94 and n., 101-106, 134, 135 n., 285 n.

"PILLARS OF FIRE," 184.

PINCKNEY, Charles, 3, 21 n.

PITNEY, Justice, 101-104.

PLACE, Francis, 260, 271 n.

PLATFORMS, party, not be taken too seriously, 267.

GENERAL INDEX

POLITICAL DISCUSSION, doctrine that it should be confined to the legislature, 27, 28; punishment of criticism of government, chapter I.; forbidden to superintendent of schools, 11 *n.*; conventions prohibited, 11 *n.*; campaign expenses limited, 11 *n.*; in war, 48, 49, 62, 63. See SEDITION.

POLITICAL TRIALS, 85 *n.*, 94, 116, 132-137. See SEDITION.

POLLARD, E. A., on confederate censorship, 117 *n.*

POST, Louis F., Assistant Secretary of Labor, 233 *n.*, 239 *n.*, 243, 272 *n.*, 291 and *n.*, 292; controversy with Palmer, 250-252.

POST-OFFICE, subject to First Amendment, 34, 108, 109, 218; conclusiveness of administrative decisions, 45, 54, 106-109, 199, 233, 234; powers under Espionage Act, 6, 12 *n.*, 43, 45, 46-56, 106-109, 115, 229, 335; in peace-time sedition bills, 197-199; control of express and telegraph, 109 *n.*; no jury, 158, 199; powers to exclude matter inciting to murder, etc., 214, 229; opening mail, 241 *n.*

POUND, Roscoe, on freedom of speech, 8 *n.*; on rights and interests, 35 *n.*

PREIS, Engelbert, deportation, 256-261, 268.

PRESIDENT, 252; powers under Alien Law of 1798, 29; criticism of, punished under Sedition Act of 1798, 29, 204, under Espionage Act, 129, 138; protection of life, see UNITED STATES OFFICIALS; threats against, 202, 207, 214, 215. See JEFFERSON; LINCOLN; WILSON.

PRESIDENT'S MEDIATION COMMISSION, report of, 113 *n.*, 163, 272 *n.*, 292.

PRESS, freedom of, 5, 17, 18, 21. See CENSORSHIP; SPEECH, FREEDOM OF.

PREVIOUS RESTRAINT, 8-32; definition of freedom of speech. See SPEECH, FREEDOM OF.

Price We Pay, pamphlet, 101-106. See PIERCE.

PRIMARIES, political, 11 *n.*

PROBER, prosecution, 144. See ABRAMS.

PROCEDURAL SAFEGUARDS. See SPEECH, FREEDOM OF.

Procès de tendance, 175 and *n.*

PROFANITY, 170 *ff.*

PROFITEERS, discussion of criminal, 50, 58, 59, 68, 95, 102, 103, 119, 225; possible raids on, 308.

PRO-GERMANS, 2, 59 *n.*, 64, 70 and *n.*, 73, 94 *ff.*, 107, 194, 224, 296.

PROHIBITION, 66 *n.*, 114, 209.

PROPERTY, judicial protection, 106.

PROSECUTING ATTORNEYS, effect of free speech clause on, 5; in the war with Germany, 73-76; under Sedition Act of 1798, 78; in Abrams case, 126, 144, 145.

PROUDHON, 221.

Public, excluded from the mails, 107.

PUBLIC INFORMATION, COMMITTEE ON, 108, 132.

PULLING, *Defense of the Realm Manual,* 42 *n.*

QUAKERS, 197, 277.

QUEBEC, address to people of, 17, 170.

RADICALS, freedom of speech for, 1, 2, 52; duty of restraint, 187; mob violence against, 44, 45, 46; under Espionage Act, 77, 81 *ff.*, 162; on juries, 78-80; attitude of judges toward, 81-84, 85 *n.*; in Abrams case, 120-160 *passim;* prevalent after the War, 161, 162; relation to the criminal law in peace, chapter IV., 161-228 *passim;* see SEDITION and succeeding headings; deportation of, 229-293; exclusion from legislatures, 329, 332 *ff.*

RAI, Lajpat, book on India excluded from mails, 108.

RAIDS, on Communists, 230, 241-254, 292, 293; on I. W. W., 242 *n.*, 260, 274; time of Wilkes, 296-299; in war, 115, 229, 302; by Lusk Committee, 302-310; in

GENERAL INDEX 425

Massachusetts, 310, 311. See SEARCHES AND SEIZURES.

RAND SCHOOL, 204, 257 n., 308-310, 356, 361.

RANDOLPH, John, 23.

RAY, Judge, 13 n., 214.

READING, Lord, 325.

RECHT, Charles, 272 n., 275 n., 278 n.

RED CROSS, criticism of, punished, 57; refusal of contributions, punished, 109, 110.

RED FLAG LAWS, 180-187.

REFERENDUM, before war, discussion criminal, 57, 64, 65.

RELIGION, toleration, 2, 3, 172, 176, 177, 196, 197, 276, 277, 370; Virginia statute, see VIRGINIA; federal control prohibited, 5, 170; Christianity called inconsistent with war, 6, 57, 61, 62; religious meetings, 183, 184; Catholic Association, in Ireland, 264. See MORMONS.

REPRESENTATIVE GOVERNMENT, right of, 17, 296. See LEGISLATIVE EXCLUSIONS.

Review (now, *Weekly Review*), on Abrams case, 152 n.; on Socialist assemblymen, 338; on Lusk bills, 362 n.

REVOLUTION, 97, 139-142, 164-169, 173-179, 199-201, 205-207, 212, 219, 257-262. See SEDITION BILLS; PALMER; RUSSIA; AMERICAN and FRENCH REVOLUTION.

RHODE ISLAND, demands federal free speech clause, 4; soul liberty, 177, 276, 283; Berger, 321; property qualification, 372.

RHODES, J. F., 116 n., 117 n., 177 n., 290 n., 330 n.

RIGHTS, and interests, 34-38, 366 ff.

RIOTS, 164, 177, 178, 182-186, 203, 212.

ROBERTS, Brigham H., exclusion case, 345 n., 347 n., 350 n., 352 and n.

ROBINS, Raymond, 132-137, 181 n.

RODENBERG, Representative, on Berger case, 331.

ROCKEFELLER, John D., 146.

ROGERS, H. W., Judge, 54 n., 56 and n., 108 n., 278-280.

ROLLAND, Romain, 367.

ROMAN CATHOLICS, abuse of, 184; legislation against, 264, 265, 281, 283.

ROOSEVELT, Theodore, 316, 325; (the younger), 361.

ROOT, Elihu, 86, 355, 359.

ROOT, Erastus, 21 n.

ROSANSKY, H., prosecution, 123, 127, 144, 147 n., 148. See ABRAMS.

ROUSSEAU, J. J., 52.

ROXBURY RIOT, 182-186, 212.

RUGG, 186 n.

RUSSELL, Bertrand, prosecution, 242 n., 59 and n., 295; *Proposed Roads to Freedom*, 222, 223, 276, 284.

RUSSELL, Lord John, 227.

RUSSELL, G. W. E., 227 n.

RUSSELL, Pastor, sect, prosecutions, 83 n., 101.

RUSSIA, 10, 290; Russians in U. S., 82, 120-160 *passim*, 230, 235, 256; Czarist policy toward discussion, 176, 178, 191, 211 and n., 269, 294 n.; effect of Russian Revolution in U. S., 26, 58, 81, 82, 86, 95, 120-160 *passim*, 162, 178, 196, 289, 293, 334, 360 ff., 371; truth needed, 158; Harvard library on Revolution, 221; documents censored in U. S., 107, 221, 311; German participation, 132 and n., 135, 147; Soviet Government Bureau in N. Y., 287, 305-308; American intervention, 94, 129-132; criminality of opposition, 130, 137 ff., 160; questionable effect of our deportations policy upon Russia, 286, 287.

Russian-American Relations, cited, 131 n.

RUTHERFORD, Livingston, *John Peter Zenger*, 23 n.

RYAN, J. M., Asst. U. S. Attorney, 126, 145.

SABOTAGE, 163; Federal statute, 152 n., 163; state statutes, 163, 274, 276; advocacy of, 190-194; deportations, 231 n., 272-275.

SALVATION ARMY, rioting against, 183 and n.

SANFORD, Chancellor, 342, 354.

GENERAL INDEX

SCANDELLA, American deported from Venezuela, 288 n.

SCHAEFER, *Tageblatt* prosecution, 85, 87, 94-101, 106, 207, 216, 218, 265.

SCHENCK, prosecution, 9 n., 16 n., 88-93, 98, 99, 102, 155, 178, 179, 191, 192, 285.

SCHOFIELD, Henry, *Freedom of the Press in the United States*, 4 n., 8 n., 20 n., 21, 24 n., 30 and n., 31 n., 56.

SCHOOLS, political speeches by superintendent, 11 n.; freedom for teachers, 365-376.

SCHWARTZ, prosecution, 124, 125, 126, 146. See ABRAMS.

SCIENCE, promoted by freedom of speech, 17, 31, 32, 170, 370, 374.

SCOTLAND, sedition trials in, 28.

SCOTT, Austin W., on atheism, 172 n.

SCRUTTON, Lord Justice, 119.

SEARCHES AND SEIZURES, warrants authorized by Espionage Act, 43, 45, 302; raids in the war, 115, 229, 302; Russia, 176; importance of warrants, 140, 159; in deportation proceedings, 241 and n., 242 n., 244-247, 302; at time of Wilkes, 295-298; Supreme Court decisions on Fourth Amendment, 299-301; consequences of illegality, 300-302; when legal, 242 n., 301, 310 n.; Lusk Committee raids, 302-310; N. Y. law, 303-310; Massachusetts raids, 310, 311.

SEARS, Clara E., 172 n.

SEAS, FREEDOM OF THE, 17.

Seattle Union-Record, raided, 115, 229, 302.

SEDITION, common law of, and free speech, 8, 9, 11, 14, 19-32, 170; not federal common law crime; British trials, 22, 23, 26-29, 118, 146 n., 157, 175, 296 ff.; colonial trials, 19, 22, 23; societies to suppress, 71, 72, 357; in war, see WAR, ESPIONAGE ACT; punishment in peace, chapter IV., 161-228; normal criminal law sufficient, 161-169; criminal law of obscenity, breaches of peace, etc., distinguished, 169-173; criminal law of violence distinguished, 173-180, 196; suppression of agitation by law unwise, 219 ff.; distinguished from treason, 325-328. See SPIES.

SEDITION ACT OF 1798, 1, 17, 25, 65 n., 109, 116, 157, 162, 194, 199, 208, 223, 229, 329, 345; summary of text, 29, 30; constitutionality, 20-22 and nn., 30, 200, 204; comparison with Espionage Act, 56, 128; juries, 78 and n.; judges, 80, 81.

SEDITION ACT OF 1918, 44. See ESPIONAGE ACT.

SEDITION BILLS, FEDERAL, 81, 140, 194-228, 229, 230, 231; summary, 194-199; constitutionality, affirmative federal power, 199-201, treason clause, 201-203, first amendment, 203-207; wisdom, 207-228, 268.

SEDITION STATUTES OF STATES, in war, 57, 74 n., 110-113, 163; in peace, 163, 169, 173-194, 204, 212, 216, 224, 246; red flag laws, 180-187; anarchy syndicalism, and sedition, 187-194, 261, 265, 268; constitutionality, 191-194; recommended by Palmer, 195; enforced by Palmer, 229, 249.

SELF-INCRIMINATION, rule against, 69, 303 and n., 307.

Sentenced to Twenty Years Prison, 145 n.

SENTENCES, English and Scotch sedition trials, 28 and n., 87 n.; Defense of the Realm Act trials, 118 n.; India, 159 n.; Espionage Act trials, 58-62, 87 and n., 147, 148, 159, 160, 220; long sentences as cruel and unusual punishment, 148 n.

September Morn, suppression of, 175.

Sermon on the Mount, and war, 55, 119.

SERVICE-LETTER STATUTES, 3 n.

SERVITUDE, involuntary, sometimes constitutional, 7, 35, 36.

SEWARD, W. F., arbitrary arrests, 116; on intervention, 160 n.

SEX, discussion, 171, 172.

SHAKESPEARE, William, 14, 55; censored, 175, 214.

GENERAL INDEX

SHAW, Bernard, 32; censored, 175, 283.
SHAW, Lord, 42 n.
SHAY'S REBELLION, 164.
SHELLEY, 172.
SHERMAN ANTI-TRUST LAW, 53 n., 106.
SHIPLACOFF, A., prosecution, 125.
SHIPMAN, Clare, 190 n.
SHIPS, discussion of sinking of, 57, 60; parables of, 276, 286.
SHIPYARDS, limiting war-time discussion, 7, 58.
SIDIS, W., 186 n.
SIMS, Admiral, 64.
SISSON, Edgar, Russian documents, 132 and n.; in Abrams case, 133.
SISTERS, discouragement of, in war, criminal, 103.
SLANDER, no previous restraint possible, 14; not immune, 15. See LIBEL.
SMITH, Alfred, Governor, 362 and n.
SMITH, F. E. (now Lord Birkenhead), criticism of, excluded from mails, 108.
SMITH, Jeremiah, on intent, 149 n., 150 n.
SMITH AND WESSON CO., 153.
SMOOT, Reed, Senator, exclusion case, 347 n., 352, 353.
Socialist Review, 319 n., 331 n.
SOCIALISTS, 2, 10, 27, 260; need for judicial comprehension, 82-84, 86; in the War, 81, 83, 162; St. Louis Platform, 162, 315, 316, 334; peace-time prosecutions, 188, 210, 216, 224; secession of left-wing, 256, 262; exclusion as a party from legislature, 306, 329-338, 355-364; in schools, 365 *ff.*; in Germany, 262. See DEBS; PIERCE; STOKES; SYRACUSE; BERGER; RAND SCHOOL; LIPMAN; LEGISLATIVE EXCLUSION; COMMUNISTS.
SOCIETIES, to suppress sedition, 71, 72.
SOCRATES, 367, 370.
SOLICITATION, criminal, relation to freedom of speech, 25, 165, 166, 173, and to Espionage Act, 49, 51-53, 88, 89, 155; to non-criminal interference with the government's war activities, 53, 169; in federal crimes, 166 and n., 201.
SOLOMON, Charles, N. Y. Socialist assemblyman, 333, 356, 357.
SOUTH CAROLINA, constitution, free speech clause, 4 n.
SOVIET GOVERNMENT. See RUSSIA.
SPEECH, FREEDOM OF.
  Constitutions: guaranty in U. S. Constitution, 3-5, 18, 200, demanded by states, 3, 4, 19, 156; in Congressional debates, 3; in state constitutions, 3 and n., 4 and n., 17, 18, 21 n., 30 n., 374; exception of "abuse" implied if not expressed, 4 n.; clauses a guide to interpretation of constitutional statutes, 5, 6, 46, 48, 193, 194, 207; and also invalidate statutes, 3, 4, 11 and n., 16, 111 n., 156, 192 n.
  Meaning: 1-39, 155-158, 366-372; subject to limits, 2, 7; necessarily extends to unpopular persons and causes, 3, 156, 157, 294, 366; Blackstonian censorship view, 8-12, 19, 21-23, 31, 32, 38, 108, 199; liberty and license view, 12-16, 210, 211, 368; history of principle, 17-32; inconsistent with common law of sedition, 14, 22-24, 170; social and political function, 34-36; conclusions on meaning, 34-39, 156 *ff.*, 368 *ff.*; view of Judge Hand, 50, 51; of Justice Holmes, 88, 155, 156; an issue between two tests of criminality, danger v. bad tendency, 24-31, 37-39, 49-52, 154-159, 173-180, 213-219, and elsewhere; not secured by juries, 24-28, see JURY TRIAL; meaning not fixed in 1791, 14, 32, 35, 36; does not exclude intemperate and foolish discussion, 48, 83, 114, 140 n., 173, 206, 219, 220; applies to political research, 370, 371; but not limited to political discussion, 156, 170; does not depend on merits of existing government, 210; suppression ineffectual, 118, 119, 219, 220, 226, 227.

Procedural safeguards: 39, 49, 66-69, 92, 93; Fox's Libel Act, etc., 24, 39, 69; precise offense must be specified, 49, 92, 93; objective test of criminality of words, 49-51, 54 *ff.*, 216 *ff.*; exclusion of psychological questions and disputes of opinion, 52, 66-69, 73, 103-106; judicial guidance of jury, 85, 86, 94-100; evils of bad intention as test of guilt, 63-68, 86, see INTENTION; culling sentences, 100, 102, 220; right to counsel, 236 *ff.*, 247 *ff.*; narrow range of administrative power in criminal law, 75. See HUMAN MACHINERY.

Relation to other branches of the law and concrete applications: libel, see same; nuisance, 52, 171, 205; breaches of the peace, 24, 25, 74 and n., 102 n., 110 n., 111, 171, 172, 205, 208; war, 6, 7 and n., 25, 26, 32-38, 46-56, 63-66, 88-90, 96, 104-106, 176, 179, 369 *ff.*; obscenity, blasphemy, etc., 169-173, and see same; peace-time sedition laws, 173-180, 191-194, 199-228; deportations, 280-291; legislative exclusion, 328-332, 362-364; schools, 368-376. See ATTEMPT; SOLICITATION; ESPIONAGE ACT; POST-OFFICE; ASSEMBLY.

Summary of recent events in U. S., 296, 336-339.

SPENCER, Herbert, 226, 276.

SPIES, German, 6, 70-72; opponents of war as, 41, 42; government spies and informers 59, 71, 72, 227, 268-272, 302, 357.

SPIES, August, anarchist, 165, 205, 206.

Spirit of '76, moving picture case, 10, 38 n., 43, 60, 61.

STAMP TAX, restraint of press by, 19 n., 32.

STANCHFIELD, J. B., on guilt by association, 360.

STANTON, E. M., arbitrary arrests, 116.

STAR CHAMBER, 32, 232, 238.

Star-Spangled Banner, alleged prosecutions for not standing up, 102 and n., 103.

STATE SEDITION LAWS, in war and peace. See SEDITION STATUTES OF STATES.

STATE WAR CASES, miscellaneous, 110 n.

STEAD, W. T., "The Maiden Tribute," 171.

STEIMER, Molly, prosecution, 123, 126, 143 and n., 144, 145, 147 n., 148. See ABRAMS.

STEPHEN, James Fitzjames, 13, 20 n., 23 n., 24, 26 n., 29 n., 56, 201 n., 263 n.

STERLING BILL, 197, 207.

STEVENSON, J. A., 269 n.

STEVENSON, R. L., on Braxfield, 146 n.

STIRNER, 221.

STOKES, Rose Pastor, prosecution, 13 n., 28 n., 58, 59, 67, 87 n., 92, 118, 119, 225.

STONE, F. D., 19 n.

STOREY, Moorfield, on intervention, 160 n.

STORY, Joseph, 8 n., 341, 345 n.

STREET MEETINGS. See ASSEMBLY.

STRIKES, 53, 164, 218, 220; under Espionage Act of 1918, 74, 269, 273, 274; coal strike, 82, 260; advocacy of general strike, 122, 125, 139, 140, 149-153, 163, 188, 216, 257-261, 271. See LABOR UNIONS.

STRONG, A. L., 115 n.

SUBMARINE WARFARE, discussion of criminal, 57, 60.

SUGARMAN, prosecution, 88 n., 89, 90.

SUHR, an I. W. W., 163.

SUMNER, Charles, 210, 330.

SUMNER, William G., 97, 362.

SUNDAY, Rev. Wm., 260.

SUPREME COURT OF THE UNITED STATES, Espionage Act cases, 15, 16, 87-106, 116, 120-160 *passim*, 178, 191, 207, 285; other free speech cases, 9, 12; on conscription, 7, 35, 40, 57; on postal power, 108; protection of lives of judges, 197, 200, 206; on power over aliens, 230 *ff.*; on anarchist exclusions, 275 *ff.*; on guilt by association, 265; on searches and seizures, 299-301, 335; on federal peace-time sedition bill, 207.

GENERAL INDEX 429

SWEDEN, free speech in, 286.
SWEET, Thaddeus C., N. Y. Speaker, 333-339, 357, 361 ff.
SWEETHEARTS, discouragement of, in war criminal, 58, 103.
SWITZERLAND, free speech in, 286.
SYNDICALISM, statutes against, 163, 190-194, 197, 212, 265.
SYRACUSE SOCIALISTS, prosecution, 115.

TACITUS, quoted, 118 n.
Tageblatt, Philadelphia. See SCHAEFER.
TANEY, Chief Justice, 34 n.; against lawlessness in war, 81 n.
TARDE, 163.
TAXATION, 106, 233; restraint of free speech by, 19 n., 32, 282; discussion of war taxation suppressed, 57, 64, 65, 95, 107.
TELEGRAPH, censorship of, 109 n.
TENDENCY, bad, as test of criminality of words, fatal to freedom of speech, see SPEECH, FREEDOM OF; social and economic tendency unsuitable for decision by judges and juries, 49, 52, 68, 69, 104, 132-136, 158.
TEST OATH, restricted by U. S. Constitution, 3; in R. I., 77; in N. Y., 333, 342, 343, 354 n.
TEST OATH ACT, 328, 330, 349-351, 353.
TEXAS, war sedition law, 111 n.
THAW, H. K., trial, 136 n., 163.
THAYER, J. B., 6 n.
THAYER, W. R., 203.
THEATER, shouting fire in, 16; censorship of, 172, 175.
THIRD AMENDMENT, 33.
THIRTEENTH AMENDMENT, 7, 35, 36.
THOMAS, A. V., 218 n.
THREATS. See PRESIDENT.
TIBERIUS, Emperor, censorship, 118 n., 268.
TIGHE, Ambrose, on war powers, 33 n., 117 n.
TILDSLEY, John L., 365 ff.
TOBACCO, 209.
TOLEDO, 191.
TOLSTOY, 276, 279, 294 n.
TORTS, outside free speech clauses, 14, 15. See LIBEL.

TOWNLEY, prosecution, 78 n., 85 n., 111 and n.
TRACHTENBERG, A., 257 n.
TRADE UNIONS. See LABOR UNIONS.
TRADING WITH THE ENEMY ACT, 108 n., 195.
TRAINING CAMPS, limiting wartime discussion, 7, 57, 119; sanitary conditions, 64.
TREASON, 97; levying war, 166, 201, 265; aid and comfort to enemies, 148 n., 202, 324-328; in war with Germany, 41 and n., 50, 74, 91, 325 n.; against U. S., states cannot prosecute, 111; effect of clause on federal sedition statutes, 201-203, 218; Berger and relation of treason to Espionage Act, 325-328.
TREATIES, 36, 233; with Germany, 1, 119; secret, 36, 37 and n.
TREVELYAN, G. O., 295, 312.
TROTSKY, Leon, 135, 144, 147, 311.
TRUMBULL, Lyman, Senator, on expulsion, 346, 347.
TRUTH, social interest in, 34-39, 155-160, 176, 368 ff.; importance in war, 36, 37, 46, 63, 65, 66, 96; not concerned in mere advocacy of violence and lawlessness, 49, 50, 63, 173, 204; not a defense under Espionage Act, except false statements clause, 56, 115; relation to criminal law of obscenity, profanity, etc., 169-173. See LIBEL.
TUCKER, St. George, 8 n.
TUCKER, St. John, 101.
TUNNEY, T. J., Inspector, 123, 169 n., 181 and n., 182.
TURNER, John, anarchist excluded, 275-283 *passim*.
TYLER, Moses C., 276 n.

UNDER-COVER INFORMANTS, 269-272.
UNITED STATES, inciting resistance to, opposing cause, see ESPIONAGE ACT; division of state and federal jurisdiction over crimes, 113 ff., 171; political parties, see PARTIES; absence of intellectual divergencies, 289, 363.
UNITED STATES CONSTITUTION, absence of free speech clause and

ratification, 3, 4, 156; affirmative power over speech and sedition, 3, 34 and *n.*, 199-201; abuse of, crime, 45, 114. See various topics, e.g., SPEECH, FREEDOM OF; TREASON; DEPORTATIONS; BILLS OF RIGHTS; also the various amendments by number.

UNITED STATES COURTS, no common law crimes, 22. See SUPREME COURT; DISTRICT COURTS; JUDGES; FEDERALIST JUDGES.

UNITED STATES OFFICIALS, protection of, from violence, 163-169, 196-207, 213-215, 251. See PRESIDENT; PROSECUTING OFFICIALS; JUSTICE, DEPARTMENT OF.

UNITED STATES STATUTES, adequacy against utterances in war, 40-42, 46, 50; against revolution and attacks on officials, 165-169, 194, 196; accessories, 52 and *n.*, 53, 166 *n.;* attempts and incitement, 166 and *n.;* judicial code, 269, 149 *n.;* Explosives Act, 169.

UNTERMYER, Samuel, on Rand School, 309, 310.

VALLANDIGHAM, 97, 117 and *n.*, 325, 330.

VANCE, W. R., on freedom of speech, 22 *n.*, 76 *n.*

VAN VALKENBURGH, Judge, 13 *n.*, 28 *n.*, 58, 59, 87, 225.

VEBLEN, Thorstein, book on Germany excluded from mails, 108.

VENEZUELA, deportation of American, 288 *n.*

VERMONT, constitution, free speech clause, 4 *n.*

VESSELS, merchant, sinking of, 57, 60. See SHIPS.

VIOLENCE, draft riots, 40, 50; mobs in war, 44-46; law against, 165-169; advocacy of, by radicals, chapters IV., V., *passim;* by conservatives, 260, 261; suppression of opinion by, 196, 197, 219, 260, 264. See "FORCE AND VIOLENCE"; SOLICITATION; RIOTS.

VIRGINIA, demands federal free speech clause, 4; constitution, free speech clause, 4; religious toleration statute, 17, 18, 31, 66, 67, 170, 217; Resolutions, 20 *n.*, 211 *n.*, 240 *n.*

VOTERS' LEAGUES, restrictions on, 11 *n.*

WADE, Judge, 13 *n.*, 62, 63, 64, 83.

WAITE, Chief Justice, 325 *n.*

WALDMAN, Louis, N. Y. Socialist assemblyman, 333, 356.

WALDRON, C. H., prosecution, 61, 62.

WALLACE, D. H., prosecution, 13 *n.*, 62.

WALLAS, Graham, 271 *n.*, 294 *n.*

WAR, extended scope to-day, 6, 7; criticism of flogging in army, 27, 28, 68; of general by troops, 50; trial of civilians by military courts, 33 *n.*, 42; censorship on military news, 10, 98, 99; Bills of Rights in, 32-34; importance of the truth in, 36, 37, 46, 63-66, 114; psychological effects, 225; mob violence, 44-46; causes of war not subject to judicial proof, 104-106; state war cases, 110 *n.;* effect on legislative exclusion, 328-332; on schools, 366 *ff.;* technical war, 113-119; future wars and free speech, 46, 64, 113 *ff.;* federal war powers, 88, 200. See SPEECH, FREEDOM OF, *Concrete applications;* CONSCRIPTION; ESPIONAGE ACT; ARMY; NAVY; SEDITION STATUTES OF STATES; ASSEMBLY; names of various wars.

WAR DEPARTMENT, *Report of Activities in Field of Industrial Relations,* cited, 153 *n.*

WAR OF 1812, opposition to, 64, 330 *n.*

War College Publications, cited, 98, 99.

War-time Prosecutions and Mob Violence, cited, 45 *n.*, 57 *n.*, 74 *n.*, 102 *n.*, 110 *n.*, 302 *n.*

WARD, Judge, 54 *n.*

WARRANTS, general, 296, 297, 299, 311. See ARRESTS; SEARCHES AND SEIZURES; DEPORTATIONS.

WARREN, Charles, on treason, 325 *n.*, 326 *n.*, 327 *n.*

WASHINGTON, prosecution for libel

GENERAL INDEX

on the dead, 172; red flag law, 181 *n.*; anarchy act, 188.

WASHINGTON, George, 147; libel on, 172.

WATKINS, Gordon S., 256.

WEBSTER, Daniel, 330.

WEINBERGER, Harry, 126, 132, 133 *n.*, 146.

WEST VIRGINIA, red flag law, 181; sedition law, 190; moving picture law, 203 *n.*

WESTENHAVER, Judge, 91.

WESTERN FEDERATION OF MINERS, 267.

WESTERN UNION TELEGRAPH CO., 109 *n.*

WHARTON, Francis, quoted, 52, 73.

WHITE, E. D., Chief Justice, 12, 148 *n.*

WHITE SLAVE TRAFFIC, discussion punished, 171.

WHITNEY, Anita, 190 *n.*

WICKERSHAM, G. W., 133.

WIGMORE, J. H., *Evidence*, 85 *n.*; on Abrams case, 130 *n.*, 141 *n.*

WILCOX, E. H., *Russia's Ruin*, 132.

WILKES, John, 23, 295; searches and seizures, 295-298, 301; exclusion from House of Commons, 250, 295, 296, 311-315, 321, 328, 329, 338, 343, 349, 355, 356.

WILLES, Justice, 9 *n.*

WILLIAMS, A. R., called in Abrams case, 133.

WILLIAMS, Roger, 176, 227, 276, 277, 286, 321, 372.

WILLOUGHBY, W. W., 230 *n.*, 233 *n.*

Willy and his Papa, cartoons, 52.

WILSON, William B., Secretary of Labor, 243, 247, 248, 250, 252; decisions on Communist Labor Party and Communist Party, 256-262, 268; on I. W. W., 272, 273; Martens case, 287, 288; on deportation policy, 290, 291.

WILSON, Woodrow, President, on Sedition Act of 1798, 25; ignorance of secret treaties, 37 *n.*; opposes court martial for pacifists, 62; speeches as evidence in Espionage Act cases, 57, 103-106; exercise of pardoning power, 60, 61, 62 *n.*, 73, 87 *n.*, 117; war aims hindered by policy of suppression, 113, 119; attacked in Abrams case, 120-122, 138; Russian policy, 131, 132, 151; message on Federal Sedition Bill, 211-213, 220; threats to kill, 215; responsibility for deportations, 249; on economic nature of the War, 321; free speech record, 336; miscellaneous, 60, 225, 315, 363.

WITCHES, Salem, 356, 351.

WOLVERTON, Judge, 83.

WOMEN, discouragement of, in war, criminal, 57, 58, 103; nationalization of, 154.

WOOD, Baron, 27, 28.

WOODS, Arthur, 177, 178 and *n.*

WORDS, and acts, relation to freedom of speech, 49-51, 164-180; criminal law of language, 169-173.

WORKS, John D., on federal judges, 84.

"WORK OR FIGHT" STATUTE, constitutional, 7.

WURSTERBARTH, denaturalized, 109, 110 *n.*

WURTS, John, on federal juries, 80 *n.*

YOUNG MEN'S CHRISTIAN ASSOCIATION, criticism of, criminal, 57, 70; refusal of contributions, punished, 109, 110.

YOUTH, social interest in training of, limits freedom of speech, 34, 170, 179, 180, 368, 374 *ff*.

ZENGER, Peter, trial, 23 and *n.*